Qualities That Count

Heber J. Grant as
Businessman, Missionary, and Apostle

Biographies in Latter-day Saint History

An imprint of BYU Studies and the
Joseph Fielding Smith Institute for Latter-day Saint History

Brigham Young University
Provo, Utah

Qualities That Count

Heber J. Grant as
Businessman, Missionary, and Apostle

Essays by
Ronald W. Walker

Brigham Young University Press
Provo, Utah

This volume is part of the Smith Institute and BYU Studies series
Biographies in Latter-day Saint History

Other volumes in this series:

T. Edgar Lyon: A Teacher in Zion
"No Toil nor Labor Fear": The Story of William Clayton

© 2004 Brigham Young University Press

Cover images:
Heber J. Grant at different ages, courtesy Church Archives,
The Church of Jesus Christ of Latter-day Saints
Cover design by Kimberly Chen Pace

Library of Congress Cataloging-in-Publication Data

Walker, Ronald W. (Ronald Warren), 1939–
  Qualities that count : Heber J. Grant as businessman, missionary, and
apostle / by Ronald W. Walker.
    p. cm.
  ISBN 0-8425-2550-5 (alk. paper)
  1. Grant, Heber Jeddy, 1856–1945. I. Title.

BX8695.G7W35 2004
289.3'092–dc21

2003011090

Printed in the United States of America
10 9 8 7 6 5 4 3 2 1

To friends and collaborators at the Smith Institute,
who have so fully enriched my life.

Contents

Missionary

Illustrations

Introduction

I remember the telephone call well. Picking up the receiver, I heard my secretary's voice telling me of an incoming call. "Brother Walker," she said, "Grover Cleveland is on the phone and wants to speak with you."

In a way, that phone call began this book.

Of course, Grover Cleveland—the long-deceased President of the United States—was not on the telephone. My caller was actually Leonard J. Arrington, Church Historian at the time, and he was phoning in his usually cheery way to ask me to join his staff. At the time, I was working at the Salt Lake City headquarters of the Church Education System, helping to write curriculum. Leonard, who enjoyed a little of the cloak and dagger, used President Cleveland's name as a means to give privacy to our negotiation. My secretary, an able worker but not much of a historian, never broke the code. After several weeks of his entreaties, I finally joined his staff.

I was only a day or two on the job when Leonard gave me a proposition. "How would you like to write a biography of President Heber J. Grant?" he asked. "Look over the preliminary register of President Grant's papers and give me an idea of how long it will take."

Just beginning my career, I was hardly on scholarly speaking terms with President Grant. However, there were some things that I knew. I knew, for instance, that he had presided longer than any other Church president, except Brigham Young, whose thirty-year tenure exceeded President Grant's by just three years. So long was

President Grant's career and tenure, his life spanned Mormonism's second, third, and fourth generations, from 1856 to 1945. I also knew my Primary stories about President Grant's grit and persistence. Also, I could recall, as a six-year-old living in Cedar Rapids, Iowa, hearing the radio bulletin announcing his death. My mother said that this news was important, and I knew that it must be so. News about Latter-day Saints was an unusual in the mid-twentieth century in the American Midwest. I understood this fact even as a small boy.

Yet, beyond such incidental and skeletal things, I knew little about the man, though I understood the professional and religious opportunity that Leonard was giving me. Here was a chance to get acquainted with a major Church leader and to learn about Mormon history for more than two-thirds of the Church's existence. Following Leonard's instruction about examining the register, I glanced at its many pages and, hardly understanding the summit to be climbed, told him that the research could be managed in two years, with another year needed for writing. My rough estimate reflected no reality except my own desire and ambition.

The mountain proved to be a steep one. The Grant papers turned out to be monumentally large. Beginning with his call to preside over the Tooele Stake in western Utah at age twenty-three, President Grant kept a diary. It was a task he undertook with little relish but with steeled determination. He felt that journal keeping was a duty that he must answer. Readers of Grant's diaries will find in it many passages of complaint—no one, he thought, would possibly wish to read his record. On other occasions, he asked why should a busy man like himself, often juggling a half dozen Church or business projects, keep a journal? Yet day after day and month upon month, he carried on until his personal diary occupied more than sixty years of Church history, an achievement that hardly can be overstated. In scope and detail, Grant's diaries are one of the Church's great treasures.

He was as careful with his correspondence, which again bulked large. From his early twenties, he retained most letters sent to him, and, still more impressive, he retained copies of his own letters. On both accounts—incoming and outgoing letters—the volume of material was large because he enjoyed an active and full career. But a personal dimension also made his correspondence remarkable, too.

Voluble and people-interested, President Grant liked to talk to others, and in this case, liked writing to others—in fact, writing a *great deal* to others. His lifelong insomnia furthered the inclination. Unable to sleep but enjoying a good conversation, President Grant spent many nights "talking" his correspondence into the various recording devices he kept by his bedside, enough to keep a secretary scurrying. These nocturnal dictations have proven extraordinarily important to a historian and biographer. Often remarkably detailed, frank, and personal—they are almost a stream-of-consciousness—they aid in understanding Grant's emotions, thoughts, and expectations and do much to reveal and revive his character. For once, a biography is able to get "inside" a character, beyond the usual, impenetrable shell that conceals most historical figures from view.

To be sure, the Grant collection was an embarrassment of riches, both in quality and in quantity. For a worker in the biographical trenches, they represent extraordinary effort. Tens of thousands of diary pages had to be read as well as hundreds of thousands of pages of correspondence, and these estimates did not include President Grant's account books, the many pages of his published sermons, photographs, and miscellany. Indeed, the voluminous Grant collection requires almost two hundred archival boxes, occupying an esti-mated sea of almost one hundred linear feet of shelving. In addition to Grant's collection, auxiliary collections had to be looked at, not to mention Grant's extensive book collection (MSS 2853) housed in L. Tom Perry Special Collections, Harold B. Lee Library at Brigham Young University. When finished with all this research, my files bulged with more than ten thousand five-by-eight-inch note sheets.

So rich a collection of information before me, I moved step-by-step from my "hardly speaking acquaintance" with President Grant to an easy but respectful familiarity, and I must say, in this case, familiarity bred respect, not the opposite. I found my biographical subject to be "human" in the best sense of the term. Certainly there were frailties, but generally these were products of what I saw as compounded virtues. President Grant's rush and enthusiasm some-times left behind him a stormy torrent that required calming. Deter-mined to push "good causes," he sometimes bore down hard and demanded from others the same lofty standard of effort and giving that he held for himself. No intellectual, he seemed uncomfortable with thoughts, ideas, distinctions, qualities manifest in his preaching: he was always more an exhorter than a teacher or explicator. Yet at the center of his person—President Grant would say, "in his heart of hearts"—he had a remarkable charity for a man of fluctuating but generally modest means. Rumors of his great wealth were largely the creation of his open-handedness. Could a man be so free with his means without an abundance, some asked? In fact, it was true, for his life answered the measure of his religion, that men and women must be judged by the abundance of their heart when dealing out their means. In this great criterion, he was exemplary.

To uncover the "Heber J. Grant story," I resolved on a piecemeal, step-by-step strategy. I planned to write a series of articles—position papers as it were—from which a larger, perhaps several-volume biography could later be built. During the several years that I worked on the project, I wrote more than a dozen articles about the man and his times, mostly about his "early years." Then, due to intervening circumstances at the Historical Department, I was required to put aside the biography and move to other publishing tasks.

Recently, I have looked back upon these early essays and wondered, pending my formal biography, whether they should be made accessible to a general reader in a single volume. Considering the idea, I realized these writings actually had about them a uniting theme. They were largely about the making of the man, described by a phrase used by President Grant himself at the time of his call into the Quorum of the Twelve. At the time, he was a scant twenty-five years old (no Apostle since has been younger). He was unseasoned and unsure of himself, something of which he was acutely aware. Musing on the theme, he wondered in correspondence to his boyhood chum and lifelong confidant, Richard W. Young, whether he had "the qualities that count." However, "there is one thing that sustains me," he told Young, "& that is the fact that all powers, of mind or body, come from God and that He is perfectly able & willing to qualify me for His work provided I am faithful in doing my part."[1] That hope became a lifelong journey.

This book, then, is encompassed by its title. It is about "qualities that count," how qualities were planted by his parents, friends, and early experiences; how qualities took root and grew in the course of business, family, and church service; and how qualities grew and matured in the man who became the President of the Church. Some still may remember him: his ramrod-straight posture at the pulpit, his stentorian voice extending to the farther reaches of the Tabernacle, and the fundamental values that he taught. During his lifetime, detractors saw some of these qualities as old-fashioned in the New Deal world of change; however, at the beginning of the twenty-first century they appear traditional and time tested. Certainly, these qualities helped to navigate the Church through the troubled sea of economic bad times and world war. This book is about how these traits came to be.

The story opens with a discussion of President Grant's heritage, especially the story of the tutoring of that unusual widow, Rachel Grant—improvident, handicapped by a hearing loss, yet sunny in disposition and brimming with social and cultural values that her son would inherit and then later transmit in Church service to the twentieth century. The essays "Heber J. Grant's Years of Passage" and "Growing Up in Early Utah: The Wasatch Literary Association, 1874–1878" tell what it was like to be a boy and adolescent in post–pioneer Utah, and they suggest that, despite the family's relative poverty, Rachel and Heber were part of a growing social elite that not only changed Utah and Mormon society but provided young Grant a network of important contacts as he moved along in his career.

The next section introduces one of the tugs that conflicted Grant throughout his career. He came of age during America's "Golden Age of the Entrepreneur," and he was unmistakably drawn to the balance sheet and to business. This section displays President Grant's fascination with business and how he used his natural talent to save or aid Church credit in the depressed 1890s, particularly when he assumed the hero's role in the Panic of 1893 when Mormon finances stood at the brink of ruin.

The next section suggests a counterpoint. While Elder Grant loved business activity, Church leaders saw the young man's talent and spirit and wanted to enroll him in Church matters. The resulting tension is conveyed in the title: "Young Heber J. Grant and His Call to the Apostleship." While he enjoyed his ministry, there were also times when Grant wondered if his Church service was almost unnatural and unreasonable. How could it be that someone of his inborn business relish and talent be taken from his element? Another essay in this section, dealing with his marriage to Emily Wells Grant during the anti–plural marriage crusade in the 1880s, shows Grant, the Apostle, through the prism of his family life during this difficult personal and Church era. Finally, the essay, "Heber J. Grant and the Succession Turmoil of 1887–1889," reveals the tension among Elder Grant's competing loyalties—business, church, and family—during an extraordinary episode in Church administrative history.

The last section of the book presents Elder Grant in the foliation of vigorous manhood, serving proselytizing missions to Japan and England.

Throughout, Elder Grant's traits march across the page. He is successively devoted, energetic, honest, and idealistic. He is also direct and outspoken, perhaps to a flaw. An enthusiast, he enjoys a campaign for a good cause. As he matures, he increasingly yields himself to Church activity and to the requirement and restraints placed upon him because of his calling. Whatever his earlier ambivalence between business and religion, in later years it seemed increasingly resolved, in part by events. He assumed Church leadership in 1918 precisely at the time when his gifts could best be used for his religion: Utah's economic downtown in the 1920s and the Great Depression of the 1930s.

In presenting this collection of essays, I have deleted some of the redundancies that inevitably occur in articles written for a variety of purposes, and my editors have also suggested occasional minor rephrasing for style and clarity. The articles have undergone minimal editing for uniformity of style, and in a handful of places, new information, which has become available since the essay was first published, has been inserted to bring the piece up to date. Nevertheless, the articles remain mainly as I first wrote them and contain my early views. One exception to this rule is the previously unpublished article dealing with Grant's role in the Woodruff succession. Written over a decade ago for presentation at a historical conference and then set aside to fallow, as this book took form I felt the need to smooth this story, although my original interpretation remains. This important but largely untold story was pivotal in Elder Grant's early experience—and the Church's as well—enforcing upon him the need for apostolic collegiality. Finally, this book also includes "helps," such as a family pedigree chart and numerous photographs not used during the first publication of the articles.

Any book is an unconscious recipient of favors, and this one is no exception. I am thankful to Leonard Arrington for asking me to undertake this task, to members of the large and friendly Heber J. Grant family who have indulged my requests for interviews and comment, and to the small phalanx of research assistants, past and present, who have aided me in so many ways. The staff of the Historical Department of The Church of Jesus Christ of Latter-day Saints has been unfailingly helpful, most recently by allowing me re-access to the Grant collection so that I might confirm the accuracy of more than six hundred citations. This last endeavor required the service of several people, including research assistants Benjamin Austin and James Lambert. Over the years, my colleagues at Brigham Young University's Joseph Fielding Smith Institute for Latter-day Saint History have read my Heber J. Grant essays and given me helpful comments. Richard L. Jensen remains unexcelled for his facility with a red pen; past and present directors of the institute, Ronald K. Esplin and Jill Mulvay Derr, have generously offered encouragement and assistance. However, as always, the usual and necessary disclaimer must be made: I alone am responsible for this book's presentation and views.

In bringing the manuscript to publication, I have been particularly pleased to work with publication staff of Brigham Young University Press. Professor John W. Welch, Director of Publications for the Smith Institute and Editor in Chief of *BYU Studies,* lent his support; Heather Seferovich, managing editor of the Smith Institute Series, pushed the project along while at the same time allowing me to profit from her invaluable eye for precision, clarity, and grace in expression. Skilled editors are as rare. Kimberly Chen Pace, prodution editor for the Smith Institute, made the volume look attractive—inside and out—prepared the illustrations for the press, and even created the family tree (p.11) and the map (p.280). Stephen J. Fleming, having an available summer to help before continuing graduate study, played a key role in laying out the manuscript and selecting photographs. Marny K. Parkin compiled an index, itself an art form. Finally, the BYU Studies staff assisted with various editing duties and production assignments.

Qualities that Count is more than a title of a book or a description of President's Grant's qualities. The phrase of course is also a suggestion for proper living, and, as such, it is a reminder of a past when books were read for personal "growth" as well as for understanding a figure or an era. President Grant, we think, would be pleased with such a phrase, for it captures much of what he and his era were about.

Note

1. Heber J. Grant to Richard W. Young, November 16, 1882, Grant Letterpress Copybook, 5:62–63, Heber J. Grant Papers, Church Archives, The Church of Jesus Christ of Latter-day Saints, Salt Lake City.

Jedediah and Heber Grant

On December 1, 1856, Elder Wilford Woodruff and Elder Franklin D. Richards left the Church historian's office for the home of Jedediah Grant, less than a block away. The hour was late, about 10:30 in the evening. It had snowed several inches during the day, and the weather was turning cold.

For over a week Elder Woodruff had maintained a vigil at his friend's adobe home, constantly praying and blessing Jedediah's weakened body. Now he learned that there would be no recovery. Before arriving at their destination, the two Apostles heard the dreaded news: Jedediah Morgan Grant—one of President Young's counselors and the mayor of Salt Lake City—was dead. "Lung disease," a combination of typhoid and pneumonia, had taken him at the early age of forty.

Elders Woodruff and Richards hastened their steps. They found the Grant household on Main Street in distress. Jedediah's wives and children were "weeping bitterly."[1] They had lost a kind husband and father but also their provider in Utah's young and still uncertain society. Less than ten years had elapsed since Brother Brigham and the others had first entered the Salt Lake Valley. This year, 1856, had been especially hard. Indian turmoil, handcart tragedies, and bad crops had plagued the Saints. Now there was Jedediah's death.

Upstairs, concealed from the view of the Apostles, lay another grieving woman. Only nine days before, Rachel Grant had borne her husband a son—her first child. Her labor had been difficult, and for a time her attendants feared for her life. At the moment of Jedediah's death, she remained bedridden, recovering her strength. The commotion downstairs must have set her thinking. She had left her home in New Jersey for the gospel's sake. Jedediah had not been a wealthy man. What might her future be? What would become of her son?

On that dark, troubled night, no one could have guessed the answers to her questions.

Jedediah Grant—the Beginning

Both Joshua Grant and Athalia Howard, Jedediah's father and mother, came from families that had farmed Connecticut's stony soil for at

Courtesy Church Archives, The Church of Jesus Christ of Latter-day Saints

Illus. 1-1. Jedediah Morgan Grant (ca. 1856), counselor to Brigham Young and father of Heber J. Grant.

least four generations. They married in Sullivan County, New York, and then frequently uprooted their growing household in a steady westward migration. When the Latter-day Saint missionaries found the Grants, Joshua and Athalia had twelve children. "Jeddy," as he was usually known, was their seventh (illus. 1-1).

Like many early converts, the family embraced the gospel after a dramatic spiritual experience. During winter 1833, Elders Amasa Lyman and Orson Hyde came to the Grant family home near Erie, Pennsylvania. Athalia lay paralyzed with rheumatism. "I remember how tall Elder Lyman looked as he stood by the side of Mother's bed telling us of the gifts and blessings of the restored Gospel and that these blessings follow the believer," a daughter recalled many years later.

> My mother asked why she could not be blessed as she had perfect faith that God could heal her. The elders placed their hands on her head and prayed for her recovery. Later that evening my mother got up, dressed herself, went out of doors and climbed the stairs, which were on the outside of the house and, with my help, prepared a bed in which the elders slept that night.[2]

By March 2, 1833, seventeen-year-old Jeddy had seen and heard enough to desire baptism. The weather was not accommodating, but Jeddy was determined. The winter temperature was so biting that the young man's clothing froze to his body after he came up out of the river. Eventually most of the family, parents as well as children, followed him into the new faith.

At first glance Jeddy seemed to offer little promise. "He was a frontier boy," his biographer wrote, "one whose hopes went no further than the wrinkled face of his father and the earthy struggle for life into which he was born."[3] His nose, broken early in life, descended properly to its bridge and then angled noticeably to the left. His sinuous frame looked fragile, almost delicate.

But there was more here than met the eye. Frontier schooling gave him only a shaky command of commas, periods, and the perplexing science of orthography; yet as a teenager he ambitiously read from such religious and philosophical thinkers as Wesley, Locke, Rousseau, Watts, Abercrombie, and Mather.[4] And he early learned to make his slender body respond to his commands. Young Jeddy could fell large trees single-handedly and more than keep pace in his father's shingle making business. He had intelligence, willpower, and a flood of nervous energy.

Mormonism completely captivated him, and he enthusiastically responded to its calls. A year after his baptism, he marched with Zion's Camp to Missouri. Winter 1835–36 found him working on the Kirtland Temple. At nineteen he began the first of four proselyting missions, which largely occupied the years 1835 through 1842. In 1843 he received the appointment of Presiding Elder of the Philadelphia Branch and a year later became a member of the First Council of Seventy and of Joseph Smith's General Council at Nauvoo.

He found his talents multiplying. During his long missionary tours in the Virginia and Carolina back country, Jeddy's wit and eloquence won scores of converts—and a preaching reputation that became a local legend. He also earned high marks for loyalty and leadership. "I think he has saved the church in Philadelphia," Wilford Woodruff wrote as dissension swept many of the eastern branches following Joseph Smith's death. "Elder Grant is a man after my own heart. He is true in all things."[5] Likewise during the 1847 migration to Utah, Jedediah was given responsibility. He captained the "Third Hundred" pioneers across the plains and into the valley.

Only two members of his father's family permanently followed Jedediah to the West. The rough-hewn George D. distinguished himself as a scout and militiaman; Grantsville, Utah, was named in his honor following an Indian skirmish. Joshua Jr., Jeddy's frequent missionary companion, settled in Salt Lake City, where he died in 1851.

However, the remainder of the family stayed behind. Jedediah's parents had "gathered" at Kirtland and later in Far West, but for them the Missouri persecutions were a searing experience. Joshua and Athalia eventually located near Altona, Knox County, Illinois, about sixty miles northeast of Nauvoo. Removed from the Saints, their faith in the gospel gradually withered.

Jedediah's other brothers and sisters followed a similar pattern. Some drifted into Universalism. Two sisters successively married William Smith, brother of the Prophet. Several accepted the reorganized church's doctrines of Joseph Smith III. When one of Jeddy's sons many years later visited his aging aunts and uncles in the Midwest, he found them to be "good people," but no different in attainments and character than the folk that surrounded them.

Rachel Ivins

Rachel Ivins met the dramatic, twenty-three-year-old Jedediah Grant when she was about eighteen.

She was the sixth of eight children born to Caleb Ivins and Edith Ridgeway. Both parents had died before she was ten, and Rachel was then raised by a succession of relatives.

The Ivins and Ridgeways were similar—serious-minded merchants who had migrated to America in the late seventeenth century. Rachel's relatives generously filled her childhood wants and instilled within her the virtues of hard work, neatness, discipline, and Christian kindness.

However, Rachel had trouble accepting her family's Quaker seriousness. She saw herself as "religiously inclined but not of the long-faced variety."[6] Moreover, she liked to sing. While living with a straight-laced cousin who banned music from his home, the orphan would steal off to a small grove of trees where she sang as she sewed for her dolls.

When Rachel first heard Jedediah Grant and Erastus Snow teach the restored gospel, she wondered if these might be the "false prophets" that the Bible spoke of. She returned home after one Mormon preaching session, knelt down, and pleaded for the Lord's forgiveness for deliberately listening to false doctrine on the Sabbath.[7] But more searching prayer and study convinced her otherwise. In 1840 she was baptized, and two years later, with relatives who also had accepted the faith, she traveled to Nauvoo.

The well-bred Rachel Ivins, just twenty-one, must have turned more than one head during her Nauvoo visit. A friend later described her:

> She was dressed in silk with a handsome lace collar, or fichu, and an elegant shawl over her shoulder, and a long white lace veil thrown back over her simple straw bonnet. She carried an elaborate feather fan. . . . One could easily discern the subdued Quaker pride in her method of using it, for Sister Rachel had the air, the tone, and mannerisms of the Quakers.[8]

Actually Rachel stayed longer in Nauvoo than she planned. She witnessed the kaleidoscopic last days of Joseph and Hyrum Smith and was present when Brigham Young spoke with the voice and mannerisms of his predecessor. This last event long remained a testimony to her. Some of her Ivins cousins were a part of the *Nauvoo Expositor* intrigue, which eventually led to Joseph's death, and they later strayed into James J. Strang's apostasy. Rachel herself did not doubt where the Lord's authority lay. She had seen Joseph's mantle fall upon Brigham.

Rachel did not follow the Saints westward at first but instead returned to New Jersey. However, by spring 1853 she joined a company of New Jersey Saints in their migration west. Doctors warned that the journey might turn a persistent cough into something dangerous; her family had a medical history of "consumption," or tuberculosis. Most of Rachel's relatives also attempted to dissuade her. They even offered her a lifetime annuity if she would remain.

When the New Jersey pioneers arrived in Salt Lake City, they turned up Main Street and found lodging with their old friend Jedediah Grant. He had retained ties with his New Jersey flock and had returned several times to his old missionary area to determine their welfare.

Rachel would return to Jedediah's adobe house a little more than a year later, this time as his seventh and last wife.

Jedediah Grant's Children—the Second Generation

From the beginning, Rachel's young son seemed a child of promise. When Bishop Edwin Woolley christened him "Heber Jede Ivins Grant," the spirit of the occasion was unusual. "I was only an instrument in the hands of his dead father . . . in blessing him," Bishop Woolley later remarked. Heber Grant "is entitled to be one of the Apostles, and I know it."[9]

However, the childhood of Heber Jeddy Grant, time quickly shortened his name, was not an easy one. After the death of Jedediah, Rachel briefly married his brother George D. Grant. Their divorce left her again impoverished.

Heber later looked back upon his youth. There were blustery nights with no fire in the hearth, months with no shoes, never more than a single homemade outfit of homespun at a time, and except for an adequate supply of bread, a meager fare which allowed only a pound of butter and not many more pounds of sugar for an entire year.[10] Although Rachel's education, personality, and intelligence placed her among Deseret's "first ladies," sewing became her means of avoiding charity. "I sat on the floor at night until midnight," Heber remembered of many evenings, "and pumped the sewing machine to relieve her tired limbs."[11] The machine's constantly moving treadles became a symbol of the Grant family's stubborn independence.

Young Heber J. Grant quickly displayed his talents in a remarkable fashion. At the age of fifteen, he joined the insurance firms of H. R. Mann and Company as an office boy and policy clerk. After business hours, he marketed fire insurance. By nineteen, he had bought out his employers and organized his own successful agency. During his early twenties he broadened out into other business activities. At twenty-three he was called to preside over the Tooele Stake. And two years later, in October 1882, he filled the destiny seen by Bishop Woolley when he was set apart as a member of the Quorum of the Twelve.

While Rachel's son became the most prominent of Jedediah's children, there were actually ten others from six other plural wives

(Caroline Van Dyke, Susan Fairchild Noble, Rosetta Robinson, Sarah Ann Thurston, Louisa Marie Goulay, and Maryette Kesler). Two daughters died in their youth; the two other daughters, Rosette (Marshall) and Susan Vilate (Muir), settled on out-of-the-way Utah farms.

Jedediah's seven sons pursued a variety of paths (illus. 1-2). After a long and successful mission to England, George was killed in a hunting accident a few months short of his thirtieth birthday. Lewis McKeachie, an adopted Scottish orphan, managed the Grant family lands in Davis County, Utah, where he also served as a justice of the peace, county selectman, city judge, and bishop. Jedediah Morgan Grant Jr. farmed for several decades in Rich County, Utah, and later pioneered in the Big Horn Basin of Wyoming, concluding his Church service as a patriarch.[12]

Joshua, Joseph Hyrum, and Brigham Frederick played a role in many of Heber's businesses, but these brothers also made their own way. Joshua helped found Utah's largest wagon and implement business, served on the Salt Lake Board of Education, and later managed the American Steel and Wire Company.

Illus. 1-2. Six of Jedediah Grant's sons, 1877. Top row (*left to right*), Brigham F., Heber J., Joshua F. Bottom row (*left to right*), Jedediah M., Joseph H., George S.

Hyrum's fine eye and gentle way with horses made him for a time the manager of the Grant Brothers' Livery and Transfer Company. Later, while farming in Bountiful, he contracted jaundice. The disease wasted his body to about seventy pounds, and doctors, failing to detect a pulse, pronounced him dead. Yet a priesthood blessing promised him both life and the opportunity to serve as Davis Stake President. Hyrum realized both promises.[13]

The life story of B. F. Grant reads like a romance novel. Abandoned by his mother as an infant and apprenticed to a stern and heavy-handed Cache County farmer at six, the boy fled to Montana as a stowaway in a freighter's wagon at the age of twelve. The lad then traveled throughout the West as a miner, cowboy, and laborer. When B. F. arrived back in Salt Lake City at the age of about fifteen, Brigham Young extended a helping hand, giving him work and schooling. But it was not until B. F. was about forty—after bankruptcy and thoughts of suicide—that he returned to the faith of his father. B. F. concluded his career as a convincing preacher to wayward youth, as Salt Lake City's chief of police, and later as general manager of the *Deseret News*.

Elder Marriner W. Merrill of the Quorum of the Twelve had an explanation for B. F.'s return to Church activity. The night after his Cache County neighbors learned that the boy had run away, Elder Merrill had a dream about B. F. He saw him in all kinds of wicked company, but B. F. was always surrounded by a light. When Elder Merrill wondered about the meaning of the light, he was told: "It is the influence of the boy's father who, having been faithful, is permitted to protect him from being contaminated with the sins of the world, so that he can return to the fold of Christ."[14]

Whatever the reason, it is remarkable that despite the disintegration of Jedediah's family after his death, all his children except Joshua became active Church members.

Moreover the Grant second generation achieved a remarkable unity, particularly the sons. "We are all the very best of friends and have never had any family difficulties to speak of and we work with pleasure to aid each other in our business affairs," Heber said of the Grant boys' relationship thirty-five years after Jedediah's demise. "There are none of us who have the same mothers so it is not to be supposed we would be as much alike in dispositions as some brothers are and yet I think that we are greater friends and more united than many brothers where there was but one mother."[15]

Jedediah would have been pleased.

Heber's Family—the Third Generation

"What, are you writing home again?" Brigham Young Jr. asked Heber J. Grant. "I must say that I have never seen a man so badly cracked on the home question as you are." The two members of the Quorum of the Twelve were traveling through Arizona Territory, and the new Apostle had taken every opportunity to write to his family. Elder Grant admitted feeling homesick. "This is my first experience in being away from home and I am free to confess that I . . . long for the time that I can embrace my darling wife and mother and kiss three little girls."[16]

Despite many subsequent years of Church travel, Grant always felt lonely when away from his family. His return home was usually a joyous occasion. "What a jubilant time we had when he came home!" a daughter remembered. "We would all gather around and listen to his experiences. I can see him now walking around the house with a child on each foot, or tossing the children up on his knee."[17]

Grant came to have a large family—three wives and twelve children (illus. 1-3). The lovely and hard-working Lucy Stringham was his first wife. Young Heber vowed to capture her before his twenty-first birthday and succeeded with three weeks to spare. Seven years later he also married Huldah Augusta Winters and Emily Wells (illus. 1-4).

The three Grant wives were remarkably similar. They were well educated for the times. All had taught school. Augusta in fact conducted classes ten years before her marriage and was reputed to be the ablest and highest-salaried schoolmarm in the territory. Each of the women bore a quiet but firm belief in her religion, and each descended from pioneer families. Lucy's father was a former counselor in the Thirteenth Ward bishopric, the taciturn Bryant Stringham. Augusta came from early settlers who farmed in Pleasant Grove, Utah. The shy Emily was the daughter of Daniel Wells, Jedediah Grant's successor in the First Presidency.

These three women, their husband, and Rachel, who lived into her eighty-eighth year, set the tone for the Grant household. Church

Illus. 1–3. Heber J. Grant's ten daughters, ca. 1902. Back row (*left to right*): Anna (Midgley), Florence (Smith), Martha Deseret "Dessie" (Boyle), Edith (Young). Front row (*left to right*): Susan Rachel "Ray" (Taylor), Mary (Judd), Frances Marion (Bennett), Emily (Mansen), Grace (Evans), and Lucy "Lutie" (Cannon). Heber's two sons died young.

Illus. 1-4. Family Tree of Jedediah M. and Heber J. Grant

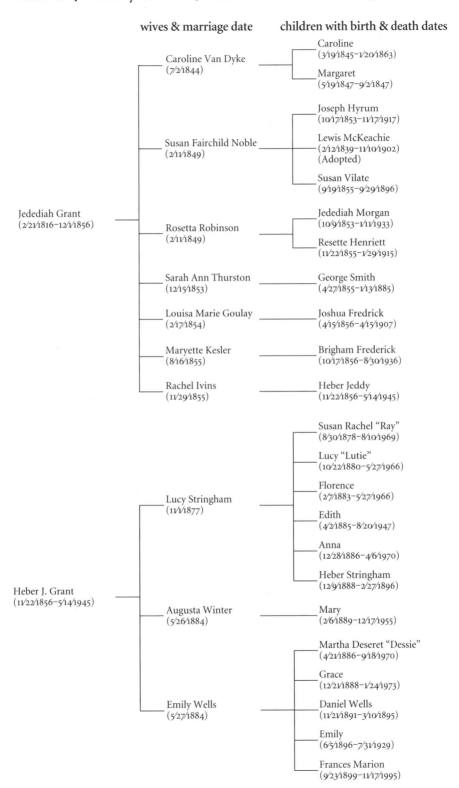

wives & marriage date   children with birth & death dates

Jedediah Grant
(2/21/1816–12/1/1856)

- **Caroline Van Dyke** (7/2/1844)
  - Caroline (3/19/1845–1/20/1863)
  - Margaret (5/19/1847–9/2/1847)

- **Susan Fairchild Noble** (2/11/1849)
  - Joseph Hyrum (10/17/1853–11/17/1917)
  - Lewis McKeachie (2/12/1839–11/10/1902) (Adopted)
  - Susan Vilate (9/19/1855–9/29/1896)

- **Rosetta Robinson** (2/11/1849)
  - Jedediah Morgan (10/9/1853–1/11/1933)
  - Resette Henriett (11/22/1855–1/29/1915)

- **Sarah Ann Thurston** (12/15/1853)
  - George Smith (4/27/1855–1/13/1885)

- **Louisa Marie Goulay** (2/17/1854)
  - Joshua Fredrick (4/15/1856–4/15/1907)

- **Maryette Kesler** (8/16/1855)
  - Brigham Frederick (10/17/1856–8/30/1936)

- **Rachel Ivins** (11/29/1855)
  - Heber Jeddy (11/22/1856–5/14/1945)

Heber J. Grant
(11/22/1856–5/14/1945)

- **Lucy Stringham** (11/1/1877)
  - Susan Rachel "Ray" (8/30/1878–8/10/1969)
  - Lucy "Lutie" (10/22/1880–5/27/1966)
  - Florence (2/7/1883–5/27/1966)
  - Edith (4/2/1885–8/20/1947)
  - Anna (12/28/1886–4/6/1970)
  - Heber Stringham (12/9/1888–2/27/1896)

- **Augusta Winter** (5/26/1884)
  - Mary (2/6/1889–12/17/1955)

- **Emily Wells** (5/27/1884)
  - Martha Deseret "Dessie" (4/21/1886–9/18/1970)
  - Grace (12/21/1888–1/24/1973)
  - Daniel Wells (11/21/1891–3/10/1895)
  - Emily (6/5/1896–7/31/1929)
  - Frances Marion (9/23/1899–11/17/1995)

activity was always stressed. As one daughter said of the family's commitment to the Church: "In our home we seemed to observe an unwritten law that Church service came first and home duties second. We early became aware that the best way to show our love and appreciation for our parents was to do our best to help in Church organizations. There was no way we could make them happier than to be faithful in Church duties."[18]

The children were also introduced to cultural influences. Elder Grant for many years owned the controlling interest in the majestic Salt Lake Theatre, and the family attended its performances at least weekly. Following a play, the children were asked to discuss the production at the family dinner table, a practice that led one Grant child to "count the theater second only to [her] actual schooling in educational value."[19]

The printed word likewise had a high place among the Grants. Books filled Elder Grant's homes. "It was as natural for us to read as to eat or sleep," Augusta's daughter Mary later wrote.[20] Like the morality plays of the Salt Lake Theater, the Grant library taught "right and wrong." Emphasis was upon Victorian didacticism rather than "great works."

The dictum "spare the rod and spoil the child" never had much of a place in raising the Grant children, so Lucy recalls. Rachel had indulged young Heber, balancing light discipline with loving but demanding expectations. The formula was now tried upon another generation. "They will only be children once," Elder Grant explained, "and I want them to get as much pleasure as they can out of life as they go along."[21]

The Panic of 1893 removed any possibility of spoiling the children. Wealthy before its onslaught, Elder Grant was left with crushing debts. Nickels now seemed worth dollars. Domestic help became an unaffordable luxury. The children, particularly Lucy's older family, rose to the challenge. They helped with household chores and even with their father's debts. "As soon as we were old enough," one remembered, "we started to work in his office, and it was the greatest satisfaction of our young lives to feel that we were helping him by caring for ourselves and in that way sharing his heavy burden of debt."[22] The depression of the 1890s brought increased family purpose and solidarity.

The Grant home life had other challenges. Elder Grant admitted that even in the best of times plural marriage was difficult. And the 1880s and 1890s, with Congress and the federal courts attempting to stop the practice, were not the best of times. While the Grants succeeded in achieving genuine love within the system, it also placed great strain upon the family. At times there were weeks and even months when Elder Grant was separated from his loved ones.

The Grant family felt the tragedy of death. Both of the Church leader's sons died in childhood. His beloved Lucy passed away at the age of thirty-four, leaving five children between the ages of four and fourteen (Anna, Edith, Florence, Lucy, and Rachel; Heber was deceased). Emily's early death in 1908 occurred when her two youngest children were eight and eleven (Frances and Emily, the others were Grace and Martha Deseret; Daniel had passed away). Yet the family remained united, just as the second generation had. "Aunt" Augusta (her child was Mary) helped raised Lucy's family, while Emily's young children were brought up by older sisters.

The ten Grant daughters remembered a happy early life. There were family outings such as picnics and drives through the city, ward parties where their much-in-demand father danced only with his children, and fatherly letters that counseled but never carped.

Indeed, Elder Grant always seemed to say the right things at the right time. Once Augusta suggested that each of them point out the annoying habits of the other. Her husband agreed. She mentioned several of Heber's idiosyncrasies and waited for his suggestions. There was "a slight twinkle in his eye," she remembered, and then he replied, "You haven't one."[23]

Such tact calms even the most troubled matrimonial waters.

The Fourth Generation—and Beyond

On November 20, 1978, 252 members of the Heber J. Grant family met in the Federal Heights Ward building in Salt Lake City. As part of the program, a pamphlet profiling the characteristics of the family was distributed.[24] The pamphlet showed how this branch of the Jedediah Grant family had multiplied and prospered. The booklet recorded 454 descendants of Heber J. Grant (607 if spouses were counted). There had been 166 marriages, but only 13 divorces— less than one-fifth of the current United States national average. The family mirrored the Church's post–World War II migration trends. While 60 percent of the descendants continued to live in Utah, Grants now resided in twenty-one other states.

The Grants have continued to serve their church. Five of President Grant's daughters were called either to an auxiliary general presidency or a general board: Lucy Cannon, YWMIA General President; Dessie Boyle, Primary presidency; and Rachel Taylor, Mary Judd, and Frances Bennett of the YWMIA, Relief Society, and Primary general boards. Two of the Grant daughters married men who became General Authorities: Rachel, wife of John H. Taylor of the First Council of Seventy, and Edith, wife of Clifford E. Young, an Assistant to the Twelve. Florence Smith, another child, served as matron of the Salt Lake Temple.

Later generations have also accepted calls at the general Church level. Florence Jacobsen followed her aunt as a president of the YWMIA. George I. Cannon, later President of the Salt Lake Temple and an Area Authority Seventy, and Lucy Taylor Anderson, later part of the Primary General Presidency, both worked as counselors in the YMMIA General Presidencies. At least eight other descendants have served on Church general boards, while another three have presided over missions.

The Grants' service at the local level has been even more extensive. The family has served in callings ranging from YWMIA and YMMIA president, to elders quorum president, to bishop and stake president. As of 1980, President Grant's descendants had filled 130 missions.

All this from a family whose beginnings in early Utah history had seemed tentative and troubled. Despite their trials and in some degree because of them, Jedediah, Heber, and the first Grant women had created a family in the image of their own hopes, personalities, and talents. Their concern for higher things—their church, family, and the ideals of education and service—engendered a similar concern in their descendants.

Notes

This article was originally published in *Ensign* 9 (July 1979): 46–52.

1. Wilford Woodruff, Journal, December 1, 1856, Church Archives, The Church of Jesus Christ of Latter-day Saints, Salt Lake City. For details on

the life of Jedediah M. Grant, I am particularly indebted to Gene Sessions in *Mormon Thunder: A Documentary History of Jedediah Morgan Grant* (Urbana: University of Illinois Press, 1982). Also see Mary G. Judd, *Jedediah M. Grant: Pioneer-Statesman* (Salt Lake City: Deseret News Press, 1959).

2. Thedy Grant Reeves, Reminiscence, as told to Joseph Hyrum Grant Jr., November 26, 1904, Lanthrop, Missouri, as quoted in Sessions, *Mormon Thunder*, 6.

3. Sessions, *Mormon Thunder*, 6–7.

4. Sessions, *Mormon Thunder*, 265.

5. Wilford Woodruff to Brigham Young, December 3, 1844, Brigham Young Collection, Church Archives.

6. Quoted by Francis Bennet Jeppson, "With Joy Wend Your Way: The Life of Rachel Ivins Grant, My Great-Grandmother," 3, typescript, 1952, Church Archives.

7. Mary Grant Judd, "Rachel Ridgway Ivins Grant," *Relief Society Magazine* 30 (April 1943): 228–29. Both family and printed sources differ in the spelling of "Ridgeway"; I have used the form that appears on the earliest family records. See also Joseph Smith, *Young Woman's Journal* 16, no. 12 (December 1905): 550.

8. Emmeline B. Wells, as quoted in Judd, "Rachel Ridgeway Ivins Grant," 229.

9. Preston W. Parkinson, *The Utah Woolley Family* (Salt Lake City: Deseret News Press, 1967), 126. The christening is recorded in the Thirteenth Ward Historical Record, Book B: 1854–59, January 1, 1857, Church Archives.

10. Heber J. Grant, "Faith-Promoting Experiences," *Millennial Star* 93 (November 19, 1931): 760; "Two Octogenarians," *Improvement Era* 39 (November 1936): 667; Heber J. Grant, "Charity Enjoined," *92nd Semi-Annual Conference of The Church of Jesus Christ of Latter-day Saints* (Salt Lake City: The Church of Jesus Christ of Latter-day Saints, 1921), 13; Relief Society Minutes of the Thirteenth Ward, Book B; 1898–1906, February 13, 1902, 95.

11. Grant, "Faith-Promoting Experiences," 760.

12. For brief biographical sketches of the Grant family, see Sessions, *Mormon Thunder*, 293–97.

13. Heber J. Grant, "The Dead Were Raised," *Improvement Era* 30 (November 1926): 11–12.

14. Heber J. Grant to Joseph Hyrum Grant Jr., December 3, 1917, copy, in author's possession.

15. Heber J. Grant to Ann Smith, June 4, 1892, Grant Letterpress Copybook, 13:248, Heber J. Grant Papers, Church Archives. See also *114th Annual Conference of The Church of Jesus Christ of Latter-day Saints* (Salt Lake City: The Church of Jesus Christ of Latter-day Saints, 1944), 7.

16. Heber J. Grant to Lucy Grant, February 26, 1883, Lucy Stringham Grant Papers, Church Archives.

17. Lucy Grant Cannon, "A Father Who Is Loved and Honored," *Improvement Era* 39 (November 1936): 681.

18. Cannon, "Father Who Is Loved," 681.

19. Mary Grant Judd, "A Mormon Wife: The Life Story of Augusta Winters Grant," *Improvement Era* 49 (March 1946): 153.

20. Judd, "Mormon Wife," 153.

21. Heber J. Grant to Anna L. Ivins, January 1, 1895, Grant Letterpress Copybook, 18:464.

22. Cannon, "Father Who Is Loved," 681.

23. Augusta Winters Grant, "My Husband," *Relief Society Magazine* 23 (November 1936): 671.

24. [Carol C. and Gordon A. Madsen], *The Heber J. Grant Family: A Study* (Salt Lake City: privately printed, 1978).

Rachel R. Grant:
The Continuing Legacy of
the Feminine Ideal

We can imagine ourselves visiting Aunt Rachel Grant, long-time president of the Thirteenth Ward Relief Society and one of The Church of Jesus Christ of Latter-day Saint's "leading ladies," at her home on Salt Lake City's Second East Street. In the year of our visit, 1890, her two-story, plastered adobe home partakes of the prevailing feminine ideal that stresses homemaking and handicraft. The stove is highly burnished, while the arms of each chair are covered with homemade lace crocheting. A corner "whatnot" meticulously displays pictures, small framed mottoes, wax and hair flowers, and other curios. Rachel's person also reflects her times. Despite her sixty-nine years, her skin remains supple and clear. She credits her preservation to a lifetime devotion to skin hygiene—no sunlight without a protecting bonnet, no dusting or sweeping without gloves.[1]

We visit Rachel Grant not wishing to find fault with her domesticity and primness nor with the other Victorian values she so fully embodies. Rather, we seek to understand her and her age—and in a sense, ourselves. Aunt Rachel may not be as celebrated a feminist as her contemporaries Eliza R. Snow, Bathsheba W. Smith, or Emmeline B. Wells, but she has influenced later generations certainly as much and perhaps a great deal more. In our age, which often overlooks the obvious, we forget the power that a nineteenth-century woman often wielded from her home. Rachel's only child, Heber J. Grant, with whom she enjoyed a particularly close relationship, led the Church for twenty-seven years of the twentieth century, preaching and practicing the values he had learned from her.

To understand Rachel Grant is to learn something about the personality of present-day Mormonism.

Rachel Ridgway Ivins was born at Hornerstown, New Jersey, March 7, 1821, the sixth of eight children. She would have few memories of her parents. Caleb, her father, evidently involved himself in the family's expansive business concerns, which included Hornerstown's distillery, country store, and grist and saw mills. Due to apparent sunstroke, Rachel's mother, Edith Ridgway, died when Rachel was six. To compound the tragedy, Rachel's grandmother, Keziah Ivins, described by her contemporaries as a "lovely, spirited woman, liked by all," died just four years later.[2]

The orphan was subsequently raised by a succession of her close-knit relatives. For several years she remained at Hornerstown with Caleb Sr., her indulgent grandfather. However, she found the stringent household of her married cousins Joshua and Theodosia Wright at Trenton more to her liking. The Wrights' home was set off by gardens complete with statuary and wildlife and meant no diminution in her lifestyle. Moreover, much to Rachel's delight, the house was run by cousin Theodosia with precision, industry, and regularity. Under the older woman's demanding, six-year tutelage, teenage Rachel learned both personal discipline and the domestic arts. An able student, she returned to Monmouth County when she was about eighteen as a housekeeper for Richard Ridgway, her widower uncle.[3]

She must have marveled at the religious changes in her neighborhood. Like upstate New York's earlier and more famous "Burned-Over" district, central New Jersey experienced wave after wave of religious excitement during the first half of the nineteenth century, with the newfangled and despised Mormons competing with the more established Methodists, Baptists, and Presbyterians. By the late 1830s, a cadre of some of Mormonism's ablest missionaries, including Jedediah Grant, Erastus Snow, Benjamin Winchester, Wilford Woodruff, and Orson and Parley Pratt, had founded a half-dozen Latter-day Saint congregations in central New Jersey, several with their own unpretentious chapels.[4]

Rachel's kin played a major role in this activity. Young Israel Ivins was the first Latter-day Saint convert from Monmouth County.

Merchants Charles and James Ivins soon followed. Parley Pratt described James as a "very wealthy man" and enrolled him, along with himself, as a committee of two to reissue the Book of Mormon in the East. But no conversion was as telling upon Rachel as that of her older sister, Anna Lowrie Ivins. Optimistic and stoical, Anna was her alter ego and would remain so to the end of Rachel's life.[5]

Whatever the sociology and psychology of conversion, Rachel, despite her initial belief that the Latter-day Saint preachers were "the false prophets the Bible speaks of," seemed ideally prepared to accept the new religion. She always had been "religiously inclined, but not of the long-faced variety" and had enjoyed reading the Bible. Yet in a century that cultivated such things, she was a young lady without strong ties to a visible religious establishment. For generations her progenitors had been practicing Quakers, but by the nineteenth century this commitment had begun to wane; Rachel herself bridled at the Friends' prohibition against song. Therefore, at the straitlaced Wrights', who banned music from their home, she would retreat to a small grove of trees where she would sing as she sewed for her dolls. This penchant for music may have contributed to her conversion at sixteen to the more musically inclined Baptists, though her commitment failed to go very deep. She later claimed to have "never learned anything from them."[6]

When Anna and a friend from Trenton told her that Erastus Snow and Joseph Smith, the Church's Prophet, would preach at the "Ridge" above Hornerstown, she concluded after some hesitation to go. Though she found Joseph to be a "fine, noble looking man . . . so neat," she was by her own account "prejudiced" and thus paid little heed to his message. Only politeness to her Trenton friend persuaded her to return the following day, Sunday, to hear Joseph Smith once more. Thereupon she returned to her room and pled for the Lord's forgiveness for deliberately listening to false doctrine on the Sabbath. But Joseph Smith's preaching planted a seed that continued to grow. "I attended some more meetings," she recalled, "and commenced reading the Book of Mormon [so enthralled she began reading one evening and did not stop until almost daybreak], *Voice of Warning,* and other works," and was soon convinced that they were true. "A new light seemed to break in upon me, the scriptures were plainer to my mind, and the light of the everlasting Gospel

began to illumine my soul." When a Baptist minister's funeral sermon consigned an unbaptized youth to hell she noted with favor the
contrast of Orson Hyde's discourse on the innocence and salvation
of young children.[7]

Rachel's interest was neither isolated nor unique. A local historian wrote of Joseph Smith's preaching foray, "Hundreds attended
the [Mormon] meetings," and Joseph "sealed [in baptism] a large
number." The drama of the moment was heightened when the
Prophet anointed a lame and opiated boy, promised him freedom
from both his pain and crutches, and saw the results as promised.
Alarmed at the rising tide, the old-line clergy used stern methods to
put down the new faith. Rachel's Baptist minister admonished her
that if she continued attending the Latter-day Saint meetings, she
could retain neither her pew nor her fellowship in the congregation.
"This seemed to settle the question with me," Rachel remembered,
"I soon handed in my name [to the Latter-day Saints] for baptism
and rendered willing obedience."[8]

"Oh, what joy filled my being!" she exclaimed. Her conversion
opened a floodgate of suppressed emotions that brought her Quaker
relatives to the point of despair: "When she was a Baptist, she was
better, but now she is full of levity—singing all the time." She
delighted in the words of Joseph Smith and those of another
young dynamic preacher, Jedediah Grant, and became completely
enmeshed in the Saints' close-knit society. In addition to the Ivinses,
of whom probably a dozen joined the new faith, many of her neighbors were also baptized. "What good times we had then," she proclaimed years later.[9]

Nevertheless, Rachel wanted to settle in Nauvoo, Illinois, the
hub of Mormon activity during the early 1840s. Already Charles and
James Ivins had reconnoitered the area and returned with plans to
move their families there. Driven by "the spirit of gathering," Rachel,
along with several of her Ivins relatives, ventured to the Mormon
capital in spring 1842.[10]

"The first year of my stay was a very happy one," she remembered. Her cousins Charles and James Ivins rose to immediate prominence. As two of the richest capitalists in the young city, they resumed
their merchandising, met in council with Church leaders, and eventually operated the Nauvoo ferry. Their imposing, Federal-style,

three-building complex on the corner of Kimball and Main streets was used for retailing and small community gatherings and served as a home as well. Here, Rachel lived with James and his family in comfort and relative high style.[11]

Well-bred and in her early twenties, Rachel must have turned the head of more than one admirer. While she herself denied having been a belle, she possessed charm and quiet refinement. Emmeline B. Wells remembered her Nauvoo appearance:

> She was dressed in silk with a handsome lace collar, or fichu, and an elegant shawl over her shoulder, and a long white lace veil thrown back over the simple straw bonnet. She carried an elaborate feather fan . . . I recall the fascination of that fan. One could easily discern the subdued Quaker pride in her method of using it, for Sister Rachel had the air, the tone, and mannerisms of the Quakers.[12]

There was more than a subdued and attractive façade. While little is known of her daily Nauvoo activities and interests, her bosom companion was Sarah Kimball, which suggests a great deal. Several years Rachel's senior, this young and affluent matron entertained Church leaders with memorable elegance. Significantly, Sarah was a thoroughgoing feminist who sought stimulation beyond the thimble and needle and who helped to initiate the Nauvoo Female Relief Society. The intimate friendship of Sarah and Rachel would continue the rest of their lives.[13]

During these Nauvoo days, Rachel came to see the Church and its leaders at close view. Her understanding and acceptance of Latter-day Saint teachings deepened. Because of her love of family and tradition, she especially found the newly declared doctrine promising salvation to the worthy dead "very precious to my soul." Yet, Joseph Smith proved to be an enigma. When he preached, his power deeply affected her. But in private and informal moments, he seemed distressingly "unProphet-like." Outgoing and playful, his personality was the polar opposite of Rachel's—and contradicted her view of what a prophet should be.[14]

There were interludes when Joseph whittled away at her sectarian seriousness, and she came to admire him, along with his brother Hyrum, more than any men she had ever known. She was often at the Prophet's home for parties, although he was present only occasionally. "He would play with the people, and he was always cheerful and happy," she remembered of these occasions. Once while visiting the Ivinses on the Sabbath, he requested the family girls sing the popular "In the Gloaming." Rachel believed singing and newspaper reading breached the Sabbath and responded with a mortified, "Why Bro. Joseph, it's Sunday!" Smith swept her objections aside with a smile and the comment, "The better the day, the better the deed."[15]

These pleasant moments were not long lasting. Smith's opponents, some of whom were in Rachel's own household, were gathering force. Charles and apparently James Ivins joined the Law, Foster, and Higbee brothers in resisting the growing economic and doctrinal complexity of Mormonism. Charles, who, despite his original capital worth, had not prospered in Nauvoo and reacted with particular outrage to rumors that some Church leaders were teaching and practicing plural marriage.[16]

Rachel also knew of these rumors in a very personal way. When Joseph sought an interview with her, she believed he wished to ask for her hand in plural marriage. Her personal turmoil over this prospect must have been excruciating. Her initial response was offended outrage, and she vowed with untypical shrillness that she would "sooner go to hell as a virtuous woman than to heaven as a whore." On one hand, there was the weight of outraged tradition, her cautious and puritanical instincts, and her family's clamor that she withdraw from the Church with them. (Charles Ivins's name appeared on the anti-Smith *Nauvoo Expositor* masthead as one of its publishers.) Yet in other moments she must have considered her still-strong feelings for Mormonism and her respect for Joseph. In her emotional distress, Rachel found it impossible to throw off a persistent fever that eventually threatened her life.[17]

The historical record during these difficult times is inconsistent, perhaps reflecting Rachel's own ambivalence. She refused to meet with Joseph Smith, yet years later she insisted that her faith never wavered. In fact, she repeatedly requested that the elders rebuke her illness; each time she felt strengthened. When Sidney Rigdon sought to lead the Church after the Prophet's assassination, she saw Joseph's mantle fall instead upon Brigham Young. "If you had had your eyes shut," she later testified of President Young's remarkable speech, "you would have thought it was the Prophet [Joseph]. In fact he looked like him, his very countenance seemed to change, and he spoke like him."[18]

Notwithstanding these remarkable experiences, Rachel left Nauvoo in late 1844 bewildered and emotionally scarred. As her son later revealed, "When plural marriage was first taught, my mother left the church on account of it." She returned to New Jersey, ailing physically as well as spiritually and planning never to mingle with the Saints again. She would be gone almost ten years.[19]

In Victorian symbolism, a dried white rose had an unmistakable meaning: better be ravaged by time and death than to lose one's virtue. While Church leaders insisted that plural marriage was heaven-sent and honorable, Rachel, like most women of her generation, initially rejected the practice. She was, in fact, the quintessence of the nineteenth century's prevailing feminine ideal. Where and how she absorbed these values can only be suggested. Her first school was an eighteen-by-twenty-four-foot affair with a ceiling hardly high enough for an adult to stand, but nothing is known about what really counts—her teachers, primers, and curricula. She continued her formal studies while living in Trenton. Schools for young women in the area, like the Young Ladies' Seminary at Bordertown, emphasized as their most important duty "the forming of a sound and virtuous character." Rachel was schooled in the heart, not necessarily the mind. She also assimilated the ideal image of womanhood by reading popular religious literature and almost certainly women's magazines and gift annuals—the common purveyors of the reigning feminine ideal.[20]

Following her Nauvoo experience and her return to the East, Rachel first ran the old Hornerstown household. When her brother Augustus married, she transferred her talents successively to the homes of her sisters Anna, Edith Ann, and particularly Sarah. Very much in her natural element, Rachel became a devoted spinster-aunt. She sang to her nieces and nephews the melodies of her own youth, sewed their clothing, and did more for them, according to their hard-pressed mothers, than their mothers could do. There were also times of inspiration. When consumptive Sarah lay discouraged because of her daily fevers and chills, she asked Rachel to pray and sing several Latter-day Saint hymns. When Rachel rendered

"Oh, Then Arise and Be Baptized," Sarah found the unexpected strength to sing with her and, remembering the hymn's message, requested baptism. Thereupon Sarah's fainting spells ended.[21]

The New Jersey branches that previously had yielded Latter-day Saint converts so bounteously still had some members. Sam Brannan recruited some of the New Jersey Saints to join the *Brooklyn*'s 1846 voyage to California. Two years later Elder William Appleby returned from the West to revive the local flocks and, incidentally, to administer to Rachel for her periodic bronchitis. But this activity was a pale imitation of the excitement that had once burned through the region. Seeking to integrate the gospel more fully with their daily lives, Anna Ivins, her husband-cousin Israel, and several other members of the Ivins family still loyal to the new faith decided in 1853 to join a large company of New Jersey Saints gathering to Utah.[22]

The request forced Rachel into a final weighing of the Church and plural marriage. For a time after Nauvoo she had compartmentalized the two. Even in her early distress about polygamy, she had refused to listen to William Smith, Joseph's schismatic brother, when he had come to the Ivinses' Hornerstown home preaching "another Gospel." When possible she continued her outward Latter-day Saint activity. But for at least several years she struggled with plural marriage, until at some point through prayerful self-searching she found she could accept the doctrine. Although anti-Mormon family members warned that the westward journey would endanger her health and offered a lifetime annuity if she would stay, Rachel turned her face once again to the Mormon promised land, and this time she did not look back.[23]

She prepared carefully. Anticipating frontier scarcity, she filled a chest with bedding, wool and calico piece goods, and a practical wardrobe of bonnets, gloves, and dresses. Other members of the emigrating party, all relatively prosperous, were equally well stocked. By their preparations they were in fact saying good-bye to their life in the East.[24]

The emigrants traveled comfortably. Rachel had the familiar society of several of her Ivins relations, including her cousins Theodore McKean and Anthony Ivins as well as Anna and Israel. Leaving Toms River on April 5, 1853, the party—comprising "a large number of persons from Toms River and other places in the state"—made its way to Philadelphia, boarded the train to Pittsburgh, and then floated on river steamers via Saint Louis to Kansas City. After visiting sites of interest in Jackson County, they purchased mule and wagon outfits (remembered as "one of the best equipments that ever came to Utah in the early fifties") and began the trek west.[25]

The two-and-a-half months on the plains passed equally pleasantly. Anna and Israel traveled with a milk cow and two heavily provisioned wagons. One of these was furnished as a portable room, complete with chairs, a folding bed, and stairs descending from its tailgate. Rachel walked, and while walking spent much of her time knitting, and when tired mounted the stairs and the bed for a rest. Rachel believed the arid Great Plains air permanently thinned and dried her hair, but it also cured her long-standing bronchitis. After about a 130-day journey from New Jersey the Ivins pioneers arrived in Salt Lake City on August 11 and turned up Main Street. There they found temporary lodging with their preacher-friend from years before, Jedediah Grant.[26]

Rachel was now a mature thirty-two. The bloom of youth had passed, but her statuesque charm remained. In polygamous Utah, where sex ratios were perhaps slightly in her favor, she must have had her admirers. But the Ivinses seemed unhurried and cautious about such things. Three of her four brothers never married, and the fourth waited until he was in his thirties. Two of her sisters married cousins. For Rachel's part, she discounted romance or physical attraction. "One could be happy in the marriage relations without love," she reportedly advised, "but could never be happy without respect."[27]

Whether seeking respect or more likely hoping to find a spouse worthy of her own esteem, Rachel's hopes were fulfilled by Jedediah Morgan Grant. She had known him from her late teens when "Jeddy," as he was familiarly known, barnstormed through the New Jersey camp meeting circuit as a missionary. His wit and eloquence won scores of converts and his preaching reputation became a local legend. A biographer has aptly labeled him "Mormon Thunder," but he was more than a religious enthusiast. As a teenager he ambitiously read from Wesley, Locke, Rousseau, Watts, Abercrombie, and Mather. In Salt Lake City, his charity was open-handed and widely heralded. Brigham Young chose him as a counselor and as mayor of Salt Lake City. Already much married, Jeddy sought out Rachel's hand as his seventh wife two years after her Utah arrival.[28]

Given Grant's Church, civic, and connubial duties and Rachel's practicality, their courtship was probably unceremonious and perfunctory. Brigham Young insisted that she first be "eternally sealed" by proxy to his predecessor, apparently to satisfy any obligation owing Joseph. Then on November 29, 1855, Rachel left the home of Anna and Israel, where she had lived for the last two years, and married Grant "for time [in mortality] only" in the Endowment House.[29]

Life at the Grant adobe home on Main Street (the site later occupied by the Meier & Frank in Crossroads Mall) must have been challenging to a woman so private and self-controlled (illus. 2-1). In turn, her ways and presence unsettled others. When little Belle Whitney was once sent to the Grant home for silk thread, she was startled. "I saw this strange beautiful woman sitting there," she recalled. "She looked to me like a queen, and I really thought she was one. I did not dare ask her for the silk. . . . I turned and ran [away]." Initially the other Grant wives were also caught off guard. Instead of exchanging close confidences as women of the century were prone to do, Rachel was restrained. "She writes frequently [to you]," complained one of Jeddy's wives with some edge, "but does not see fit to read them to us."[30]

Courtesy Church Archives, The Church of Jesus Christ of Latter-day Saints

Illus. 2-1. The Grant adobe home on Main Street (the site now occupied by Meier & Frank in Crossroads Mall).

Rachel was not altogether happy at the Grant household. "Remember the trials your dead grandma had and that she was only a wife for a year," wrote her son many years later to one of his own children. The fault did not lie with Jeddy. Though he was often absent on Church assignment, the two evidently enjoyed a satisfactory relationship. She remembered her tendency to "lean" upon him—perhaps too much she later wondered—and in later years she never expressed a hint of criticism of her husband. In turn, one of Grant's few surviving letters expresses concern, cautioning her "not to work to[o] hard." On November 22, 1856, she bore him a son, Heber Jeddy Grant, nine days before "lung disease," a combination of typhoid and pneumonia, took Jedediah's life at the early age of forty.[31]

For a time attendants also feared for the new mother's life. Rachel's labor had been difficult, and the shock of her husband's sudden death weakened her further. Without him she had no tangible source of security. Her cache of New Jersey "store goods" had long since been personally used or distributed to those around her, while Grant's small estate would have to be divided with her sister-wives. Her eastern relatives had promised that the latch-string would always be out for her return—if she would renounce her religion. But she rejected this; in matters of faith Rachel had made her decision.[32]

Rachel eventually recovered, and because of the two dominant forces that now shaped her life—her religion and her son—she remarried. President Young promised the Grant wives that if they would remain as a unit and accept George Grant, Jeddy's brother, as their new husband, they would successfully raise their children to be faithful Church members. Rachel and several of the Grant wives complied. However, Rachel's preference was to return to Anna's Salt Lake household. She married George on February 17, 1858, resolute in her religious obedience and hopeful for the future of her son (illus. 2-2).[33]

The union was a disaster. George, once a faithful Saint, Indian fighter, and hero of the 1856 handcart tragedy was, unbeknown to Church leaders, on a downward course. His erratic and immoderate behavior, apparently due to alcoholism, soon became public. Six months after his marriage to Rachel, George "committed an unprovoked attack on Thos. S. Williams with [the] attempt to kill." The fracas ended in a street brawl. With such incidents and George's drinking becoming more common, President Young dissolved the two-year-old marriage, but Rachel's hurt never entirely healed. "It was the one frightful ordeal of my mother's life, and the one thing she never wishes to refer to," Heber remarked in later years.[34]

Rachel thereafter rejected every opportunity for remarriage. Although prizing her independence, her overriding concern was Heber. Nothing—not a new father nor any other uncontrollable circumstance—must inhibit his promise. For several years she and her son remained at the Grant home

Courtesy Church Archives, The Church of Jesus Christ of Latter-day Saints

Illus. 2-2. Young Heber and his mother, Rachel.

on Main Street with a couple of the other widowed and now divorced wives. But the lack of money forced the sale of that property and the break up of their extended family. With President Young's permission, Rachel took her $500 share of the transaction and purchased a cottage on Second East Street (illus. 2-3).[35]

The change in living standards was wrenching. The disappointed and disoriented six-year-old Heber wandered back to the Main Street home and vowed that some day he would live there again. Certainly the new home had no luxuries. Rachel at first had only six dining plates, two of which were cracked, an occasional cup and saucer, her bed and bedding, and several chairs. There was a meager diet, which allowed only several pounds of butter and sugar for an entire year, and many blustery nights with no fire. One Christmas Rachel wept because she lacked a dime to buy a stick of candy for her boy's holiday.[36]

Poverty, or at least scarcity, was a part of pioneer living, and Rachel's situation differed from many others only in degree. Yet being accustomed to relative affluence and to giving rather than receiving, she must have found these trials poignant. Once while visiting Anna, who had moved to St. George in southern Utah, she firmly declined President Young's offer of Church aid. Instead, she supported herself and Heber by sewing, at first by hand in the homes of others and later with a Wheeler and Wilcox sewing machine in her own house. "I sat on the floor at night until midnight," Heber remembered many evenings, "and pumped the sewing machine to relieve her tired limbs." The machine's constantly moving treadles became a symbol of the Grant family's stubborn independence.[37]

Despite her financial distress, she retained her personal style and preferences. A willing hostess, she often subjected Heber and herself to a diet of "fried bread" (slices of bread warmed in a greased frying pan) so she could "splurge" on entertaining her friends. And she continued her fastidious habits. "She could wear a dress longer than anyone I have seen and have it look fresh and nice," a relative recalled. "She always changed her dress in the afternoon and washed herself and combed her hair, and if at home put on a nice white

Courtesy Church Archives, The Church of Jesus Christ of Latter-day Saints

Illus. 2-3. A detail of the cottage on Second East Street that Rachel purchased in the 1860s.

apron. . . . It would not look soiled [for several days]." Only her providence allowed this. She often cannibalized several threadbare garments to produce something "new" and usable.[38]

About five years after moving to Second East Street, Rachel began serving meals to boarders out of her small basement kitchen. Alex Hawes, a New York Life insurance man, helped make her venture successful. Attracted by her intelligence, charm, and culinary skill, Hawes first boarded and then at his own expense outfitted a small room at the Grants for his use. His rent and warm testimonials to Rachel's cooking provided her, as the boarding business increased, with a growing margin of financial security.[39]

Conversation at the Grants' boarding table was interesting and at times lively. "How I used to chaff her on matters religious or otherwise," Hawes recalled, "& how with her quiet sense of humor she would humor my sallies! We even made bets on certain events then in the future." The intelligent, detached, and agnostic Hawes enjoyed the iconoclast's role. "I know I respected [Hawes]," remembered Miss Joanna Van Rensselaer, a Methodist boarder, "notwithstanding his belief or want of belief—and recall vividly an argument between him and Miss Hayden—as to whether there was a real Devil."[40]

Rachel was Hawes's antithesis. She permitted no smoking in her home; gentlemen were told to indulge their habit on a tree stump in the yard. She was equally firm in defending her religion before her boarders, never neglecting, as she remembered, "any opportunity to introduce Mormonism to them." W. H. Harrington, an editor of the *Salt Lake Herald,* recalled her kindly and repeated assurances of his forthcoming but never realized conversion ("at which I would smile quietly"). Her boarders came to call her "Aunt Rachel," following the lead of her two nieces who served the table.[41]

Shortly after starting her boardinghouse business, Rachel was "blessed and set apart" as the Thirteenth Ward Relief Society "presidentess." Relief Societies had been organized briefly in Nauvoo and later in Utah during the middle 1850s, but not until a decade later did the movement gain momentum. When it reached Rachel's Thirteenth Ward, she fit Bishop Edwin D. Woolley's bill of particulars for the job. "It was not his habit to be in a hurry in his movements," Woolley told the women at their organizing session, and he wished the Relief Society sisters to be likewise "cool and deliberate" and their leaders obedient in carrying out "such measures as he should suggest from time to time." His eye naturally rested upon Rachel.[42]

The burden of leadership was often heavy. She trembled to overcome her diffidence when speaking or conducting meetings. The kind Scandinavian sisters unknowingly repelled her as they grasped and kissed her hand. She "scarcely knew what to do" with some women who behaved irrationally and then demanded the Society's charity. Rachel repeatedly gave herself solace by saying "it was not the numbers that constituted a good meeting." And there was Bishop Woolley, whose bark was as legendary as his toothless bite. He scolded them for having "left undone some things that he told us to do, and we done some things that we ought not to." But his comments apparently were nothing more serious than passing irritation, for he and his two successors retained Rachel in her position for thirty-five years.[43]

The detailed minutes of the Thirteenth Ward Relief Society suggest she closely resembled the nineteenth-century ideal Latter-day Saint woman. On occasion she prophesied. She experienced uncommon faith and expression while praying. Following priesthood counsel, she used, when possible, articles manufactured in Utah, and when Brigham Young requested women to abandon their cumbersome eastern styles, she wore, despite ridicule from many women, the simplified and home-designed "Deseret Costume." Her name appeared with those of a half-dozen other prominent Latter-day Saint women protesting the passage of the anti-Mormon Cullom Bill. Likewise, she was a member of a committee of leaders representing the "large and highly respectable assemblage of ladies" thanking Acting Governor S. A. Mann for his approval of the Utah Woman's Suffrage Act.[44]

However, as her Relief Society sermons show, Rachel was more a moralist than an activist. "We all have trials to pass through," she spoke from personal experience, "but if living up to our duty they are sanctified to our best good." Her tendency was to see only the good in life. She called for obedience to authority and the avoidance of faultfinding. God's hand and his rewards were omnipresent. "I am a firm believer in our being rewarded for all the good we do," she insisted, "& everything will come out right with those who do right." She had long since made her peace with plural marriage.

While its practice might be a woman's "greatest trial," she rejoiced that she herself had experienced the "Principle." Propounding duty, goodness, obedience, toil, and sacrifice, her Quaker-Mormon attitudes blended comfortably with the era's prevailing Victorianism.[45]

Rachel and her Thirteenth Ward sisters did more than sermonize. Notwithstanding "often having to endure insults," the Relief Society block teachers canvassed the congregation to discover the needy and to secure for their relief an occasional cash donation. The sisters were usually more successful in procuring yarn, thread, calico pieces, rugs, and discarded clothing, which they transformed into stockings, quilts, and rag rugs. The Relief Society women also braided straw, fashioned hats and bonnets, stored grain, and sewed underwear, buckskin gloves, and burial and temple garments. On these items the poor had first claim; the remainder were sold with most of the proceeds going to charity. During Rachel's three-and-a-half-decade ministry, a time of scarcity and deflated dollars, the Thirteenth Ward Relief Society's liberality in cash and goods exceeded $7,750. The little money left she invested for her sisters in securities, which appreciated spectacularly after her death. By 1925 the Thirteenth Ward Relief Society had assets worth $20,000.[46]

Rachel Grant's "greatest trial" during her years as Relief Society president was her worsening hearing. She had noticed a hearing loss in late adolescence, but when she was almost fifty, an attack of quinsy[47] left her virtually deaf with what she described as a "steam engine going night and day" in her head. No longer hearing melody, much conversation, nor the proceedings of her Church meetings— among the things she valued most—she nevertheless attempted to carry on. In her Relief Society meetings she compensated for her disability with what her friends felt to be an extra sense. "She often picked up the thread of thought and conversation," commented one of her Relief Society coworkers "and voiced her own conclusions so appropriately and so ably that her associates marveled afresh at the keenness of her spiritual comprehension."[48]

Because she led the women of the prominent Thirteenth Ward, and in part because of her able manner, her influence in later years spread. She became recognized as one of Mormondom's "leading sisters" who in lieu of a centralized Relief Society staff, traveled throughout the territory speaking and advising on distaff questions, becoming "Aunt Rachel," an honored pioneer title, to more than her boarders. While never rivaling Eliza R. Snow, Bathsheba W. Smith, or Emmeline Wells as women's exponents (the latter two served under her presidency during the Thirteenth Ward Relief Society's early years), she was nonetheless esteemed as a model of proper behavior. Stately, serene, fastidious, and proper, Rachel came to be compared with Victoria herself.[49]

Rachel might have traveled and preached in the outlying settlements, but she was always uneasy at center stage—restrained not only by her natural hesitancy and lack of hearing but also by her preoccupation with Heber. She never doubted that the boy's destiny would at least equal his father's, and her urgent anticipations coupled with her light discipline did much to forge his character. If in his youth Heber took advantage of her leniency and proved to be very much a boy, in later years his attitude toward her became reverential. "There are many things about her that I could wish were different," he candidly declared in adulthood, apparently with reference to her firmly programmed ways and mannerisms, "but mother is one of the sweetest and kindest of women and as loveable as can be."[50]

In many ways, and especially in the ways most pleasing to her, Heber proved a facsimile of herself. Neither prim nor systematic, he accepted the Ivinses' business-mindedness and Rachel's Victorian values. Above all, she bequeathed to him her towering commitment to their religion along with her feelings of Latter-day Saint embattlement and persecution. As Heber rose to commercial and Church prominence, becoming during the last twenty-five years of Rachel's life a member of the Quorum of the Twelve Apostles, his career was the fulfillment of her own.

Her last years were again dominated by family concerns. Due to the long illness and eventual death of Lucy Stringham Grant, the first of Heber's three plural wives, Rachel's grandmotherly duties were heavy. For a time, the seventy-year-old woman personally tended Lucy's six children. Later she moved to an upstairs room and surrendered much of this role to her son's second wife, Augusta Winters Grant. Yet she still darned, mended, and sewed for the family and invited her grandchildren to her room for school study and silent companionship—though they learned that Rachel's displeasure might easily be aroused if they wandered too close to her immaculate and painstakingly made bed. Her deafness insulated her from the family's quarrels and prompted occasional humor. The children "had no idea," she told them, "how funny it was to see their angry faces and hear none of their words."[51]

Such a statement reveals a characteristic attempt to see the bright side of her tormenting disability. To the end she refused to accept its finality. She was repeatedly anointed and blessed. As a measure of their regard, congregations from Idaho to Arizona in 1900 fasted and prayed for her hearing. She repeatedly repaired to the temple, hoping that health baptisms in a holy place—a common practice at the time—might bring a cure. "I watched in breathless silence to see the miracle performed," Susa Young Gates recalled of one such temple experience. "I saw my miracle . . . eight long agonizing times [she was baptized with little effect] . . . the vision of Aunt Rachel's beaming smile at God's refusal to hear her prayer gripped my soul with power to bear." The miracle, of course, lay in Rachel's good nature, despite her tormenting affliction.[52]

Rachel Grant was equanimity personified. The financial panics of the 1890s crushed her son's ascendancy for several decades; to aid him, she transferred to him the stocks and properties that he had previously given her. She reacted with similar stoicism to the death of little Heber, her semi-invalid grandson upon whom she had lavished so much love and attention. In 1903 at the age of eighty-two, she retired from the Thirteenth Ward Relief Society presidency. "I am not one," her resignation read, "who wishes to hold on to an office when I can not do as I wish." She thus conceded to old age what she had steadfastly refused to grant to her deafness.[53]

During her final five or six years Rachel retired from most pursuits—with the exception of her reading, meditating, and letter-writing. She was honored by an annual "surprise" birthday party. After one such fête, a reporter from the *Woman's Exponent* found her "the picture of health and happiness. . . . It can truly be said of Sister Rachel, that she has grown old gracefully." Yet her lifetime of physical and psychological toil had its effect. Rheumatism, nerves, and the constant cacophony within her head would often not allow sleep until 3:00 or 4:00 A.M. Accordingly, she would take a hymnal from under her pillow and sing the silent sounds of the past. "I was awake early this morning & thinking of my past life," she wrote revealingly to Heber on such an occasion.

> When you were young I thought & prayed that I might live to see
> you grown then I would be satisfied, if you wer[e] a faithful
> L[.]D[.] Saint . . . when thinking of the many things I had passed
> through hard & unpleasant how happy it makes me now that I
> never complained . . . not even to my sister. I knew she would
> feel bad. I can talk about them now without caring.

Clearly her outward serenity had often been a mask.[54]

After fighting for a week with pneumonia, which brought little actual suffering, Rachel died on January 27, 1909, at 1:10 A.M.—with "absolute and perfect confidence" in what lay ahead. She was almost eighty-eight. Heber, who would fulfill his mother's faith by becoming the president of The Church of Jesus Christ of Latter-day Saints, was at her bedside. Through him and his administration of almost three decades, her personality would touch yet another generation of Saints.[55]

Notes

This article was originally published in *Dialogue* 15 (Autumn 1982): 105–21.

I am indebted to Marlena Ahanin and Peggy Fletcher Stack for their assistance in researching this paper.

1. Lucy Grant Cannon, "A Few Memories of Grandma Grant," undated manuscript, Heber J. Grant Letterpress Copybook, 65:182, 185, Heber J. Grant Papers, Church Archives, The Church of Jesus Christ of Latter-day Saints, Salt Lake City; Annie Wells Cannon, "Rachel Ivins Grant," *Improvement Era* 37 (November 1934): 643.

2. Luther Prentice Allen, *The Genealogy and History of the Shreve Family* (Greenfield, Ill.: Privately Published, 1901), 210; Frances Bennett Jeppson, "With Joy Wend Your Way: The Life of Rachel Ivins Grant, My Great-Grandmother," 1, typescript, 1952, Church Archives.

3. Jeppson, "With Joy Wend Your Way," 2; Rachel Ridgway Grant to Heber J. Grant, December 18, 1904, Heber J. Grant Papers; Lucy Grant Cannon, "Recollections of Rachel Ivins Grant," *Relief Society Magazine* 25 (May 1938): 295–96.

4. The Mormon invasion and success in central New Jersey is an important but untold story of early Latter-day Saint proselyting. The Church's chapels must have been among the earliest built by the Saints anywhere. William Sharp, "The Latter-day Saints or 'Mormons' in New Jersey," 1897, typescript of a memorandum, 3, Church Archives; Edwin Salter, *History of Monmouth and Ocean Counties* (Bayonne, N.J.: E. Gardner and Son, 1890), 253; Franklin Ellis, *The History of Monmouth County, New Jersey* (Cottonport, La.: Polyanthos Publishing, 1974), 663. Later in the 1840s,

Latter-day day Saint converts apparently founded a small fishing village on the New Jersey coast, which they named "Nauvoo." Stanley B. Kimball, "'Nauvoo' Found in Seven States," *Ensign* 3 (April 1973): 23.

5. Anthony W. Ivins, Diary, 1:3, Utah State Historical Society, Salt Lake City; Kimball S. Erdman, *Israel Ivins: A Biography* (n.p., 1969), 3; Parley P. Pratt to Joseph Smith Jr., November 22, 1839, Joseph Smith Papers, Church Archives. At the Church's conference held in Philadelphia, January 13, 1840, Ivins suggested and Joseph Smith agreed that the Book of Mormon should be printed instead in the West. Philadelphia Church Records, 1840–54, microfilm, Church Archives.

6. Rachel Ridgway Grant, "How I Became a 'Mormon,'" unpublished memorandum, Heber J. Grant Papers; Rachel Ridgway Grant, "Minutes of a Meeting of the General Boards of the Young Men and Young Women MIA," June 11, 1902, Grant Letterpress Copybook, 35:324; Rachel Ridgway Grant, "Testimonial to Sister M. L. Horne," W*oman's Exponent* 31 (December 1 and 15, 1902): 53. For women and nineteenth-century religion, see also Barbara Welter, "The Feminization of American Religion: 1800–1860," in *Clio's Consciousness Raised: New Perspectives on the History of Women,* ed. Mary S. Hartman and Lois Banner (New York: Harper & Row, 1974), 137– 57; Mary P. Ryan, "A Woman's Awakening: Evangelical Religion and the Families of Utica, New York, 1800–1840," *American Quarterly* 30 (winter 1978): 602–23.

7. Rachel Grant, "How I Became a 'Mormon,'" 1; and Rachel Ridgway Grant, "Joseph Smith, the Prophet," *Young Woman's Journal* 16 (December 1905): 550–51.

8. Sharp, "'Mormons' in New Jersey," 1–2; Salter, *Monmouth and Ocean Counties,* 253; Rachel Grant, "How I Became a 'Mormon,'" 1–2.

9. Rachel Grant, "How I Became a 'Mormon,'" 1–2; Rachel Grant, "Minutes of a Meeting of the General Boards," Relief Society Minute Book, 1875, Thirteenth Ward, April 1, 1875, 10, Church Archives. In addition to the Ivins family, the Appleby, Applegate, Bennett, Brown, Curtis, Doremus, Horner, Implay, McKean, Robbins, Sill, Stoddard, Woodward, Wright, and Wychoff families mixed together without social distinction in their central New Jersey branches.

10. Erastus Snow, Journal, typescript, 2:25, Church Archives; Rachel Grant, "How I Became a 'Mormon,'" 2. Snow, who visited his New Jersey flock in late 1841, declared, "I found them strong in the faith, many having of late been added to them and several families, I found about ready to move to Nauvoo." Snow, Journal, 2:28.

11. Rachel Grant, "How I Became a 'Mormon,'" 2; Journal History of the Church, April 30, June 27, and August 14, 1842, Church Archives, microfilm copy in L. Tom Perry Special Collections, Harold B. Lee Library, Brigham Young University, Provo, Utah; Nauvoo Trustees Land Book, Part B, 29, Church Archives; Nauvoo City Tax Assessments Books, Wards 1–4, 1841–44, Church Archives; Nauvoo Restoration, Inc., *The James*

Ivins–Elias Smith Printing Complex (Nauvoo: Nauvoo Restoration, n.d.), 1–4. Visitors in present-day Nauvoo identify John Taylor as owner of the Ivins buildings, used for the printing of the *Times and Seasons,* an early Church periodical.

12. Mary Grant Judd, "Rachel Ridgway Ivins Grant," *Relief Society Magazine* 30 (April 1943): 229.

13. Their intimate friendship is repeatedly mentioned in the Heber J. Grant Papers; see Heber J. Grant to Harold A. Lafount, April 24, 1924, Grant Letterpress Copybook, 61:839. See also for a life sketch of Sarah Kimball, Jill C. Mulvay, "The Liberal Shall Be Blessed: Sarah M. Kimball," *Utah Historical Quarterly* 44 (summer 1976): 205–21.

14. Rachel Grant, "How I Became a 'Mormon,'" 2; Rachel Grant, "Joseph Smith, the Prophet," 551.

15. Rachel Grant, "Joseph Smith, the Prophet," 551; Heber J. Grant, "Remarks Made at a Sunday School Union Board Meeting," January 7, 1919, Grant Letterpress Copybook, 54:348; Rachel Ridgway Grant to Edith [Grant], September 17, 1904, Family Correspondence, Heber J. Grant Papers; Thirteenth Ward Relief Society Minutes, Book B: 1898–1906, March 17, 1902, 100–101, Church Archives.

16. Thirteenth Ward Relief Society Minutes, Book A: 1868–98, February 11, 1897, 611, Church Archives. In several letters to Brigham Young, Ivins steadfastly maintained his innocence. "I can say that I never to the best of my recollection persuaded the first person to join either Law or Sidney [Rigdon]—all I have bin guilty of is believing the doctrine of Mormonism as it was taught me in the beginning." Charles Ivins to Brigham Young, July 1845, Brigham Young Papers, Church Archives.

17. Truman G. Madsen, *The Heritage of Heber J. Grant* (Salt Lake City: privately published, 1969), 12, 30; Rachel Grant, "How I Became a 'Mormon,'" 2; Heber J. Grant to Ray O. Wyland, December 12, 1936, Grant Letterpress Copybook, 74:530–31. Erdman, *Israel Ivins,* 5–6, claims that Joseph Smith actually proposed to her.

18. Rachel Grant, "How I Became a 'Mormon,'" 2; Rachel Grant, "Joseph Smith, the Prophet," 551.

19. Heber J. Grant to Heber M. Wells, April 28, 1904, Grant Letterpress Copybook, 38:590; Heber J. Grant to E. S. Tainter, August 25, 1926, Grant Letterpress Copybook, 64:611; Heber J. Grant and Anthony M. Ivins, "Remarks at a Birthday Dinner for Heber J. Grant," transcript in Heber J. Grant Typed Diary, November 22, 1924, 314–15, Heber J. Grant Papers.

20. Barbara Welter, "The Cult of True Womanhood," *American Quarterly* 18, no. 2 (1988): 151, 153; Ellis, *History of Monmouth County,* 639. The school described here was probably Rachel's, for John Horner, as cited in Ellis, recalled attending his early grammar studies with her.

21. Cannon, "Memories of Grandma Grant," 181; Rachel Ridgway Grant, untitled and undated memorandum, Heber J. Grant Papers.

22. William Appleby, Journal, November 17, 1845; October 26; and November 1, 1848, Church Archives.

23. Rachel Grant, untitled and undated memorandum; Jeppson, "With Joy Wend Your Way," 8.

24. Jeppson, "With Joy Wend Your Way," 9; clipping from *(Toms River) New Jersey Courier*, November 9, 1934, Grant Papers.

25. Sharp, "'Mormons' in New Jersey," 2–3; Theodore McKean, "Autobiography," 2, unpublished draft, Church Archives; clipping from *(Toms River) New Jersey Courier*, November 9, 1934.

26. Jeppson, "With Joy Wend Your Way," 9–10.

27. Cannon, "Memories of Grandma Grant," 181; Wayne L. Wahlquist, "Population Growth in the Mormon Core Area: 1847–90," *The Mormon Role in the Settlement of the West*, ed. Richard H. Jackson, Charles Redd Monographs in Western History no. 9 (Provo, Utah: Brigham Young University, 1978), 116–24. Wahlquist found the female imbalance to be most significant during the years of marriageability—a tendency plural marriage must have heightened.

28. Gene A. Sessions, *Mormon Thunder: A Documentary History of Jedediah Morgan Grant* (Urbana: University of Illinois Press, 1982), 265.

29. Caleb Ivins Jr., Group Sheet, Archives, The Genealogical Society of The Church of Jesus Christ of Latter-day Saints, Salt Lake City; Grant and Ivins, "Remarks at a Birthday Dinner."

30. Belle Whitney Sears to Heber J. Grant, February 20, 1919, General Correspondence, Heber J. Grant Papers; Susan and Rosetta Grant to Jedediah M. Grant, January 7, 1855 [1856?], photocopy, Family Correspondence. Another wife complained that the frequently writing Rachel monopolized all the news.

31. Heber J. Grant to Florence [Grant], June 6, 1905, Letterpress Copybook, 39:832; Rachel Ridgway Grant, Thirteenth Ward Relief Society Minutes, Book A, July 7, 1870; Jedediah M. Grant to Susan Grant, October 14, 1856, photocopy of holograph, Grant Family Correspondence.

32. Heber J. Grant to Claus [?] H. Karlson, October 28, 1885, Grant Letterpress Copybook, 6:203–4; Jeppson, "With Joy Wend Your Way," 9. Eventually only four of the Grant wives participated in the distribution of their husband's property—those who left the Grant homestead and remarried elsewhere were excluded.

33. Cannon, "Memories of Grandma Grant," 182–83.

34. George Goddard, Journal, August 27, 1858, Church Archives; Heber J. Grant to Junius F. Wells, March 30, 1905, Grant Letterpress Copybook, 39:502; Cannon, "Memories of Grandma Grant," 183.

35. Jeppson, "With Joy Wend Your Way," 12.

36. "Two Octogenarians," *Improvement Era* 39 (November 1936): 667; Heber J. Grant, "Faith-Promoting Experiences," *Millennial Star* 93 (November 19, 1931): 760; Cannon, "Memories of Grandma Grant," 183; Rachel Ridgway Grant, Thirteenth Ward Relief Society Minutes, Book B, February 13, 1903, 95.

37. Clipping from *(Toms River) New Jersey Courier*, November 9, 1934;

Heber J. Grant, "Faith-Promoting Experiences," 760. Her refusal of aid was categorical. "I . . . told him [Brigham Young] that persons had said to me I was a fool for working as I did when your father [Jedediah] killed himself working in the kingdom. I told him I did not wish to be supported by the church. I was too independent for that." Rachel Ridgway Grant to Heber J. Grant, October 19, 1901, Family Correspondence.

38. Cannon, "Memories of Grandpa Grant," 183.

39. Heber J. Grant, *An Address Delivered by Invitation before the Chamber of Commerce, Kansas City, Missouri* (Independence, Mo.: Zion's Printing and Publishing, 1924?), 15; Heber J. Grant, Press Copy Diary, August 20, 1887, Heber J. Grant Papers; Heber J. Grant, Remarks, "President Grant's Seventy-First Birthday Party," memo, Heber J. Grant Papers. Heber was explicit on Hawes's effect upon the Grant household: "I may say that the turning point in my mother's life came when Colonel Hawes entered our home as a boarder." Heber J. Grant to Elizabeth L. Peltret, March 19, 1914, Grant Letterpress Copybook, 49:363.

40. Alexander W. Hawes to Heber J. Grant, December 28, 1912, Grant Letterpress Copybook, 48:151–52; Joanna H. Van Rensselaer to Heber J. Grant, January 21, 1925, General Correspondence.

41. Cannon, "Memories of Grandma Grant," 184; Rachel Ridgway Grant, Thirteenth Ward Relief Society Minutes, Book A, March 7, 1872, 106–7; W. H. Harrington to Heber J. Grant, December 1, 1897, General Correspondence.

42. Thirteenth Ward Relief Society Minutes, Book A, April 18, 1868, 1–2.

43. Rachel Ridgway Grant, Thirteenth Ward Relief Society Minutes, Book B, March 17, 1902, 100–101; Cannon, "Memories of Grandma Grant," 184. Thirteenth Ward Relief Society Minutes, Book A, August 7, 1873; June 29, 1876; and October 26, 1887, 154, 260, and 466. Sister Emma Goddard, the secretary, discreetly crossed out Wolley's remarks and replaced them with a more grammatical sentence, see Relief Society Minute Book 1875, Thirteenth Ward, June 3, 1875, 25–26.

44. Rachel Ridgway Grant to Heber J. Grant, January 8, 1891, Family Correspondence; Rachel Ridgway Grant to Heber J. Grant, October 12, 1901, Family Correspondence; Hannah C. Wells to Heber J. Grant, February 28, 1907, General Correspondence; Cannon, "Memories of Grandma Grant," 187; "In Memorium: Rachel Ridgway Ivins Grant, *Woman's Exponent* 37 (April 1909): 52; Heber J. Grant, "Address at BYU Centennial," October 16, 1925, Grant Letterpress Copybook, 63:533–54; Thirteenth Ward Relief Society Minutes, Book A, April 15, 1875, 227; Relief Society Minute Book, 1875, Thirteenth Ward, April 1, 1875, 9–10; Thomas G. Alexander, "An Experiment in Progressive Legislation: The Granting of Woman Suffrage in Utah in 1870," *Utah Historical Quarterly* 38 (winter 1970): 20–30.

45. Rachel Ridgway Grant, Thirteenth Ward Relief Society Minutes, Book A, March 5, 1874; June 4, 1874; September 2, 1875; and January 13, 1898; 175, 188–89, 244, and 633; Rachel Ridgway Grant, Thirteenth Ward Relief Society Minutes, Book B, March 13, 1902, 97–98; Cannon, "Recollections of

Rachel Ivins Grant," 293–98; Rachel Ridgway Grant to Heber J. Grant, May 7, 1905, Family Correspondence.

46. Rachel Ridgway Grant, Thirteenth Ward Relief Society Minutes, Book A, December 4, 1873, 164; "Rachel Ridgeway Grant," memorandum, May 28, 1903, Heber J. Grant Papers; Elizabeth H. Goddard, "Letter to the Editor, "*Woman's Exponent* 4 (December 1, 1875): 98; Elizabeth H. Goddard, "Editor Exponent," *Woman's Exponent* 5 (June 1, 1876): 5; R. C. Atwood, "Sketch of the F.R. [Female Relief] Society," *Woman's Exponent* 14 (June 15, 1885): 13, 14; Cannon, "Memories of Grandma Grant," 184.

47. Quinsy is an inflammation of the tonsils and nearby tissues and can often lead to abscesses.

48. Cannon, "Memories of Grandma Grant," 187; Jeppson, "With Joy Wend Your Way," 13; Susa Young Gates, "Relief Society Beginnings in Utah," *Relief Society Magazine* 9 (April 1922): 189; *Woman's Exponent* 31 (December 1 and 15, 1902): 52–53.

49. Mary Grant Judd, "Rachel Ridgeway Ivins Grant," *Relief Society Magazine* 30 (May 1943): 316; May Booth Talmage, "Coronets of Age: Rachel R. Grant," *Young Woman's Journal* 19 (April 1908): 182–85. The *Woman's Exponent* occasionally recorded Rachel's visits among the outlying areas, see also "Editorial Notes," *Woman's Exponent* 9 (June 15, 1880): 13; "Editor Exponent: R.S., Y.L. M.I.A. and Primary Reports," *Woman's Exponent* 12 (September 1, 1883): 55; "L.D.S. Women's Meeting," *Woman's Exponent* 12 (September 15, 1883): 60; "R.S., Y.L.M.I.A. and P.A. Reports, Salt Lake Stake," *Woman's Exponent* 14 (October 1, 1885); 70; "Relief Society Conference," *Woman's Exponent* 15 (April 1, 1887): 164.

50. Heber J. Grant to Lucy Grant, April 17, 1892, Lucy Grant Papers, Church Archives. Her parenting provided the classic conditions which often produced an entrepreneurial type of personality; see Everett E. Hagan, *On the Theory of Social Change* (Homewood, Ill.: Dorsey Press, 1962), 93; and David C. McClelland, *The Achieving Society* (Princeton, N.J.: D. Van Nostrand, 1961), esp. 353–76.

51. Jeppson, "With Joy Wend Your Way," 17; Cannon, "Memories of Grandma Grant," 188.

52. Susa Young Gates, "A Tribute to Rachel Ivins Grant," *Young Woman's Journal* 21 (January 1910): 30.

53. Jeppson, "With Joy Wend Your Way," 17–18; Rachel Ridgway Grant to Heber J. Grant, June 28, 1903, Family Correspondence.

54. *Woman's Exponent* 31 (March 1903): 77; Cannon, "Memories of Grandma Grant," 181; Rachel Ridgway Grant to Heber J. Grant, November 27, 1904, Family Correspondence.

55. Heber J. Grant, Manuscript diary, January 27, 1909, Heber J. Grant Papers; Heber J. Grant to Mrs. S. A. Collins, February 12, 1909, Family Correspondence.

Young Heber J. Grant's
Years of Passage

As Heber J. Grant came of age, Mormonism was as much a part of the Utah landscape as the territory's dusty valleys and vaulting mountain walls. Young Heber met religion everywhere—in his Salt Lake City home and neighborhood, at the Tabernacle on Temple Square, in the offices of Church and civic leaders where he sometimes ventured, and certainly in his native Thirteenth Ward, one of the most innovative and organizationally developed Latter-day Saint congregations of the time. Slowly young Heber internalized his religious culture, but not before encountering the usual perils of adolescence and coming of age. The process tells not only a great deal about Heber himself, but also about the beliefs, rituals, and worship patterns of early Utah Mormons.

Heber J. Grant was a second-generation Mormon, born November 22, 1856, at Jedediah Grant's imposing Main Street home. His father, Brigham's counselor and Salt Lake City mayor, died nine days later. In Jedediah's stead, the boy was christened by Thirteenth Ward Bishop Edwin D. Woolley, who found the spirit of the occasion to be unusual. "I was only an instrument in the hands of his dead father . . . in blessing him," the bishop later remarked. That boy "is entitled [someday] to be one of the Apostles, and I know it"[1] (illus. 3-1).

There were other harbingers of the child's future. Once Rachel, his mother, took the boy to a formal dinner at the Heber C. Kimballs'. After the adults had finished dining, the children were invited to eat what remained. Excited, little Heber was thoroughly enjoying himself when Brother Kimball suddenly lifted him atop a table and began prophesying about his future. The frightened child especially remembered the foreboding, coal black eyes of President Young's first counselor.[2] Moreover, there was the portentous Relief Society gathering held at William C. Staines's home, where Eliza R. Snow and Zina D. Young spoke and interpreted in the "unknown" tongue. Blessing each of the women present, they eventually turned to Rachel. Heber, who was playing on the floor, recalled hearing something about his becoming "a great big man." His mother's understanding,

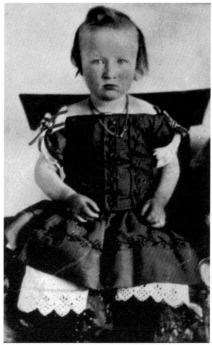

Courtesy Church Archives, The Church of Jesus Christ of Latter-day Saints

Illus. 3-1. Heber J. Grant as a baby, ca. 1858.

however, was more precise. "Behave yourself," Rachel knowingly told him as he grew to maturity, "and you will some day be one of the apostles in the Church."[3]

The Thirteenth Ward, the Grants' home congregation, made these auspicious predictions more likely. One of the largest and most culturally diverse wards in the territory, the Thirteenth Ward also boasted major human and economic resources. Among its members were some of the most prominent men in the territory, including General Authorities, prominent merchants, and land investors. These in turn brought a high level of prosperity. "The 13th Ward," observed one contemporary, "was richer than all the Saints at Kirtland when the Temple was built." Indeed, the Thirteenth Ward may have enjoyed the highest income level in the Church during the years when Heber J. Grant was growing up.[4]

Such a ward was an ideal setting for the beginning of the Church's Sunday School movement. While churchmen had earlier organized a few scattered and short-lived Sabbath schools, the Thirteenth Ward's was the first established after the city's bishops agreed, in a major policy decision, to counter the post–Civil War denominational academies with Mormon Sabbath schools.[5] A typical Sunday might find the children meeting at the Thirteenth Ward assembly rooms, where they listened to short talks, sang, and recited inspirational prose and poetry. Leaders might also "catechize" the youth with questions drawn from the Bible, Book of Mormon, or Church history, liberally awarding prizes for both correct answers and proper conduct.

Heber took advantage of the ward's new school. In fact, the ambitious and assertive boy was often at front stage. Excelling at memorization, he quickly mastered the Articles of Faith; the first five pages of John Jaques's *Catechism;* and Joseph Smith's health revelation, the Word of Wisdom, a frequent Sunday School recitation. "You were our prize Sunday School boy," remembered a classmate. "Bros. [Milton] Musser and Mabin [John Maiben] predicted great things for you."[6] On one occasion, Heber pitted his declamatory skills against Ort [Orson F.] Whitney, whose rendition of "Shamus O'Brien" proved superior to Heber's "The Martrydom of the Prophet and Patriarch." But "Heber had another card up his sleeve," Orson Whitney recalled many years later. "He answered more questions from the *Catechism* than any other student in school, and won a prize equal to mine, which was the *Autobiography of Parley P. Pratt.*"[7]

Yet Heber's confident façade concealed a desperate shyness. When first asked to pray publicly, he trembled "like a leaf" and feared imminent collapse.[8] President Young's 1868 reconnoiter at the school had similar results. Unnerved, Heber stumbled badly in his recital of the Word of Wisdom, causing his classmates great merriment. Thoroughly confused, Heber had to begin his recitation anew. President Young later salved the incident by highly complimenting him. "I was my father's own son by not being discouraged [and quitting]," Heber remembered Brigham telling him, "but demonstrated a true spirit of determination to accomplish the task given me." Heber never forgot his embarrassment nor President Young's words of praise.[9]

As in Victorian England, Latter-day Saints used their Sabbath schools for both moral and social uplift. Children were taught scripture study, Sabbath observance, honesty, family solidarity, observance of the Word of Wisdom, and, of course, general propriety. At times the instruction on propriety was specific. Boys were told to stop stealing peaches from neighborhood gardens and warned of "the evil consequences of such evil conduct." Moreover, they should quit "throwing mud from the end of a stick which disfigured buildings that had cost a great deal."[10]

Perhaps such a boyish misdeed almost drove Heber from the school. Angered by a reproof, the youth stormed from the assembly rooms, exclaiming that the school could go "plumb to hell." "Being raised as an only child," he later explained, "I was ... rather ... hot-headed . . . and I quit going." After many entreaties to return, including those of George Goddard, his neighbor and a member of the school's superintendency, Heber finally rejoined his classmates. Brother Goddard "kept me from going where I said the Sunday School could go," Heber acknowledged.[11]

Heber generally enjoyed the school and credited it as having a major shaping influence on his character. Clearly its impact went beyond rote learning and indoctrination. Goddard, Maiben, and school librarian F. A. Mitchell—who was always on hand to lend "good books to read"—were in fact role models that the fatherless boy desperately needed.[12] "Your integrity and devotion ... has been an inspiration to me," Heber wrote in mid-life to Maiben. "I look back with pleasure to the happy associations that I have had with you and Brother Goddard, Bishop Woolley and many other faithful Saints when I was a young man."[13]

Heber's youthful Thirteenth Ward experiences involved more than Sunday School exercises. The Thirteenth Ward held a plethora of meetings. Many of which, directly or indirectly, impacted on the growing boy. These included youth meetings, women's meetings, men's meetings, Quaker-type meetings that allowed broad-based participation, and preaching meetings that were held during the winter season as often as three times a week. Unlike most pioneer Mormons, who were chronically lax in their meeting attendance, Heber was often seated in a Thirteenth Ward pew. Indeed, some of his fondest memories centered on "going to meeting." There were Brother Blythe's interminable half-hour prayers and George Goddard's sweetly (and often) sung rendition of "Who's on the Lord's Side?"[14]

Courtesy Church Archives, The Church of Jesus Christ of Latter-day Saints

Illus. 3-2. Bishop Edwin D. Woolley (ca. 1854), bishop of the Salt Lake Thirteenth Ward, which Heber attended.

And then there was Bishop Edwin D. Woolley (illus. 3-2). Charitable, well-meaning, and firmly dedicated to his religion, Bishop Woolley could also be summary during a preaching meeting. During one worship service, he "spoke warmly" of those who accused him of failing to act "the part of a Father" and urged his critics to air their feelings. When William Capener did so, Bishop Woolley peremptorily cut him off from the Church. Members debated the action the following week, with half the congregation refusing to sustain the excommunication. Bishop Woolley, however, refused to budge. Railing "about the whoredom and the wickedness" of the ward, the bishop vowed "by the help of the Lord and the brethern" to cleanse it.[15]

Heber's memory of Bishop Woolley focused on more prosaic things—the bishop's heavy emphasis on tithe paying or his control of speakers and meetings. Bishop Woolley didn't like meetings to last longer than two hours and invariably warned his preachers to limit their sermons to a single hour. Heber normally positioned himself in the northeast corner of the assembly rooms where, after the obligatory hour, he would periodically snap his watch crystal as a reminder of the hour's lateness. The act usually was unnecessary. From his vantage point, Heber could witness the bishop's surreptitious hand reach out and tug at a long-winded preacher's coattails. But Woolley's behavior was not automatic. A spellbinding speaker like John Morgan, fresh from his Southern States mission, received *carte blanche*. "Bishop Woolley knows whose coat to pull," the boy thoughtfully observed.[16]

There were other speakers Heber remembered being drawn to. Young John Henry Smith, only eight years Grant's senior, seemed always to carry "the inspiration of the Lord." Joseph F. Smith, nephew of the founding Prophet and youthful counselor to President Young, also spoke impressively. Even "as a little child . . . before I could thoroughly comprehend the teaching of the authorities of the Church," Heber recalled, President Smith's Thirteenth Ward preaching would "thrill my very being."[17]

Few speakers captivated him like President Young. Somewhat over five feet eight inches tall (above average for the time), Brigham Young carried himself with conscious presence. Observers who watched his delivery emphasized his lips, which "came together like the jaws of a bear trap" and conveyed "indomitable pluck." While young Heber probably failed to detect them, Vermont provincialisms such as *leetle, beyond, disremember, ain't you,* and *they was* gave color to Brigham's remarks and punctuated his easy, conversational style.[18] Both Church members and those outside the faith generally agreed on Brigham's pulpit appeal.[19]

Heber was enthralled by Young's "wonderful capacity to hold his audience" and his ability to inspire his listeners about "the principles of life and salvation."[20] Whether behind a Thirteenth Ward pulpit or more frequently occupying the rostrum at Temple Square, President Young stated and restated his themes: build Zion; sacrifice time, talent, and means for the community; bear each other's burdens; become the Lord's steward; be self-sufficient; avoid Babylon; work hard; perform your duty; be obedient. So indelibly were they impressed on Heber's young mind that Young's themes became his own lifelong preaching texts.

Heber learned other lessons by attending the Thirteenth Ward's preaching meetings. One elder never used a simple word when several larger ones might do. On one occasion after delivering a fulsome sermon, the elder using expansive words was followed to the speaker's stand by the ungrammatical Millen Atwood. During the first sermon, Heber, who was studying English at the time, penciled on his removable cuff a long list of unfamiliar words that required study. Eyeing Atwood, he proposed to continue his self-improvement exercise by listing a few solecisms. "I did not write anything more after that first sentence—not a word," Heber vividly remembered sixty-five years later. "When Millen Atwood stopped preaching, tears were rolling down my cheeks. . . . [Atwood's] testimony made the first profound impression that was ever made upon my heart and soul of the divine mission of the Prophet [Joseph Smith]."[21]

Heber's priesthood activity also helped mold him. Unlike young men in the Church today, he apparently was never asked to break and bless the sacramental bread.[22] He did, however, serve as one of the ward's block teachers, whom Bishop Woolley admitted were not always the "best talents" or the "best men." They were, in Woolley's mind, simply the best that would "work with him."[23] This meant occasionally asking a youth like Heber to labor with an experienced companion like Hamilton G. Park. Heber's teaching activity was of more than passing importance. Park's faith was deep and visionary— he once announced that he had "seen the Savior and heard him speak."[24] As the man and boy walked around the block occupied by the imposing Salt Lake Theatre, Brother Park plied his impressionable companion with faith-promoting stories, many involving his personal experiences as a missionary to Scotland. Such moments convinced Heber that Hamilton Park was "one of the best spirited men in the Church & one that would sacrifice Everything for his religion."[25] At a time when few teenagers served as block teachers, Heber performed with uncommon diligence. In addition to his monthly teaching chores, he regularly attended the twice monthly bishops' report sessions at the Council House.[26] Every bishop, bishopric counselor, and teacher in the city was invited to these sessions, but leaders complained of "thin" and "woefully neglected" attendance. Typical meetings might find half of the city's bishops and only a handful of teachers present—Heber of course being one of them.[27]

Commensurate with this activity, young Heber was ordained a seventy, nineteenth-century Mormonism's most common lay priesthood office. At the time, Heber was very much a sapling among mature men.[28] Most Thirteenth Ward priesthood bearers were in their middle or late thirties. Even the few who held the "Lesser," or Aaronic, Priesthood were normally adults. In contrast, Heber was ordained and assigned to the Thirtieth Quorum of Seventy when he was about fifteen years old.[29]

Lessons, meetings, and priesthood duties were not the only shaping forces in the young boy's life. Books also influenced him. He found Parley P. Pratt's *Autobiography* to be "intensely interesting" and was "thrilled" by Pratt's *Key to Theology.* The Thirteenth

Ward library furnished Dr. Paley's two works, *Evidences of Christianity* and *Natural Theology*, and Heber accounted David Nelson's work, *Infidelity*, as having made a "profound impression" on him. However, none of these affected him as much as Samuel Smiles's chapbooks, *Character*, *Thrift*, and *Self-Help*, which in the Victorian style of the time idealized the self-made man. Equally important were his *Wilson* and *National* school readers. Their firm biblical values made such a powerful impact on the boy that he quoted from these elementary readers for the rest of his life.[30]

Then there was the Book of Mormon, which Anthony C. Ivins, Heber's uncle, first persuaded him to read. Pitting the fourteen-year-old Heber against his own son, Anthony Ivins promised the first boy to finish the book a pair of buckskin gloves, a wild frontier extravagance. After the first day, Heber's hopes were virtually dashed. Heber's young cousin had stayed up most of the night and read 150 pages, while Heber, who hoped to read the scriptures thoughtfully, had amassed only 25 pages. The incident, however, had a "Tortoise and the Hare" ending. "When I finished the book," Heber remembered, "I not only got a testimony [of it] but . . . the gloves as well." After his fast start, Heber's cousin never read another page.[31]

Young Heber, however, did not escape adolescence without its usual trials. By his late teens, he obviously prized his independence—even when dealing with the men whom he admired most. For example, when Bishop Woolley asked him to manage a ward social—a dance—Heber hesitated.

"I will do my best, but you need to agree to some conditions."

A bond had grown between the boy and his bishop that allowed such cheeky candor. Because of Heber's marble playing and perhaps his graver offense of ball-throwing against the Woolley barn, the bishop had labeled Heber "the laziest boy in the Thirteenth ward." But Heber had earnestly mounted a successful campaign to reclaim the bishop's confidence.[32]

Heber made his first request. The dance would require a smooth dance floor, not the rough-hewn planks of the Thirteenth Ward assembly rooms. Whittling candle wax into the cracks could make the floor smooth. Bishop Woolley had long opposed the idea for safety reasons. But he agreed to Heber's terms.

"And you must agree to pay the loss if there is one. You cannot have the party in the Thirteenth ward and make any money," Heber complained. "The young people won't come any more. . . . You have got to have three waltzes."

Neighboring wards permitted at least three of the new "round dances" such as the waltz and polka each evening. But Bishop Woolley insisted on quadrilles and cotillions, where dancers discreetly grouped themselves in old-fashioned lines or squares instead of pairing off in couples.

For a moment Bishop Woolley weighed philosophy and values against the possibility of another unsuccessful dance. An earlier party had failed to raise money for the St. George Temple fund, and the ward's proud reputation for always being in the lead had been tarnished.

"Take the three waltzes," Bishop Woolley conceded.

As his last request, Heber argued that they must hire Olsen's Band—the only ensemble in town that played the "Blue Danube Waltz" to perfection. The problem lay with the band's flutist, whose drunkenness at an earlier ward engagement had caused a great deal of disorder. As a result, Bishop Woolley had strictly forbidden the band to return. But, once again, Heber won. "Take Olsen's Quadrille Band," the bishop said. "Take your three round dances. Wax the floor."

On the night of the dance, President Young himself came. "This is for the benefit of the St. George Temple, isn't it?" he asked Heber at the door. Squeezing a ten dollar gold piece into the young man's hand, he asked, "Is that enough to pay for my ticket?" and entered the well-decorated room.

That night the Thirteenth Ward raised $80 for the new temple. No other ward earned half as much. "We scooped the town," Heber recalled years later, "and we had *four* round dances!"

When the unauthorized fourth round dance began, President Young instantly recognized the change in the program and protested, "They are waltzing."

"No," said Heber, only technically correct. "They are not waltzing: when they waltz they waltz all around the room. This is a quadrille."

Heber's sleight of hand brought a laugh from Brigham and the mild rejoinder, "You boys, you boys."[33]

A short time later President Young played a central role in one of Heber's greatest trials of faith. The Church leader had called the seventeen-year-old into his office to discuss the future, and he quickly focused their talk. "I think it is about time some of . . . [Jedediah's] boys were putting on the harness," he told Heber. "Don't you want to go on a mission?"

"That is a splendid idea, and I approve of it," Heber later recalled saying, "but I have some brothers three years older than I, and I suggest that you call them first."

At length Brigham complied but found the Grant polygamous half-brothers to be even more hesitant than Heber. As a result, Rachel's son was once more summoned to the President's office, and this time Heber agreed to accept a mission call the following spring.[34]

Actually, there were good reasons for his misgivings and mock resistance. He had left school at the age of sixteen to support his mother—and to fulfill his desire for a commercial career. His employers had promoted him rapidly, and now for the first time Rachel and her son enjoyed a measure of prosperity. But Heber's feelings were by no means consistent. Patriarch Perkins had promised him, while he was still an infant, that he would "begin the ministry when very young." Rachel and Heber had read and reread this blessing repeatedly. Now with President Young's call, the part about a youthful ministry seemed fulfilled. Excited, Heber began reading of the adventures of George Q. Cannon, Joseph F. Smith, and Erastus Snow—other teenaged missionaries—no doubt mentally comparing his skills and sinew with the young heroes who had preceded him.[35] Heber paid his debts and prepared for an immediate departure.

According to the custom of the time, formal missionary calls were announced during the official proceedings of general conference, and Heber entered the Tabernacle in April 1876 fully expecting to hear his name read. However, much to his bewilderment, the clerk failed to do so. Heber was devastated. During the next several days as he tried to complete his normal duties with Wells Fargo, he frequently wept in disappointment and perhaps in embarrassment.[36] Years later he would learn why no mission call had come. Erastus Snow and Daniel H. Wells had objected to his name when the list of prospective missionaries was submitted for General Authority approval. The boy, they claimed, was already performing "a very splendid mission" in providing for his widowed mother.[37]

The wound was slow to heal. Unbeknown to his closest friends and even to Rachel in whom he often confided such matters, during the next four or five years the episode haunted him. The problem, he believed, lay in the efficacy of Perkins's blessing—and in the larger question of religious revelation itself. Had not the patriarch erred? How "sure" was prophecy's "sure word"? "I was tempted seriously for several years to renounce my faith in the Gospel because this blessing was not fulfilled," he admitted. "The spirit would come over me . . . that the patriarch had lied to me, and that I should throw the whole business away."[38]

The Word of Wisdom also challenged the young man's faith. While his Thirteenth Ward Sunday School tutors inveighed against coffee, tea, tobacco, and alcohol, the prohibition of these commodities was never made to be a religious test. Church members could be considered "good" Mormons and still occasionally imbibe. In fact, devout Rachel's boardinghouse first introduced Heber to the taste of coffee. He soon became addicted, and despite Rachel's gentle disapproval he found that he could not abandon it. Time after time he quit, only to find his appetite uncontrollable. Finally, "Aunt" Susan Grant, one of his father's plural wives, served him a cup of her special blend of creamed coffee. Heber demurred.

"Have you promised anybody that you would quit?"

"I have promised myself a number of times that I would quit," he allowed. But "now I have said I am going to take a cup of coffee whenever I want it and I haven't drank any for months."

"This is a fine cup to quit on," said the angelic Aunt Susan, who was entirely out of character as a temptress.

"All right, my dear aunt." Heber raised the cup to his lips, his mouth watering. But after a moment the full and undrunk cup returned to the table, and with that victory his craving for the beverage ceased.[39]

The young man had an even greater difficulty with beer. Fearing an early death like his father's and convinced of the virtues of life insurance, Salt Lake City's youngest agent repeatedly sought coverage to protect his mother. Nineteenth-century actuarial tables, however, discriminated against slender girths and no company would issue Heber a policy. Determined to gain weight, Heber sought out Dr. Benedict, who had an immediate solution. If Heber would drink four glasses of beer daily, which Dr. Benedict prescribed, within two years he would have the additional twenty pounds necessary for coverage.

At first Heber found beer "bitter and distasteful," like his mother's herbal "kinnikinnick" tea. But he quickly acquired both a business and a personal taste for it. Within a year, he secured the fire insurance business of most Salt Lake City saloons and Utah breweries, an additional ten pounds, and a growing relish for the savor of hops. His daily four-glass limit became five, and occasionally grew to six.

He warred with his acute sense of conscience. Rereading the Word of Wisdom, he resolved to abandon his drinking and place his health and his mother's future with the Lord, "insurance or no insurance." But resolutions were easier made than kept. "I wanted some [beer] so bad that I drank it again," he confessed. Finally, he found strength in the same formula he had used with coffee. By telling himself he was free to take a drink whenever he wished, he overcame his obsession and ceased drinking. Just as quickly, he lost his trade with the saloons and breweries of the territory.[40]

During this time of personal struggle, Heber learned firsthand of the apparent fallibility of Church leaders. With Rachel in St. George, Utah, doing temple work, he and Frank Kimball kept "bachelor hall" at the Grant home. Frank Kimball, a moral but not an outwardly religious man, was summoned by the Fifteenth Ward bishopric and tried for his membership. After attempting in vain to testify for his friend, Heber perched himself on a fence pole outside an open window of the second-story hearing room. Kimball found it difficult to make a confession of faith, but pled for a year's probation to prepare himself. In response the bishopric, ignoring President Daniel H. Wells's counsel "to go slow" with the case, demanded guarantees about his future tithe paying and several other duties. Heber was outraged. "No, I wouldn't [agree], darn you," he found himself saying under his breath, still seated on his pole. Minutes later Frank Kimball was excommunicated, a judgment which, at least according to Grant's understanding, breached fairness and Christian kindness.[41]

Heber's several problems and scarring experiences gnawed at his spirit. Uncertain of his inherited faith, he attended at least one meeting at the freethinking Liberal Institute, probably more in curiosity than in actual discontent.[42] He also became "greatly interested" in the writings of Robert G. Ingersoll, nineteenth-century America's antichristian curmudgeon.[43] Accordingly, his network of friends reflected his growing religious ambivalence. Balancing the young man's many staunchly Mormon friends were others who he later came to regard as disreputable. They "smoked a little, and did things they ought not to do," Heber recalled, "but I liked them, they were jolly fellows."[44] He later considered his situation to be grave. "I stood as it were upon the brink of usefulness or upon the brink of making a failure of my life."[45]

Heber credited the Thirteenth Ward for his salvation. Bringing his Sunday School experience to full circle, the twenty-one-year-old was appointed a teacher. As in the earlier days of Brothers Goddard, Maiben, and Musser, Heber now stood before a congregation of "scholars," teaching, catechizing, praying, and serving as a role model. He frequently asked questions drawn from the Book of Mormon or the "Little Learner" section of the *Juvenile Instructor*. After several years' service, his responsibilities were expanded to include assistant secretary and eventually secretary of the school.[46]

The Church's first ward Young Men's Mutual Improvement Association [YMMIA] also allowed him to serve. The Thirteenth Ward YMMIA called Heber as a president's counselor at its initial meeting in 1875, and he continued in that capacity through a series of new presidencies for the rest of the decade.[47] The YMMIA's weekly sessions were first designed to give men in their late teens and early twenties the chance for self-study and speechifying, though exercises later included readings, essays, music, lectures, and answering questions on religious and cultural topics.

The Thirteenth Ward YMMIA meetings were often high toned, though once the men peremptorily refused a member's suggestion to take "the round dance pledge."[48] Gospel topics were the primary staple, with each youth expected to speak. Since fifteen or twenty men were usually present (out of an enrolled thirty-three), meetings theoretically could be long. In actuality, most participants talked briefly. "Bro. H. J. Grant said he like the rest who had spoke before him was unprepared," the minutes of one meeting recorded, "but according to the Book of Mormon he was satisfied that this was the Gospel of

Christ restored." On another occasion he was more loquacious. "If a person had any sense at all," Heber observed, "he could see that Tobacco and Whiskey was not good for the human system as nearly any one that used Tobacco had to make themselves sick the first time and[,] Second[,] how disgraceful an intoxicated person made himself."[49]

Heber had other Mutual duties concurrent with his ward assignment. He acted as Salt Lake Stake YMMIA secretary and as a Mutual "missionary" in the emerging Churchwide youth organization. The latter calling required him to speak before various Utah congregations. Unlike his later forceful, machine-gun style delivery, his first effort was a halting, two- or three-minute affair, which no doubt drew beads of perspiration. Lastly, the April 1880 general conference sustained him as secretary to the General YMMIA Superintendency of the Church. He thereby became associated with Elders Wilford Woodruff, Joseph F. Smith, and Moses Thatcher, members of the new superintendency.[50]

Grant's adult Sunday School and Mutual activities reinforced the values and faith of his heritage and permitted him to navigate successfully the difficult adolescent years of passage. No doubt he inflated the seriousness of his early crisis of belief. Bright and curious, he was subjected to a man's world when sixteen, yet his acts never trespassed pioneer Utah's basic religious norms (illus. 3-3). His gambling was with matchsticks; he permitted himself no Sunday baseball playing; and when friends offered him a sexual liaison, he fled with the rapidity of Joseph of Egypt.[51] More than he knew, his religious feeling was inbred.

"You must know[,] and I am the only person who would tell you so," he wrote to a friend, "I have got to be a very good boy. I attend meetings Sunday, generally twice a day, [and] go to the Elders Quorum [and my] Youngmen's Mutual Improvement Asstn."[52] While many of Zion's youth found it chic to renounce plural marriage, Heber wrote a long, impassioned defense. Whatever it lacked in grammar, orthography, and argument, this defense clearly set him apart among his contemporaries. "Shall we the sons and daughters of these men and women who have sacrificed so much for their religion resign any portion of that religion [viz., polygamy] to suit the notions and fancies of those who are our bitterest enemies?" He particularly scored his disbelieving friends who claimed they would never enter into its

Courtesy Church Archives, The Church of Jesus Christ of Latter-day Saints

Illus. 3-3. Heber as a young man.

practice. "Just stop and think for one minute what must be the feelings of a polygamist mother . . . [for] one of her children speaking lightly of an ordinance, by the practice of which they were born."[53] Rachel's influence was always close at hand.

Those who knew young Heber best understood his religious commitment. "He lives his religion," Richard Young reported, "but is seldom able to warm himself unto enthusiasm over a principle; his love is a practical, everyday, commonsense devotion to principles which from their superiority to all others, he chooses to believe are divine."[54]

Bishop Woolley was less analytical. When Heber was called to preside over the Tooele Stake at age twenty-three (thereby fulfilling Patriarch Perkins's blessing in an unexpected way), Bishop Woolley made a point of being at the conference. He wanted to assure the people that they were "getting a man and not a boy." Later the bishop met John Henry Smith on a Salt Lake City street. Reaching up and placing his arms around the large Apostle's neck, Bishop Woolley became emotional. "John Henry . . . [Heber J. Grant] is worthy to be one of the Apostles, don't you forget him. . . . I can't remain here much longer, but when I am gone don't you forget Heber J. Grant."[55]

Notes

This article was originally published in *BYU Studies* 24 (Spring 1984): 131–49.

1. Preston W. Parkinson, comp., *The Utah Woolley Family* (Salt Lake City: Deseret News, 1967), 126; see also Heber J. Grant, Typed Diary, September 22, 1924, and February 2, 1938, Grant Papers, Church Archives, The Church of Jesus Christ of Latter-day Saints, Salt Lake City. The christening is recorded in the Thirteenth Ward Papers, Church Archives. When citing material in the Grant collection, I have used box and folder numbers only when source identification cannot be established through the use of the collection's register.

2. Heber J. Grant to Helen Mar Monson, November 2, 1942, Grant Letterpress Copybook, 81:601, Grant Papers.

3. Heber J. Grant, "Testimony of Prophecy through the Gift of Tongues," *97th Annual Conference of The Church of Jesus Christ of Latter-day Saints* (Salt Lake City: The Church of Jesus Christ of Latter-day Saints, 1927), 17–18.

4. Zerubbabel Snow, General Minutes of the Thirteenth Ward, 1854–68, May 12, 1863, Thirteenth Ward Papers; Leonard J. Arrington, *From Quaker to Latter-day Saint: Bishop Edwin D. Woolley* (Salt Lake City: Deseret Book, 1976), 325.

5. General Minutes of the Thirteenth Ward, March 30, 1867, Thirteenth Ward Papers.

6. Belle Whitney Sears to Heber J. Grant, February 20, 1919, General Correspondence, Grant Papers. For Articles of Faith and Jacques's *Catechism* respectively, see Grant, "Remarks at the Dedicatory Service of the Pocatello Institute," October 27, 1929, p. 1, Grant Papers; and Heber J. Grant to Wilford Owen Woodruff, September 19, 1922, Grant Letterpress Copybook, 59:753.

7. Orson F. Whitney, Minutes of Birthday Celebration, November 6, 1926, Grant Papers.

8. Heber J. Grant to Thomas G. Judd, May 10, 1926, General Correspondence.

9. Heber J. Grant, undated and loose diary sheet, box 177, fd. 5, Grant Papers.

10. Sunday School Minutes, August 23, 1868, Thirteenth Ward Papers. For the social ramifications of Victorian reform, see George Kitson Clark, *The Making of Victorian England* (Cambridge, Mass.: Harvard University Press, 1962), 147–205.

11. Heber J. Grant to A. G. Gowans, July 10, 1919, Grant Letterpress Copybook, 54:826; Heber J. Grant to Hyrum H. Goddard, December 8, 1937, Grant Letterpress Copybook, 75:930.

12. Heber J. Grant, Blessing of F. A. Mitchell, September 15, 1919, Grant Letterpress Copybook, 55:70.

13. Heber J. Grant to John Maiben, July 19, 1901, Grant Letterpress Copybook, 31:98 (inserted between pp. 680–81). See also Heber J. Grant, "Remarks at the Funeral Services of Franklin B. Platt," March 18, 1928, Grant Letterpress Copybook, 66:332.

14. W. S. Naylor to Heber J. Grant, November 22, 1940, Ephemera Material (Birthday Tributes), Grant Papers; Emily Wells Grant to Heber J. Grant, August 11, 1890, Family Correspondence, Grant Papers.

15. General Minutes, December 21 and 25, 1856, Thirteenth Ward Papers. According to Bishop Woolley, Capener had previously agreed that their long-standing dispute would be settled privately. The disgruntled communicant, however, had refused to come forth.

16. Heber J. Grant to Iva Hamblin, May 23, 1935, Grant Letterpress Copybook, 72:644. For Woolley's emphasis on tithe paying, see J. H. Midgley to Heber J. Grant, May 16, 1941, General Correspondence.

17. Heber J. Grant, "Remarks at the YMMIA Board Meeting," January 29, 1919, Grant Papers.

18. For these and other contemporary descriptions of Brigham Young's speaking, see sketch by S. A. Kenner in *History of the Bench and Bar of Utah,* ed. and comp. C. C. Goodwin (Salt Lake City: Interstate Press Association, 1913), 12; *Chicago Times,* report filed February 22, 1871, printed in Preston Nibley, *Brigham Young: The Man and His Work* (Salt Lake City: Deseret News, 1936), 469; and "A 'Forty-Niner' Describes Brigham Young," in LeRoy R. and Ann W. Hafen, *Journals of Forty-Niners: Salt Lake to Los Angeles,* vol. 2 of Far West and the Rockies (Glendale, Calif.: Arthur R. Clark, 1954), 276n.

19. Ronald W. Walker, "Raining Pitchforks: Brigham Young as Preacher," *Sunstone* 8 (May–June 1983): 4–9.

20. Heber J. Grant to Susa Young Gates, March 16, 1927, Grant Letterpress Copybook, 65:167.

21. Heber J. Grant, "The Spirit and the Letter," *Improvement Era* 42 (April 1939): 201. See also Heber J. Grant, *71st Annual Conference of The Church of Jesus Christ of Latter-day Saints* (Salt Lake City: The Church of Jesus Christ of Latter-day Saints, 1901), 64; and Heber J. Grant, Reminiscences of President Heber J. Grant, n.d., p. 25, box 144, fd. 4, Grant Papers. Grant remembered the first speaker using such phrases as "We have indisputable and uncontrovertable evidences of the devine [*sic*] benignity."

22. Grant, Typed Diary, July 7, 1901.

23. Minutes of the Bishops' Meetings, April 29, 1869, and September 1, 1870, Presiding Bishopric Papers, Church Archives.

24. Anthon H. Lund, Journal, January 7, 1900, Church Archives.

25. Heber J. Grant, Manuscript Diary, May 29, 1881, Grant Papers; Heber J. Grant to the Family of Hamilton G. Park, May 3, 1912, Grant Letterpress Copybook, 45:343–44; and undated draft manuscript, p. 4, box 177, fd. 5, Grant Papers.

26. Heber J. Grant, "Sermon Delivered by President Heber J. Grant, 12 June 1921," draft in General Correspondence, Grant Papers; and Heber J. Grant, "Funeral Services for Edward W. Hunter," December 1, 1931, Grant Letterpress Copybook, 69:634.

27. Minutes of the Bishops' Meetings, esp. November 11, 1858; September 27, 1860; November 19, 1863; and July 7, 1870, Presiding Bishopric Papers.

28. A survey of ward priesthood officers in 1856, the last comprehensive Thirteenth Ward census, reveals that of the 130 boys and men over twelve years of age, fourteen held the Aaronic Priesthood (five deacons, three

teachers, and six priests) and sixty-seven held the Melchizedek Priesthood (eleven elders, forty-five seventies, and eleven high priests). Forty-nine were unordained. The average age for deacons, teachers, and priests was twenty, thirty-five, and twenty, respectively. For elders, seventies, and high priests, the average age was twenty-five, thirty-four, and sixty-eight. Only three minors were ordained to either of the priesthoods. Ordinance Records, 1856, Thirteenth Ward Papers. The paucity of Aaronic Priesthood bearers continued at least until the late 1870s when there were only 170 in the entire city—or about nine per ward. See Minutes of the Bishops' Meetings, August 31, 1877, Presiding Bishopric Papers.

29. Heber J. Grant to Edward H. Anderson, June 5, 1900, Grant Letterpress Copybook, 30:619; Grant, Typed Diary, December 16, 1930. Toward the end of Grant's life, several sources indicate that he had been earlier ordained an elder. Heber J. Grant himself never mentioned such an ordination, nor is it confirmed by extant ward records.

30. Pratt: Grant, Typed Diary, November 22, 1930; First Presidency Letterpress Copybook, 63:517, LDS First Presidency Papers, Church Archives. Paley: Heber J. Grant, "Draft of Remarks at Tabernacle," July 7, 1895, and January 26, 1896, Grant Letterpress Copybook, 21:38 and 33:28, Grant Papers. Nelson: Heber J. Grant, "Draft of B.Y.U. Centennial Address," October 16, 1925, Grant Letterpress Copybook, 63:548. Smiles: Heber J. Grant to Edward Anderson, June 5 and 6, 1900, Grant Letterpress Copybook, 30:619–20, 622. Readers: Heber J. Grant to Leo J. Muir, June 10, 1941, Grant Letterpress Copybook, 80:107.

31. Heber J. Grant, undated and untitled draft of reminiscences, box 144, fd. 4; Heber J. Grant to J. M. Shodahl, December 9, 1927, Grant Letterpress Copybook, 65:736.

32. Grant, Manuscript Diary, August 30, 1903.

33. Rachel Grant Taylor, "When Brigham Young Watched a Waltz," *Improvement Era* 44 (November 1941): 654, 678.

34. Heber J. Grant to Leland H. Merrill, June 14, 1938, Grant Letterpress Copybook, 76:611; Heber J. Grant, "Draft of Remarks on Brigham Young," June 1, 1924; Grant, Typed Diary, November 23, 1928.

35. The undated and unidentified blessing is found in box 176, fd. 23, Grant Papers. For its importance to Heber and Rachel, see Heber J. Grant to Edward H. Anderson, June 5, 1890, Grant Letterpress Copybook, 30:620; Heber J. Grant to Rachel Ridgway Grant, December 16, 1901, Grant Letterpress Copybook, 34:135; and Rachel Ridgway Grant to Heber J. Grant, May 23, 1905, Family Correspondence. For details of Heber's youthful missionary call a his reading of teenaged proselyting accounts, see Grant, "Reminiscences of President Heber J. Grant," 12, 17.

36. George H. Crosby, Jr., to Heber J. Grant, November 27, 1931, General Correspondence.

37. Heber J. Grant to Wilford Owen Woodruff, August 18, 1922, General Correspondence.

38. Heber J. Grant to Marian Cannon Bennion, March 2, 1935, Grant Letterpress Copybook, 72:284; Grant, "Reminiscences of President Heber J. Grant," 17–18.

39. Heber J. Grant to Leslie [Midgley], n.d., Grant Letterpress Copybook, 74:293–94.

40. Heber J. Grant, "Draft of Remarks Made at the Inglewood Stake Conference," February 4, 1940; Heber J. Grant to Leslie [Midgley], November 23, 1936, Grant Letterpress Copybook, 74:294; Heber J. Grant to Mr. and Mrs. E. H. Huish, April 20, 1936, General Correspondence.

41. Frank Kimball, the son of Mormon matriarch Sarah M. Kimball, refused to appeal the decision to the high council and remained out of the Church the rest of his life. Heber J. Grant to Heber M. Wells, April 8, 1937, Grant Letterpress Copybook, 75:246; Heber J. Grant to the family of Elder John Morgan, April 22, 1937, Grant Letterpress Copybook, 75:286–87; Grant, Typed Diary, October 11, 1940.

42. Grant to Henry C. Link, October 31, 1938, Grant Letterpress Copybook, 76:909.

43. Heber J. Grant to Fred [?], April 26, 1924, Grant Letterpress Copybook, 61:832; Grant, "Draft of B.Y.U. Centennial Address," 549.

44. Heber J. Grant to Thomas Judd, April 13, 1936, Grant Letterpress Copybook, 73:648; Heber J. Grant to Leona Walker, May 15, 1939, Grant Letterpress Copybook, 77:791.

45. Heber J. Grant, "Y.M.M.I.A. Annual Conference," *Contributor* 16 (August 1895): 640.

46. Sunday School Minutes, esp. May 27, August 5, December 23, 1877; January 13, March 10 and 17, May 19 and 26, July 21, August 18, October 13, November 3, 1878; April 13, 1879; Thirteenth Ward Papers. See also Grant, Manuscript Diary, January 3, 1886; Heber J. Grant to Thomas W. Sloan, August 15, 1905, Grant Letterpress Copybook, 40:50.

47. "Y.M.M.I.A.," Thirteenth Ward Manuscript History, n.d., Church Archives. From pioneer times youth "improvement" meetings were held in the ward, some as late as 1874, but its meetings of June 1875 are generally credited with being the beginning of the modern YMMIA movement. "Biographical Sketch," n.d., Grant Letterpress Copybook, 58:177, lists Heber J. Grant as having served as president, although no corroborating evidence is found in the sketchy official minutes.

48. Young Men's Mutual Improvement Association Minute Book, 1874–76, September 20, 1875, Thirteenth Ward Papers.

49. Young Men's Mutual Improvement Association Minute Book, 1874–76, September 17 and October 11, 1875.

50. Stake Secretary: Heber J. Grant to James N. Lambert, April 3, 1923, in Grant, Typed Diary, April 5, 1923, Grant Papers; Mutual Missionary: Heber J. Grant to Emil A. Berndt, July 16, 1920, General Correspondence; Church MIA Secretary: Edward H. Anderson, "The Past of Mutual Improvement," *Improvement Era* 1 (November 1897): 6.

51. Heber J. Grant to Leslie [Midgley], November 23, 1936; Heber J. Grant to Leona Walker, May 15, 1939, Grant Letterpress Copybook, 77:791; Heber J. Grant, "Sunday Baseball," 16 *Improvement Era* 16 (January 1913): 262.

52. Heber J. Grant to Fera[morz] Young, March 26, 1876, General Correspondence.

53. The address, which the nineteen-year-old apparently delivered before his seventies quorum particularly censured the disbelief of Mormondom's youth. Heber J. Grant, "Draft on Polygamy," February 12, 1876, Grant Papers.

54. Richard W. Young, Diary, 2:3–4, November 1882, Western Americana, J. Willard Marriott Library, University of Utah, Salt Lake City.

55. Heber J. Grant to Orson Woolley, February 20, 1917, Grant Letterpress Copybook, 53:667.

Growing Up in Early Utah:
The Wasatch Literary Association,
1874–1878

One day in early February 1874, Jim Ferguson, sensing the forlorn hope of advancing his courtship with Minnie Horne, suggested to Ort (Orson F.) Whitney and another of the boys that they organize a reading society. Ferguson "had heard, no doubt, of fond couples 'reading life's meaning in each others eyes,'" Whitney later mused, "and that was the kind of reading that most interested him." Since the seventeen-year-old Whitney found himself "in the same box with Ferguson on the girl question," the suggestion found a ready response. Whitney immediately invited those who "would make desirable members" to meet at the home of Sister Emmeline B. Wells, his motherly confidante. It was there on Salt Lake City's State Street that the Wasatch Literary Society was born[1] (illus. 4-1).

From such modest roots flowered one of territorial Utah's most lively and far-reaching adventures with culture. Whitney confessed that he and his friends had a long-standing interest in the highbrow. "As for essays, declamations, and musical renditions, we had been doing that all our lives."[2] Prior to the Wasatch, Whitney and Ferguson had drawn up constitutions for several cultural societies. Indeed, Whitney and a dozen of the subsequent "Wasatchers" had previously affiliated with the intellectually stimulating and controversial Zeta Gamma, Dr. John R. Park's debating society at the University of Utah and reputedly the first Greek-lettered group in the Intermountain West. Some also had joined the short-lived Delta Phi, a literary society that had flourished in 1873.[3]

Courtesy Church Archives, The Church of Jesus Christ of Latter-day Saints

Illus. 4-1. Young Orson F. Whitney (ca. 1875), founding member of the Wasatch Literary Society.

The 1870s were ripe for cultural societies. From the beginning the Latter-day Saint settlers had fostered as much culture as their pioneer economy would permit. They had sponsored the "Polysophical," "Philomathian," and "Universal Scientific" societies; they listened to the literary and scientific "Seventies' Lectures"; and they built the Social Hall and the Salt Lake Theatre to stage drama. The 1870s brought new wealth and a cosmopolitan spirit to this foundation. The Union Pacific Railroad, the antagonistic *Salt Lake Tribune,* the Tintic Mining District, the one-thousand-seat Godbeite Liberal Institute each in its own way increased Utah's diversity and prosperity. The result was significant. Mormon cultural traditions mixed with the new pluralism, and the stage was set for unprecedented creativity and ferment.[4]

The Wasatch Literary Association drew from both Mormon and wider American legacies. With few exceptions, the sixty who eventually came to enroll in the society were first generation, native-born Utahns. Many were scions with the bluest of Mormon blood. (Nearly one-sixth were Brigham Young's children, grandchildren, nephews, or nieces, while seven were sons and daughters of Daniel H. Wells, Brigham's counselor.) However, an appreciation of culture, not wealth or position, was the common denominator in the background of its members. Many of their parents were longtime mainstays of the territory's Chautauqua programs and amateur theater.[5]

The "Wasatchers" proved very much the children of their heritage. According to its constitution and bylaws, the Wasatchers desired "the social advancement and the improvement of its members in general literature, music and drama"—no small task for unsupervised youth in a semirural community of less than twenty-five thousand. To fulfill the society's mission, the usual complement of officers was put in place. A president, vice-president, secretary, treasurer, and chairman of the program committee were elected at first monthly and later every six weeks. A marshal and janitor were subsequently added to provide much needed decorum—and probably a touch of humor given the ignominy of such positions. The original ceiling of twenty-five active members was once raised to thirty-two, but all efforts to increase it still higher were soundly defeated. The bylaws called for the society to meet every Wednesday evening in one of the members' homes.[6]

The society, while dedicated to culture, had too much youth and wit in the group to admit either pretension or gravity. Most members entered the Wasatch when in their late teens or early twenties. While occasional leeway was extended to venerability, as in the brief membership of thirty-three-year-old Will Woods, exceptions were usually on the side of precocity. "Hebe" Wells was fifteen when he joined, Bud Whitney sixteen, and Dick Young just over seventeen.

With a "disposition to sacrifice everything for a laugh," the Wednesday evening programs were unpredictable. "J[ohn] B. Read, *Janitor,* assumed the chair," one meeting's minutes began. "By overwhelming majority vote of those present, Mr. Read was fined 50¢ for this assumption of authority." Normally the president—not the janitor—called for a quorum and approved the minutes. A general reading of literature began after the reading of the minutes. Each member was required to participate. They studied the Mormons' favorite Wordsworth ode, "Intimations of Immortality," several times, and they read the life or works of Byron, Goldsmith, Gray, Longfellow, Pope, Scott, and Shakespeare, often drawing the selections from school readers.[7]

Group reading proved too staid, however, so this portion of the weekly program was soon abandoned in favor of spelling matches and an expansion of the next portion of the meeting, individual cultural exercises. (The first was apparently based upon genuine need, for the secretary misspelled two words in the sentence recording the motion.) Individual exercises were assigned to members in turn a week or two prior to the scheduled performance. These might include declamations, lectures, debates, and remarks; original essays, parodies, and poetry; vocal or instrumental renditions; and dialogue, dramatic readings, and even small scale theatrical productions.[8]

The best exercises were remembered as "ambitious and meritorious," a judgment that seems fully warranted at least on the first account. Without the light touch and quick humor of his friends, H. J. Grant twice lectured on "Insurance" and backed up his remarks with the solid credentials of owning, despite his youthful nineteen years, one of the territory's leading insurance agencies. The half sisters Emily and Emmeline Wells, known as "Little and Big Em of the Wasatch," once debated "which has had the more ground for complaint, the Indian or the Negro." Ort Whitney, also versatile with flute and guitar, whistled an obbligato to the "Poet and Peasant" overture as Lena Fobes "brilliantly" performed the piece on the piano. And Stan Clawson's violin butchered the "Crystal Schottische" with such great finesse that the performance became an unforgettable memory.[9]

Bud Whitney's "The Desereted Village," an extended parody of Goldsmith's "The Desereted Village," also became a Wasatch legend. Though subsequently lost, the text was partially reconstructed from collective memory and passed in later years from member to member like a Homeric epic. Telling of the hearth of Billy Dunbar and the mien of Emily Wells, his belle, it captured the meter and idyll of Goldsmith's original:

> Removed from Brigham Street a league or two,
> The estate stands whereon our hero grew.
> Not large the lands, nor spacious are the halls,
> No costly chattels hang the simple walls.
> No shimmering font the sportive eye delights,
> No grassy lawn the travelers toil invites.
> Far far from these, the vain display of wealth
> Is here exchanged for free and rugged health.
> . . . .
> Each Sunday morn to visit Mrs. Sears,
> The lovely form of little Em appears.
> Unconscious, half of all her blooming charms,
> Yet well inured to love and loves alarms.
> White gauzy skirts pinned backward hard and tight,
> Still other charms afford the eager sight.[10]

The spell of the gaslights seemed to excite members most of all. Their cultural exercises, filled with scenes and staging, soon required a new Wasatch officer called "dramatic manager." Popular dramas became common. So did original productions that at times were directed to the intrigues of the society's current social situation.

"The whole [of next weeks' program is] to conclude with a scene from the '*fowl*' tragedy, *Waiting for the Verdict*—the *Court Scene*," the minutes read with apparent reference to an impending matrimonial decision "by Messrs R. W. Wells, O. F. Whitney, Rud Clawson, Stan Clawson, H. M. Wells, H. G. Whitney, Jno Horne, Lorenzo Young and Miss Cornelia Horne." The Wasatch's devotion to Shakespeare was more decorous. Dialogues and sometimes whole acts were performed from *Hamlet, Henry IV, Julius Caesar, King John,* the *Merchant of Venice, Othello,* and *Richard III*.[11]

The quality of the cultural exercises varied widely, according to the society's candid minutes. "The regular exercises were . . . very poor," one entry declared. On another occasion they were "only tolerably well rendered." The members' busy schedules seemed to be the chief difficulty behind failures to prepare and sometimes to perform. The society's talent was sufficient to sponsor periodic public exhibitions at the Social Hall, which generally were well received. For example, an exhibition opened in February 1876 with the society's orchestra playing an overture, assisted by the cultured schoolmarm Ida Cook and the budding vocalist B. B. Young. Wasatch President John Caine then spoke. Next, Harry Culmer, May Wells, and Bud Whitney read essays. The Wasatch chorus sang "Joy! Joy!" after which Cornelia Clayton, Mattie Horne, Libbie Beatie, Bud Whitney, Harry Emery, and Mary Ferguson provided several musical numbers. The evening concluded with dialogue from the second act of Libbie's *Marble Heart*.[12]

This performance was an embarrassment, however, at least in the dour judgment of President Caine. "Our leader, the Grand, Infallible, John T. Caine, is dissatisfied with our last," Heber Wells reported to Dick Young, then teaching school in Manti. He "has willed that we *must* do something to redeem ourselves. . . . Of course, the girls all melted at the sight of their 'beau ideal,' and of course they all voted in the manner which 'Johntee' prescribed." Caine in fact called a special meeting of the Wasatch to insist that a redeeming exhibition be scheduled, and, with the girls voting as a block, secured the authority to manage the new production personally.[13]

No Wasatch gathering was ever complete without good-natured wrangling and practical joking. When the forgetful H. J. Grant asked one Wednesday where the society was meeting, Jim Ferguson sent him to Kittie Heywood's home high on a Salt Lake City hill. "It was a good joke on me walking so far for nothing," Grant admitted after the wild-goose chase, "and I think I shall try & get even with James for playing me so."[14]

Immediate recourse was always available through the society's celebrated "budget box," the *piece de resistance* of each meeting. This "budget box" was a box in which members could anonymously place any composition, serious or most often otherwise. Edited and selected by a reader appointed at the previous meeting, the box's contents were read following the general culture exercises. The idea was not original. Will Woods, President Wells's nephew from Iowa, had suggested the society appropriate the plan from a club to which he had once belonged.[15]

The budget box "used to fairly scintillate with the brilliance of its articles," the *Salt Lake Herald* judged a decade after the Wasatch Literary Association's demise, "many of them—but for their rather personal character—would adorn the pages of any of our brightest periodicals of current literature." After a Wastacher memorized but badly executed the role of Claude Melnotte in Bulwer's *The Lady of Lyons*, the budget box began with what at first seemed a compliment:

> Now Claude was well committed, too,
> And doubly done—ay, this is true;
> You first commit the part, to prove it,
> And then commit the murder of it.[16]

Spicy rumors of members' social lives were a budget box staple. Several squibs detailed an alleged hugging incident involving Rob Sloan and the popular yet coquettish Emily Wells on her distinguished father's front porch (illus. 4-2). They graphically continued with the reactions of her distraught admirers Ort Whitney and H. J. Grant threatening vengeance and Billy Dunbar, suicide. "I would [have] given a dollar if you could have been there to hear them," Grant said when reporting the episode to a friend in the East. The budget box pieces "were too good for anything."[17]

On another occasion B. B. Young must have thought otherwise. Young apparently earned Wasatch displeasure by first affiliating with and then openly censuring the society. The budget box responded with a torrent of abuse. Bid Young, his half-brother, disclosed that B. B.'s "regular morning exercise was to run a chicken . . .

until it sweat, so that he would extract an egg without much difficulty for his morning drink." Members refused to let the lampoon die. A week later they staged a mock trial, with B. B.'s chicken-running prosecuted as a crime with "malice prepense." Not understanding legal jargon, "the defendant denied chasing the chicken with 'a mallet prepense,' maintaining that 'it was a stick with a nail in the end of it.'" Rule Wells, the judge, swept the distinction aside and sentenced the criminal to death. Still later the society fired another fusillade. Responding to B. B.'s complaint that his calculus studies were "using him up," the budget box wondered if the problem did not lie more realistically in his "getting drunk."[18]

Courtesy Church Archives, The Church of Jesus Christ of Latter-day Saints

Illus. 4-2. Young Emily Wells, member of the Wasatch Literary Society and future wife of Heber J. Grant.

New members in particular were subject to attack. "Harry Culmer," Heber Wells reported to Dick Young, "is now a member and on the next evening he may prepare to be slandered, laughed at, abused, and culumniated at the pleasure of the budget box writers." The eighteen-year-old Wells could hardly still his enthusiasm—nor keep his metaphors consistent:

> He must go through the "kinks." I have, and you have, and why should he be exempt? Let us rally! and pour such hot words into his burning ears as will scorch his very inners, and make his blood run cold with fiery indignation. I will ransack the remotest corner of my cranium for wit, and coupling this with all the eloquence my soul posesses, I'll "let him have it," loud and long, egad I will![19]

More and more, the budget box determined a meeting's success. The gathering at the Hornes' was "'way up,' one [of] the best (if not the best) we have ever had," reported one member. "There was nearly (if not quite) 50 budget box [pieces]." Contributions were vigorously solicited from out-of-town members ("Attack anybody, *me* if you like"). Other members hatched a budget box conspiracy. Using Emily Wells as amanuensis, signing themselves as Gax, Ginx, Iago, Pard, Uebec, and Yoric, and further disguising their trail by occasionally attacking themselves, they embroiled the society week after week not only with their calumnies but by the aura of mystery surrounding their true identities.[20]

While intended as "innocent merriment," the Wasatch barbs occasionally inflicted wounds upon the sensitive. For example, H. J. Grant, a widow's son without the opportunity for formal schooling, remembered shedding "many bitter tears when my gramatical errors & other mistakes were laughed at" and at times felt "the least beloved and respected of any of the members of the Club." Unfortunately, many were not as resilient as Grant. After running the verbal gauntlet, probably a tenth of the society's incoming members quickly dropped out. Realizing the excesses of the budget box, the fun-loving Wasatch old-timers finally adopted a formal resolution declaring "personalities" a misdemeanor and banned them, subject to fines, from all proceedings.[21]

However, the fines themselves became a source of amusement. Assessed each meeting after the budget box reading, the fines often touched most members' pockets, as the minutes of October 21, 1874, testify:

> Fine of 5 cents were imposed of Kate Wells, R. S. Wells, and Kittie Heywood for not contributing to [the] B[udget] B[ox]. Fines of 20 cents were imposed on Kittie Heywood, H. G. Whitney, C. B. Swift, Jote Beatie, Emily Wells, Nellie Whitney, R. S. Wells[,] Emmie Wells & O. F. Whitney for disorder. It was moved and seconded that O. F. Whitney behave himself during the remainder of the evening. Mr. Swift was fined 25 cts for rudeness. Moved that Messr[s] Swift, H. G. and O. F. Whitney be fined for disrespect for president, 10¢. H. G. Whitney was fined 15¢ for disorder. Jote Beatie, Emily Wells & R. S. Wells were fined for whispering.

The fines, added to the club's dues, proved an ample revenue source. During its four-year history, the society met expenses and maintained a burgeoning account at Zion's Savings Bank.[22]

The Wasatch's prosperity occasioned an alleged letter from John R. Winder, Salt Lake City's Collector of Taxes. Members had not realized that their money was subject to levy. Concerned, the society appointed a committee of Ort Whitney, John B. Read, and D. C. Young to negotiate a settlement. Week after week passed with the committee temporizing or making partial reports. Realizing he could spin the matter out no further, Whitney finally admitted the truth—the letter was a hoax.[23]

The critic's report, the final Wasatch agenda item, attempted to conclude meetings on a decorous note. The "critic," appointed weekly at the outset of each meeting, judged both the culture exercises and budget box reading. His animadversions could be delivered "very sarcastically" and at times were "very plain and to the point." Once the budget box was judged to contain a number of meritorious pieces "but its wit and interest were not equivilent to its length." After the Wasatch's burlesque of B. B. Young, critic Emma Wells, Emily's half-sister, so railed at the abuse of "our friends" that participants felt "like a Mexican dollar with seventy cents deducted." John Caine was equally scathing when ill-timed laughter marred a dramatic dialogue between Iago and Othello. "You who have laughed at these gentlemen and their commendable efforts to entertain us this evening," Caine opened, "have applauded worse acting upon the boards of the Salt Lake Theatre." Such a high-tone demeanor, however, was not always maintained. Once when John Read's critique was called for, he sardonically refused any response—and was fined 25¢ for neglecting duty.[24]

Not surprisingly, given the society's impetus, socializing played an important role. Members might meet informally at the home of Emmeline Wells or of the popular Beaties, where the parlor bulged each Sunday evening with "the crowd." On weekdays, members pared apples or danced the slightly disreputable waltz. If the conversation lagged, Carl Young would play the William Tell Overture or Ort Whitney would sing "Thoughts." With autograph albums the rage, swains vied to be sentimental and witty. Harry Emery, quoting Othello, wrote in Jote Beatie's album: "Excellent wench, but I do love thee / And when I love thee not, chaos has come again." The charm was lost when he indelicately penned the same lines in rival albums.[25]

A year after its organization, the society officially started sponsoring social activities. There were weekend outings to City Creek

Canyon, Wells's Farm, and Black Rock House on the Great Salt Lake. On one occasion big, buff Harry Emery swam from the beach house to Black Rock and back despite a raging storm—to the ladies' admiration but to the dismay of several men who nearly drowned trying to also complete his feat. At Calder's Park, now Nibley Park, the Wasatchers alternately ice-skated or boated as the seasons permitted. One time Mary Jones's skiff capsized and she was rushed to the shore to dry out. As her teeth chattered and body quivered from coldness, Bud Whitney asked with more nervous sympathy than forethought if she cared for ice cream. "Her reply," a member recalled, "was an Artic glance that 'froze the genial current of his soul.'"[26]

Members approved proposed social events only after "a lively and lengthy discussion," and there were times when their caution appeared wise. In January 1876 the young women, supported by John Caine and Harry Emery, hoped to stage a grand ball at the Wasatch Hotel. The proposition had been approved and a committee on arrangements appointed when the men began to question the plan's feasibility. "The boys all know that we girls <u>want</u> to have a party and <u>we think</u> it is mean in them to predict that it will be a failure," an impassioned Mary Jones declaimed. "We know that if the boys <u>want</u> it to be a f[a]ilure and do all they can to make <u>it one</u> of course it <u>will be one</u>." Despite her forensics, the project was voted down on basically straight male-female lines. The matter did not end there. Although men and women usually shared leadership positions in the Wasatch, at the next election of officers the women vigorously exercised their franchise. An entire distaff slate was elected—with four of the men receiving fines for disorderly conduct during the election.[27]

As the ladies' reaction indicated, socials were serious business—especially when directed toward courting. Victorian romance and sensibility exaggerated emotions and stylized behavior. Wasatch men openly pled their troths. In turn, the girls' flirtatious glances and carefully phrased letters dropped telltale hints of reciprocated affection. Final marital decisions brought extravagant misery to rejected parties. There was mock (and perhaps some real) fear that Bud Whitney was suicidal when Alice Young eloped with Charlie Hopkins. Luella Cobb plunged several Wasatch beaux into despair by becoming the fifth plural wife of middle-aged John W. Young.

Some pains did not heal quickly. In later years when members recalled their Wasatch experience, memories of "heartaches" and "upsetting love affairs" remained to taint their otherwise happy nostalgia.[28]

Church leaders and parents understandably had some misgivings about the association. Its activities were unsupervised, and its spirit seemed too secular, carefree, and at times bruising. Too few men within the society accepted mission calls. Others, like Ort Whitney, appeared to postpone "real life" for prose and drama. Many members rejected polygamy, the nineteenth century's badge of total Latter-day Saint commitment, and when they did marry, some chose spouses who were lapsed Saints or not even Church members.[29] When prominent Wasatcher John Read joined the staff of the *Salt Lake Tribune,* the Mormons' strident journalistic foe, the worst fears of the older generation seemed confirmed.

"The Wasatch has already, through the gab and energy of certain mischief makers, attained in the eyes of our parents, the unenviable notoriety of an institution for the promotion of infidelity and sacriligiousness," Heber Wells noted. But he insisted parental concerns were overdrawn. Most of the Wasatch nonbelievers were "of that cast . . . before they were Wasatchers. It is simply absurd to think that an association where nothing of . . . [a religious nature] is discussed but where a few persons meet and go through exercises for literary culture, could be the means of turning out nothing but infidels."[30]

In truth, in matters of behavior and religion the society left its members largely as it found them. Certainly there was little outward piety. When it was suggested that meetings be opened and closed with prayer, the motion evoked so little support it never came to a vote. Another suggestion that the society tithe its revenue met a similar fate. Yet there were no carping complaints about the Church either. For example, prior to Ort Whitney's planned departure for a New York dramatic career, the society staged a farewell benefit at the Social Hall. When a mission call intervened, they cheerfully gave Whitney another testimonial in the Fourteenth Ward Hall. When Rule Wells left on a mission, the group secured a private railroad car and traveled to Ogden to see him off on the Union Pacific[31] (illus. 4-3).

Whatever its religious failings, the Wasatch excited "the admiration and envy of the literary, dramatic and musical portions of the town" and presumably the young social set as well. Its imitators were numerous. Some youth organized a "reading association." Others formed the Azalea Society, a cultural group that divided its membership into the "Democrats" and "Republicans" more than a decade before national political parties entered Utah. Each of the latter groups then competed against the other in presenting cultural exercises. Still more imaginative was the all-male Decennial Philadelphian Society. It planned to meet each decade, "renewing and perpetuating the friendship of early life." Finally, the Church-sponsored Mutual Improvement Associations (M.I.A.) began in the middle 1870s. Sensing an obvious vacuum and wishing to avoid the Wasatch's excesses, Brigham Young called Junius Wells to reinvigorate the previously organized youth Retrenchment Societies and commence Churchwide M.I.A. activity.[32]

Courtesy Church Archives, The Church of Jesus Christ of Latter-day Saints

Illus. 4-3. Rulon Wells (*seated, center*) and Orson Whitney (*standing, right*) leaving for their missions, ca. 1875.

The organization of the M.I.A. was a death knell. With young Salt Lakers being drawn into Church youth activities, the Wasatch no longer had a pool of potential new members. For a time the two rival organizations existed side by side, but by the winter of 1877–78 the Wasatch was losing momentum. Meetings were abbreviated so members could leave to make "Lasser Candy" or canceled in lieu of the St. Mark's Cantata or the "Kellogg Cary Combination" appearing at the Salt Lake Theatre.

As members married they resigned, and those who remained seemed changed by time and new experiences. When Ort Whitney returned from his mission, there was a new, unfamiliar gravity about him. "Yes, I have been down East for the past year and seven months and have not felt very well," he typically replied to all inquiries with un-Wasatch seriousness, "but I hope soon with the help of Heaven and the mountain air to . . . regain my native health." This was not the stuff from which the society had been built and was a sign both of the members' growing maturity and of the Wasatch's consequent decline.[33]

For a time, the beleaguered association tried to regroup. Not having met for several months, members in late spring 1878 drafted a new constitution, pledged biweekly meetings, and elected new officers. Ort Whitney, who had been the first Wasatch president and—despite his several absences from Salt Lake City—once again assumed the chair. But old enthusiasms could not be relit. The final session of the Wasatch Literary Association met at the Wells's South Temple Street home on May 29, 1878.[34]

Yet, it was *not* the last meeting. Twelve years later, in June 1890, members held a reunion. Amid rose bowers, Chinese lanterns, refreshment-filled tables, and wafting melodies of the band, the Wasatch met at a familiar gathering place, Frank and Kittie Heywood Kimball's home on Heywood Hill. The intervening years had not extinguished the Wasatch spirit. "It is to be hoped," read the ludicrously printed formal invitation, that "the same rigid decorum which formed so conspicuous a feature of the Wasatch in other days will be observed at this meeting."[35]

Members were called to order by Ort Whitney. The roll was called and the minutes of the May 29, 1878, meeting were read. Then Whitney imposed wide-ranging fines and introduced the general exercises, which included Stanley Clawson's celebrated "Crystal Schottishe." The budget box contained "a host of humorous skits, poems and allusions to the status of the members and their adventures, loves, courtships, etc., of a dozen years ago." Reportedly it was "immensely enjoyed by all—even those who were hardest hit." Sometime before 2:00 A.M. the party concluded and the Wasatch adjourned *sine die*.[36]

The reunion must have occasioned moments of personal reverie and appraisal. In the past lay their youthful exuberance, when their exaggerated words and consciousness of style had become the foundation for many members' subsequent able prose. Likewise, the Wasatchers must have realized that their amateur theatrics had borne fruit. Nine former Wasatch members had formed the core of the Home Dramatic Club, a stock company that contributed largely to late nineteenth-century Utah drama.[37] Looking at the reunion's guest list, members must have also understood the importance of the association's socializing. Almost half of the society had married fellow Wasatchers.[38]

More dramatically, the Wasatch's legacy was the success its members enjoyed in adult life. The list is impressive. *Art and architecture:* J. Willard Clawson, portraitist; H. L. A. Culmer, civic booster, editor, and landscape painter of the grandiose; and Don Carlos Young, Church architect. *Public Affairs:* Heber M. Wells, Utah's first state governor and treasurer of the U.S. Shipping Board; William W. Woods, Idaho legislator and magistrate; and Richard W. Young, attorney, U.S. Commissioner of the Philippines, and Utah's first general of the U.S. Regular Army. *Education:* John T. Caine Jr., proponent of "scientific" agriculture and Utah State College professor of history and English; and Joseph Toronto, University of Utah professor of mathematics and history. *Journalism:* John B. Read, editor of the Butte [Montana] *Miner;* Robert W. Sloan, Democratic State Chairman, broker, editor of the Logan *Journal;* and Horace G. Whitney, managing editor and nationally recognized dramatic and lyric editor of the *Deseret News. Businessmen:* Charles S. Burton; Laron A. Cummings; James X. Ferguson; John F. Horne; Frank D. Kimball; and Herbert M. Pembroke.

In spite of their earlier unruly and profane reputation, Wasatch members made their most distinguished contributions in the field of religion. Kittie Heywood Kimball found a satisfying faith in Christian Science, and she became Salt Lake City's first practitioner of the religion and its most forceful organizer. Wasatch *bete noir* Bicknell (B. B.) Young worked in the same movement on a broader scale. Abandoning a promising career as a baritone vocalist, Young delivered Christian Science lectures in Australia, England, and the United States, taught the denomination's prestigious Normal Class, and later served as First Reader of the Mother Church in Boston.[39]

Not surprisingly, Wasatchers were called to Latter-day Saint ecclesiastical positions more than perhaps anyone, including themselves, foresaw. Cornelia Horne Clayton and Minnie Horne James served on the Primary and Relief Society General Boards. Martha Horne Tingey labored forty-nine years in the presidency of the Young Women's Mutual Improvement Association, including twenty-four years as president. Richard W. Young and Brigham S. Young led the Ensign Stake and the Northwest Mission, respectively. Four Wasatchers were called as General Authorities: Rulon S. Wells as Senior President of the First Council of Seventy; poet and historian Orson F. (Ort) Whitney as a member of the Quorum of the Twelve; Rudger Clawson as President of the Quorum of the Twelve; and Heber J. Grant served twenty-seven years as President of the Church.[40]

The Wasatch Literary Association obviously played a role, however modest, in the remarkable achievement of its members. Probably its members were ordained for "success" long before Jim Ferguson talked to Ort Whitney on a Salt Lake City street. But the society schooled its members in culture and trained them in public speaking and writing. And during their careers, like the graduates of British public schools, Wasatchers often turned to each other for professional or financial help. In fact, in later years the association became something of an alma mater, a halcyon time, "the happiest days of my life," wrote one Wasatch octogenarian. Heber Wells, who usually said things best, albeit with hyperbole, admitted his Wasatch days touched his senses like "the almost forgotten fragrance of burning sagebrush." Or perhaps his memories were better expressed by "the odor of the honeysuckles that used to grow in Uncle Brigham's upper garden."[41]

Notes

This article was originally published in *Sunstone* 6 (November/December 1981): 44–51.

1. Orson F. Whitney, "The Wasatch Literary Association," *Improvement Era* 28 (September 1925): 1017–19; Orson F. Whitney to Heber J. Grant, January 27, 1912, General Correspondence, Heber J. Grant Papers, Church Archives, The Church of Jesus Christ of Latter-day Saints, Salt Lake City. I am indebted to Ronald O. Barney of the Church Historical Department.

Having a longtime interest in the Wasatch Literary Association of his own, he nevertheless graciously made many useful suggestions, which improved my essay.

2. Orson F. Whitney to Heber J. Grant, January 27, 1921, General Correspondence.

3. Orson F. Whitney to Heber J. Grant, January 27, 1921, General Correspondence. The names of the first Zeta Gamma members can be found in "The Original Zeta Gamma Society," *Deseret News,* January 4, 1902, 9. The minutes of the Delta Phi are deposited at Western Americana, Special Collections, J. Willard Marriott Library, University of Utah, Salt Lake City.

4. The impulse was manifold: the evangelical and private school movement; the historical writing of Edward Tullidge and T. B. H. Stenhouse; the increasingly public and active role of Latter-day Saint women; the commencement of the publication of the *Woman's Exponent* and its male counterpart, the *Contributor;* the Latter-day Saint auxiliary movement; and the itinerant ministry of the free-thought spiritualists at the Liberal Institute are examples of these new cultural currents.

5. The minutes of the association suggest a little more than sixty members, although a listing prepared for the 1890 reunion has only fifty-six names. See the Wasatch Literary Association Minute Book (hereafter Wasatch Minutes), Church Archives.

6. Wasatch Minutes, May 29, 1878, pp. 174–75, see also pp. 6, 17, 24, 36, and 47.

7. Whitney, "Wasatch Literary Association," 1019; Wasatch Minutes, November 7, 1877, 157; italics added. For examples of the general reading exercises, see October 14 and 21, November 11, December 23 and 30, 1874, January 6, 20, and 27, February 3, April 7 and 21, 1875, pp. 1, 2, 5, 11–12, 16–17, 19, 21, 32, and 35.

8. Marba C. Josephson, "President Grant and the Wasatch Literary Club," *Improvement Era* 44 (November 1941): 659, 690; Wasatch Minutes, June 2, 1875, p. 441.

9. Heber J. Grant: Wasatch Minutes, May 31, 1876, and May 2, 1877, pp. 44, 98, 139. Wells's debate: Wasatch Minutes, March 21, 1877, p. 134. Orson F. Whitney, *Through Memory's Halls: The Life Story of Orson F. Whitney as Told By Himself* (Independence, Missouri: Zion's Printing and Publishing Company, 1930), 112. Stan Clawson: Wasatch Minutes, May 31, 1876, p. 99; Emily Wells Grant to May Wells, May 7, 1890, Family Correspondence, Grant Papers. Clawson originally was accompanied by Bud Whitney on the flute and J. Willard Clawson on the guitar. Performed several times later, its inaugural "created an im[m]ense amount of laughter."

10. Heber J. Grant to C. Bryon Whitney, November 17, 1920, General Correspondence; F. D. Kimball to Heber J. Grant, December 15, 1937, General Correspondence. Whitney's poem even became the object of literary criticism by Wasatcher H. L. A. Culmer, Wasatch Minutes, December 6, 1876, p. 120.

11. Wasatch Minutes, April 14, 1875, p. 34; Whitney, "Wasatch Literary Association," 1020.

12. Wasatch Minutes, January 27, March 10, 1875; February 2, March 1, and June 28, 1876, pp. 19, 28, 78–79, 84, and 105.

13. Heber M. Wells to Richard W. Young, March 4, 1876, typescript, Richard W. Young Papers, Western Americana; Wasatch Minutes, March 8, 1876, p. 86.

14. Heber J. Grant to Feramorz Young, March 26, 1876, General Correspondence.

15. Whitney, "Wasatch Literary Association," 1019.

16. Orson F. Whitney was even more laudatory: "Some of the [budget box] sketches, by such writers as Horace G. Whitney, Heber M. Wells, and John B. Read—wits of the first water—rivaled Goldsmith, Dickens and Mark Twain. This is positively no exaggeration, and it constituted one of the main reasons for the society's popularity." Whitney, "Wasatch Literary Association," 1020–21; "Wasatch Redivivus: Reunion of the Old-Time Literary Society," Salt Lake Herald, June 22, 1890, 5.

17. Heber J. Grant to Feramorz Young, fragment about 1876, Grant Papers.

18. Lorenzo D. Young to Richard W. Young, April 9, [1876?], typescript, Grant Papers; Whitney, "Wasatch Literary Association," 1021.

19. Heber M. Wells to Richard W. Young, December 18, 1877, typescript, Richard W. Young Papers.

20. Heber J. Grant to Feramorz Young, September 25, 1876, Grant Papers; Wells to Young, December 18, 1877; Orson F. Whitney, "Verbatim Report of Funeral Services in Honor of Emily Wells Grant," May 27, 1908, Frank W. Otterstrom, reporter, Church Archives.

21. Heber J. Grant to Heber M. Wells, January 29, 1892, Heber J. Grant Letterpress Copybook, 12:170, Grant Papers; Heber J. Grant to J. Golden Kimball, April 23, 1903, Grant Letterpress Copybook, 36:83; Wasatch Minutes, March 10, 1875, p. 28.

22. Wasatch Minutes, October 21, 1874, May 12, 1875, pp. 3 and 40.

23. Wasatch Minutes, March 24 and 31, April 7, 14, and 21, 1875, pp. 30–31, 33, and 35.

24. Wasatch Minutes, April 21, December 29, 1875; January 12, October 4, 1876, pp. 36, 71, 75, 108; Whitney, "Wasatch Literary Association," 1020–21.

25. Emmeline Wells, Diary, September 29, November 8, 1874, Emmeline B. Wells Collection, L. Tom Perry Special Collections, Harold B. Lee Library, Brigham Young University, Provo, Utah; Heber M. Wells, Reminiscence, n.d., Rulon S. Wells Papers, Church Archives.

26. Whitney, "Wasatch Literary Association," 1022.

27. Heber J. Grant to Richard W. Young, January 29, 1876, General Correspondence; Wasatch Minutes, June 30, 1875, January 12 and 26, 1876, pp. 50, 74–75, and 77.

28. Heber M. Wells to Richard W. Young, February 10, 1876, General Correspondence; John T. Caine to Heber J. Grant, May 3, 1939, General Correspondence.

29. The marriages of Alice Young to Charles Hopkins and Melvina Whitney to William Woods were examples of children of prominent Latter-day Saint families finding spouses outside their faith. For information on Ort Whitney and John Read, see Orson F. Whitney to Richard W. Young, February 13, 1876, typescript, Grant Papers; and Heber M. Wells to Richard W. Young, December 18, 1877, typescript, Richard W. Young Papers. The Wasatch opposition to plural marriage is recorded in Heber J. Grant, Diary, November 28, 1881, Grant Papers.

30. Wells to Young, December 18, 1877.

31. Whitney, *Through Memory's Halls*, 67, 72; Heber J. Grant, Remarks read at the funeral of Rulon S. Wells, transcript, Grant Papers; Heber J. Grant, Typed Diary, October 28, 1935, Grant Papers; and Whitney, "Wasatch Literary Association," 1021.

32. "Wasatch Redivivus," 5. Reading Association: Horace G. Whitney to Richard W. Young, July 15, 1874, typescript, Grant Papers. Azalia: Heber J. Grant to Feramorz Young, March 26, 1876, General Correspondence. Decennial Philadelphian Society: M. M. Young to Richard W. Young, February 7, 1876, typescript, Grant Papers. Some "Wasatchers" had little doubt that their association had occasioned the Mutual Improvement Association movement. See Whitney, "Funeral Services in Honor of Emily Wells Grant."

33. Wasatch Minutes, October 29, November 7 and 26, 1877, January 30, 1878, pp. 155, 158, 161, 169; Heber M. Wells to Heber J. Grant, December 4, 1920, General Correspondence.

34. Wasatch Minutes, May 29, 1878, pp. 174–75; Whitney, *Through Memory's Halls*, 112.

35. "Wasatch Redivivus," 5. For a copy of the reunion program, see Wasatch Minutes, p. 179.

36. Wasatch Minutes, June 18, 1890, p. 175; "Wasatch Redivivus," 5.

37. Wasatch Members participating in the Home Dramatic Club included Orson F. Whitney, Heber M. Wells, Laron A. Cummings, H. L. A. Culmer, Horace G. Whitney, Birdie Clawson Cummings, Brigham S. Young, Mary Jones Clawson, and Keetie Heywood Kimball. See Whitney, *Through Memory's Halls*, 117–18; and Horace G. Whitney, *The Drama in Utah: The Story of the Salt Lake Theatre* (Salt Lake City: Deseret News Press, 1915), 38–39.

38. I obtained marriage data by examining the obituaries of club members printed in Salt Lake City newspapers.

39. "Mrs. Lucretia H. Kimball Passes Away in Boston," *Deseret News*, February 24, 1920, 2; Mark Cannon III's forthcoming article on B. Bicknell Young in *Utah Historical Quarterly*.

40. Other members of the association not listed in the last several paragraphs include Ellen Richardson and Hampden S. Beatie, Josephine Beatie Burton, Agnes Sharp and Albion Caine, Birdie Clawson Cummings, James L. Clayton, Mary Jones Clawson, Stanley H. Clawson, Belle Clayton, C. Q. U. Irwin De Vere, Harry Emery, Francis Fox, Emily Wells Grant, Joseph L. Heywood, Alice Young Hopkins, Mattie Hughes, A. B. Kimball, Mary Ferguson Keith, Joseph Pitt, Carl D. B. Swift, Edna Clawson Tibbitts, Ned Wallin, Catherine Wells, Emmeline Wells, Elizabeth Beatie Wells, Susan Annette Wells, Rose Sipple Weighman, May Wells Whitney, Nell Woods, Allibo [Alice?] Young, Luella Cobb Young, Lorenzo D. Young. Those often attending meetings but not actually enrolled were Annie Wells Cannon, Martha Paul Hughes Cannon, William Dunbar, Fergus Ferguson, William A. Morton, George D. Pyper, John D. Spencer, Feramorz Young, and Mahonri M. Young.

41. Frank D. Kimball to Heber J. Grant, March 1940, General Correspondence; Heber M. Wells to Heber J. Grant, October 3, 1925, General Correspondence. Even the staid Rudger Clawson found that the Wasatch "more than justified its existence." See Rudger Clawson, "Autobiography," manuscript, Utah State Historical Society, Salt Lake City.

Young Heber J. Grant:
Entrepreneur Extraordinary

When lecturing at the Harvard Law School, Justice Oliver Wendell Holmes told students they could do anything they wanted to in life, if only they wanted to hard enough. Later in a private aside he added, "But what I did not tell them was that they had to be born wanting to."[1]

Heber J. Grant was born wanting to be an entrepreneur. Young Heber consumed the commercial news of the *New York Weekly Ledger* as avidly as other boys might have read the sports page. He and his close companion Heber Wells ventured into an ambitious but disastrous egg business (harried by neighborhood dogs and infested with the pip, the hens refused to lay). Heber even became a youthful employer. His keen eye and steady fingers won him a trove of marbles, and he used his winnings with Tom Sawyeresque skill. Less nimble companions were hired to cut wood, haul water, and do his other distasteful chores.[2]

Business ambitions boiled within the youth. "As a boy of seventeen, I dreamed in my mind about my future life," he later recalled. "I had never thought of holding a Church position; I had other plans." These plans he plotted with precision. First, he would master the tasks of business clerk and bookkeeper while still a teenager. Next, by his twenty-first birthday he would have his own business concern. He projected that by the age of thirty he would be a director of Zion's Cooperative Mercantile Institution (ZCMI), Utah's largest wholesale and retail outlet. Other youthful plans were to found a local insurance company, preside over a Utah bank, or sit on the board of one of the transcontinental railroads.[3]

Why did Grant have such a passion for business? One obvious answer to this question is that this passion was a part of the times. During the last decades of the nineteenth century, the business of America *was* business. Daring entrepreneurs reaped fortunes by masterminding such exciting new industries as steel, oil, and electricity. These new captains of industry stamped their personalities upon their era and made private property, competitive enterprise, and corporate wealth appear as eternal verities. The cult of the self-made man arose. The English writer Samuel Smiles and his American counterparts William Makepeace Thayer and Horatio Alger wrote books that promised any determined, hardworking boy material success. As Alger penned in a couplet that included 6 of his 119 book titles:

> *Strive and Succeed*, the world's temptations flee—
> Be *Brave and Bold*, and *Strong and Steady* be.
> Go *Slow and Sure*, and prosper then you must—
> With *Fame and Fortune*, while you *Try and Trust*.[4]

Smiles's books on *Character, Thrift,* and *Self-Help* found their way into young Heber's hands, and the boy drank thirstily from the self-help draught. Local schools taught such precepts as duty, success, and moral truth from the widely used *Wilson* and *National* readers.[5] So indelible was the mark of these elementary school texts that Grant quoted from them the rest of his life. The devout Rachel Ivins Grant, Heber's widowed and subsequently divorced mother, hoped that her son might give himself to church service, but she by no means resisted the prevailing commercial climate. She herself came from a long line of Quaker merchants.

The nation's business spirit spilled into Utah's previously isolated valleys. In the twenty years following its founding, Utah had been a pioneer community. Survival, settlement, and the propagation of Latter-day Saint ideals were its concerns. But during the 1870s, the years when young Heber came of age, the territory began to enter the American mainstream. Across the tracks of the recently completed Union Pacific Railroad flowed products and ideas. Utah's mines began to prosper and Salt Lake City acquired for the first time a commercial district, which was rapidly growing. Many Latter-day

Saint leaders caught the entrepreneuring fever, and their business activities impressed young Heber.

Among the enterprising young men who provided the boy with behavioral models was Joseph Elder, who owned a "little frame grocery store" a half block down Main Street from where the Grants lived. Heber, not yet six years old, spent hours at Elder's store, listening, talking, and being initiated into the mysteries of commerce. Another mentor was the crusty and indefatigable Edwin Woolley, the Grants' Thirteenth Ward bishop and a man of many business endeavors. The bishop left such an impression that Heber later described him as "a good man, an honest man, a hard-working man—and a man I loved." But no acquaintance exercised a stronger business influence on Heber than the affable Alex Hawes. As the New York Life Insurance Company's agent for Salt Lake City and later for the Pacific Coast and England, Hawes typified the hardworking and principled nineteenth-century business ideal. For six months when Heber was twelve years old, Hawes boarded at the Grants, beginning a life-long bond between the two. Hawes recognized in the boy a budding talent of the first order and for years afterward showered letters of fatherly encouragement upon his protégé.[6]

Of course Heber's youthful experiences and contacts were not an alchemy that mysteriously and automatically produced an entrepreneur. Similar influences worked to no avail upon his boyhood friends. Tony (Anthony W.) Ivins, Dick (Richard W.) Young, Hebe (Heber M.) Wells, Fera (Feramorz) Young, Ort (Orson F.) Whitney, and Rud (Rudger) Clawson, although they later would prove themselves to be remarkably talented, were not compulsively drawn to the balance sheet or ledger like Heber Grant.

Clearly there was something in Grant's personality that drew him to business. Whitney bemusedly remembered the boy as "a persevering sort of chap whose chief delight seemed to be in overcoming obstacles."[7] Despite a natural clumsiness, Grant determinedly set out to win the second base position with the Red Stockings, only to lose interest when the team gained the territorial championship. His fine penmanship developed only after classmates laughed at his blots and scribbles. Never a serious reader or scholar, he nevertheless had no rival when a concrete task or contest lay at hand, such as the memorization of the Deseret Alphabet or Jaques's *Catechism*.

After Bishop Woolley branded him a ne'er-do-well, Grant earnestly set out to win the bishop's approval and succeeded.[8] "I confess there is something in being at the head," the compulsive achiever later admitted, "that has always favorably impressed me."[9]

Young Heber was also developing other entrepreneurial virtues. His towering ambitions spoke loudly of his outward optimism and cocksurety. Such traits were later diagnosed by the celebrated and perceptive phrenologist Henry Fowler, who told the young man to reduce his "bump of hope" by half and be satisfied. Moreover, Heber embodied diligence. He found that he could not "help working and that in a hurry." Upon securing his first office job at fifteen, Heber quickly mastered his tasks and asked for more. Four years later he almost resigned because of nothing to do. The young man in fact worked nights to complete his duties and was rewarded by his grateful employer with a $100 bonus for industry. "I did it," he explained without acknowledging there was anything unusual in his behavior, "because . . . I did not like to sit around idle."[10]

He learned self-reliance early, literally at his mother's knee. Despite her stately charm, Rachel Grant had not married until her mid-thirties, only to be widowed when her only child was nine days old. Although Rachel's education, personality, and intelligence placed her among Deseret's "first ladies," the death of her husband, Jedediah Morgan Grant, and her unsuccessful remarriage to his dissolute brother, George D., left her impoverished. Young Heber recalled blustery nights with no fire in the hearth, months with no shoes, never more than a single homemade outfit of homespun at a time, and, except for an adequate supply of bread, a meager fare that allowed only a pound of butter and four pounds of sugar for the entire year.[11] Sewing became Rachel's means of avoiding charity. "I sat on the floor at night until midnight," Heber remembered, "and pumped the sewing machine to relieve her tired limbs."[12] The machine's constantly moving treadles became a symbol of the Grants' stubborn independence.

"A man who has been the indisputable favorite of his mother," theorized Freud, "keeps for life the feeling of conqueror, the confidence of success which often induces real success." Indeed there grew between mother and son a special bond that permanently etched a spirit of independence upon Heber's character (illus. 5-1).

Courtesy Church Archives, The Church of Jesus Christ of Latter-day Saints

Illus. 5-1. Heber J. Grant as a young boy with his mother Rachel.

On the one hand she indulged him, an advantage the boy later regretted exploiting. "Being both son and daughter to my mother," he remarked, "I suppose I may have been partially spoiled in the raising."[13] But on the other hand, she showered upon him her adult interests and high expectations. She never doubted that the boy's destiny would exceed that of his father, who had served as mayor of the city and as one of Brigham Young's counselors. Her light discipline and heavy confidence encouraged Heber in his experiments to raise chickens and to hire other boys with marbles. The consequence was a growing sense of mastery, a feeling that he could and should get things done.

To help his mother, the boy at fourteen worked twenty straight Saturdays at fifty cents a day to earn the ten dollars required to insure her modest home. Although Bishop Woolley protested that Rachel's many friends would quickly rebuild her home in case of a disaster, Heber replied that the Grants could do without such help. "I don't care to live in a house built by charity," he said. "I would be a little pauper, living in a house not knowing who furnished the money to build it, and therefore not being able to pay it back."[14]

Such fierce independence bred within Heber a resilience to popular opinion. "When certain people start to say kind things about me," he confided many years later, "I say, 'Heber Grant, what's the matter with you? If you were doing your duty that man wouldn't say good things about you.'"[15] His willingness to defend an unpopular position had taken root early. While reading the Book of Mormon at age fifteen, he strongly identified with the outspoken Nephi who often preached against the popular grain. The Nephite prophet became his hero, more influential in his life, he admitted, "than . . . any other character in ancient history, sacred or profane—save only the Redeemer of the world."[16]

The influence of Book of Mormon characters was only one part of the Church's impact upon Heber. "As a boy he was inclined always to religion," recalled his intimate boyhood friend Richard Young. Rachel had nourished Heber from infancy upon Mormonism's milk. Some of his earliest memories were of "going to meeting" to hear Brother Brigham. As a boy he proudly sat next to Bishop Woolley in the Thirteenth Ward meetinghouse to time speakers and meetings. When healthy and in town, the youth never missed attending general conference. As a young man he was careful with his tithing and donations. Nor could he remember an instance of playing Sabbath baseball. At fifteen he was ordained an elder, several years later was chosen as a seventy, and at nineteen was called as a counselor in the first ward Mutual Improvement Association organized. "He lives his religion," Richard Young reported, "but is seldom able to warm himself unto enthusiasm over a principle; his love is a practical, everyday, common-sense devotion to principles which from their superiority to all others, he chooses to believe are divine."[17]

As well as supplying the young man with a system of religious ethics, the Church gave purpose and energy to his life. While he did not have an intellectual's appreciation for his religion with its promises of human worth and a divinely ordered world, he nevertheless felt the empowering spirit of his faith. The sermons in the Tabernacle taught him that Latter-day Saints were a special people with a special mission. Thus the character of Nephi appealed to Grant not simply because of the ancient prophet's outspokenness, but also because of his sense of mission—"his faith, his determination, his spirit to do the will of God."[18] Grant became such a disciple himself, possessed with the enormous energy given to those who are confident of their providential duty and destiny.

In summary, a modern behaviorist might use Grant as a case study of an innovative or entrepreneurial personality. Here was a bright boy with the deep needs of an achiever. Buoyant, self-confident, industrious, self-reliant, and tough-minded, he had acquired these entrepreneurial traits in a nearly classic textbook manner. He was the only child of a mature woman who had dominated him with loving indulgence and high standards. Heber's father figures—Joe Elder, Bishop Woolley, Alex Hawes, and Erastus Snow, an Apostle who took an unusual interest in the boy—supplied the quiet, pliant paternal influence that usually characterizes an innovator's childhood. Like most contemporary entrepreneurs, Grant rose from the urban middle class—if not in wealth, certainly in values and status. As was also true of many entrepreneurs, Grant's early reading and school-ing taught him firm values, authority, and a beneficent and yielding world. Lastly, Grant's sense of religious mission followed closely the general pattern. "Innovators in the early stages of growth seem to be characterized by a common ethic which is appropriately termed religious in nature, whatever their religious dogma," Everett Hagan has written. "They feel a personal responsibility to transform the world that far transcends a profit motive."[19]

There was an additional ingredient in the boy's motivation. Hidden behind his brusque self-confidence and compulsion to succeed were the fears and uncertainties of a poor boy proving him-self. Anxieties usually push the highly motivated, and for Heber they had begun early. When he was about six, he and his mother were forced to move from the spacious home on Main Street that they shared with Jedediah's other wives and children into a widow's cottage. Later the little boy wandered back to his old home and wept. Shaking his fist he vowed that someday as a man he would possess the place.[20] In a sense he eventually did—not as a homeowner, but as principal investor and chairman of the executive committee of ZCMI, the large department store that came to occupy the old

Grant homestead. The contrast symbolized much of Grant's business career. He was ever at heart a poor boy reaching uncertainly but determinedly beyond himself.

The comet began its ascent early. On June 5, 1872, when only fifteen years old, Grant found employment as a bookkeeper and policy clerk at H. R. Mann and Company, Insurance Agents. The position had not come by chance. The boy had prepared himself. Several years earlier he was downtown playing marbles when a lanky young man strolled past. "Do you see that chap there?" asked a companion. "He works in Wells Fargo's Bank and gets $150 a month." Heber's quantitative mind quickly grasped what this meant. He currently was shining shoes at a nickel a pair. To equal the bank clerk's salary, he calculated that he would need more than 240 feet of shoes, 6 days a week, 4 weeks a month. He immediately enrolled in a bookkeeping class.[21]

To forego secondary and college education and enter business at an early age was then not uncommon, but Grant had had an attractive educational option. He refused an appointment to the United States Naval Academy (which would have required considerable remedial schooling) because of his mother's entreaties and perhaps, one suspects, because of an accurate sense of his own limitations.

Heber found his first taste of insurance and financial matters appetizing. He mastered his job easily and quickly. During the day he worked tirelessly. At night he sold policies. Mann and Company occupied the front basement portion of the banking firm A. W. White and Company, and, when duties allowed, Grant volunteered his services at the bank. He offered "to do anything and everything I could to employ my time, never thinking whether I was to be paid for it or not, but having only a desire to work and learn." Mr. Morf, the bookkeeper of A. W. White, in turn schooled Grant's penmanship. Soon Grant's Spencerian hand enabled him often to earn more after office hours writing cards and invitations than he gained from his insurance salary.[22] Three or four years after coming to Mann and Company, Grant assumed the "entire charge of the business" with the exception of writing an occasional letter and actually signing the policies. He bought the company at age nineteen, after Rachel Grant mortgaged her home to provide the necessary $500.[23]

A less confident eye might have seen Grant's purchase as fool hearted. H. R. Mann and Company's assets consisted entirely of goodwill, or the inside track in securing policy renewals. In this case goodwill might have no value at all. Would policy holders trust their future business to a nineteen year old? Would the national insurance companies transfer their business from Mann and Company to Grant? The young man might have customers but no insurance to sell them. Also, there were piranhas waiting to strike. Four other insurance companies in Salt Lake City now commanded the same volume that Mann had once possessed. Agents like the vigorous and clever Hugh Anderson could be expected to attack both Grant's customers and the seven national agencies supporting his business.

Grant quickly proved that he had talent to match his daring. He strengthened his position by forming a partnership—Jennens, Grant and Company—with another Salt Lake insurance agent, B. W. E. Jennens. If Grant required the additional luster of Jennens's maturity and experience, the fast-selling Jennens needed access to the national insurance policies offered by Mann and Company. Six of these Grant managed to retain. To help him do so, Hawes and Henry Wadsworth, Grant's former employer at Mann and Company, actively pulled strings in San Francisco, but Heber's personality also played a key role. When the field representative for one insurance firm arrived to transfer his agency from Mann and Company to another local firm, Grant personally met him at the railroad depot and dissuaded the startled agent from his decision before he was able to lodge at a local hotel. A month and a half after he began business, Grant's correspondence showed a firm hand at the helm. "You think when Mr. Farr [the national representative] returns [to Salt Lake] he will explain the matter to my satisfaction," the adolescent wrote when one insurance company and its representative attempted to defraud him of a small premium. "The only way the matter can be explained to my satisfaction is to have the draft paid. I shall forward it for collection again and trust it will be honored."[24]

Heber found admiring friends in the Salt Lake business community. "Few young men here are held in higher esteem by all classes than he," the *Salt Lake Herald* wrote in praise of Mr. Grant and his new insurance venture.[25] Prominent bankers Horace S. Eldredge and William S. Hooper signed his insurance bonds.

Businessmen Hiram Clawson, W. S. McCornick, and Thomas Webber vouched for Grant's ability and integrity. Webber went further, promising him ZCMI's insurance account. Even the Rev. G. D. B. Miller trusted the youth's salesmanship and insured the St. Mark's School.

Presiding Bishop Edward Hunter taught the fledgling a lesson in public relations. The colorful bishop did not care for Grant's initial business advertisement. "H. J. Grant, H. J. Grant, insurance agent, insurance agent," Hunter spoke in his customary staccato echoes. "Who is he? Thought I knew all the Grants, thought I knew all the Grants." When told that H. J. Grant was none other than Heber J., Jedediah's son, he commented in his terse double speak, "Why don't he say so, why don't he say so? . . . Might mean Helen J., might mean Helen J." When informed of the bishop's views, Grant immediately and permanently changed his business name to "Heber J. Grant."[26]

Buying insurance in nineteenth-century Utah required a personal conversion tantamount to changing one's religion. The industry was only beginning to enter the Utah market, and many hard-line conservatives saw an insurance policy as a violation of family and social responsibility. Besides, Eastern- and European-based companies drained dollars from Utah's colonial economy, a practice despised by Latter-day Saint leaders. Grant himself could not warm to life insurance for many years. But fire protection made sense, and he had few peers in the marketing of it. He sensed the psychological moment to close a deal. The evening after Salt Lake City's destructive 1882 fire, he recorded in his journal: "While standing watching the fireman throwing water on the ruins, [today] I insured L[orenzo] D. and A[lonzo] Young for 5000 and Jos[eph] L. Richards for 5000."[27] Grant's energy was inexhaustible. When he left the office one morning his partner challenged him to make $25 in premiums. "I told him I could make twice that much. I started in at 9 a. m. and talked until after 7 P.M. . . . The total profits for the firm were $101."[28]

He could be equally tenacious in defending a client's claim. When adjusters refused any settlement on a fire at the Woolley Brothers' property in Paris, Idaho, Grant decided to make a personal appeal. "Realizing my inability to fully explain the matter in a letter," he wrote the president of the German-American Assurance, J. F. Downing,

"I have decided to visit Erie [Pennsylvania], feeling confident that during a personal interview I can so plainly show to you the unjust and arbitrary manner in which W. Bros were treated."[29] As Grant's train sped eastward, Downing repeatedly wired that he would be out of town and unavailable for an interview. Grant as persistently telegraphed his prospective time of arrival. When the two finally met, their strained relations rapidly improved, and the German-American eventually paid two-thirds of the contested claim.

However, success with sales and claims did not immediately bring personal prosperity. When Grant married Lucy Stringham on November 1, 1877, over a year since the founding of Jennens and Grant, he stood deeply in debt. The newlyweds therefore spent most of their first year in Rachel Grant's small home. Insurance success, then as now, was a slow accretion, so Heber looked for supplemental income. Jennens, Grant and Company branched out to peddle books. Grant also sought Utah retailers for the Chicago grocery house Franklin MacVeagh and Company. He briefly considered a brokerage partnership with Richard Young. Grant did odds and ends for the Deseret National Bank, and he taught penmanship and bookkeeping at the University of Deseret. Teaching gave Grant one of his first opportunities to support home industry. Local merchants had previously refused to sell George Goddard's homemade ink, describing it as inferior. "I know better," Grant remembered telling them, "I am a judge." The professor insisted that his students use the Goddard variety, and the merchants quickly stocked the product to meet the unexpected demand.[30]

However, the most important of these second jobs (it would have occupied almost anyone else full time) was at the Church-owned Zion's Savings Bank and Trust Company (illus. 5-2). In August 1877, with the vigorous support of the dying Brigham Young, Grant was appointed assistant cashier. The position was literally a one-man show: cashier, bookkeeper, paying and receiving teller, after-hours note collector—and janitor. For a young man not quite twenty-one, the selection was impressive, although Grant himself took a different view. "I would not have had the job as a gift," he recalled, "had it not been that it gave me a chance to talk insurance to the depositors." His $75-a-month at Zion's was only a third of his other income.[31]

Courtesy Church Archives, The Church of Jesus Christ of Latter-day Saints

Illus. 5-2. Zion's Savings Bank and Trust (corner building), where Heber worked as a young man.

At Zion's Savings, Grant received one of the major shocks of his life. While reading the *Deseret News* one evening he learned for the first time of his "resignation" from the banking concern. Zion's Savings had fired him. The bank board's action probably owed less to Grant's selling of insurance during office hours than to the return of Bernhard H. Schettler from a mission. Schettler had New York banking experience and he had served as Zion's assistant cashier prior to his proselyting tour. With President Young now deceased, the board apparently felt free to choose the more experienced of the two men. The achievement-oriented Grant was shattered, although he responded, typically, with even greater zeal. "I am half inclined to think that the kicking me out of the Savings Bank was the making of me," he later reflected, "as it started me out to rustle with greater energy than ever before."[32]

Grant's hard work gradually began to pay handsome dividends. A typical Utah wage earner of the time might make annually between $400 and $600. In contrast Grant, still in his early twenties, earned $3,800 in 1878, $5,480 in 1879, and over $6,800 in 1880. He opened another agency in Ogden and dominated Utah insurance. At the same time he began to fulfill his dreams of furthering home industry. Along with Lorenzo W. Richards, he purchased the Ogden Vinegar

Works. Grant invested $6,500 of his own earnings and borrowed another $10,000 for the investment.

Grant's business climb, however, was not without interruption. On October 30, 1880, just before he turned twenty-four, Grant was appointed president of the Tooele Stake. The new assignment proved enormously difficult and trying. For one thing, Grant's finances deteriorated. His new ecclesiastical duties required much personal time and energy, and his Salt Lake City business declined proportionately. Nor was he able to find any supplemental income in his village home. "I never made a dollar in Tooele during the two years I was president of that stake," Grant recalled, "and my expenses were much greater than they had been before." He was forced for the first time to keep a team and buggy for his official Church travel within the stake. There were also the costs of commuting between Tooele and Salt Lake City. Whenever possible Grant spent weekdays in the Utah capital, traveling to and from Tooele on Saturdays and Mondays. In addition he found that as a leading citizen of both communities, he was expected to donate freely in each.[33]

Another far more serious factor in Grant's strained finances involved the Ogden Vinegar Works. The venture was not even meeting costs. By November 1880, Lorenzo Richards had extricated himself from the operation, forcing Grant to incorporate the factory and personally shoulder most of the financial burden. Utahns simply refused to patronize the home-manufactured product. The harried Grant ordered chemical tests on his imported competition and announced that the rival brand was doctored with acetic acid. Still merchants would not push his product. Grant facetiously asked one businessman if he did not wish to purchase Utah Vinegar in two-thirds-full barrels, add his own "mineral poison," and make even greater profits. "He thought that would be wrong," Grant recounted, "but he went on selling the stuff manufactured that way. I could not get the patronage."[34]

Then, on April 22, 1881, the vinegar factory burned to the ground, wiping out virtually all Grant's assets. All that remained were smoldering ruins with a salvage value of several thousand dollars and $9,000 in debts. To add professional embarrassment to his financial distress, the fire insurance salesman found that he was underinsured! The vinegar works, worth between $16,000 and

$18,000, was protected by only a $7,000 policy. And it was uncertain whether this insurance was actually in force, for Grant had forgotten to alter the policy's beneficiary from his old partnership to the new corporation. Furthermore he feared the possibility of arson. Had Frank Rother, his manager, intentionally set the fire to conceal his inability to turn a profit? Grant's distress led some to wonder if there might not be a higher meaning in the calamity. Elder Francis M. Lyman bluntly told his friend that the fire was a possible heavenly warning to keep his speculations within bounds and to give more prayerful attention to gospel study.[35]

Grant did see a few hints of hope among the dark shadows. Not one of his creditors demanded payment upon his notes. Three of them actually promised further credit, while a new creditor, James Wrathall of Grantsville, began a long relationship with the businessman by lending a large sum. "I found that I had much better credit than I had ever expected," Grant exulted.[36] Of course, his creditors were not entirely selfless. By requiring payment they would have invited Grant's bankruptcy, a course that would have given them only a fraction of the cash due them. They, along with Wrathall, were betting their money on Grant's skills and honesty to pay them someday in full.

Grant was able to minimize the disaster at the Ogden Vinegar Works. After seeking Lyman's counsel, he decided to come clean to the insurance carriers. He told the investigating adjustor the full particulars of the improperly assigned beneficiary and was relieved that the companies would pay regardless. Also the plant's manager, Frank Rother, promised several thousand dollars to buy the damaged machinery and real estate.[37]

Nevertheless, for a time Grant's finances remained precarious. Expenses continued to mount and his income continued to decline. He had borrowed money to buy his Tooele home only ten days before the Ogden fire, and Rother was failing to make his payments. Grant's friends now suggested that he make an assignment on the vinegar works and throw the disastrous project to the wind. By December 1881, in a desperate attempt to salvage his finances, Grant was working almost every night until midnight and sometimes until 2 A.M. "I would be simply delighted," he often told Lyman, "if [the General Authorities] would call me on a mission for ten years, with the privilege after ten years of going back to Salt Lake to be born again, financially speaking, instead of being buried alive out here."[38]

Grant's image of death and burial was more than a passing remark—it evidenced deep distress. He later admitted that during his Tooele Stake presidency he felt so blue that he didn't know "what to do or where to turn."[39] The fact that his insurance and business dealings had not prepared him for his ministry threw him off balance. And worse, serious illness now entered his home. After only a week in their new Tooele residence, the Grants' second daughter came close to dying. Then Lucy, Heber's wife, began a lingering stomach illness and female disorder that twelve years later claimed her life. These accumulated pressures finally brought Grant himself near to death. His six-foot, 140-pound frame almost yielded to "nervous convulsions," after which an attending doctor solemnly warned if the young man did not slow his pace he should certainly experience a "softening of the brain."[40]

Less than two years after his arrival in Tooele and ten months after his nervous collapse, Grant received a telegram that once more affected his business goals. He was asked to attend a 3:30 P.M. council meeting on October 16, 1882, in President John Taylor's office. Taylor announced a revelation concerning the filling of two vacancies in the Quorum of the Twelve Apostles. As the document was read, Grant learned of his own appointment. At twenty-five he was a member of the Church's second-ranking body.

There were whispers and innuendoes surrounding his selection to the Twelve. While close associates like Anthony Ivins, Richard Young, Edwin Woolley, Alex Hawes, and Charles Savage, the pioneer photographer, had believed his appointment was only a matter of time, Grant learned it had taken President Taylor's written revelations to convince others that he was apostolic timber.[41] No one doubted his ability or integrity—only his business preoccupation. Grant understood that President George Q. Cannon's prayer of ordination was more than a gentle reminder. "Thou must look upon this calling and this Apostleship," Cannon warned, "as paramount to everything else upon the earth; money, stocks and all kinds of property must fade into insignificance."[42]

Such comments weighed heavily upon Grant, and during the next several months he experienced a dark night of the soul. To friends he acknowledged that perhaps he should place his business ambitions aside. He resolved to follow the noble example of Elder Erastus Snow, who labored impecuniously in the service of others. Grant recognized that money had dominated his short career. Nevertheless he insisted that *"never* in my life have I seen the time that I was not willing to change my plan of action at the word of command from God's servants." To prove this he pointed out that he had gone to Tooele at fearful financial sacrifice. And while there, he repeatedly offered to sever his remaining Salt Lake City business ties if his Church leaders so desired. *"Cash* has not been my God," he stoutly maintained; "my heart has never been set on it, only to do good with what might come into my possession."[43]

At other moments Grant's abnegation wavered. He wondered whether he could cast himself in the image of Erastus Snow. Must not he be himself? He understood that Apostles of his time were allowed to do considerable private work. He also knew that he had a rare business gift and enjoyed making money. Should he totally ignore his talents and interests? Significantly, Grant occupied in the Quorum of the Twelve the vacated seat of the scholarly Orson Pratt, whose death had left his wives and children impoverished. The new Apostle did not want a similar fate for his own family. He remembered both his childhood poverty and his recent critical illness. Might he be closer to Pratt's example than he realized? Weighing all these factors, Grant set for himself a new goal: whenever his ecclesiastical responsibilities permitted, he would work at amassing $100,000, then with that money in the bank, he would devote all his time to the ministry.[44]

While not personally avaricious, Grant did confess to a very strong desire for wealth and believed that someday he would have it. Yet he scrupulously insisted upon an accompanying proviso: "Heavenly Father . . . [must] give me wisdom to make a proper and beneficial use of the same." His pet ambition was "to have a lot of money and to have no love for it and to do good with it."[45]

Grant's ideas on beneficial wealth were the Latter-day Saint version of the Gospel of Wealth then sweeping America. The Reverend Russell H. Conwell, who delivered his lecture *Acres of Diamonds* some six thousand times, described the viewpoint of the Latter-day Saint entrepreneur to a tee. "To secure wealth is an honorable ambition, and is one great test of a person's usefulness to others," Conwell asserted.

> Money is power. Every good man and woman ought to strive for power, to do good with it when obtained. Tens of thousands of men and women get rich honestly. But they are often accused by an envious, lazy crowd of unsuccessful persons of being dishonest and oppressive. I say, get rich, get rich! But get money honestly, or it will be a withering curse.[46]

Grant may have first received these doctrines from his exemplar Brigham Young, who preached in a similar vein. But their popularization throughout America at the time Grant launched his career undoubtedly put resolve in his spine. The young man planned to personify the proper uses of wealth.

From his youth he lived simply. Moreover, unlike many tycoons of the era who spent lifetimes accumulating money and their few last years dispensing it, Grant's generosity bloomed early. For example, when the boy-businessman heard Bishop Woolley appeal for donations, he gave $50 despite other pressing demands. At first Woolley demurred, saying it was too much. Grant insisted and paid his money.[47] Even when the debts of his vinegar works pressed upon him, he donated liberally; almost one-fifth of his income in 1881 went to the Church, civic projects, and the needy.[48]

During the 1880s his gifts to friends and worthy purposes were often twice as great as his tithing—so his charity totaled over 30 percent of his income. Even the liberal-minded Francis Lyman could not fully approve Grant's course. While Lyman believed that the young man should do his full share in aiding others, he wondered if Grant's donations weren't out of proportion to his means. Still Grant continued to give. "I do try to feel another's pain and to aid all that I can to lessen it," he wrote in his journal after a friend had written expressing appreciation for an "anonymous" gift. "He [the friend] is correct in thinking I aided him. . . . I sent his family $300 by James H. Anderson while he was in the penitentiary [on cohabitation charges] but I requested brother Anderson not to inform them from whom the donations came."[49] However, the scale of Grant's giving sometimes made anonymity difficult.

Grant believed his capitalist stewardship involved more than the giving of alms. In the decade following his call he embarked upon what he described as a temporal ministry, using his money and talents to defend and prosper the Saints. First he preached and continued to practice home industry. In sermon after sermon he raised his voice to defend Brigham Young's old battle cry to support the local economy. Nor was he content with mere words. Grant-manufactured and Grant-sold products became familiar Utah items. He himself always tried to wear "homemade." When the Utah assembly fêted its Wyoming counterpart, Grant's legislative duties required that he purchase an imported black suit and Prince Albert coat. However, fearful that his continued example might impair the home-industry cause, immediately after the ball he gave the expensive attire to a relative. "I have been called a crank on home made goods," he admitted, "and I am pleased to have the title."[50]

The second element in his temporal ministry was more combative. During the 1880s the Church was pushed to the wall. Residents of Utah who were hostile to the Church, and who were often merchants, attempted to wrest economic and political control from Church leaders, while congressmen in Washington passed punitive legislation against the Saints. Grant defended the Latter-day Saints by founding "home institutions," businesses that would deprive antagonistic elements of their commercial profits and power. Of course, home industry and home institutions went hand in hand. "I hope to see . . . [home industries] come into general favor not only because they are good and worthy of the support of the people," Grant once explained, "but because the money which is spent for them stops in the country and assists me and others to maintain home institutions and to start others . . . that is the dream of my life in a business line."[51]

The tension between ministry and money continued to agitate Grant for many years. However, once he came frankly to assess his talents and embark upon his temporal ministry, his self-doubts and melancholy noticeably lifted. Clearly this was not an Apostle in the traditional mold. Other men might speak publicly on theology or see visions and dream dreams. Heber, though he might have had similar private experiences, expressed his religion publicly in duty, observance, charity, and building the temporal kingdom. When a newspaper caustically suggested that Grant's favorite hymn was "We Thank Thee, O God, for a P-r-o-f-i-t," the Apostle cheerfully conceded some truth in the remark.[52] Grant acknowledged that the Church required men of differing talents. His talent was financial. He would improve the material well-being of the Saints.

Upon returning to Salt Lake from Tooele in 1882, Grant appraised his moneymaking to date. His success had been moderate at best. "I have had many ups and downs in the past five years," he wrote his cousin Anthony W. Ivins. "During the five years I have made, including $2,000 from Father's Estate, about $26,000—perhaps $27,000." He actually had little to show for his income. His assets might have been valued at $6,000 or $7,000, with most of his cash tied up in the real estate of the two homes occupied by his mother and his own family. Grant took consolation for what he described as his poor showing in knowing that during the period "I have paid a full tithing; donated liberally to the poor, temples, assembly hall, missionaries, etc.—and that none of my money has been spent in gambling, purchasing liquor, [or] tobacco."[53]

He also had high hopes for his financial future. In addition to his yearly General Authority living allowance of $2,000, he could count on his insurance business annually netting him $2,500. Since his original partnership with Jennens, Grant had taken his insurance company through a series of reorganizations. Each had made it more profitable. Furthermore, Grant had found a new investment. His half-brother, B. F. Grant, had gratuitously given him a half share in his forwarding and commission business at Milford in southern Utah. This, Heber calculated, would bring in another $1,500 and $2,000 a year. "I see no reason, provided I do not have to give up my business[es]," he summarized, "why I should not have [saved] fully $10,000 in hard cash when I am 30 years old."[54] He was giving himself only four years.

Milford was a railroad terminus that served the wild and rich Frisco Silver Mining district, less than twenty miles to the north-west. Grant Brothers wholesaled and plied supplies to the mines. For several months the Milford business seemed a bonanza. Heber received his first intimation that the venture might be flawed when he inspected its books and found that his half-brother had overpaid $500 when buying the concern. The oversight was symptomatic. Within less than a year B. F. Grant was bankrupt and his half-dozen Milford businesses in disarray. From his distant office in Salt Lake City, Heber for several years vainly tried to salvage something. But his new partner in Milford not only failed to collect the business's accounts, to Grant's mortification he also rented part of its premises to a saloon. Finally the Apostle cut his losses and sold out.

Grant could not have considered the Milford forwarding business more than a commercial skirmish. In January 1844 he launched what actually was his first major commercial venture. Along with Joshua Grant (his half-brother) and George Odell (his cousin-in-law), Grant purchased the implement business of B. Mattison and formed Grant, Odell and Company. "The special legislation that has been enacted against our people was the cause, as much as anything else, which led me to engage in the wagon and machinery business," he later explained.

> Prior to the formation of the firm of Grant, Odell & Co. almost the entire control of the wagon and implement business was in the hands of men whose interests were inimical to our people; and in some cases these parties used a portion of the means which they had made from the Mormon people to try to procure special legislation detrimental to their interests.[55]

Grant had surveyed a strategic salient, like a general reconnoitering a battlefield, and then attacked. Grant, Odell and Company was his first home institution.

The selling of buggies, wagons, and farm machinery in Utah had a shaky history, and Salt Lake City bankers were cautious when Grant asked for financing. The company was forced to turn to private lenders such as James Wrathall of Grantsville and to pay usurious interest. Within a year after its organization, without ample capitalization and financing, Grant, Odell and Company was almost at the end of its financial tether.

But Odell proved an able manager, and business from the first was unexpectedly brisk. By April 1885 the partnership was broadened into a corporation. A year later the company was rechristened the Cooperative Wagon and Machine Company, a change Grant believed would improve its public image and marketing. "Human nature is such that many men don't like to see a firm succeed but they don't object to a Cooperative Company succeeding."[56] By the end of the 1880s bankers were asking the company to take loans, and the conservative moneyman James Sharp climbed aboard as a major investor. During its first seven years, the company became the largest wagon and implement dealer in Utah, accumulated $100,000 in reserves, and consistently paid an annual 12 percent dividend. It made Grant's business reputation.

From its beginning the wagon company was a semireligious venture, a business of the Latter-day Saint people. It paid tithing to the Church before issuing dividends. Officials curbed swearing by employees and threatened to dismiss the former muleskinner B. F. Grant if he didn't desist. One major reason for incorporating was to attract prominent Church leaders as investors. Grant wrote stake presidents offering them stock, reduced his own holdings to allow others to invest, and personally guaranteed against loss stock options for the First Presidency. Such action not only placed profits in the proper hands but enhanced the firm in the eyes of Mormon con-sumers. "I feel that the . . . men that are now associated together in our firm are much more worthy of the patronage of the Saints than those who are not of us," Grant pointedly wrote to one local bishop. "There has never in my opinion been a time when it was more nec-essary for me to support our friends only, than now."[57]

The Cooperative Wagon and Machine Company provided Grant an ample field for his salesmanship. But he insisted that there was not religious arm twisting. "I know quite an amount of business naturally comes to me on account of being an Apostle," the young businessman admitted. "This I am willing to accept but nothing that comes because a person feels that he is under any obligations."[58] The *Salt Lake Tribune* had a more jaundiced eye. "Apostle Heber J. Grant . . . sells wagons and mowing-machines to Saints on the score that he is an Apostle and he will deal by the brethren better than any wicked Gentile would," the paper wrote with begrudging admiration. "He sells threshing-machines and horse rakes to Gentiles on the score that he has so great a custom among his own people that he can afford to sell to Gentiles cheaper than any Gentile man or firm can."[59] Grant would replay the wagon company scenario several times with other companies: inadequate financing, desperate scrambling to meet obligations, and then triumphant success.

In fall 1885, only a few months after the wagon and implement company turned solidly into the black, Grant embarked on a still more difficult mission—involvement in the newspaper business. The Church's *Salt Lake Herald* had threatened to suspend publication.

Since 1870 Church leadership had informally sponsored the morning newspaper as a foil to the anti-Mormon press. By remaining in private hands, the *Herald* could grapple with its opponents on their own terms while the Church-owned *Deseret News* sedately preached in the evenings. The *Herald* owners estimated that the newspaper required a transfusion of $51,000, which they attempted to raise by issuing new stock. But to invest invited future liability, and by the middle of November the campaign for new investment money stalled $16,000 short of the goal.

Grant and other Church leaders worked desperately to save the newspaper. The anti-Mormon clamor of the 1880s was reaching tumultuous proportions, and the kingdom needed a journalistic defender. By November 15, President John Taylor issued a circulating letter pleading for the Saints to take more stock. Four days later, Grant asked the assembled *Herald* stock subscribers to dig deeper into their pockets, but he found no takers. Grant himself was finding sleep difficult. In the early morning of November 20, he made a personal resolve: "I would either go under with the *Herald* or save it."[60]

With that resolve came a plan of action. Grant offered personally to raise the remaining money if paid $3,000 in *Herald* stock. His first day of soliciting brought $11,200. He had already borrowed heavily to invest in the wagon company but found that by mortgaging his home he could raise $2,000 more. Grant, Odell and Company chipped in another $3,000, and the rest came from men who had refused Grant several days before. "Certainly I have great cause to be thankful to my Heavenly Father for the success of today," he penned in his diary. "Only two persons have refused to increase their subscriptions."[61] Within ninety days he completed his fundraising.

Heber had saved the *Herald*—at least temporarily—but the question remained whether the newspaper would be as kind to its new and now largest stockholder. It had never been consistently profitable. Its owners bought stock out of civic and religious duty and not because of hoped-for profits. Likewise Grant invested to protect the kingdom, but his risk was far greater than that of the other investors. He had imperiled his own credit and that of his fledgling wagon company. If the newspaper continued to sink, it could take him with it. It is no wonder that several days after Grant decided to intervene personally he was prostrated by nerves. "I had intended to go to North Jordan to preach [today]," he wrote, "but did not consider it wisdom to do so, on account of my extreme nervous condition."[62]

During the late 1880s no business project claimed more of Grant's time than the *Herald*. First as vice-president and later as president, he took charge. Within a year he had installed a new editor, Edward H. Anderson, and a new business manager, Horace G. Whitney. Grant himself wrote slashing, off-the-top-of-the-head editorials that surprised his friends with his writing ability. In 1889 the newspaper adopted a more pleasing format, and a year later it was printed on a newfangled perfecting press. As profits began to accrue, Grant expanded features and coverage. Within five years the *Herald* was a new journal.

Grant later admitted that he felt "a particular charm" in controlling the newspaper, a privilege he would willingly pay for.[63] But by the end of 1889 his ownership was no longer a financial sacrifice. Reflecting its new management and the territory's booming economy, the *Herald* now repaid what Heber described as immense profits. On December 30, 1889, the firm's directors surprised Grant with a $1,500 bonus. Not only had he secured large advertising increases, he also had netted the newspaper over $3,500 for its special Christmas issue. He had personally authorized an increase for the issue from 10,000 to 25,000 copies—and then sold 13,000 of the papers himself. The price of the *Herald*'s stock responded accordingly. From the time Grant assumed control of the newspaper in 1886, its shares rose almost four times in value.[64]

This was a prologue to Grant's greatest financial coup. In the first days of March 1887, a month after completing the *Herald* subscription drive, Grant offered to manage the sale of the Church's 3,500 ZCMI shares, worth more than $300,000. Two weeks before, by enacting the draconian Edmunds-Tucker Act, Congress had threatened to seize all Church property in excess of $50,000. Church leaders scurried to sell holdings so they would not have to turn them over to the government. President Taylor had already tried to market the ZCMI stock, but cautious financiers judged the times perilous and demanded a large drop in the stock's price.

In contrast, Grant ebulliently brushed these doubts aside. His mission was to defend Latter-day Saint institutions. Besides, he saw a personal financial opportunity. The Edmunds-Tucker turmoil had depressed the price of ZCMI stock, making it an irresistible bargain—even if the price did not drop to levels demanded by the more cautious.

On March 10, 1886, only three days after receiving President Taylor's go-ahead, Grant informed the First Presidency that he had arranged the sale. He planned to take 500 shares himself and sell the remaining 3,000 to a hastily formed investment syndicate, eventually known as Armstrong, Farnsworth, and Company. The latter was composed of ten Mormon financiers, including Grant and such prominent figures as Francis Armstrong, George Romney, Philo T. Farnsworth, John Murdock, Francis Lyman, and John Henry Smith. Grant refused President Taylor's suggestions that the firm also include Horace Eldredge, James Little, and Jesse Sharp—the most prominent businessmen in the city. The benefits of the purchase, Grant believed, should go to men "with more faith and less money," kingdom-builders of his own stripe.[65] The Armstrong, Farnsworth, and Company partners paid a scanty 10 percent down and pooled their credit for five years to meet the remainder of the purchase price. They hoped that in the interval ZCMI's annual 10 percent dividend would more than meet the loan costs while the stock rose to its actual value.

John Taylor responded warmly to Grant's action. For the first time since his appointment as a General Authority, Grant felt the distance narrow between himself and his leader. Previously Taylor had cautioned Grant for his business mindedness; Taylor's manner toward the new elder had seemed cold and unappreciating. But during the ZCMI negotiations, the Church President cordially placed his arm on Grant's shoulder and praised his dedication to God's kingdom.[66] Grant never forgot the moment. It was one of those spontaneous, private gestures symbolic of something larger than itself. Grant's religious leader—the man whose opinions he prized most—had come to appreciate his temporal mission. The act seemed to sanction Grant's deepest drives and ambitions.

The late 1880s were kind to Grant and his enterprises. Utah prospered as never before. Its mines enjoyed heavy demand and high prices. The value of Salt Lake City real estate skyrocketed—two, three, and in some cases more than six times their values of a decade earlier, and speculators declared even these prices to be cheap.[67] Credit was readily available. Banks might charge between 7 and 9 percent on loans, but a well-run business might annually return 10 percent on an investment. Reflecting the good times, the flagship of Grant's stock portfolio—ZCMI—navigated a steady upward course. By 1891 the stock was selling at over $140 a share—twice what Grant had paid for it.[68]

With fortune so easily yielding her charms, the young businessman-Apostle worked passionately. New inventions were an irresistible lure (by 1900 he calculated that he had lost $2,000 in buying patents that proved worthless).[69] He bought the Utah rights to make and sell the Little Joker Washing Machine. He marketed Utah Southern Railroad bonds. He considered and then rejected, for a variety of reasons, building a Salt Lake City hotel, purchasing Idaho farm lands, and starting a local jewelry store. Instead he invested in a Salt Lake City mercantile business, Mexican timber lands, the Mountain Summer Resort Company, an Idaho flour mill, beehives in Tooele, a ranch in southern Utah, and Charles W. Nibley's highly profitable Oregon lumber business. He collected directorships as naturally as Penelope gathered suitors. Zion's Savings and Deseret National, the two main Church-affiliated banks of the 1880s, claimed him as a director. He also served on the board of the *Contributor* (a magazine for young Latter-day Saint men), Zion's Benefit Building Society (a building and loan institution), the Social Hall Society (Salt Lake City's oldest recreational facility), and the Salt Lake Literary and Scientific Society (a semi-Church holding company with title to such properties as the Council House and the Deseret Museum).

However, these activities were sidelights to Grant's main concerns. He continued to found and maintain home institutions. Less than a month following his ZCMI purchases, Grant was asked by his fellow quorum member Wilford Woodruff to arrange "carriages from among our friends" for his wife's funeral cortege.[70] Grant found the request difficult to satisfy. The Salt Lake livery business was tightly controlled by Gentiles with a reputation for slandering the Church. In fact, in the minds of the Latter-day Saint leaders, the city's hack drivers (along with the editorial writers of the *Salt Lake Tribune* and the proprietors of local hotels) were largely responsible for the Church's tarnished public image.[71] Grant's immediate frustration in securing

Illus. 5-3. Grant Brothers' Livery and Transfer Company.

"friendly carriages" sparked him to action. In April 1886 he organized the Grant Brothers' Livery and Transfer Company and began a furious war to control the local cab and transfer business (illus. 5-3).

The business actually had little to recommend it. Livery profits usually were low, and in Salt Lake City the prospects of a company owned by Church members were dim. The city's main hotel owners, who controlled a principal source of cab and transfer traffic, were frequently hostile to the Church. Predictably, at the outset, Grant Brothers Livery absorbed heavy losses, and after two years Latter-day Saint leaders, who had invested $22,500 in Church funds in the project, bailed out at eighty cents on the dollar.

But Heber plunged ahead. Grant Brothers Livery advertised vigorously, bought the latest equipage, including the magnificent forty-passenger Raymond Coach. By the end of 1888, Grant played his trump card. He dangled ZCMI's profitable freight business before the territory's two competing railroads, the Union Pacific and the Denver and Rio Grande, suggesting ZCMI's contract might depend on Grant Brothers receiving the railroads' local transfer trade. The tactic was decisive. By 1890 Grant had his railroad contracts and Grant Brothers Livery was undisputed master of the terrain.

A flurry of other home ventures followed. In fall 1886, Grant organized the Home Fire of Utah and proceeded three years later with the Home Life of Utah. The entrepreneur hoped that the two insurance companies would plug the drain of insurance premiums from the territory and also provide money for local investment. In 1888, when the Provo Manufacturing Company needed a transfusion of cash and energy, the 125-man firm named Grant a director. These woolen works were the largest producer west of the Mississippi. By 1889, Grant secured control of the majestic but unprofitable Salt Lake Theatre (illus. 5-4). The Church had built the playhouse twenty-seven years earlier and had retained tacit control through a series of friendly owners. With no one else willing to assume the burden, Grant took control. And in 1890, when he sensed that the two Latter-day Saint banks inadequately served their Mormon clientele, he founded the largest capitalized bank ($500,000) in the territory, the State Bank of Utah. "There is no business that can aid [home] institutions . . . so much as a bank," he wrote characteristically, "and I think an effort should be made to retain as much as possible all of the business of every class in the hands of our people."[72]

Courtesy Church Archives, The Church of Jesus Christ of Latter-day Saints

Illus. 5-4. The Salt Lake Theatre (ca. 1864), which was acquired by Heber in 1889.

By the end of 1890, Grant's economic kingdom-building had won him a remarkable array of titles and powers. As chairman of ZCMI's executive committee, he oversaw the territory's largest whole-sale and retail business. In addition he served as president of an insurance agency, a wagon and implement dealership, and a livery stable—each of which dominated their respective fields. He also headed two insurance companies and one of Salt Lake City's largest banks, published the Mormons' most influential newspaper, and owned the city's main recreational attraction. Grant had in fact amassed the $100,000 he had set out to obtain eight years earlier. His youthful ambitions had not been in vain. At least for the moment, he had climbed the summit of Salt Lake City's commercial mountain.

Notes

This article was first published in *The Twentieth Century American West: Contributions to an Understanding*, ed. Thomas G. Alexander and John F. Bluth (Provo, Utah: Charles Redd Center for Western Studies, 1983), 85–102.

1. Quoted in Catherine Drinker Bowen, *Biography: The Craft and the Calling* (Boston: Little, Brown, 1969), 145.

2. Heber J. Grant, in *89th Annual Conference of The Church of Jesus Christ of Latter-day Saints* (Salt Lake City: The Church of Jesus Christ of Latter-day Saints, 1919), 119. Heber M. Wells, "President Grant—The Business Man: Business Ventures and Church Financing," *Improvement Era* 39 (November 1936): 687. On its most common level, the word entrepreneur means "someone who is risk taking in the pursuit of business." Such behavioralists as Everett Hagen and David McClelland, as I shall cite later, also use the term to describe a special personality type often found in the world of business. In this essay I intend both meanings.

3. Heber J. Grant, "Dream, O Youth! Dream Nobly and Manfully," *Improvement Era* 44 (September 1941): 524; Heber J. Grant, Manuscript Diary, August 3, 1886, 7:275, Heber J. Grant Papers, Church Archives, The Church of Jesus Christ of Latter-day Saints, Salt Lake City; Heber J. Grant to Lucy Grant, April 17, 1890, Lucy Grant Collection, Church Archives; and Heber J. Grant to Allie Ford, September 6, 1899, Heber J. Grant Letterpress Copybook, 29:400, Grant Papers.

4. Quoted in Merle Curti, *The Growth of American Thought* (New York: Harper and Row, 1964), 629.

5. Heber J. Grant to Edward Anderson, June 5 and 6, 1900, Grant Letterpress Copybook, 30:619–20, 622.

6. Heber J. Grant, "Recollections Awakened by the Late Semi-Centennial Celebration," *Improvement Era* 1 (April 1898): 395–96; Grant, Manuscript

Diary, October 16, 1881, 3:194. Heber J. Grant, "Knowing and Doing," *Improvement Era* 42 (June 1939): 329; Heber J. Grant, Typed Diary, August 20 and 25, 1887, Grant Papers; Heber J. Grant to Alex Hawes, March 28, 1896, Grant Letterpress Copybook, 21:662–63; Heber J. Grant to Alex Hawes, September 29, 1896, Grant Letterpress Copybook, 23:345–46.

7. Orson F. Whitney, *Through Memory's Halls: The Life Story of Orson F. Whitney as Told by Himself* (Independence, Mo.: Zion's Printing and Publishing, 1930), 43.

8. Whitney, *Through Memory's Halls*, 43, 66–67; Heber J. Grant to Edward H. Anderson, June 5, 1900, Grant Letterpress Copybook, 30:621; Heber J. Grant, "One Man's Memory of an Honored Mother," *Improvement Era* 39 (May 1936): 268.

9. Heber J. Grant, in *78th Annual Conference of The Church of Jesus Christ of Latter-day Saints* (Salt Lake City: The Church of Jesus Christ of Latter-day Saints, 1908), 56.

10. Heber J. Grant to Allie Ford, June 9, 1895, Grant Letterpress Copybook, 20:487; Heber J. Grant to Lucy Grant, April 18, 1892, Lucy Grant Collection; Heber J. Grant, "The Nobility of Labor," *Improvement Era* 3 (December 1899): 83; Heber J. Grant, "For Service Rendered," *Improvement Era* 43 (March 1940): 137.

11. Heber J. Grant, "Faith-Promoting Experiences," *Millennial Star* 93 (November 19, 1931): 760; Rudger Clawson, "Heber J. Grant: The Apostle and President of the Church," *Improvement Era* 39 (November 1936): 668; Heber J. Grant, in *92nd Semi-Annual Conference of The Church of Jesus Christ of Latter-day Saints* (Salt Lake City: The Church of Jesus Christ of Latter-day Saints, 1921), 13; Relief Society Minutes, Thirteenth Ward, Book B: 1898–1906, February 13, 1902, 95, Church Archives.

12. Grant, "Faith-Promoting Experiences," 760.

13. Heber J. Grant to Heber M. Wells, January 29, 1892, Grant Letterpress Copybook, 12:170–71. See also Heber J. Grant to Lucy Grant, March 13, 1883, Lucy Grant Collection.

14. Grant, "One Man's Memory," 268. See also Heber J. Grant to Rachel Grant, November 4, 1899, Grant Letterpress Copybook, 29:632.

15. Quoted by Harold B. Lee, "Qualities of Leadership," an address to the Latter-day Saints Students Association, August 1970 Convention (published privately), 6.

16. Heber J. Grant, "As I View the Book of Mormon," *Improvement Era* 37 (March 1934): 160; Heber J. Grant, in *70th Annual Conference of The Church of Jesus Christ of Latter-day Saints* (Salt Lake City: The Church of Jesus Christ of Latter-day Saints, 1900), 23; Grant, in *78th Annual Conference*, 1908, 58.

17. Richard W. Young, Diary, November 4, 1882, 2:3, Western Americana, Special Collections, Marriott Library, University of Utah.

18. Grant, in *70th Annual Conference*, 1900, 23.

19. Everett E. Hagen, *On the Theory of Social Change: How Economic Growth Begins* (Homewood, Ill.: Dorsey, 1962), 93. For data on child-rearing, see particularly David C. McClelland, *The Achieving Society* (Princeton, N.J.: Van Nostrand, 1961), 356–73, who summarizes at least a dozen studies as well as providing information of his own. For reading and schooling patterns of achievers, see Thomas C. Cochran, "The Entrepreneur in Economic Change," *Explorations in Entrepreneurial History* 3 (fall 1964): 26. On the urban, middle-class backgrounds of promoters, see F. W. Taussig and C. S. Joslyn, *American Business Leaders: A Study in Social Origins and Social Stratification* (New York: Macmillan, 1932); and Frances W. Gregory and Irene D. Neu, "The American Industrial Elite in the 1870s: Their Social Origins," in William Miller, *Men in Business: Essays in the History of Entrepreneurship* (Cambridge, Mass.: Harvard University Press, 1952), 193–211. I am unacquainted with any motivational studies dealing directly with the child-rearing practices of Mormon society, despite the subject's obvious importance. During the nineteenth century, the influence of Mormon fathers no doubt was restricted by involvement in plural marriage, years-long proselyting tours, and local Church leadership.

20. Heber J. Grant, "My Days in School," *Improvement Era* 44 (November 1941): 665.

21. Heber J. Grant, *Address by President Heber J. Grant to the Deseret News Carriers during Their Annual Roundup* (Salt Lake City: n.p., 1921), 7. See also Grant, "Nobility of Labor," 82.

22. Grant, "Nobility of Labor," 83.

23. Heber J. Grant to J. B. Hall, June 10, 1876, Grant Letterpress Copybook, 3:55. This copybook is the most important source for Grant's early insurance dealings.

24. Heber J. Grant to T. M. Benedict, July 22, 1876, Grant Letterpress Copybook, 3:268.

25. "Insurance Agency," *Salt Lake Herald*, June 23, 1876, [3].

26. Heber J. Grant to Edward H. Anderson, July 9, 1901, Grant Letterpress Copybook, 31:667.

27. Grant, Manuscript Diary, January 5, 1882, 4:103. The Mormon analogy of converting Utahns to insurance is Grant's. See Heber J. Grant to W. G. Bickley, April 12, 1890, Grant Letterpress Copybook, 8:313.

28. Grant, Manuscript Diary, June 24, 1881, 2:69–70.

29. Heber J. Grant to J. F. Downing, July 24, 1885, Grant Letterpress Copybook, 6:128–29.

30. Heber J. Grant, in *80th Annual Conference of The Church of Jesus Christ of Latter-day Saints* (Salt Lake City: The Church of Jesus Christ of Latter-day Saints, 1910), 40–41.

31. Grant, "Dream, O Youth!" 524. See also Wells, "President Grant—The Business Man," 687.

32. Heber J. Grant, Press Copy Diary, July 18, 1890, 2:407, Grant Papers. See also Heber J. Grant to Thomas G. Webber, December 31, 1890, Grant

Letterpress Copybook, 10:124; and Heber J. Grant to George T. Odell, January 30, 1892, Grant Letterpress Copybook, 12:735–36.

33. Heber J. Grant, "Criticism," *Improvement Era* 44 (April 1941): 203. Later in the century, with Grant himself serving on the committee making the recommendation, stake presidents did receive a small living allowance. The practice was subsequently discontinued.

34. Grant, in *80th Annual Conference*, 1910, 39.

35. Francis M. Lyman, Diary, April 25, 1881, Church Archives.

36. Grant, Manuscript Diary, April 22, 1881, 2:27, and entries for several days thereafter.

37. Grant, Manuscript Diary, April 29, 1881, 2:36–38.

38. Grant, "Criticism," 203; Heber J. Grant, in *87th Semi-Annual Conference of The Church of Jesus Christ of Latter-day Saints* (Salt Lake City: The Church of Jesus Christ of Latter-day Saints, 1916), 31.

39. Heber J. Grant to B. F. Grant, July 21, 1896, Grant Letterpress Copybook, 23:77.

40. Heber J. Grant to W. H. Harrington, February 18, 1890, Grant Letterpress Copybook, 8:186. Also Heber J. Grant to Brown, Craig and Company, December 18, 1890, Grant Letterpress Copybook, 9:178; Grant, Typed Diary, November 1, 1887; and Lyman, Diary, January 7, 15, 16, and 23, 1882.

41. Grant himself understood that many did not feel sympathetic to his call. See Heber J. Grant to Willard Young, February 1, 1892, Grant Letterpress Copybook, 12:240. On another occasion he wrote: "I think I am safe in saying that about half of the Latter-day Saints if not two-thirds of them were simply dumbfounded when I was chosen to be a member of the Apostles." Heber J. Grant to John C. Cutler, December 2, 1891, Grant Letterpress Copybook, 9:423. For rumors circulating among his friends prior to his appointment, see Ronald W. Walker, "Young Heber J. Grant and His Call to the Apostleship," *BYU Studies* 18 (fall 1977): 121–22, published herein on pp. 167–73.

42. A copy of Cannon's blessing is found in Grant, Manuscript Diary, November 27, 1882, 5:89–96.

43. Heber J. Grant to Anthony W. Ivins, October 22, 1882, Grant Letterpress Copybook, 5:7–10.

44. Grant, Typed Diary, November 4, 1899.

45. Grant to Ivins, October 22, 1882, 5:2; Heber J. Grant to B. F. Grant, August 18, 1895, Grant Letterpress Copybook, 21:64. See also Heber J. Grant to Anthony W. Ivins, December 29, 1895, Grant Letterpress Copybook, 22:27.

46. Quoted in Ralph Henry Gabriel, *The Course of American Democratic Thought* (New York: Ronald, 1956), 158.

47. Abraham H. Cannon, Diary, January 18, 1891, L. Tom Perry Special Collections, Harold B. Lee Library, Brigham Young University, Provo, Utah.

48. Grant, Manuscript Diary, November 1, 1881, 4:27.

49. Grant, Manuscript Diary, April 3, 1886, 7:269. Lyman's caution is found in Grant, Typed Diary, January 31, 1887.

50. Grant, in *80th Annual Conference,* 40. Grant told the story of his short-lived attire several times. See for example Grant, in *92nd Semi-Annual Conference,* 10.

51. Heber J. Grant to John T. Smellie, January 13, 1895, Grant Letterpress Copybook, 20:11.

52. Grant, in *78th Semi-Annual Conference,* 24–25.

53. Heber J. Grant to Anthony W. Ivins, November 13, 1882, Grant Letterpress Copybook, 5:48.

54. Grant to Ivins, November 13, 1882, 5:43–44.

55. Heber J. Grant to E. H. Valentine, February 12, [1887], Grant Letterpress Copybook, 7:328.

56. Heber J. Grant to Joseph F. Smith, June 4, 1886, Grant Letterpress Copybook, 6:485.

57. Heber J. Grant to Horton D. Haight, May 29, 1885, Grant Letterpress Copybook, 5:495–96.

58. Grant, Manuscript Diary, 8:27–28, January 11–15, 1888.

59. *Salt Lake Tribune,* June 2, 1890, 4.

60. Heber J. Grant to Charles L. Anderson, December 8, 1885, Grant Letterpress Copybook, 6:247–48.

61. Grant, Manuscript Diary, November 21, 1885, 7:212–13.

62. Grant, Manuscript Diary, November 22, 1885, 7:213.

63. Heber J. Grant to Horace G. Whitney, March 21, 1892, Grant Letterpress Copybook, 13:66.

64. Heber J. Grant to Horace G. Whitney in Grant, Typed Diary, January 2, 1900. Grant, Press Copy Diary, December 30, 1889, 2:242.

65. Grant, Manuscript Diary, March 15, 1886, 7:253. Originally the leading partner was Henry Dinwoody, but following a fire in his furniture establishment he retired from the firm. Other partners included William H. Rowe, Charles S. Burton, and Junius F. Wells.

66. Grant, Manuscript Diary, March 10, 1886, 7:254.

67. Cannon, Diary, February 28 and March 6, 1890; Hezekiah Eastman Hatch, Autobiography, typescript, 37, Church Archives; Heber J. Grant to Joseph H. Richards, February 22, 1890, Grant Letterpress Copybook, 8:215–16; Heber J. Grant to Alfred L. Giles, March 26, 1890, Grant Letterpress Copybook, 8:287–91; Heber J. Grant to Anthony W. Ivins, December 13, 1890, Grant Letterpress Copybook, 9:171–72; and Heber J. Grant to R. D. Foltz, November 28, 1891, Grant Letterpress Copybook, 9:394.

68. Heber J. Grant to Moses Thatcher, April 29, 1886, Grant Letterpress Copybook, 7:93–94. Immediately after the announcement of the sale, the stock rose $10 to $15 a share, apparently due to the view of financial men that Church ownership during the difficult days of the raid had depressed its value. For the stock's 1891 price, see Heber J. Grant to J. B. Powell, April 2,

1891, Grant Letterpress Copybook, 10:647.

69. Heber J. Grant to David K. Udall, May 30, 1901, Grant Letterpress Copybook, 31:523. As was Grant's practice when calculating losses, this figure included money that might have been made had his patent investments been conservatively invested elsewhere.

70. Grant, Press Copy Diary, December 27–31, 1886, 1:92; Heber J. Grant to Joseph F. Smith, April 10, 1886, Grant Letterpress Copybook, 6:453.

71. Grant, Typed Diary, April 12, 1894; Cannon, Diary, April 12, 1894.

72. Heber J. Grant to Moses Thatcher, February 22, 1890, Grant Letterpress Copybook, 8:210.

Crisis in Zion:
Heber J. Grant and the Panic of 1893

In late June 1893, Heber J. Grant, a pencil-thin, bewhiskered young man, waited nervously in the downtown office of New York businessman John Claflin. Thirty-six years old and conservatively dressed, Grant was a member of the Quorum of the Twelve Apostles of The Church of Jesus Christ of Latter-day Saints and president or director of at least a dozen Salt Lake City–based businesses. A financial panic had struck the nation and the Mormon businessman was urgently seeking a loan to save himself and his church from bankruptcy. Although similar dramas were being enacted in business and banking houses across the United States during that summer, this episode had special significance for the West. Grant's loan efforts marked the entry of Mormondom and Utah into the nation's financial mainstream. During the panic, the Mormon community in Utah discovered that the premises of economic independence and isolation upon which it had been founded fifty years earlier were now untenable. By the time the crisis had run its course, Latter-day Saints would change their church's public image as well as their own attitude toward the outside financial world.[1]

The Panic of 1893 was among the most disastrous in American history. Stocks tumbled throughout the summer, and an unprecedented 15,252 businesses went into receivership. By winter 1893 about 18 percent of the national work force was without jobs. Those who remained employed found their wages slashed by almost 10 percent. The financial storm struck the West with particular fury. As Eastern

115

money contracted, the normally cash-starved banks of the West collapsed. Of the national bank failures in 1893, only 3 institutions in the Northeast suspended operations, while 38 in the South closed their doors. In the West, however, 115 banks went into receivership—66 in the Pacific states and Western territories alone.[2]

Even before the panic, Utah had experienced hard times. During the territorial boom of 1889–90, the value of land and of business and residential property had skyrocketed to as much as ten times pre-1889 prices. Speculators reaped enormous paper profits, and real-estate transactions in Salt Lake City alone reached an unprecedented $100,000 daily. To meet voracious demands for credit, nine new banks opened in the city. Then, in December 1890, the collapse of London's Baring Brothers burst Utah's speculative bubble, leaving behind depressed prices, lowered profits, overextended credit, and tight money. "The neighborhood seems to be infested with thieves," one diarist wrote in 1891, "as coal, wheat, lumber and many other things have disappeared."[3]

The Church's economic fortunes suffered along with those of the territory. A drop in tithing revenue, from $878,394 in 1890 to $576,584 in 1893, charted the general economic decline. But Church leaders had to cope with more than diminishing revenue. The Edmunds-Tucker Act of 1887 had financially crippled the Church. The law stripped the organization of its legal standing and hindered Church management, especially its ability to secure loans. By disfranchising some Saints and placing election machinery in the hands of their opponents, the act enabled those outside the Latter-day Saint faith to gain political control and to transfer city, county, and territorial funds from Mormon-owned banks to other banks, further undermining the Church's ability to obtain local loans. Moreover, by demanding the surrender of all Church assets in excess of $50,000, the law deprived the Latter-day Saints of property worth over $1,000,000, as well as revenue and possible loans derived from Church property.[4]

Initially, Latter-day Saint officials attempted to defuse the Edmunds-Tucker Act by selling or giving in trust Church property to faithful members who would act as stewards for the religious community. The combination of government officers, the courts, and court-appointed receivers, however, proved too powerful for

Church leadership. By the early 1890s receivers controlled most of the Church's marketable property, including some $500,000 deposited largely in Salt Lake's non-Mormon banks. Meanwhile, lawyers' fees, lost revenues, and property manipulation due to the Edmunds-Tucker Act plunged Zion $300,000 in debt. Denied legal standing and the use of its own resources, the Church stood virtually defenseless before the coming panic.[5]

Although Church finances in the early 1890s demanded retrenchment, the venerable and otherworldly Church President Wilford Woodruff, who from boyhood had avoided debt as a life-long rule of conduct, added to the Church's economic problems. For thirty-five years he had quietly cherished the knowledge, given in visions of the night, that he would complete the construction of the monumental Salt Lake Temple. When the octogenarian Woodruff dedicated the temple in April 1893, his administration alone had spent over $1,000,000 on the $4,000,000 project. Woodruff's social conscience, moreover, led to other ambitious enterprises financed largely by borrowed capital. As Woodruff's second counselor, Joseph F. Smith, explained: "We began to feel that there was a responsibility resting upon us which required something to be done, in a small way at least, in the direction of giving employment to our people." As a result, $1,000,000 was invested in public works projects such as the Saltair Pavilion on the Great Salt Lake shoreline, the Saltair Railway Company (later known as the Salt Lake and Los Angeles Railway), and the Utah Sugar Company.[6]

To meet the Church's growing debt, leaders turned increasingly to Heber J. Grant. During his short business career, Grant had promoted insurance, soap, newspapers, machinery and implements, horses and carriages, and even vinegar; now he was called upon to promote loans. During autumn 1890, almost three years before the panic hit, the dangerously overextended Salt Lake banks demanded payment on outstanding loans, and Grant scrambled not only to meet his own heavy financial obligations but also to rescue the two banks that discharged the Church's interests—Zion's Savings Bank and Trust and the State Bank of Utah (illus. 6-1 & 6-2). Grant had founded the latter and was now its president.

Desperately needing $100,000, Grant grasped "at a straw" and traveled east in late fall 1890. Omaha and Chicago bankers smiled at

Illus. 6-1. Templeton building where the old State Bank was located (*bottom right corner*).

Illus. 6-2. Detail of the Templeton building showing the State Bank's sign above the window.

his audacious request for a low-interest loan, pointing out that short-term interest rates on the New York Stock Exchange had risen to one-half of 1 percent a day or 182 percent per year. In New York, however, Grant played several trump cards. He not only insisted that bankers consider the State Bank's past and future business but also offered as security the highly regarded notes of the Zion's Cooperative Mercantile Institution (ZCMI), Utah's multibranched department store (illus. 6-3).

In the end, Grant's grit and aplomb won over the New York bankers. When J. H. Parker, vice president of the National Park Bank, received him coolly, Grant addressed a personal message to the bank's directors:

> I am offering you four notes of $12,000 each of Zion's Co-operative Mercantile Institution. These notes are guaranteed by thirteen Directors and also by the State Bank of Utah, which has a capital of half a million dollars. . . . These notes are worth at least a couple of million dollars. If two million dollars of personal endorsement, together with the endorsement of a half a million dollar bank, with the note of an institution that has never failed

Courtesy Church Archives, The Church of Jesus Christ of Latter-day Saints

Illus. 6-3. Zion's Cooperative Mercantile Institution (ZCMI) in downtown Salt Lake City.

to meet its obligations, is not considered good I will telegraph
and secure you some additional endorsement. If you do not care
to cash these notes take my advice and stop doing business with
people so far away from home as Utah.

The National Park Bank extended the loan and became one of
Grant's warmest New York contacts. Within two weeks after his
arrival in the East, the Mormon businessman turned the key to a
total of eight New York and Hartford banks, wired $240,000 to Salt
Lake City, assisted in another $60,000 loan, and secured the promise
of yet another $36,000. "I think I can say," he wrote one of his
daughters in early January 1891, "that the past seven days have been
as successful as any in my life."[7]

Grant's spectacular success catapulted him into the center of
Latter-day Saint finance. When Grant returned to Salt Lake in early
January, President Woodruff asked him to raise money for the
floundering Utah Sugar Company. Sugar financing led in turn to his
appointment as the Church's chief loan agent. Grant realized that the
Church's short-term, constantly maturing debts created a precarious
financial foundation, which the slightest tremor could reduce to
rubble. As a possible remedy, he hoped to attract Eastern or British
capital to Utah by greatly increasing ZCMI's capitalization. The
money from new investors would eventually flow into Mormon
banks, which could then lend to the Church. When ZCMI's directors,
fearful of losing control to new stockholders, refused to cooperate,
Church leaders in July 1891 suggested an alternate plan: they asked
Grant to proceed to London or Paris and secure a $500,000 long-
term, low-interest loan. Due to the serious illness of his wife Lucy
(illus. 6-4), however, Grant repeatedly postponed the long trip.[8]

Formation of the investment firm of Cannon, Grant & Company
(CG & Co.) provided a stopgap remedy for Church financial problems. Leading Mormon businessmen had for some time discussed
such an enterprise; but to get them to agree, Grant complained, was
like "the pulling of a cat by the tail over a carpet." Finally, in December 1891—only hours before he was to leave Salt Lake City on one
of his money-raising missions—Grant organized the firm. He and
George Q. Cannon, First Counselor in the First Presidency, became
senior partners, with thirteen prominent Mormon financiers serving as associates in the venture.[9]

Illus. 6-4. Heber with his first wife, Lucy, and their children in 1887: (*left to right*) Lucy "Lutie" (Cannon), Florence (Smith), Anna (Midgley), Edith (Young), and Susan Rachel "Ray" (Taylor). The handwriting across the top reads, "H. J. Grant & family 10th wedding anniversary."

CG & Co. sought to strengthen the credit of Church-related businesses by endorsing their financial paper. With the partners' pooled stock as collateral, the signature of CG & Co. could place a gilt edge on even an unattractive Utah Sugar Company note. In order to secure maximum leverage, each partner also agreed to assume, if necessary, the entire surety of the firm. Both R. G. Dun and John Bradstreet granted CG & Co. a $1,000,000 double-A rating. With this endorsement, Grant secured $232,000 in loans from San Francisco banks, and in May 1892 returned to New York to ask for an additional $260,000.[10]

Like the legendary Hudson's Bay and East India companies, CG & Co. mixed private and public affairs. The partners welcomed the prospect of personal profit, and much of their business reflected the spirit of the Age of Enterprise. However, as the threat of the Edmunds-Tucker Act forced the Church to conduct its business informally through intermediaries, the investment firm also became a semiofficial agency. During its brief period of prosperity in the early nineties, the company often held meetings in President Woodruff's office and under his supervision. It signed Church-related loans, which Eastern financiers considered morally binding upon the Mormon community. Its directorship interlocked with those of most other Mormon businesses, and the firm maintained an especially close relationship with the two Mormon banks. CG & Co. invested heavily in ZCMI and the State Bank of Utah and advertised itself as "Financial Agents, with State Bank of Utah." The firm also used money borrowed from Zion's Savings Bank to purchase over half of that bank's stock.[11]

However, when signs of an economic contraction appeared in late December 1892, CG & Co.'s power proved illusory. The State Bank not only carried a large amount of past-due paper, but it also had borrowed large sums payable "on demand." Consequently, its cash reserves were precarious. The bank's cashier and Grant's brother-in-law Heber M. Wells, who soon would be Utah's first state governor, confessed "trepidation" that CG & Co. might not be able to resolve the financial crisis (illus. 6-5).[12]

Wells's apprehensions were well founded. The Church owed at least $500,000 in short-term, rapidly maturing notes and had not the slightest prospect of paying. Moreover, the insatiable Utah Sugar

Company, on which the Church had staked its reputation, continued to devour cash. The only relief available was to dip the bucket once again into the financial well. On April 25, 1893, Church leaders authorized the First Presidency and Heber J. Grant to "raise means & handle stock of the Sugar Co. . . . whether in the States or in Europe." CG & Co. partners found it "imperatively necessary to look hurriedly to our business lest we be submitted to disgrace and serious loss."[13]

Courtesy Church Archives, The Church of Jesus Christ of Latter-day Saints

Illus. 6-5. Heber M. Wells, brother-in-law to Heber J. Grant. Wells became Utah's first state governor.

By mid-May, Grant was aboard a Denver & Rio Grande train bound for New York. He carried $300,000 in notes to be renewed, $200,000 of which bore the CG & Co. signature. A single defaulted note could destroy the Mormon credit rating and make it impossible to arrange further renewals and loans. Neither Grant nor his associates were optimistic. "This is the most difficult mission bro. Heber has ever undertaken," Francis M. Lyman wrote on May 10, "now that financial affairs are tumbling in all directions."[14]

Two weeks later, Grant was exultant. Although finding the loan market much worse than during the previous crisis and money men "frightened half to death," he nevertheless had renewed almost $150,000 of the most pressing loans and had secured an additional $25,000. The devout Grant saw in this the divine hand. Before leaving Salt Lake City, President Cannon had pronounced upon him an electrifying blessing that promised success. "I hope and pray that I may never forget . . . the blessing promised me before I came away from home," Grant wrote in his journal. "Without the blessings of the Lord. . . . I could not have succeeded with the market in the condition that it is in."[15]

Outwardly, the situation in Salt Lake Valley was also encouraging. Bank clearances in May increased slightly over the previous year, business failures were relatively low, and newspapers speculated that the Panic's destroying angel might spare Utah. Church leaders, meanwhile, continued their policy of enterprise to aid the region's economy. On June 1 they decided to sponsor—but not underwrite—a $75,000,000 railroad from Salt Lake to Los Angeles. To finance the project, and to secure long-term loans for the Church itself, officials revived their plan to obtain British capital. To this end, George Q. Cannon was given power of attorney over all remaining Church assets and was instructed to join Grant in New York. From there, the two men hoped to proceed to London.[16]

But beneath the business-as-usual atmosphere in Utah, the 1893 crisis was building steam. During the first week in June, local bankers reported a run on the banks. "Never while reason lasts or immortality endures do I wish to have repeated the experience I have undergone the last two days," a thoroughly agitated Heber M. Wells informed Grant. "Our deposits melted down over $25,000 and our available resources tonight have reached the minimum of 22%. All day long I have sat and smiled and acted (thanks to my stage experience) as if nothing unusual was happening. . . . You can not realize what a plight we are in—it is simply terrible."[17]

Wells's graphic prose revealed clearly the deteriorating conditions at the State Bank. Within a year, the bank's ratio of cash to deposits dropped from 65 to 22 percent—and 22 percent was artificially high. Several years earlier the State Bank and Zion's Savings had agreed to share quarters and customers. The State Bank had surrendered its savings accounts and Zion's Savings had given up its commercial business. Also as part of the agreement, Zion's Savings had deposited its cash reserves—over $125,000—with the State Bank. A run on both banks would mean that the State Bank's melting reserves would have to supply each. Conceivably, several large withdrawals from either bank could sink both. "Such a condition," Grant confessed, "is enough to make a man wild with the blues."[18]

Grant had long recognized that Church finances were jerry-built, but he now knew how unsound the structure actually was. Everyone intimate with Church finances realized that a single defaulted note endorsed by CG & Co. could spell the end of Church credit. Now it was suddenly apparent that the company's shadow fell ominously over the two Mormon banks as well. Because of the interlocking directorates, the collapse of CG & Co. would ruin the reputation of the leading men connected with the banks—the partners were individually responsible for the firm's debts—and precipitate a panic. Moreover, the Mormon banks had loaned CG & Co. at least $350,000. If the company went to the wall, the banks' uncollectible loans would surely force them to follow.[19]

The dominoes could also fall in the opposite direction. Bank failures would probably destroy CG & Co., which had invested heavily in the State Bank and Zion's Savings and had used bank securities as collateral in securing loans. Although the Mormon banks' assets outweighed their liabilities, even a temporary suspension due to lack of liquidity would send shivers up the spines of Wall Street capitalists, causing them to demand additional security for past and future loans—security that CG & Co. could not provide. In short, Latter-day Saint finances faced assaults from both directions and were vulnerable at each point. The only recourse was another loan.[20]

On June 7, 1893, Grant reappeared at the National Park Bank of New York. In just ten days the hard-pressed New York bankers would begin issuing clearinghouse loan certificates, rather than money, to their depositors. Not surprisingly, E. K. Wright, the bank's president and chief stockholder, flatly refused a loan. Undaunted, Grant expressed regret that the State Bank's business would have to go elsewhere and asked Wright's permission to appeal to the bank's vice president and cashier. "I feel to thank the Lord that I captured them completely," he wrote Wells. "They put their heads together as to how to capture Mr. Wright and while they were chatting together Mr. Wright stepped up and said, 'Mr. Grant if those men are favorable I shall say yes.'" Grant obtained $50,000.[21]

For the moment, the new loan seemed an ample transfusion for the Mormon banks. Relaxation might now be mixed with business, and, on June 8, Grant wired his plural wife Augusta to join President Cannon's London-bound entourage. But before the Cannon party arrived at New York, Grant decided that he could not desert his post. The panic was raging in full force, and Church notes in Hartford banks would soon mature. On June 17, Cannon's party sailed without Grant.[22]

Grant's decision to remain in New York was providential. Four days after Cannon departed for England, the damoclean sword poised over Church finances fell. For months Church leaders had feared that W. S. "Mack" McCornick, Salt Lake City's friendly non-Mormon banker, would request payment on his "demand" loans. On June 22, McCornick insisted that CG & Co. pay $20,000. Two days later, in another transaction, he required and received $37,500 from the State Bank. "Shakespeare says 'MacBeth doth murder sleep,'" Wells mordantly wrote Grant. "If he had lived till this day he would have made it a different scotchman . . . 'McCornick doth murder sleep.'" Wells won a few days' postponement by informing McCornick that the $20,000 was deposited in New York, and that Grant was using the money as leverage to renew the firm's notes.[23]

Even before McCornick's payment demands, the situation in Utah was critical. The run on Salt Lake City's banks had accelerated, and the banks in turn had closed the windows of their loan cages and tightened credit. Even Elder Abraham H. Cannon, a director of both the State Bank and CG & Co., found it impossible to obtain a loan. Stringent banking, however, proved counter productive. By forcing business to a standstill, it caused deposits to decline even faster. By the end of June, the State Bank had lost $125,000. "To those who knew the facts," Wells wrote, "apprehension and dread of direful consequences have been plainly discernible in every feature and every look, like the faces of attendants in a sick room in the presence of death, but as stated our outward demeanor has been full of buoyancy and cold bluff."[24]

The Salt Lake news almost overwhelmed Grant, who had already been driven to his physical limits. Expecting to be absent three weeks from Utah, he had now spent six weeks in the East, and he wondered whether his strength would allow him to continue his efforts. Each Salt Lake letter and telegram had a bluer cast. The Mormon bank vaults were emptying. Grant Brothers' Livery Company, unable to meet its notes, was threatened with bankruptcy. McCornick had stayed CG & Co.'s execution four times but was growing ever more impatient. Gladly, Grant thought, he would trade high finance for a bookkeeper's ledger—anything would be better than having once again "to get down on one's knees" before the bankers. Besides, he had no idea where to kneel. The State Bank's New York correspondent had already refused his demand for special consideration. "I think that I would almost be wild tonight," Grant wrote George Q. Cannon in England, "did I not know that the Lord has helped me in the past and I have faith that he will do so in the future."[25]

As a last resort, Grant turned to John Claflin, president of H. B. Claflin Company of New York, the "leading dry goods merchant in the United States." In normal or even slightly difficult times, the merchant might have rushed to the Mormons' aid. He had previously dealt with Grant and trusted him. Moreover, while others viewed the Mormons in far-off Utah as slightly bizarre if not downright disreputable, Claflin, interested in the exotic and the profitable, had invested in them. In 1889 he had loaned the Saints $40,000, followed two years later by another $100,000. His offer in 1892 of a $200,000 standing or perpetual credit had been declined.[26]

Grant did not come to Claflin empty-handed. He held as possible collateral $100,000 in ZCMI notes—the best security Utah could offer. These had come from Thomas Webber, ZCMI's manager and an unpublicized CG & Co. director. Believing the times required that "we must help one another," Webber, without consulting his directors, had made the loan to the Church. Grant hoped these securities would fortify his main argument that the State Bank–CG & Co. directors were also the leading men in ZCMI, the company that bought Claflin's goods. Their ruin—or even disfavor—might destroy H. B. Claflin Company's Mormon business.[27]

While Grant waited in Claflin's office through the long afternoon of June 27, the fate of both the Church and Grant's businesses weighed on his shoulders. Finally, after 4:00 P.M., the merchant listened to Grant's impassioned appeal. In response, Claflin explained that the season demanded that ice flow in the veins of even the most favorably disposed merchant, and that a loan was "utterly impossible." Claflin softened his refusal by promising his good offices, and the next morning he personally escorted Grant to several banking firms. When the high-risk and high-profit Blake Brothers offered to purchase a single $5,000 ZCMI note at an exorbitant 18 percent, Grant grabbed the chance. Later, he extracted an additional $5,000 from Claflin, who had just penned a strong letter declaring: "If the Z.C.M.I. is not good the merchants of the United States generally might as well go out of business."[28]

Events in Salt Lake City, meanwhile, seemed to climax. Grant's efforts in New York left McCornick only half appeased—he still demanded the $10,000 outstanding on his $20,000 loan to CG & Co. On June 28, George M. Cannon, Zion's Savings cashier, privately feared catastrophe "to many of our institutions." On Saturday, July 1, Heber Wells gloomily noted that the Mormon banks had begun the day with $40,000 in their vaults and closed with only $10,000 remaining. That same day two Provo banks collapsed, while Salt Lake's Bank of Commerce escaped failure only by securing aid from the bankers' clearinghouse. "Before you receive this," Wells wrote Grant, "it is possible—nay probable you will hear of our suspension."[29]

Despite Wells's dire prediction, the Mormon banks weathered this wave of the storm. Beginning on Monday, July 3, Zion's Savings Bank, along with Salt Lake City's other savings institutions, required a thirty-day notice of withdrawal for deposits of less than $100 and a sixty-day notice for larger sums. Although extraordinary, the action was legal. "At first there was a lull," Wells remembered,

> then the storm broke in all its fury. Depositors swarmed around Zion's side [of the bank]. . . . Some went out sullenly muttering that something was wrong, some said they expected it, some stormed, demanded their money and said the bank must [be] shaky; but the medicine worked.

No one suspected that the problems of the city's savings banks touched the State Bank, which was actually able to increase slightly its reserves.[30]

Grant, meanwhile, was determined to secure money in the East. On Monday morning, he unsuccessfully appealed to his insurance friends; called at two banks; approached W. H. Coler, a New York financier who for several days had considered making a $100,000 loan; and visited the New York Life offices, only to find them closed because of the approaching July 4 holiday. Finally, he again tried Blake Brothers, begging them "to find one of their customers who would purchase the notes I had to offer at some price." In a few moments, he secured $20,000 at a whopping 24 percent discount. Grant immediately wired news of his success to Salt Lake City. Mindful of McCornick's unpaid $10,000, Heber Wells dolefully twirled his mustache—"the only remnant of hair I have left"—as he opened the latest telegram from New York and saw the words "GLORY HALLELUJAH." Two days later, Grant was still celebrating with friends over the popular nineteenth-century dessert, water ice, at Delmonico's.[31]

The crisis of July 3 had passed, and for several weeks Grant felt certain that the worst of his difficulties was behind him. Not only had he resolved all the Church's pressing obligations, but he had also secured from several New York banks an additional $150,000. By the end of July, however, Grant realized that his tour de force had only postponed catastrophe. The panic still raged, and his new loans were of only two, three, or at best four months duration. Furthermore, Grant recognized that additional renewals probably would be impossible. Like Zion's Savings' delayed deposit payments, the New York loans were short-fused time bombs set to explode at the end of August.[32]

For a while, Mormon fortunes seemed to rest with George Q. Cannon's English mission. On July 3, the day on which Church finances were barely salvaged, Cannon had talked at Whitehall with the Earl of Roseberry, the British foreign secretary. Although twenty years had passed since their last meeting—apparently while Cannon was serving as Utah's territorial delegate in Washington—the foreign secretary, soon to be prime minister, cordially received the Mormon emissary and wrote a letter of introduction to Baron Rothschild. On July 7 a tersely worded telegram—"UNSUCCESSFUL"—dashed Mormon hopes for a long-term loan. Cannon had met with Rothschild, his brothers, and other leading financiers, but the prevailing American panic and the Europeans' ignorance of Utah affairs made a loan impossible.[33]

Utah, meanwhile, was slipping into a severe economic depression. Banking contraction was only partly to blame. A late winter had heavily damaged local agriculture, particularly the important cash-producing wool clip, making 1893 Utah's worst sheep year to date. Moreover, the plummeting price of silver forced the closing of many mines, further reducing the local money supply. By the end of June, Utah businessmen began laying off workers and reducing wages. Such prominent citizens as John Morgan, Abraham O. Smoot, and Ben Rich went bankrupt, and real-estate speculator George A. Meears committed suicide for the lack of $1,000. "From every side arises the cry of hard times," wrote one diarist.

> I have never witnessed a greater stagnation in business enterprises than has manifested itself during the last month. Money is not to be had, confidence seems to have disappeared, and credit is denied by nearly all tradesmen. Public works are stopped, and . . . thousands of men are out of employment.[34]

A kaleidoscope of personal, human acts reflected the hard times. A needy seamstress, fearing starvation for her children, appealed to the patriarchal Franklin D. Richards. "I encouraged her the best I could," Elder Richards remembered, "& she wiped away her tears & went with apparently increased bravery." The Salt Lake County tax collector—also a bishop and a CG & Co. director—mismanaged $32,000 in public funds and then asked protection from the General Authorities to avoid embarrassing the Church. Elder Francis Lyman spent one August morning in his bed, immobilized by the awful prospect of bankruptcy and regretting his debts to family and friends. George Q. Cannon, back from England, abandoned his multifamily communal kitchen, kept his boys from school to do the work of released hired hands, and transferred his few unencumbered assets to his wives. By contrast, during the State Bank's desperate days in July, young George F. Richards bolstered its reserves with $1,500— the bulk of his savings.[35]

The depression paralyzed the Church. By late June, cash donations had almost ceased. On July 1 the Church failed to meet its payroll, forcing the General Authorities to draw their living allowances in tithing commodities. In Salt Lake City, mission president J. Golden Kimball described himself as at "the <u>end</u> of the rope" and pleaded for "<u>anything</u>" to aid him in returning to his assignment in the Southern states. Appropriations for Church education were halted, twenty schools were closed, and the opening of the new Church University in Salt Lake City was postponed indefinitely. Clerks struggled to pay even the low-priced fares of returning missionaries, and sometimes failed. "Every day urgent demands for cash are made of us, which we cannot meet," wrote the First Presidency, "for the simple reason that we have no money. . . . We never saw such a time of financial stringency as there is now."[36]

Endeavoring to maintain the Church's balance, leaders sent letters to local congregations directing that tithing commodities or other property be cheaply sold and the cash sent to Church headquarters. Buyers were few, however, and local charity consumed most of the money raised. During a prosperous year, over 50 percent of all tithing flowed into Church offices; in 1893 the Church received only 19 percent. For several weeks the General Authorities considered borrowing over $100,000 from 126 wealthy Saints, but they evidently realized that the plan would cripple the Mormon banks. There seemed to be no solution, only a gaping crevasse.[37]

On August 2 the leading Latter-day Saint money men met to take "stock." The weary Grant had returned the previous day from New York, and at an 8:00 A.M. CG & Co. meeting he reported on his labors. "We only live now on sufferance of those we owe such large sums to," Francis Lyman summarized after Grant's narration. But the investment firm had larger problems than note renewals in the Eastern market. It had endorsed the paper of Burton-Gardner Company, and the latter's recent bankruptcy seemed a mortal blow. CG & Co. directors decided to transfer the Sugar Company's heavy indebtedness elsewhere—perhaps, somehow, to the Church itself. A joint meeting of the directors of the two Mormon banks that afternoon was equally grim. Cashier Wells revealed that without new deposits the banks would close within several weeks. He dispiritedly wondered whether an earlier closing might not be the wisest course.[38]

The Lord had given and now he seemed ready to take. Church leaders solemnly entered their new temple and prayed for relief. "All the Lord requires of us," President Woodruff exhorted, "is to do the very best we can, and He will then take care of the remainder." On August 12, President Woodruff made his last public attempt to resolve the crisis. At a meeting attended by the First Presidency, seven Apostles, the Presiding Bishopric, and nineteen stake leaders, Woodruff reviewed the emergency and urged an increase in donations. When possible, the Church would borrow from the Saints at 10 percent. Two weeks later, sublimely calm amidst the Church's crumbling finances, Woodruff appropriated $15,000 recently found in the Church's accounts in England and Hawaii, and led the rest of the First Presidency and the Tabernacle Choir on a long-planned public relations tour of the World's Fair in Chicago. Before leaving Utah, President Woodruff nominated Grant and George Q. Cannon somehow to resolve the crisis. Since Cannon was part of Woodruff's party, the responsibility fell to Grant.[39]

Again, Grant's mission was critical. Within two weeks, Zion's Savings must begin paying the large withdrawals requested sixty days earlier. And at about the same time, the Church's many loans would start to mature. Meanwhile, Wells Fargo had unexpectedly demanded that the Church reduce its $25,000 overdraft privilege at the bank by $10,000. When, on August 24, the Brigham Young Trust Company failed to pay $50,000 owed Wells Fargo, Heber Wells tried to resolve the problem with a new loan from Mack McCornick. "Yesterday we bearded the former lion in his den," Wells related. "We told him everything; pleaded, entreated, cajoled, warned, threatened, and afterwards damned him. He was callous, obdurate, unyielding." Finally, with an eye on future Mormon business, McCornick yielded $10,000 as a temporary sop. Toward the end of August, the Church notified Wells Fargo in San Francisco that it would probably default on its September 2 loan payment.[40]

By August 24, Grant was back pounding the streets of New York in search of a large, long-term loan. This time, he realized, a pound of flesh would be necessary to save Church finances. With margins of reserves to assets in New York banks at 20.5 percent in mid-August—their lowest point of the crisis and well below the 24 percent legal limit for national banks—nothing less than a huge bonus would entice bankers into risking a long-term loan. But even when he promised a 20 or 25 percent commission, Grant found no takers. "I am getting blue by the hour," he informed Wells. "I wish that there was something bright in the distance that I could look forward to."[41]

In Utah the final crisis was at hand. On Friday, September 1, the Mormon banks held only $20,000, a scant 3 percent of deposits. By closing time $5,000 had been drained from the vaults, and Wells frantically wired Grant that the State Bank could not survive another two days. Earlier that same day Grant had finally wrangled a promise for a $100,000 loan. But he had pressed too hard, and the frightened banker had delayed payment until Wednesday, September 6. Now Grant learned that the Mormon banks could not last that long. He had come so close![42]

Since arriving in New York, Grant had tried to follow President Woodruff's counsel to neither worry nor complain about the financial crisis. But as events pounded down upon him, he again wondered whether he might not break under the strain. He had exhausted all possibilities for a loan; there seemed to be no stone left to turn. Before him loomed the "perfect horror" of another Kirtland Bank failure, which had rent Church finances and caused widespread apostasy fifty-six years earlier. Several times during the early morning of September 2, he shed bitter tears as he "supplicated the

Lord with all the earnestness and power which I possessed." After 3:00 A.M. he lapsed into a few hours of fitful sleep.[43]

Events of the next day seemed drawn from a surrealistic drama. Grant appeared to move in slow motion, almost in defiance of the prevailing high stakes and emotions. Arising after 8:00 A.M., an unusually late hour for the vigorous Grant, he knelt in morning prayers and offered to forfeit his life in exchange for the preservation of the banks. Experiencing a calming assurance, he bathed and breakfasted deliberately and then, without a destination in mind, boarded an elevated railway train. At the station nearest H. B. Claflin Company, he decided to stop and shake John Claflin's hand. The merchant was not in his office, but had left word that he wished to see Grant. Grant proceeded on to the National Park Bank, but missed the right station. Backtracking, he entered Blake Brothers, and there found John Claflin with a proposition.

Claflin had watched closely over the past several weeks as New York bank reserves finally stabilized and edged above the 24 percent legal minimum. Recognizing that the worst of the national money crisis was over, and aware of Grant's willingness to pay an extravagant bonus, the New York businessman sensed the time was ripe to save the finances of his Mormon friends, secure for himself a handsome commission, and ensure for his company ZCMI's lucrative trade. His terms were terrifying: $500,000 for two years at 6 percent with a $100,000 bonus going to Claflin—almost 33 percent of the loan would be lost to interest or commission (illus. 6-6). A desperate Grant refused to "split straws." He asked only that the deal be halved: $250,000 for two years, same interest, with $50,000 given to Claflin. Within hours the State Bank learned that it could draw upon its New York correspondent for an initial installment of $50,000. The Mormon banks were saved.[44]

The attractiveness of Claflin's loan varied with the beholder. On the grounds of the Chicago World's Fair, Grant explained his actions to the First Presidency. "Prest. Woodruff did not appreciate . . . getting only $200,000 and yet paying interest on $250,000," Grant remembered. In fact, the Church president found the loan's terms "fearful." Although Church leaders formally approved the note, and many personally signed it, the more cautious believed that Grant had gone too far. In their eyes the loan had ruined Grant's

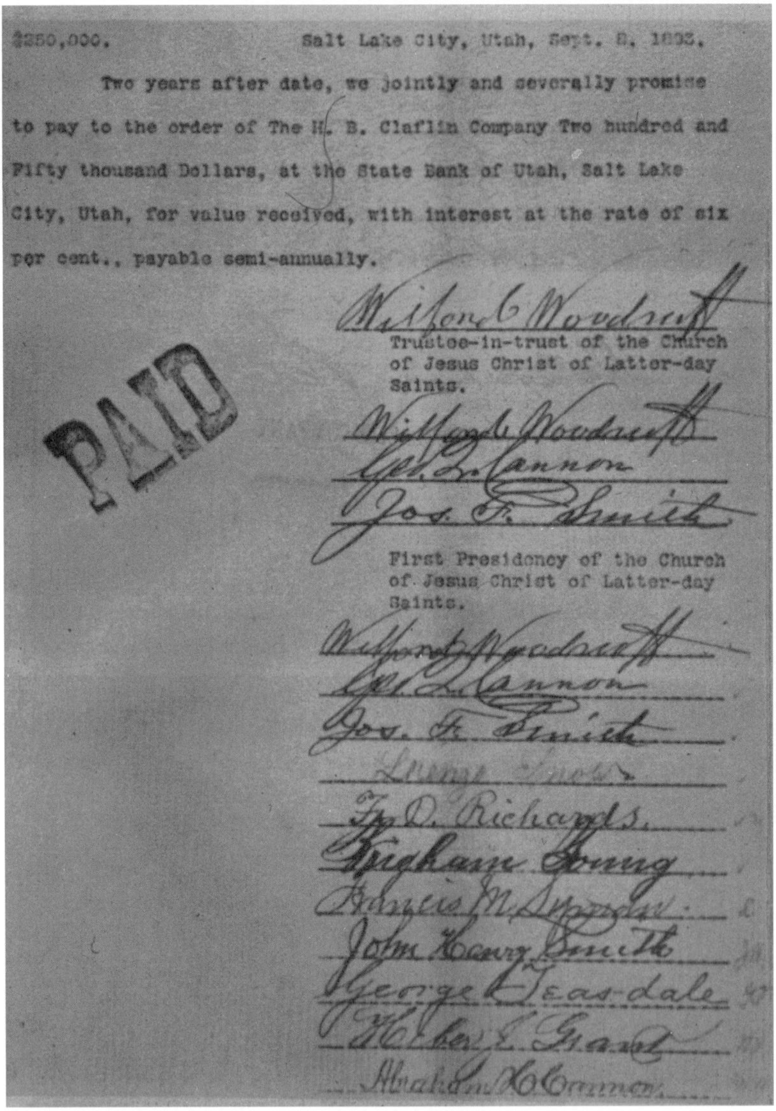

$250,000.   Salt Lake City, Utah, Sept. 8, 1893.

   Two years after date, we jointly and severally promise
to pay to the order of The H. B. Claflin Company Two hundred and
Fifty thousand Dollars, at the State Bank of Utah, Salt Lake
City, Utah, for value received, with interest at the rate of six
per cent., payable semi-annually.

PAID

Wilford C Woodruff
Trustee-in-trust of the Church
of Jesus Christ of Latter-day
Saints.

Wilford C Woodruff
Geo. Q. Cannon
Jos. F. Smith
First Presidency of the Church
of Jesus Christ of Latter-day
Saints.

Wilford Woodruff
Geo. Q. Cannon
Jos. F. Smith
Lorenzo Snow
F. D. Richards
Brigham Young
Francis M. Lyman
John Henry Smith
George Teasdale
Heber J. Grant
Abraham H. Cannon

Illus. 6-6. The note, signed by the First Presidency and Twelve Apostles, from H. B. Claflin Company loaning the Church money during the economic depression of the 1890s.

financial reputation. "They did not comprehend the exigencies of the case," Grant later argued, "but I would gladly have given twice as much had it been necessary in order to save our banks."[45]

Grant scarcely overstated matters. Although the Church would require loan after loan during the troubled 1890s, the Claflin money had allowed the banks to navigate their most dangerous passage. The safety of the banks in turn had prevented the bankruptcy of CG & Co., its individual partners, and—morally at least—the Church itself. Such failures would have had far-reaching consequences of their own. There is no possible way of estimating the eventual catastrophe had the floodgates not held.

The trauma of 1893—with its foundering banks, pinched finances, and heroic loans—was never related publicly. As each new wave of the crisis had threatened, the Salt Lake newspapers had reassuredly pronounced the financial foundations of Zion as unshakable as the granite walls of the Wasatch Range. Officially the Saints were never told otherwise. When President Cannon addressed their October conference, he stated only the obvious. "We have had, since we last met," he reported, "considerable trouble in financial matters. . . . You have no doubt felt it individually, as we have felt it as a church. Probably at no time in our previous experience have we had to contend with pecuniary embarrassments as we have had of late." Only a few in the audience understood that Cannon spoke of more than the Church's unpaid bills. Nor did the Mormon public learn of the Claflin loan. Fearing a reputation as a Shylock, John Claflin had demanded secrecy.[46]

This Mormon story had a sequel. Although Grant's loans may have saved Zion and its money men from bankruptcy, the panic was ruinous. "A few years ago," Grant admitted in 1898, "we thought less of spending $100 than we do now of a $5 bill." Although the pacified national government returned what was left from the Edmunds-Tucker confiscations, Utahns and the Church staggered through the misnamed "Gay Nineties." When the entire Claflin note fell due in 1895, the Church was able only to make the first payment on the loan's principal. It eventually canceled its debt largely by transferring to H. B. Claflin Company some of the Church's shares in the Saltair Beach and the Salt Lake and Los Angeles Railway companies. Final payment on the Claflin note was not made until 1899.[47]

Beyond contributing to the distress of the nineties, the panic left a lasting imprint upon the Church. The Church in the nineteenth century had styled itself a unique religious commonwealth apart from mainstream America. Grant's own business career itself had reflected Brigham Young's preaching on Zion's self-sufficiency and independence. Yet Grant's New York loans wrapped the cords of American finance tightly around Utah's Zion. Thereafter, Church leaders would not only feel increasingly at ease with the ways of American capitalists, but they would be beholden—at least in the short run—for their services. Within another decade these influences would go so far that muckraking journalists would begin to cast the Church in the role of a Wall Street plutocrat. Along with other economic forces working to nationalize America, the Panic of 1893 changed not only the economics of the Church but also indirectly its public image.

There was a final, personal irony to the episode. The mighty H. B. Claflin interests became overextended and in 1914 fell into receivership. John Claflin spent his last twenty years in retirement— prosperous enough to winter on the palmy Jekyll Island resort in Georgia, but stripped of personal or financial influence. Heber J. Grant, in contrast, became financially stable and the Church's president. One of the hallmarks of his administration, even during the Great Depression of the 1930s, was fiscal stability. The harrowing summer of 1893, with its lessons for careful finance, clearly had left its mark. Indeed, for its participants, like old comrades-in-arms, the Panic of 1893 became a topic to cherish and celebrate. "Those were the days," Heber Wells mused to Grant almost thirty years after the event, "when we fought and bled and nearly died together."[48]

Notes

This article was originally published in *Arizona and the West* 21 (Autumn 1979): 257–78.

1. Western historians have generally either ignored the Panic of 1893 or have treated it as a prelude to the Silver and Populist agitations. A close examination of the impact of the financial upheaval upon the specific community of Salt Lake City suggests that the panic was indeed a major turning point in the history of the nineteenth-century West.

2. Charles Hoffmann, *The Depression of the Nineties: An Economic History* (Westport, Connecticut: Greenwood Publishing, 1970), 54–71, 97,

109; W. Jett Lauck, *The Causes of the Panic of 1893* (Boston: Houghton-Mifflin, 1907), 107.

3. Heber J. Grant to Joseph H. Richards, February 22, 1890, Heber J. Grant Letterpress Copybook, 8:215–16, Heber J. Grant Collection, Church Archives, The Church of Jesus Christ of Latter-day Saints, Salt Lake City; Heber J. Grant to Alfred L. Giles, March 26, 1890, Grant Letterpress Copybook, 8:287; Heber J. Grant to Anthony W. Ivins, December 13, 1890, Grant Letterpress Copybook, 9:172; Heber J. Grant to R. D. Foltz, November 28, 1891, Grant Letterpress Copybook, 9:394; Abraham H. Cannon, Diary, February 28, March 6, 1890, and May 13, 1891, Church Archives; Hezekiah Eastman Hatch, Typescript autobiography, 37, Church Archives; Roland Stucki, *Commercial Banking in Utah, 1847–1966* (Salt Lake City: University of Utah Press, 1967), 27.

4. The precipitous drop in tithing revenue is in Cannon, Diary, October 5, 1894; and "Annual Reports of the Presiding Bishopric, 1901," 26, Papers of the Presiding Bishopric, Church Archives. These tithing summaries do not include donations from the Church's missions and branches or money paid into a special "Defense Fund," informally collected by Church leaders to facilitate statehood. Leonard J. Arrington, *Great Basin Kingdom: An Economic History of the Latter-day Saints, 1830–1900* (Lincoln: University of Nebraska Press, 1966), 360–73, discusses the Edmunds-Tucker Act and its economic consequences. Historians have overlooked the importance of the transfer of government funds from non-Mormon banks, but contemporaries understood its seriousness. "The losing of the funds of the City, County & Territory," Grant informed George Q. Cannon on January 26, 1892, "has done as much to place the Mormon party of the community in a financial corner as the fearful draw on our resources by the government having stolen the Church property. . . ." Grant Letterpress Copybook, 12:94.

5. Arrington, *Great Basin Kingdom*, 400–401.

6. *Deseret Evening News*, March 27, 1889, 3; President Joseph F. Smith, "True Economy," *Deseret Evening News*, December 16, 1893, 1; Cannon, Diary, April 5, 1895; Arrington, *Great Basin Kingdom*, 386–93, 400–401, provides details on Church expenditures of the period. Confirmation that these projects were largely deficit financed is in Heber J. Grant, Typed Diary, August 5, 1893, Grant Collection, Church Archives; Heber J. Grant to George M. Cannon, July 12, 1893, Grant Letterpress Copybook, 17:162.

7. Heber J. Grant to Spencer Clawson, December 20, 1890, Grant Letterpress Copybook, 9:186; Heber J. Grant to John C. Cutler, December 17, 1890, Grant Letterpress Copybook, 10:7; Heber J. Grant to E. K. Wright, January 7, 1891, Grant Letterpress Copybook, 10:204; Heber J. Grant to Ray [Rachel] Grant, January 7, 1891, Grant Letterpress Copybook, 10:210; Heber J. Grant, Reminiscence, box 177, fd. 3, Miscellaneous Papers, Grant Collection. A reminiscence of Grant's trip to the East is in Bryant S. Hinckley, *Heber J. Grant: Highlights in the Life of a Great Leader* (Salt Lake City: Deseret Book, 1951), 54–60.

8. Heber J. Grant to Brigham Young Jr., July 13, 1892, Grant Collection, 11:409; Heber J. Grant to Rachel Grant, January 28, 1893, Grant Collection, 12:131; Heber J. Grant, Press Copy Diary, July 9, 1891, Grant Collection; and Cannon, Diary, July 2, 1891.

9. In addition to Cannon and Grant, the partners were: Joseph F. Smith, Second Counselor in the First Presidency and director of ZCMI, Zion's Savings Bank, and the State Bank of Utah; Abraham H. Cannon, member of the Quorum of the Twelve and manager of the printing firm of George Q. Cannon & Sons; John H. Smith, member of the Quorum of the Twelve and businessman; Francis M. Lyman, member of the Quorum of the Twelve and businessman; George M. Cannon, cashier of Zion's Savings and principal shareholder of the State Bank; Leonard G. Hardy, bishop and county collector; Thomas R. Cutler, manager and director of the Utah Sugar Company; Thomas G. Webber, superintendent of ZCMI, president of Zion's Benefit Building Society, and director of Zion's Savings, Utah Sugar Company, and Home Fire Insurance; Philo T. Farnsworth, mining speculator; William H. Rowe, assistant superintendent of ZCMI and director of ZCMI and the State Bank; and Henry A. Woolley, Nephi W. Clayton, and Jesse W. Fox, all Utah businessmen. Webber and Farnsworth kept their participation from public view and did not allow their names on CG & Co. stationery. Investments of the partners are in Memorandum, April 18, 1892, CG & Co. Papers, Church Archives.

10. Heber J. Grant to Charles Deare, January 4, 1892, Grant Letterpress Copybook, 10:682; Heber J. Grant to Heber M. Wells, January 29, 1892, Grant Letterpress Copybook, 11:168; Heber J. Grant to J. F. Grant, May 15, 1892, Grant Letterpress Copybook, 13:122.

11. Cannon, Diary, May 3, 1892. Heber J. Grant to G. Q. Cannon, June 5, 1892, Grant Letterpress Copybook, 11:371, indicated that CG & Co. probably controlled 80 percent of the stock of Zion's Savings.

12. Heber M. Wells to Heber J. Grant, December 22, 1892, Grant Letterpress Copybook, 13:649–50; Heber M. Wells to Heber J. Grant, February 14, 1893, Grant Letterpress Copybook, 16:19.

13. Franklin D. Richards, Diary, April 24, 25, 1893, Church Archives; Francis M. Lyman, Diary, May 3, 1893, Church Archives; Cannon, Diary, May 3, 1893.

14. Lyman, Diary, May 10, 1893.

15. Grant, Press Copy Diary, May 19, 23, 31, 1893.

16. *Salt Lake Tribune,* June 1, 1893, 6; Lyman, Diary, June 1, 1893; Marriner W. Merrill, Diary, June 1, 1893, Church Archives. Lyman suggests that in addition to easing unemployment, Church officials saw the proposed railroad as a means of increasing Church influence and prestige as well as a way of keeping "some of the important enterprises of the west in our hands."

17. Heber M. Wells to Heber J. Grant, June 3, 1893, in Grant, Press Copy Diary, 519. Grant frequently copied correspondence in his diary.

18. Heber J. Grant to Heber M. Wells, June 11, 1893, in Grant, Press Copy Diary, 538–39; Heber J. Grant to Alexander G. Hawes, September 22, 1893, Grant Letterpress Copybook, 17:487; Cannon, Diary, December 8, 1891, January 15, 1892.

19. Heber J. Grant to Anthony W. Ivins, August 14, 1893, Grant Letterpress Copybook, 17:244–45. Eight of the thirteen CG & Co. partners were State Bank directors: J. F. Smith, A. H. Cannon, H. J. Grant, H. A. Woolley, W. H. Rowe, Elias Morris, Nephi Clayton, and P. T. Farnsworth. The interrelationships were almost as tight with the Zion's Savings board, with six of its thirteen directors being CG & Co. partners: G. Q. Cannon, J. F. Smith, H. J. Grant, F. M. Lyman, G. M. Cannon, and L. G. Hardy.

20. Grant believed throughout the crisis that the fates of CG & Co. and the two Mormon banks were inseparably connected. Heber J. Grant to Heber M. Wells, June 27, 1893, Grant Letterpress Copybook, 18:63; Heber J. Grant to G. Q. Cannon, July 5, 1893, Grant Letterpress Copybook, 18:102; Heber J. Grant to J. F. Smith, August 28, 1893, Grant Letterpress Copybook, 18:317.

21. Heber J. Grant to Heber M. Wells, June 7, 15, 1893, in Grant, Press Copy Diary, 542–43, 531, respectively; Heber J. Grant to Wilford Woodruff and J. F. Smith, June 19, 1893, Grant Letterpress Copybook, 17:18.

22. Grant, Press Copy Diary, June 8–17, 1893.

23. Heber M. Wells to Heber J. Grant, June 22, 1893, in Grant, Press Copy Diary, 520–21.

24. Heber M. Wells to Heber J. Grant, June 28, 1893, excerpts in Grant, Press Copy Diary, 525; Cannon, Diary, June 17, 21, 23, 24, 28, 1893; John Henry Smith, Diary, June 13, 26, 28, 29, 1893, Church Archives. On June 29, Smith wrote: "Money matters continue exceedingly close. Everybody is calling for money and seemingly none to be got."

25. Heber J. Grant to Wells, June 21, 1893, Grant Collection; Heber J. Grant to G. Q. Cannon, June 23, 1893, Grant Letterpress Copybook, 17:41, 53–54, Grant Collection, Church Archives.

26. *New York Times,* June 26, 1914, 1; *New York Times,* June 12, 1938, 39; Edward D. Page, "Lessons of the Claflin Crash," *The Independent* 79 (July 13, 1914): 76–78; Muriel E. Hidy, "John Claflin," in Robert Livingston Schuyler and Edward T. James, eds., *Dictionary of American Biography,* 22 vols. (New York: Charles Scribner's Sons, 1958), 22:104–5. Claflin's Mormon contacts are in Heber J. Grant to Wilford Woodruff, G. Q. Cannon, and J. F. Smith, January 5, 1891, Grant Letterpress Copybook, 10:184; Heber J. Grant to Thomas G. Webber, May 24, 1892, Grant Letterpress Copybook, 13:221; Heber J. Grant to James B. Powell, June 28, 1893, Grant Letterpress Copybook, 17:72; John Claflin to Heber J. Grant, January 7, 1891, Grant Letterpress Copybook, 10:977; Cannon, Diary, May 13, 1891.

27. Wells to Grant, June 22, 1893. When the ZCMI directors met on July 5, Webber's action proved "very grinding upon the brethren," and some complained of its illegality. However, they eventually approved the

Church's use of the notes. Lyman, Diary, July 5, 1893, Church Archives. Mormon business interconnections are in Heber J. Grant to James B. Powell, June 28, 1893, Grant Letterpress Copybook, 17:72.

28. Heber J. Grant to G. Q. Cannon, July 5, 1893, Grant Letterpress Copybook, 17:100–108. Claflin's ZCMI letter of recommendation is in John Claflin to Heber J. Grant, June 28, 1893, Grant Letterpress Copybook, 17:71.

29. *Salt Lake Tribune*, July 1, 1893, 6; *Salt Lake Tribune*, July 2, 1893, 3; Heber J. Grant to G. Q. Cannon, July 5, 1893, Grant Letterpress Copybook, 17:100; Heber M. Wells to Heber J. Grant, July 1, 1893, in Grant, Press Copy Diary, 574; Cannon, Diary, June 28, 1893. The Walker Brothers' Union National Bank reportedly was also dangerously low in cash reserves.

30. Heber M. Wells to Grant, July 3, 1893, in Grant, Press Copy Diary, 574–75, Grant Collection; Cannon Diary, July 3, 1893. Some of the directors of both banks had urgently desired to require notice of withdrawal on June 28, but Woodruff at the time "did not think it wisdom to do so" and the plan was shelved. Wilford Woodruff, Diary, June 28, 1893, Church Archives.

31. Wells to Grant, July 3, 1893, 574; Grant to G. Q. Cannon, July 5, 1893, 17:107; Heber J. Grant to Heber M. Wells, July 5, 1893, Grant Letterpress Copybook, 17:110.

32. Heber J. Grant to J. F. Smith, July 18, 1893, Grant Letterpress Copybook, 17:193.

33. Cannon's telegram is recorded in F. D. Richards, Diary, July 7, 1893, Church Archives. Additional information about his mission is in G. Q. Cannon to Wilford Woodruff and J. F. Smith, July 3, 7, 1893, Wilford Woodruff Papers, Church Archives.

34. "Wool Men Are Blue," *Deseret Evening News,* June 17, 1893, 1; *Salt Lake Tribune,* June 27, 1893, 1; *Salt Lake Tribune,* June 28, 1893, 1; *Salt Lake Tribune,* June 29, 1893, 1; *Salt Lake Tribune,* July 9, 1893, 1, 11; Cannon, Diary, October 4, 1893; Lyman, Diary, June 28, July 7, 1893; John Henry Smith, Diary, July 1, 1893; James E. Talmage, Diary, August 23, 1893, L. Tom Perry Special Collections, Harold B. Lee Library, Brigham Young University, Provo, Utah.

35. F. D. Richards, Diary, August 31, 1893; Lyman, Diary, July 6, August 3, 1893; George F. Richards, Diary, July 25, 1893, Church Archives.

36. J. F. Smith to Heber J. Grant, June 30, 1893, extract in Grant, Press Copy Diary, 562; J. G. Kimball to Wilford Woodruff, July 19, 1893, Woodruff Papers; George Reynolds to George F. Browning, July 18, 1893, First Presidency Letterpress Copybook; Wilford Woodruff, G. Q. Cannon, and J. F. Smith to W. T. Stewart, November 13, 1893, First Presidency Letterpress Copybook; Wilford Woodruff and J. F. Smith to Canute Petersen and Counselors, June 29, 1893, First Presidency Letterpress Copybook, Church Archives; Talmage, Diary, August 11, 23, 1893.

37. J. F. Smith to Heber J. Grant, June 30, 1893; William B. Preston, R. K. Burton, and John R. Winder to L. W. Shurtliff, July 1, 1893, Presiding

Bishopric Letterpress Copybooks, Church Archives; Presiding Bishopric Annual Reports, 1900, 30, Presiding Bishopric; John R. Winder to Wilford Woodruff and Council, July 7, 1893, Woodruff Papers; Woodruff, Diary, July 20, 1893; Cannon, Diary, July 20, 27, 1893.

38. Cannon, Diary, August 2, 1893; Lyman, Diary, August 2, 1893; Woodruff, Diary, August 2, 1893.

39. Matthew Noall to the First Presidency, August 29, 1893, Woodruff Papers; Anthon H. Lund to Wilford Woodruff and Counsel, November 2, 1893, Woodruff Papers; Woodruff, Diary, August 9, 12, 1893; Cannon, Diary, August 12, 1893; Lyman, Diary, August 12, 1893; Merrill, Diary, August 12, 1893. Lyman believed the Chicago "undertaking quite unreasonable to entertain under present circumstances," but Woodruff strongly desired the trip. Lyman, Diary, August 12, 1893. In late August, the Church took over and successfully marketed $225,000 of the Utah Sugar Company indebtedness. Eastern bankers, believing that the government would soon return the Edmunds-Tucker confiscations, came to prefer the Church's credit to that of CG & Co. Woodruff, Diary, August 23, 1893.

40. J. E. Dooley to Wilford Woodruff, August 2, 22, 1893, Woodruff Papers; Grant, Press Copy Diary, August 27–31, 1893; Heber M. Wells to Heber J. Grant, August 24, 1893, in Grant, Press Copy Diary, 617; Wilford Woodruff, G. Q. Cannon, and J. F. Smith to Henry Wadsworth, August 24, 1893, First Presidency Letterpress Copybook.

41. Heber J. Grant to Heber M. Wells, August 25, 1893, Grant Letterpress Copybook, 17:292; Lauck, *Causes of the Panic of 1893*, 101.

42. Heber J. Grant to Heber M. Wells, September 1, 1893, Grant Letterpress Copybook, 17:325; Heber J. Grant to J. F. Smith, September 1, 1893, Grant Letterpress Copybook, 17:332; Heber M. Wells to Heber J. Grant, September [3?], 1893 (telegram), in Grant, Press Copy Diary, 620.

43. Heber J. Grant to J. F. Smith, September 1, 1893, Grant Letterpress Copybook, 17:332; Grant, Press Copy Diary, August 27–31, 1893; Memorandum, January 8, 1916, in Grant, Press Copy Diary, 1893, preceding 402; Grant, Typed Diary, October 3, 1893.

44. Memorandum, January 8, 1916; Grant, Typed Diary, October 3, 1893; Cannon, Diary, February 14, 1895; Lauck, *Causes of the Panic of 1893*, 101.

45. Heber J. Grant to Heber M. Wells, September 4, 1893, extract in Grant, Press Copy Diary, 623; Heber J. Grant to Hiram B. Clawson, September 20, 1898, Grant Letterpress Copybook, 28:68; Heber J. Grant to John Claflin, December 29, 1897, Grant Letterpress Copybook, 26:237–38; Woodruff, Diary, September 4, 1893. During the crisis, Church leaders actually had approved the paying of an extravagant bonus for a loan, but many apparently forgot or wished to deny personal responsibility. Cannon, Diary, August 2, 1893.

46. *Deseret Evening News*, July 3, 1893, 4; *Deseret Evening News*, July 8, 1893, 3; *Deseret Evening News*, July 11, 1893, 1; *Deseret Evening News*, July 19, 1893, 1, 3; *Deseret Evening News*, July 20, 1893, 4; *Deseret Evening News*, August 24,

1893, 1; *Deseret Evening News,* November 25, 1893, 9; *Salt Lake Tribune,* June 2, 1893, 6; *Salt Lake Tribune,* July 1, 1893, 1, 6; *Salt Lake Tribune,* July 4, 1893, 1; *Salt Lake Tribune,* July 20, 1893, 1; *Salt Lake Tribune,* July 21, 1893, 1; *Salt Lake Tribune,* July 27, 1893, 1; *Salt Lake Herald,* June 13, 1893, 8; *Salt Lake Herald,* July 2, 1893, 4; *Salt Lake Herald,* July 4, 1893, 8; *Salt Lake Herald,* July 20, 1893, 4; *Salt Lake Herald,* July 21, 1893, 4; *Salt Lake Herald,* August 4, 1893, 4; *Salt Lake Herald,* August 6, 1893, 4; *Salt Lake Herald,* August 9, 1893, 4.

47. Heber J. Grant to Allie Ford, April 13, 1898, Grant Letterpress Copybook, 26:406–7; Memoranda on Claflin Note, Church Properties, Financial Department Papers, Church Archives.

48. Heber M. Wells to Heber J. Grant, [March 1921], Grant Letterpress Copybook, 57:671.

Heber J. Grant and
the Utah Loan and Trust Company

Before 6:00 A.M. on May 29, 1897, the portly and veteran Apostle Brigham Young Jr., himself ailing due to an attack of dropsy, called at the Heber J. Grant household to pray a blessing upon his associate. He found that "Bro Grant . . . had a poor night but he was going to the hospital with firm faith that all would be well." The day before, Grant awoke with severe lumbar and abdominal pain. The doctors diagnosed a ruptured appendix and advanced peritonitis and advised immediate surgery. As the hour-and-a-half operation progressed, the nine attending surgeons found "extraordinary suppuration and commenced mortification." After rotting the appendix and part of the colon, the infection had discharged a quart of pus throughout the stomach cavity. The chief surgeon turned to Joseph F. Smith, who was present at his friend's critical hour, and said, "My [Dear] Smith, you do not need to think of the possibility or probability of this man recovering." Only the doctor who monitored Grant's remarkably vigorous pulse disagreed.[1]

A fortnight later Elder Grant was propped on his pillows at the Catholic St. Mary's Hospital, celebrating the miracle of extended life. His recovery had been extraordinarily rapid, and his personal crisis had brought him an unexpected tide of sympathy and well-wishing. There was an added reason for rejoicing. His two visitors had a proposition that might mean the beginning of the end of his almost ninety thousand dollar indebtedness. The one with the dark mustache and slight Bristol accent began directly and hopefully. "Heber,"

Courtesy Church Archives, The Church of Jesus Christ of Latter-day Saints

Illus. 7-1. Elder Abraham H. Cannon attempted to save the Utah Loan and Trust Company in June 1896.

Thomas J. Stevens said, "would you like to make $15,600?"[2]

Stevens was bishop of Ogden City's Fifth Ward and Grant's long-time friend and brother-in-law (both had married daughters of Briant Stringham). Stevens and his companion, Matthew Browning, were respected Ogden citizens, but more to the point, they were directors and members of the executive committee of Ogden's Utah Loan and Trust Company (UL&T). In addition, two days before Stevens had been appointed the bank's cashier or general manager. The UL&T was on the verge of failure, and the two men had come to Grant hoping that a mutually advantageous deal might be struck.

The bank had proven an albatross to its owners almost from its founding in 1888. Charles Comstock Richards and Franklin S. Richards, sons of Ogden's Apostle and leading Latter-day Saint citizen, Franklin D. Richards, had taken the lead in establishing the firm. Utah was then booming and a spate of new banks was organized throughout the territory. But a banking panic in 1891 burst the speculative bubble, and the UL&T paid its last dividend in 1892. The following spring a fire gutted the interior of its handsome, five-story building.[3] Several months later, the severe Panic of 1893 almost delivered the *coup de grace*. Nevertheless, despite the bank's shrinking deposits and the decreasing values of its investment portfolio, the Richards brothers and their fellow investors managed to hold on for the next several years.[4]

When Elder Abraham H. Cannon (illus. 7-1) offered to buy controlling interest in the bank in June 1896, the Richards family relinquished their controlling interest at sixty cents on the dollar of their original investment. The depressed '90s had not been any more kind to Elder Cannon than to the Richardses, and he hoped to recoup his fortune by promoting a Salt Lake City to Los Angeles railroad, which, by using the UL&T as its financial agent, would revive the ailing bank. The details of the transactions reflected mutual desperation of both the buyer and the seller. To secure money to pay off the Richardses, the UL&T loaned Cannon $40,000 from its scanty reserves, with the Church leader offering as collateral his newly acquired UL&T stock along with some previously owned shares. As both partners in the transaction must have known, unless Cannon could quickly come up with money to pay off his debt, the deal seriously jeopardized the bank's liquidity.[5]

Six weeks later Abraham Cannon was dead, the result of a general inflammation to his head due to complications from ear surgery. Despite a $50,000 life insurance policy, his estate could not begin to pay his many debts, including the UL&T note, the most substantial debt. Since the default on Cannon's UL&T loan promised eventual bankruptcy to the financial institution, the UL&T stock that supposedly secured the loan was itself worthless.

At least for the moment, Elder Cannon's posthumous insolvency was concealed from public view. However there was another, more immediate factor working to undermine the bank. Two employees, Leon Graves and Clarence Barton, removed $5,200 from its vaults and fled east. Although Joseph A. West, then serving as cashier, mortgaged his home and quietly replaced the money, Utah newspapers discovered the truth and made the theft banner news. As a result, rumors began to circulate that the UL&T was in distress, and a slow but accelerating run on the bank commenced.[6]

Stevens and Browning believed they had an instant solution. If Grant would assume Cannon's note, the bank could then borrow on the strength of his signature and relieve its difficulties. In return, Grant could have all Cannon's forfeited collateral that, if the bank could be made sound, might be worth $15,600 more than the assumed loan. Grant expressed great interest. Despite his recent illness and short recuperation, he promised that he would soon go to Ogden to examine the matter more fully.

Grant seemed a logical candidate to help (illus. 7-2). Only his two families and a handful of intimate advisers knew the desperation of his own finances. As president or director of at least a dozen

Courtesy Church Archives, The Church of Jesus Christ of Latter-day Saints

Illus. 7-2. Elder Heber J. Grant rescued the UL&T from financial ruin, which also secured both the state's and the Church's financial standings.

Salt Lake City–based businesses, he appeared to the public to epitomize success. Besides, he had built a reputation for being a Mormon financial Horatius-at-the-bridge, successively saving ZCMI, the *Salt Lake Herald,* and the Utah Sugar Company from their respective problems. He had also compiled a successful record of special fundraising. In the late 1880s, he was one of five Saints who raised the legal and lobbying fees for Utah's statehood drive. Following the 1893 panic, when Salt Lake City's tax collector, who served as a bishop, mismanaged $32,000 in public funds, Grant led the campaign to pay off his debts quickly without embarrassing the Church. Indeed, when Church leaders saw a special need for money, Brother Heber increasingly received their call.

Elder Grant described what he found in Ogden as "a paralyzer." After he and Stevens scrutinized the bank's accounts, they concluded that many of them, to the amount of $75,000, were uncollectible. The prevailing hard times made it difficult for even honorable men to meet their obligations, and the UL&T clearly had been less than tough-minded in demanding payments on its outstanding loans. Worse, Grant found that the Ogden bank's financial statement was grossly inaccurate. Directors had spent most of the institution's assets in erecting the Utah Loan and Trust Building, but during the depression, along with most other Utah real estate, the imposing landmark suffered a calamitous deflation in value. Nevertheless, the bank carried the building on its books at the original construction cost of $275,000, although its actual market value scarcely exceeded the $75,000 lien that David Eccles had carried on it since its construction.

"If I were as sure of getting to heaven as Dave Eccles . . . will get that [bank] corner," Elder Grant told his fellow General Authorities several weeks later in one of their Thursday meetings, "I would think I had a ticket paid for." The UL&T's reconstructed balance sheet bore out the likelihood of a foreclosure. Liabilities were listed at $162,000 and assets at $107,000, but half of the latter were judged to be of questionable quality. Grant reported that the bank's capital was "wiped off the earth" and that depositors were sure to lose most of their money.[7]

The Twelve did not immediately grasp how chilling this news actually was. Driven by his passion for building and protecting the material things of the kingdom, Grant had spent several days investigating before he himself had understood. He now shared his grim findings. A UL&T failure would bring great personal loss to its owners and depositors, and as these effects rippled outward, the result would be a sharp blow to Utah's already faltering economy. Moreover, while the Church itself owned no stock in the institution, its interests and those of its leaders were very much at stake. Since its founding, the UL&T had been regarded as "a Mormon institution," one of Utah's private businesses that functioned in behalf of the Church. Its officers, directors, and leading stockholders were a "Who's Who" of Ogden's Church officials. In addition, General Authorities Joseph F. Smith and Francis M. Lyman owned stock and served as directors—Elder Smith in fact had briefly succeeded Abraham Cannon as president of the banking firm. The times were so precarious that a UL&T failure, to the great embarrassment of the Church, would bring bankruptcy upon most of its Mormon shareholders as well as reveal the posthumous insolvency of Abraham Cannon.[8]

Unfortunately, difficulties did not stop here. Since the early 1890s, the Church's finances had rested precariously, partly because of the earlier Edmunds-Tucker confiscations of Church property, but more significantly because the First Presidency had responded to the depression with a series of deficit-financed public works. Every several months and sometimes more often, Mormon debt managers performed extraordinary feats just to meet payments and preserve credit. Now came the warning from the Church's loan agent in the East that because of the Ogden bank's links with ecclesiastical officials, its failure would "almost sure[ly]" cause eastern bankers to demand payment on existing Mormon loans—a development tantamount to forcing the Church into receivership. Grant would later learn something just as explosive. Utah law made bank officers criminally culpable for receiving deposits after an institution's liabilities exceeded its assets. While such a question lent itself to endless litigation, the statute exposed Smith, Lyman, and virtually the entire Church hierarchy in Ogden to criminal prosecution. Given the reigning Mormon-Gentile hostility in the "Junction City," with Church opponents firmly in control of the levers of local power, the possibility could not be idly waved aside.[9]

Grant's grim and forceful report to the Twelve was convincing. On July 2, 1897, a committee of George Q. Cannon, Joseph F. Smith, Lorenzo Snow, Francis M. Lyman, John Henry Smith, and Grant met for three hours to consider the problem again. The men finally agreed that "it would be a great misfortune if disaster should overtake the Bank" and if necessary Church influence should be exerted to strengthen the institution. Four days later, the General Authorities further embroiled the Church in the UL&T affair. The two Mormon banks in Salt Lake City, Zion's Savings Bank and the State Bank of Utah, were asked if they would assume respectively the UL&T's savings and commercial banking business. In case of failure, Stevens reported, "they promised to stand behind us . . . so that the depositors will be paid in full." What had begun as a possible private investment for Grant had become a project embraced by the Church.[10]

Grant had discovered the UL&T problem and sounded the tocsin, but having done so, he temporarily, although involuntarily, retired from the field. About six weeks after his appendectomy, he contracted "pleuro-pneumonia." Again his friends feared for his life, and for three months the convalescing leader retired from public affairs.

The UL&T crisis did not ease in his absence. Encouraged by promises from Church headquarters, Thomas Stevens briefly stemmed the run on the bank's reserves by looking depositors in the eye and pledging the safety of their money. Still, his behavior did nothing to change the huge imbalance between the bank's assets and liabilities. Nor did Zion's Savings and the State Bank, the two Salt Lake City banks affiliated with the Church, alter the situation. Neither Zion's Savings nor the State Bank, themselves little more robust than their sister institution, desired to sink under the heavy and perhaps fatal weight of the UL&T accounts. By August, President Wilford Woodruff admitted that the UL&T case was "not very encouraging," and offered as a hand-wringing expedient the formation of a two-man committee to study possible solutions.[11]

Former cashier Joseph West was the first to show how weak the bank really was. For several weeks he had badgered the hard-pressed directors to reimburse him for the $5,200 he had paid to cover the Graves-Barton theft. Frustrated by their lack of action and by his dismissal from the firm only hours before, he took the amount from the safe and was leaving town when his son Walker West compelled the return of the money. If he had left, the act could have brought an immediate closing.[12]

West's desperation was an indication of how difficult the times were becoming. The worst of the depression occurred in winter 1893–94, when Utah's urban unemployment exceeded 25 percent and some laborers in Salt Lake City marched to demand "bread or blood." At the same time fourteen hundred unruly "Commonwealers"—out-of-work Californians traveling East to protest the prevailing scarcity—were camped in Ogden City. However, for many Mormon institutions and men the years 1897–98 were almost as severe. Earlier these men had been able to parry their debts, but as real estate and stock values continued to fall, the men no longer had collateral to renew their loans. By late 1897 the Church itself owed over two million dollars and was looking for another loan of like amount.[13]

Thus, the UL&T crisis peaked at the very time when the Church and its leading men were least prepared to deal with it. During the last week of January 1898, Stevens repeatedly importuned the First Presidency for something more than moral or makeshift help, but he was turned away. A week later there could be no more temporizing. Stevens flatly told the General Authorities that the bank could not open the next day without assistance.[14] After protracted and agonizing discussion, aid was forthcoming. Zion's Savings loaned $5,000, and the Church itself eventually took a $15,000 second mortgage on the UL&T building and apparently advanced the bank about $7,500 besides.[15]

Everyone realized that such aid was a stopgap, which ran the risk of throwing good after bad money. Grant, whose regained health and consuming interest won him his church's commission to

Illus. 7-3. David Eccles, president of the Ogden First National Bank, a competitor of UL&T.

resolve the UL&T problem, saw two possible long-range solutions. First, he hoped to interest enough public-spirited Latter-day Saint capitalists to buy the UL&T building at $150,000 or twice its existing value. While such a proposal made little sense to men used to maximizing personal profits, Grant reasoned that as the depression eased and property values rebounded, investors eventually would be out little and might receive a small return for their philanthropy. Meanwhile, the bank could use the money to cover its two mortgages (the first to Eccles for $75,000 and the second to the Church for $15,000), pay off its other loans, and perhaps have enough working capital to ride out the rest of the hard times.[16]

Grant's alternative idea involved David Eccles, Utah's first bona fide tycoon. Son of a nearly blind and impoverished wood turner, the handsome Eccles had his fingers in most financial pies in Ogden (illus. 7-3). Since 1894 he had served as president of the Ogden First National Bank, situated across the street from the UL&T building on 24th Street and Washington Avenue. Grant proposed that Eccles be allowed to foreclose on his mortgage and secure the UL&T building at a bargain basement price. In return, the First National Bank would assume its neighbor's accounts and allow it to retire honorably from business. For some time Eccles's bank had apparently thought of splitting off its savings business and starting a new institution. The splendid UL&T building would provide excellent quarters.[17]

Elder Grant vigorously pursued both options during late winter and early spring 1898. He repeatedly approached his friends to invest in the UL&T building, and in an attempt to provide financing for such a sale, he traveled to San Francisco and wrote letters to prospective lenders throughout the Intermountain West. In addition, he personally propositioned Eccles at his Baker City, Oregon, lumber headquarters. Unfortunately his work yielded little fruit. His drive to get $150,000 to purchase the bank building stalled one-third short of the goal, though Grant himself promised $10,000 and the Church another $25,000. On the other hand, the canny Eccles, whose considerable charities rarely trespassed upon the bounds of "sound business," listened impassively to Grant's appeals. Barring something unforeseen, he knew he had the building already—without making further commitments. By April, Grant was having trouble keeping the flame of his enthusiasm lit. "Looking at it naturally," he admitted, "there is little prospect of success crowning my efforts."[18]

Finally, another of the Ogden bank's intermittent crises broke the logjam. Anders Larsen, a disgruntled depositor who believed that his money had been negligently loaned, filed a lawsuit that declared the bank to be "utterly insolvent," with "no property with which to pay its debts."[19] With confidence in the bank already fragile, Larsen's suit precipitated another run on reserves. By the first of August, Stevens was again before the General Authorities, hat in hand, pleading that without help he would be unable to open the next day.[20]

On August 8, with three UL&T directors present, Church officials now began their most decisive discussion of the question. "The object of the interview," the Journal History of the Church recorded, "was to make a last representation of the bank's condition, in the hope—almost forlorn with these [UL&T] brethren—that the Presidency might be able to see their way clear to do something to save it." Joseph F. Smith began with an eloquent appeal for further Church aid, but when President Woodruff refused to countenance the idea, Smith moved that the bank be allowed to fail. Not wishing to appear self-serving or disloyal, he plaintively admitted: "We honestly put up our money, and let us [now] take our medicine."[21]

Grant's was the only voice that spoke against the overwhelming consensus. "I hope that no one will second that motion," he asked as he pled that the earlier comments of Smith and Woodruff be stricken from the record. His previous loan brokering in the East gave him a sense of the crisis that his colleagues did not have. Besides, he was typically loath to abandon any fixed idea or determined project. Confronted by his strong opposition, the General Authorities moved to a middle ground. Rather than have the financially strapped church give aid to the bank, Smith proposed that Grant be deputized to solicit money from its most prosperous members. Grant willingly consented but believed he required help. He asked the First Presidency to call Elder Matthias Cowley to assist him and to sign a strongly worded letter endorsing the project. Grant remained outspoken. "You can either sign," he said to the First Presidency, "or let the bank go to pot." Accordingly they not only signed the letter Grant had written but also appended a paragraph that blessed those complying with its request.[22]

Grant's demands were reasonable given the magnitude of his assignment. Earlier he had attempted to organize a UL&T syndicate, which promised investors the hope of a small gain. Now hard-nosed businessmen, who were not disposed to cover the mistakes of others, were to be asked for gratuitous donations that would have to exceed $75,000. Furthermore, he was handcuffed by the demands of sensitivity and confidentiality. To reveal the actual condition of the bank invited additional pressure upon its deposits. Nor could he, without defeating his purposes, fully explain how the UL&T's health directly related to the reputation of some of the leading brethren and indirectly to the credit of the Church. At best he could ambiguously appeal to patriotic Saints to maintain "an institution of Zion" and to sustain "the brethren."

Before the meeting of the General Authorities adjourned, Elder Grant began his fundraising. Hoping to realize a profit on the sale of his last remaining, under-mortgaged real estate, he personally pledged $2,500 and challenged his brethren to follow suit. President George Q. Cannon, whose Bullion-Beck and Champion Mine dividends made him more prosperous than the rest, promised another $5,000 and drafted a $2,000 check as first installment. Grant's donation came at genuine financial peril to himself and his creditors. "I donated $2,500," he recalled, "when all I had on earth . . . would not pay my debts within $88,800 and this donation made me over ninety thousand dollars worse off than nothing." He spent the rest of the day gaining the approval of the men who had countersigned his many notes. Because of his donation, his creditors stood one step closer to having to cover his debts.[23]

Within the week Grant was stalking his quarry. First he asked $2,500 from Alfred W. McCune, a successful mining speculator and soon to be a candidate for the U.S. Senate. McCune's family of origin and his wife were Church members, but his moods and behavior were those of a sourdough miner who had found the proverbial rich strike. "Not one damned dollar," was the rough-hewn miner's first response. It was not that McCune was parsimonious; his lavish spending and occasional philanthropy fit into the Gilded Age's high style. But he was deeply prejudiced against banks. He had never placed money in one and never expected to do so. Rebuffed, Grant tried to shift the question to high moral ground. He pulled the First Presidency's UL&T letter from his pocket and in the name of McCune's believing wife asked if he wished to deny the request of the Lord's representatives?[24]

"O hell, you cannot scare me with a thing like that," the mining man answered. He acknowledged his desire to be liberal but not to conceal the incompetency of a parasitic banker.

"Alf, I defy you to look me in the eye as man to man and tell me that you do not know the Gospel is true," Grant replied. "You do know it. You gamble and swear when you get mad, and you drink whiskey and raise hell generally, . . . and you say there is nothing in religion. But I defy you to tell me that you do not know the Gospel that your father embraced is true."

"I do not," McCune began strongly, then mellowing, he said, "I will make a confession to you. I will be honest with you. Damned if I am not afraid it is."

Unfortunately, McCune's tepid confession failed to loosen his purse strings, and Grant resolved on stronger measures. Like Nephi before the drunken Laban, he felt inspired to descend to a lower standard. "Abuse him," his inner voice seemed to direct, "tell him he is not generous, that he is close-fisted, use his own language, go right after him in his own vernacular, and you will get your money."

"You are a hell of a generous cuss," Grant began his assault with an idiom quite beyond his normal use. "The idea of you with all your money refusing to give me two days' income from one mine. . . . What am I doing? I am giving $2,500. How am I fixed financially? I am a hell of a poor manager financially. I have two wives, and neither one has a home. I have a home for my mother that is mortgaged. . . . I have the children of a dead wife to support and I am over $50,000 worse off than nothing, yet I am giving the equivalent of two years and a half of my net surplus. I am only earning a thousand dollars a year above my expenses, . . . and you are so generous that you won't give two days' income from one mine. You are a generous cuss."

"Damn you," McCune responded. "Tell that story over again." When Grant rehearsed his tale, which actually minimized his debts, the incredulous McCune called for his secretary to pay Grant $5,000. "Damned if I am not going to pay your donation and mine too."

For a moment Grant was elated by McCune's generosity and thanked the Lord for the unexpected aid. But he quickly changed his mind, reasoning that if he let McCune pay his own donation, he would lose the "power to appeal to others . . . and that the Bank must break." Despite feeling "a very great temptation," he refused the offer.

Claiming that Grant was "the strangest man he had ever met," McCune took the check from his secretary, briefly looked at it, and finally extended it. "You have a hell of a job on your hands, damned if I will tear it up. I cannot understand why you won't let me pay your donation. [But] give your bank the $5,000."

Later when Grant, in one of his few partisan ventures, stoutly campaigned for McCune's senatorial candidacy, there were rumors that he had been bought. But Grant's politics were more than an appreciation for a $5,000 donation. Despite their polar differences in personality and character, Grant had found in their banter a human tie that, at least for the moment, made them friends.

Having done so well with McCune, Grant approached Jesse Knight. A short man with a walrus mustache and given to wearing Homburg hats, Knight was the son of two of Mormonism's earliest converts, Newel and Lydia Knight. However Jesse had waited until middle age to bud his own faith, which was shortly thereafter followed by good fortune. Friends had cried "humbug" when Knight told of a voice which he interpreted was directing him to stake out a mining claim—a claim he later said would save the Church's credit. But in 1896 the appropriately named "Humbug mine" became a bonanza. Obedient to his presentiment, he began to pay tithes and benefactions, which in their time became legendary.[25]

But if Grant expected an easy touch he was mistaken. After listening to his impassioned recital of the UL&T's problems and his request for $5,000, Knight was unyielding.

"Brother Grant, I do not think the Lord wants me to give anything to make good the mistakes of people who put their money in a bank and lost it. I am willing to help the poor and to pay an honest tithing, and to help in all things like universities [his donation to Brigham Young Academy in Provo kept the incipient institution alive], but I do not feel that I ought to do this. I won't give you a dollar."[26]

"Jesse, I will not take no for an answer. I shall come back again."

"There is supper, bed and breakfast for you here any time," the Provo resident responded, "Come along, but you won't get any money."

During Grant's third interview with Knight in as many weeks, Reed Smoot was present. A young businessman-politician who was soon to be called to the Quorum of Twelve Apostles, Smoot was trying to pacify Grant with a $500 donation. "If you send me a check for $500, Reed, I shall send it back to you," was Grant's reply. "I won't have it. This mission is a very hard one, and I cannot put you in the $500 class, you belong in the $1000 class. . . . Let me give you some parental advice. When you get home tonight get down on your knees and pray to the Lord to give you enlargement of the heart, and send me a check for $1,000."

Knight could not suppress his delight and laughed. It was a relief to have someone else on Grant's skewer for a moment. Knight and Smoot were long-standing political opponents, and Knight felt a devilish relish in having his friendly foe under attack. But Grant's challenge to Smoot bothered the devout Knight. "Why didn't you ask me to pray?" he asked the Apostle.

"I would if you had offered me $2,500, but what is the good of asking a man to pray who won't give you anything?"

Knight turned defensive. "Well, Heber Grant. I pray to the Lord, and I think the Lord has given me all that I have. I will pray, and I won't pray with my lips, I will pray with my heart to the Lord, and if he impresses me to give you $5,000 you shall have it as free as the air."

"Jesse, I am just as sure of getting that $5,000 as that guns are made of iron, if you will honestly pray to the Lord about it."

Two days later, Grant received in the mail a check for $11,000; $10,000 from Jesse Knight and another $1,000 from Reed Smoot. Knight explained:

Heber, if you ever come to me again with a letter from the Presidency of the Church, calling you on a mission to raise funds, whatever you ask me for I am going to give it to you; I am not going to pray about it. When I got through praying, it rang in my head just like a tune, over and over again, "give Heber ten thousand dollars; give Heber ten thousand dollars; give Heber ten thousand dollars." I got out of bed and told the Lord that I was not praying about any $10,000. Heber hadn't asked me for $10,000. I went to bed again. "Give Heber ten thousand dollars; give Heber ten thousand dollars; give Heber ten thousand dollars."

With the refrain continuing to reverberate through his mind, Knight withdrew the bulk of his savings the next morning and successfully pressed Smoot for his $1,000. More than aiding the UL&T, their contributions came as a soothing balm to the "tired and nervous" Grant, who for the past week could sleep no later than 5 A.M. and was often up two hours earlier. "When I got your letter [and check] I could have shouted for joy," he wrote Smoot and Knight. "I have never doubted my ability to succeed in connection with Brother Cowley in making this mission a success. I have, however, looked forward with anxiety and dread to the labor ahead of us."[27]

Having employed his persuasive powers to their fullest upon McCune, Knight, and Smoot, Elder Grant must have viewed William H. Smart's donation as latter-day manna. Smart was a thirty-six-year-old Idaho livestock dealer who had been called to preside over the Brooklyn Conference in the Eastern States Mission. When his niece Luella Cowley had written that her husband, Matthias Cowley, had been assigned to help save the UL&T, Smart offered between the wide range of $1,000 and $20,000. "I thank God He has made it possible for us to make this donation," he wrote in his diary, "but more especially do I thank Him for the faith He has given to prompt it." Smart eventually settled on $5,000 for his gift, half of which his business partner James W. Webster volunteered to pay.[28]

At last, the tide seemed to be turning in the Ogden bank's favor. While the Smart-Webster contribution remained confidential at Smart's request, Grant used the gifts of McCune and Knight, as well as his own, to build momentum and to rally the Saints. He and his wife Augusta personally typed hundreds of letters, often working late into the evenings, asking prominent Mormons to follow their example. Even more effective were the entreaties of Grant and Cowley as they visited the stakes of Zion. After presiding over the meetings of a stake conference, Grant typically would invite Church leaders and prosperous members to a special meeting. After reading the First Presidency's letter and touching upon UL&T matters (the comprehensiveness of his explanation seemed to vary with the occasion), he would then solicit an immediate and public response. "When my name was called," complained one participant who believed that he pledged beyond his means, "I did not feel like saying that I could not or would not do anything. Others had proffered to give one hundred dollars and I told Brother Grant that he might put $100 opposite my name." The hard-sell formula worked. "I am meeting with splendid success in getting the funds needed to save that Ogden business," Grant reported.[29]

Many Saints didn't need any more persuasion than the news that the Church was in need. "Brother Grant, don't you ever waste your time," Ephraim Ellison replied after the Church leader personally requested his donation in Layton, Utah: "It takes you all day to ride up here and back again—two days. If you are ever called on a[nother] mission by the Presidency of the Church, if you feel that I ought to give you $200 or $300 or some other amount just write me a letter and I will give it to you. Do not take the time to come up." Another Church member, John Scowcroft of Ogden, gave $500 and promised to double the amount if his new business prospered. Later the additional $500 was forthcoming without Grant's reminder.[30]

As usual, Grant was a forceful and determined campaigner. When the financially strapped George F. Richards offered $100 (to do so he was forced to sell three hundred bushels of his stored grain), Grant complained to Richards's ecclesiastical superiors that he was not doing his share to save the institution his family had founded. Grant later apologized to Richards for presuming to prescribe the bounds of another's generosity. He was particularly scathing with UL&T stockholders who, despite their liability for part of the firms debts, refused to give anything until Grant strongly implored them. And Grant was apoplectic when his old-time friend, George Romney, announced second thoughts about donating. After Grant's paroxysm of temper, Romney's business firm made good its $1,000 pledge.[31]

After five months of such fundraising. Grant triumphantly paid off Abraham Cannon's note. Executors of his estate had scraped together $15,000, but the bulk of the money came from Grant's campaigning. "I have labored earnestly in this matter," Grant wrote Stevens, "and one of the main reasons for doing so has been my desire to maintain Abraham's good name. I feel confident that had I passed away from life, and he been permitted to live, that he would have labored with equal zeal to try and preserve my honor and good name in the community." Indeed, Grant's zeal in behalf of the UL&T owed at least some of its intensity to the realization that his own poor health and debts had almost decreed for him a similar fate.[32]

However, after his success with the Cannon note, the remainder of Elder Grant's crusade was entirely uphill. Earlier fundraising had skimmed off most of the ready donations, while tight-fisted businessmen now used rumors of the bank's mismanagement to excuse themselves from making or fulfilling pledges. For instance, when one member of a stake presidency grandiloquently promised "his time, his talent, [and] his substance" to the Kingdom in a public prayer, Grant immediately closed in for a donation. But he soon learned that the man's dedication of means "was done believing that the Lord would not come to ask for any part of it." Such categorical refusals became common. Instead of money, Grant complained he now received "insults and slurs," with some of his fellow church leaders speaking at cross-purposes behind his back. As a result, he frankly and dejectedly labeled his assignment as "one of the most unpleasant tasks of my life."[33]

With the bank losing customers and cash daily, Grant reexamined his options. Eccles again refused any tangible help, citing the need to maintain proper and conservative business dealing, but he did promise any buyer of the UL&T building a $5,000 discount on his $75,000 mortgage. As a year earlier, Grant could find no one with the money to purchase the structure or refinance it. In October 1899, there seemed but one remaining possibility. At great risk to himself financially, Grant offered to take over the business. The plan had nothing to recommend it save audacity, and like his Utah Sugar Company financing a half decade earlier, he was in effect laying everything he possessed upon the altar. "You and I are engaged in the work of the Lord," he would explain later to a correspondent. "We are called upon from time to time to make sacrifices, and in no case where we do our duty will we fail in being rewarded." However, he put the scheme aside upon realizing that if he should revive the business and make it profitable, some UL&T donors would suspect that he had used their money to enrich himself.[34]

In early 1900, Grant returned from an extensive tour of the Mormon settlements in Arizona and Mexico to learn the reality of his worst fears. The UL&T was once more on the edge of collapse, threatening this time to take with it the money Grant had so arduously raised. With his efforts appearing futile and misspent, he retired to the Apostles' Room of the Salt Lake Temple to supplicate the Lord to save the bank. The bank examiner's report showed good reason for prayer. For over a month the bank's cash reserves had fallen well under the legal limit. "This bank ought to fix up its affairs," the examiner wrote, "or go out of the business entirely." Only the examiner's leniency forestalled immediate legal action.[35]

At the UL&T's moment of final peril, the Church's new president, Lorenzo Snow, moved to rescue it. Snow believed that it was unthinkable to allow a failure, especially since the Church had committed itself and its members in the semipublic efforts of Elders Grant and Cowley to assist it. Fortunately, he had the resources available to cauterize the long-festering wound. During his brief leadership, he had reduced ordinary expenditures, slashed at deficit-financed programs, and preached tithing with a fury. With his efforts happily coinciding with a general economic upturn, the Church assumed a financial stability it had not known for a decade.

As a preliminary step, President Snow requested Elders Grant and Smoot to audit the Ogden bank's books again. Their report was an oriental dish of sweet and sour. Despite Utah's worst to-date depression and the unpopularity of the cause among many businessmen, Grant and Cowley had raised over $50,000 in hard cash and estimated that at least $15,000 of the remaining pledges were good. However, after adding these figures to the bank's $30,000 assets, the institution still lacked $30,000 to cover its deposits. President Snow promised to provide most of this figure if the pledges were vigorously prosecuted.[36]

"I will not know how to express my feelings of relief and gratitude if I am ever successful, in connection with my assistants, in honorably winding up this business," Grant lamented as he took again to the circuit. During spring and summer 1900, in the absence of Cowley who was elsewhere on assignment, Elders Grant and Smoot repeatedly traveled to Ogden to persuade the recalcitrant to donate and to manage the UL&T's final act. The outstanding commitments to support the bank were generally paid. The Browning family fulfilled its $5,000 pledge and Eccles, after three years temporizing, promised to do likewise, contingent upon the bank's final closing. Ironically, the UL&T directors closed up the business and requested depositors to call for their money on the same day, August 31, 1900, that Thomas Stevens, whose probity and reputation had done so much to keep the bank afloat, died.[37]

With the exception of the UL&T shareholders who lost their investments, most of the participants in the crisis did remarkably well. Joseph West, who as cashier approved Abraham Cannon's loan and began the crisis, recovered the $5,200 he had lent the bank, and after a lawsuit he apparently secured interest on the amount as well. David Eccles proved anew his Midas touch. Six months after receiving the UL&T property for his $75,000 mortgage, he had the opportunity of selling the building for a 20 percent premium. Within a few years, it was worth twice that amount. Grant also prospered, despite his three-and-a-half year preoccupation with the UL&T. By purchasing every option, future, and share of the rapidly appreciating Utah Sugar Company that he could get his hands on, Grant was solvent with a slight margin to spare when he sailed for his Japanese mission in 1901. Finally, the Church, which spent $50,000 in subsidies and lost loans on the UL&T, paid a small price for rescuing its depositors, shoring up Ogden City's economy, saving the financial reputations of some of its leaders, and maintaining its own credit.

Fifteen years later, Francis M. Lyman called Elder Grant into his office. Lyman was dying and wished to say good-bye to the man whom he believed would soon be Church President. "Heber," he said,

> I have been reviewing your life and your accomplishments, and I want you to know that I owe my honor and my good name, and so does the prophet of God, Joseph F. Smith to you. . . . No matter whatever comes to you of importance, no matter what great labor you may perform, in my judgment you will never do anything greater than the saving of that bank, and having men put their money in a rat hole.

Even though public subscriptions by themselves were inadequate, Grant's efforts had gained the UL&T time and certainly the bank would have broken without him.[38]

During his later years as Church President, Grant did not disagree with Lyman's estimate. He realized that he had saved Mormon finances and preserved the reputations of many friends, including three General Authorities whom he deeply respected. Moreover, he seemed to perceive how the episode had changed his own life. "I had faith that the Utah Loan and Trust Co. could be saved when I fear that every member of the Presidency and Apostles were lacking in faith," he concluded. "We are all made different and have different degrees of faith on different matters. It takes all kinds for our quorum."[39] Elder Grant had long felt apprehensive and even at times unworthy of his calling because of his financial and practical orientation. Yet, because of his labors with the UL&T, he learned to accept his talents rather than to apologize or feel frustrated because of them.

Notes

This article was originally published in *Journal of Mormon History* 8 (1981): 21–36.

1. Brigham Young's observation: Brigham Young Jr., Diary, May 29, 1897, Brigham Young Papers, Church Archives, The Church of Jesus Christ of Latter-day Saints, Salt Lake City. Announcement of the operation: "Hon. H. J. Grant Ill," *Deseret Evening News*, May 29, 1897, 2; "Heber J. Grant Very Ill," *Salt Lake Herald*, May 29, 1897, 8; and Franklin D. Richards, Diary, May 29, 1897, Franklin D. Richards Papers, Church Archives. Prognosis: Penciled Heber J. Grant Memorandum, undated, box 177, fd. 3, Heber J. Grant Papers, Church Archives.

2. Thomas J. Stevens, Diary, typescript, June 12, 1897, Church Archives; Heber J. Grant, "An Interesting Experience as Related by President Grant," March 18, 1941, 1, Grant Papers.

3. Miscellaneous Notes, in Bank Examiner's Report, July 29, 1897, Bank Examiner's Reports, 1891–99, Administrative Reports of the Secretary of State, Utah Archives, Annex, Salt Lake City.

4. Stevens, Diary, March 14, 1893. Trouble in 1893: Heber J. Grant to Heber M. Wells, July 11, 1893, Grant Letterpress Copybook, 17:155, Grant Papers.

5. Charles Comstock Richards, *Autobiography of Charles Comstock Richards* (n.p.: privately printed, n.d.), 178–80; Journal History of The Church of Jesus Christ of Latter-day Saints, February 5, 1901, Church Archives, microfilm

copy in Harold B. Lee Library, Brigham Young University, Provo, Utah; Grant, "Interesting Experience," 1. While Franklin D. Richards, who owned a few UL&T shares himself, described the transaction as giving "a precious relief to a few who have borne the crushing burden in and during the past Financial Panic," the deal left the Richards family with heavy debts. In its aftermath the Apostle sought personal financial relief from the Church. See Richards, Diary, June 1, 1896; Franklin D. Richards to Presidents Wilford Woodruff, George Q. Cannon, and Joseph F. Smith, June 1896, Letterbook 1896–98, Richards Papers; and Stevens, Diary, June 17, 1897.

6. Stevens, Diary, March 27, April 26, 27, and May 1, 1897.

7. Grant, "Interesting Experience," 1–2; Richards, Diary, July 6, 1897.

8. In addition to those already mentioned, Lewis W. Shurtliff, Charles F. Middleton, Nils C. Flygare, John Watson, Henry H. Rolapp, Frank J. Cannon, Ephraim H. Nye, Thomas D. Dee, James H. Moyle, and Daniel Hamer were at various times associated with the bank. The first three constituted the Weber Stake Presidency.

9. For a preliminary study of Utah finances during the nineties, see also Leonard J. Arrington, "Utah and the Depression of the 1890's," *Utah Historical Quarterly* 29 (January 1961): 3–18. The timing of the statement of the Church's loan agent, who must have been Frank J. Cannon, is unclear. See Heber J. Grant and Matthias F. Cowley to George Osmond and Counselors, December 6, 1898, Grant Letterpress Copybook, 28:357. Culpability: Heber J. Grant, Typed Diary, February 24, 1898, Grant Papers.

10. Journal History, July 1, 2, and 6, 1897; Richards, Diary, July 6, 1897; Stevens, Diary, July 6, 1897; Charles Middleton, Diary, July 6, 1897, Church Archives.

11. Steven's conduct: Grant, Typed Diary, September 2, 1900. Woodruff: Wilford Woodruff, Diary, August 10 and 26, 1897, Wilford Woodruff Papers, Church Archives.

12. Stevens, Diary, August 16 and 17, 1897.

13. 1893–94 Depression: Abraham H. Cannon, Diary, typescript, February 14, March 28, and May 29, 1894, Church Archives; Stevens, Diary, April 8 and 11, and July 8, 1894. Church debt: John Henry Smith, Diary, typescript, December 23 and 24, 1897, Church Archives.

14. Stevens's importuning: Stevens, Diary, January 22, 24, and 26, 1898. Joseph F. Smith wanted to extend aid but had "no hope for sympathy or encouragement from bros. C[annon] and W[oodruff]," Joseph F. Smith to Thomas J. Stevens, January 25, 1898, Joseph F. Smith Letterbook, Joseph F. Smith Papers, Church Archives.

15. General Authority meeting: Richards, Diary, February 4, 1898; Grant, Typed Diary, February 4, 1898. Aid to UL&T: Heber J. Grant to John Watson, April 2, 1898, Grant Letterpress Copybook, 26:392–93. Second mortgage: Copy of memorandum on Transfer of Second Mortgage, Grant Letterpress Copybook, 31:512.

16. Heber J. Grant to J. A. Murray, February 26, 1898, Grant Letterpress

Copybook, 26:356, illustrates his UL&T proposals.

17. Leonard J. Arrington, *David Eccles: Pioneer Western Industrialist* (Utah State University: Logan, 1975), 5–6, 257–58; Heber J. Grant to Thomas J. Stevens, April 13, 1898, Grant Letterpress Copybook, 26:410.

18. San Francisco: Stevens, Diary, February 21, 1898. Letters: Heber J. Grant to J. A. Murray, February 26, 1898. Eccles: Heber J. Grant to Utah Loan & Trust Company, May 14, 1898, Grant Letterpress Copybook, 26:496. Little prospect: Heber J. Grant to W. W. Maughan, April 20, 1898, Grant Letterpress Copybook, 26:416.

19. Suit: Anders Larsen v. Utah Loan and Trust, filed May 25, 1898, Case #723, Third Circuit Court, Utah State Archives.

20. Suit: Anders Larsen v. Utah Loan and Trust, filed May 25, 1898, Case #723, Third Circuit Court, Utah State Archives; Middleton, Diary, April 4, 1900. Bank reserves: Stevens, Diary, August 7 and 8, 1898.

21. Journal History, August 8, 1898; Grant "Interesting Experience," 2.

22. Grant, "Interesting Experience," 2; Heber J. Grant, "President Grant's Story about Saving the Ogden Bank," Memorandum, box 177, fd. 7, Grant Papers; Grant, Typed Diary, August 8, 1898. All diaries suggest that the climaxing meeting of the brethren was held on August 8, 1898, although the extract in Grant's Letterpress Copybook, 26:639–40 is dated two days later. The text reads as follows:

> This letter will be presented to you by Elders Heber J. Grant and Matthias F. Cowley, and we ask you to treat as confidential all communications which they may make to you.
>
> We have called these brethren on a mission to raise the funds necessary to save one of the institutions of Zion from making an assignment. We feel that it would be a great calamity to have it fail as it would injure the credit of the Latter-day Saints as a community, and to maintain the community credit is something that should appeal to the patriotism of every true Latter-day Saint.
>
> We appeal to you to render to these brethren all the financial aid that your circumstances will admit of, and also to assist them to the full extent of your ability to secure means from any of the saints residing in your Wards whom you feel are able to aid in this matter.
>
> We fully appreciate the fact that the saints have very many calls made upon them, but notwithstanding this, as sacrifice brings forth the blessings of heaven, we do not hesitate to appeal to you for aid in this matter, knowing that every sacrifice made in aiding any of the institutions of Zion will be sure to bring an ample reward from our Father in Heaven.
>
> We assure you that we shall appreciate very much indeed all you shall do to aid the brethren in making their mission

a success.

A subsequent version of the text without detailing its relationship to the Utah Loan and Trust Company is found in James R. Clark, ed., *Messages of the First Presidency* (Salt Lake City: Bookcraft, 1966), 3:305–6.

23. Donations: Stevens, Diary, August 8, 1898; Grant, Typed Diary, August 8, 1898. Statement on debts: Heber J. Grant to John Henry Smith, January 18, 1902, Grant Letterpress Copybook, 34:267, Grant Papers. Clearing with endorsers: Heber J. Grant to Anthony W. Ivins, August 19, 1898, Grant Letterpress Copybook, 26:666.

24. The following episode with its dialogue is preserved in Grant, "Interesting Experience," 3–8; Grant, "Saving the Ogden Bank," 3–6; Grant, Typed Diary, August 13, 1898; and Heber J. Grant to Rudger Clawson, July 1, 1903, Grant Letterpress Copybook, 36:462–63.

25. Andrew Jenson, *Latter-day Saint Biographical Encyclopedia: A Compilation of Biographical Sketches of Prominent Men and Women in The Church of Jesus Christ of Latter-day Saints,* 4 vols. (Salt Lake City: Andrew Jenson History, 1901–36), 2:776–77; Jesse William Knight, *The Jesse Knight Family: Jesse Knight, His Forebears and Family* ([Salt Lake City]: Deseret News Press, 1841), 37–41, 82–87.

26. See Grant, "Interesting Experience," 10–12.

27. No sleep: Heber J. Grant to Spencer Clawson, September 3, 1898, Grant Letterpress Copybook, 28:5; Heber J. Grant to Jesse Knight and Reed Smoot, September 3, 1898, Grant Letterpress Copybook, 28:1–2; Heber J. Grant, Manuscript Diary, December 20, 1898, Grant Papers.

28. W. H. Smart to Matthias F. Cowley, September 7, 1898, Grant Letterpress Copybook, 28:165–66; William H. Smart, Diary, September 30, October 3, 10, 12 and 31, and November 1 and 22, 1898, Church Archives.

29. Heber and Augusta letter writing: Grant, Manuscript Diary, December 9, 1898; and Grant Letterpress Copybooks for the period. Complaint: William E. Bassett to Lorenzo Snow, George Q. Cannon, and Joseph F. Smith, December 7, 1898, Lorenzo Snow Papers, Church Archives. Meeting with success: Heber J. Grant to Anthony W. Ivins, August 27, 1898, Grant Letterpress Copybook, 26:678.

30. Grant, "Saving the Ogden Bank," 6–7.

31. Richards's payment: George F. Richards, Diary, October 10, 1898, Church Archives; Heber J. Grant to George F. Richards, undated, in Grant, Manuscript Diary, October 8, 1898. Romney: Grant, Manuscript Diary, December 15 and 17, 1898.

32. Heber J. Grant to Thomas J. Stevens, January 6, 1899, Grant Letterpress Copybook, 28:524–25.

33. Merchant refusal: Heber J. Grant, "Selfishness and the 'Generous Giver,'" *Improvement Era* 42 (December 1939): 713. Unpleasant task: Heber J. Grant to Brother Cutler, July 28, 1899, Grant Letterpress Copybook, 29:239. Insults and slurs: Heber J. Grant to Rudger Clawson, July 1, 1903, Grant

Letterpress Copybook, 36:459.

34. Heber J. Grant to Joseph Howell, May 4, 1900, Grant Letterpress Copybook, 30:561.

35. Grant, Typed Diary, April 2, 1900; Bank Examiner's Report of the Utah Loan and Trust, April 21, 1900, Bank Examiner's Reports, 1899–1900, Administrative Reports of the Secretary of State, Archives, Utah State University, Logan, Utah.

36. Grant, Typed Diary, April 20 and May 18, 1900.

37. Grant, Typed Diary, April 30, August 31, and September 2, 1900.

38. Grant, "Interesting Experience," 13–15.

39. Heber J. Grant to John Henry Smith, December 31, 1901, George A. Smith Papers, Western Americana, Marriott Library.

Young Heber J. Grant
and His Call to the Apostleship

A year following his call to become president of the Tooele Stake, twenty-four-year-old Heber J. Grant stopped by the Salt Lake studio of Charles Savage, the pioneer photographer. The conversation took an unexpected turn. Elder Grant wrote in his journal that Savage told him "to put it down that within one year I would be a member of the Twelve Apostles."[1]

One year and a few days later, young Heber received his call. The assignment led the new Apostle's two closest friends, Anthony W. Ivins and Richard W. Young, to write letters of encouragement. Their correspondence reveals that Savage's prediction was by no means unique. "I have long felt that your destiny was sure," Ivins wrote from his mission in Mexico, "but hardly looked to see you go into the Quorum so soon. The sooner in, however, the sooner you become accustomed to the harness and to the life of usefulness which is before you."[2] Likewise Young's letter, parts of which appear herein, suggests that only the timing of Grant's apostolic call surprised his friends; in addition it etches a revealing character portrait of the future Church president.

Despite his youth Heber J. Grant had already displayed his talents in a remarkable fashion (illus. 8-1). At the age of fifteen, he had been employed as a policy clerk by the insurance firm of H. R. Mann & Co. After business hours, he marketed fire insurance. By nineteen, he had bought out his employers and organized his own successful agency. During his early twenties he broadened into other business activities. And at twenty-three he was called to preside over the Tooele Stake.

Now this already successful and confident man was forced to take personal stock. Whatever his friends' vaunted opinions, he understood his own weaknesses and strengths. Would his talents be equal to the task at hand? Could his towering business ambitions be properly channeled? In what ways did his new assignment cause him to reflect upon his faith? The young Apostle sought to answer these questions as he replied to his friends' letters.

Courtesy Church Archives, The Church of Jesus Christ of Latter-day Saints

Illus. 8-1. Heber J. Grant in 1883, just after he was called to be an Apostle.

Elder Grant's star eclipsed those of Young and Ivins, but each later achieved prominence. Young, a grandson of Brigham, was a graduate of both West Point and Columbia Law School (illus. 8-2). Later he would distinguish himself in the American occupation of the Philippine Islands and by his civic and Church service in his native Salt Lake City. Ivins, in turn, was Grant's cousin and proved to be his closest confidant. In 1907, Ivins himself was selected to be an Apostle (illus. 8-3). Fourteen years later, Heber Grant—now as the Church president—chose Ivins to sit beside him in the First Presidency.

1. Excerpts from the Letter of Heber J. Grant to Anthony W. Ivins, SLC, October 22, 1882.[3]

> Well Tony, your predictions, made last March, as we were going to Saint George, that I would be one of the Apostles, has been fulfilled. You know the true sentiments of my heart on this subject, (as well as many others) and that they were not in accord with your prediction, not that I feel to shrink from any duty, but because I did not, nor do I now, feel that my knowledge, ability, or testimony are of such a character as to entitle me

Courtesy Church Archives, The Church of Jesus Christ of Latter-day Saints

Illus. 8-2. Richard W. Young, grandson of Brigham Young and close friend to Heber.

to the position of an Apostle, The Lord knows what is for the best and I have always trusted in Him for aid and assistance in the past and shall continue to do so in the future, As advised in my last letter, on the 16th George Teasdale and myself were ordained as Apostles, the 1st Presidency and Twelve officiating, Bros Rich, Carrington and Thatcher were absent, Prest Taylor was mouth in Bro Teasdale's ordination, Prest Cannon in mine, I shall return to Salt Lake in the morning, when I expect to get a copy of the revelation calling Bro Teasdale & myself as Apostles.[4] Bro. S.B. Young as Prest of Seventies, etc, also a copy of my ordination, and I will forward these documents with this letter.

I don't know how things will shape with me in the future from a financial standpoint. You will notice that Prest Cannon warned me particularly about setting my mind on the things of this world. While I have devoted most all of my time to acquiring this world's goods in the past, I can truthfully say that never in my life have I seen the time that I was not willing to change my plan of action at the word of command from God's servants, I did not do so much good in Tooele as I might, had I not been engaged in business,[5] I know this and several times expressed my willingness to drop my business if thought best by the authorities. While I have worked hard for Cash, you know as do all of my friends that have a full knowledge of the inmost sentiments of my heart, that Cash has not been my God and that my heart has never been set on it only to do good with what might come into my possession, I most earnestly desire that I may always feel this way. Bro. Erastus Snow comes the nearest to my idea of what an Apostle should be of any member of the Twelve, When I recall his life and labors and stop to think how little time and attention he has for his family or his financial interests, and how much time he has for the people and their interests, and how freely, and without a word of complaint, he neglected his own comfort & worldly welfare for the benefit of others, I am fully convinced that should I follow his noble example, and I shall try to do so, that my financial interests are comparatively speaking at an end. My heart is full of thankfulness to my Heavenly Father for his goodness and mercy to me, I have not language to express the feelings of gratitude in my heart, but I have made up my mind that from this time forth, my life shall be devoted to the work of God upon the Earth, If He

Courtesy Church Archives, The Church of Jesus Christ of Latter-day Saints

Illus. 8-3.   Anthony W. Ivins, cousin and close friend of Heber. Ivins later became Grant's counselor in the First Presidency.

gives me time to do my duties in his Kingdom and also make money, all right, if not all right. I feel in my heart to say "Father thy will not mine be done." Dear Cousin, I feel with God's aid & the faith and prayers of my friends, especially those that know me as you do, that I shall be able to accomplishing some good, without this assistance I shall fail in my calling as an Apostle. I can hardly realize that I am an Apostle, Suppose the fact will become more real as I get down to work. I will now stop talking of myself. . . .

2. Letter from Richard W. Young to Heber J. Grant, November 7, 1882, written from Fort Columbus on Governors Island, New York.[6]

My Dear Heber:

I will pardon you for thinking my long silence strange:— my only excuse to offer is that I have been moving and endeavoring to get settled since receiving your brief note and the news of your appointment—So you are one of the Twelve—Well, it is sooner than I looked for it, but certainly not sooner than meets with my approval, It has long been my impression that all that stood between you and that excellent body was time and some more experience

You have every reason to be ~~thankful~~ congratulated upon your success, so much the more from the fact that it is merited— As a young man, the youngest of the Quorum and as a man without a very extensive experience in matters of preaching, I can imagine that you feel impressed with your unworthiness for the position, but let me give it you as my frank opinion that the selection was one of the very best that could be made, I have no desire to flatter you, but simply to assist you in feeling more confidence in your newly acquired dignity,—when I say that I regard your judgment as about the finest of any of my acquaintances, and I consider your talent in general business, and your quickness to see a point and to unravel one up to the like qualities of any one, Your conversation to me has always been as free from vapor and as full of common sense, boiled down, as I have always been told your father's was,

I consider that your generosity, moral worth and fidelity are all that could be asked—Now take a summing up of these qualities and manufacture a young man of 26 and in my estimation, not as your friend, but as a disinterested party, you will have the best candidate for a vacancy in the Twelve to be found in the Church—And such I am certain is the opinion of everyone, I have not had an opportunity of conversing with many of our people but those I have seen—John Henry (Smith), Wm Groesbeck, Orson Arnold & Jimmy Clinton, While questioning the superiority of Bro Teasdale's worth do not hesitate in approving your selection, I was told by Bro John Henry that the selections were given in so many words by revelation. Heber, you are truly a blessed man, If I am not wrong but few of the appointments in late years have been by direct revelation,

Fancy it—our belief that God, the Good, the Almighty ruler of the Universe, He at whose pleasure the worlds move & the stars give light He whom so many generations have sought— our belief is that He is the fountain of our Church—this is as firmly my belief as it is my belief that He rules,—and He has been so far pleased with your integrity and worth as to name you personally as one of His representatives on Earth,

I scarcely know how and what to write—there is not language which will do adequate justice to such an occasion, I can only say, my friend, that if joy is not yours, that if resolve to sacrifice all to the Gospel is not yours, it is because you fail in your conception of the infinitely priceless nature of your selection,

My wish is that you may devote yourself to study, for no adornment of the mind is unnecessary to this work—that you may be blessed with the fulness of testimony of God and His Work, and that this may be the case and that you may be deeply impressed with the nature of your calling and become eminently useful therein is my earnest prayer. . . .

Nervie (R.W.'s wife) wishes to congratulate you and we both desire remembrances to your wife and to your mother Do. to Ray[7] & Lucy remember their so called Uncle Richard—Write soon for I shall look for you to.

Your friend with more good luck to you.—R.W.—

(Richard W. Young.)

3. Excerpts from Heber J. Grant's reply to Richard W. Young, SLC, November 16, 1882.[8]

With reference to my new calling and my abilities to magnify the same, I must say that I consider my position much in advance of my knowledge—I regret very much that I have not a better knowledge of grammar, as I murder the "Queens English" most fearfully—my orthography is perfectly <u>Emense</u> to say the least—I have not a good memory, or if I have it has been so badly neglected that I have not found it out that it is good, My information on subjects relating to the advancement of a community amts to nothing, I know little or nothing of History— and were it not that I have from 15 to 25 yrs. in which to study to overtake such men as Lyman, Jos. F. Smith and others, and knowing that I have the right to call upon our Heavenly Father for assistance I assure you that I should feel almost like backing out—A knowledge, of grammer and orthography is necessary for a public speaker and one that has more or less writing to do,—I naturally dislike both of these studies and have not much faith in becoming proficient in either—Your inventory of my abilities is "way up." I should like to have you get someone to accept of your ideas but think it would be a difficult task, I may have a little common sense—In fact I know that I have, I also know that my first ideas, impressions, or quickness to see a point which ever you see fit to call it, is not bad, but this really amts to but very little when you are looking for a substantial leading man. Reasoning powers and depth of thought are the qualities that count—There is one thing that sustains me, however, & that is the fact that all powers, of mind or body, come from God and that He is perfectly able & willing to qualify me for His work provided I am faithful in doing my part—This I hope to be able to do faithfully—I am also pleased to know that I shall have the faith & confidence of the people—This is a great thing as I know from personal experience while laboring in Tooele County—The folks join in regards & best wishes for your continued health & prosperity also that of your wife—Time will not permit my writing more—Again thanking you for your good wishes I remain

Your Friend & Bro

H.J. Grant

Notes

This article was first published in *BYU Studies* 18 (Fall 1977): 121–26.

1. Heber J. Grant, Journal, October 7, 1881, Church Archives, The Church of Jesus Christ of Latter-day Saints, Salt Lake City.

2. Anthony W. Ivins to Heber J. Grant, November 6, 1882, in Grant, Journal, November 25, 1882.

3. Heber J. Grant Letterpress Copybook, 5:7–10, Church Archives.

4. For a copy of the revelation calling Elders Grant and Teasdale to the Twelve, see James R. Clark, comp., *Messages of the First Presidency of The Church of Jesus Christ of Latter-day Saints,* 6 vols. (Salt Lake City: Bookcraft, 1965), 2:348–49.

5. After his call to the Tooele Stake Presidency, Elder Grant had moved his family to the western Utah village but had continued to conduct his Salt Lake business affairs. The result was that he spent as much time in Salt Lake as in Tooele, and local Church affairs sometimes suffered.

6. Copied in Grant, Journal, November 17, 1882. The explanations in parentheses and the end punctuation are apparently Grant's. The roughly educated churchman never seemed to master the use of the period.

7. "Ray" or Rachel and Lucy were the two eldest children of Heber and Lucy Stringham Grant.

8. Grant Letterpress Copybook, 5:62–63.

A Mormon "Widow" in Colorado:
The Exile of Emily Wells Grant

As the southbound Denver & Rio Grande train pulled out of the depot at Salt Lake City in November 1889, Emily Wells Grant breathed a sigh of relief, and relaxed. As a plural wife of Elder Heber J. Grant, she was used to dodging United States marshals. Her recent crisis, she admitted, was of her own making. Why had she insisted on attending her father's seventy-fifth birthday celebration in the Twelfth Ward after five years of secrecy? She had been spotted there, the grand jury had reopened her husband's cohabitation case, and she had been forced to flee again. The federal government was increasing its pressure on The Church of Jesus Christ of Latter-day Saints to end polygamy. Emily was now leaving Utah and entering a year-and-a-half exile in Manassa, Colorado. From there, she would regularly correspond with her husband, her lively letters conveying a rare view of the feelings of the "privileged" plural wives who were allowed to set up separate households. Since such a practice required considerable means, these women comprised the social and economic elite of the practicing polygamists. The story of Emily Grant's exile illustrates the human side of the Church's transition from a regional sect that practiced plural marriage to its more expansive and "American" form of today.[1]

Emily Wells had known and liked Heber J. Grant from her earliest memory. She was born in Salt Lake City on April 22, 1857, next door to the Grant family's homestead on Main Street. A daughter of former Salt Lake City mayor and current General

Authority Daniel H. Wells and his plural wife Martha, she had become an early friend of Heber, five months her senior, who was the son of Rachel Ivins and Jedediah Grant, also a former Salt Lake City mayor and church leader who had died when Heber was nine days old. In their late teens, the friendship between Emily and Heber cooled after they sharply disagreed on the question of plural marriage. At the time, she was a student at the University of Deseret and the coquette of the Salt Lake City crowd, slender and of medium height, with chestnut brown hair and blue eyes (illus. 9-1). She might be a Wells, and the offspring of a plural marriage, but nothing could persuade her to enter polygamy.[2]

Courtesy Church Archives, The Church of Jesus Christ of Latter-day Saints

Illus. 9-1. Emily Wells and Heber J. Grant had been childhood friends. Decades later Emily became Heber's third wife.

Finding Emily adamant on the subject of plural marriage, Heber married Lucy Stringham in 1877. Seven years later, by then a prominent Church leader and rising businessman, he decided to take Augusta Winters as his second wife. But there remained the unrequited attraction of Emily. When Heber first proposed marriage to her in 1883, she stoutly denounced him and the idea. But Heber persevered and Emily began a prayerful study of the principle. Within a year her opposition to Heber and polygamy ended, and she became his third wife on May 27, 1884, the day after his marriage to Augusta.[3]

Emily faced great obstacles as a plural wife. Two years before her sealing to Heber, Congress had passed the Edmunds Act, which subjected men convicted of plural marriage or living polygamously (defined as "cohabitation") to fines and imprisonment. In 1887 the government stiffened its opposition. The Edmunds-Tucker Act disincorporated the Church and forced it to surrender its properties. With Benjamin Harrison and the Republicans elected on an anti-Mormon platform, and with more draconian measures apparently on the way, the times were unpropitious for the illegal wives, or "widows" as they were called. If captured with their offspring, they were deemed sufficient evidence to convict their husbands (illus. 9-2). Consequently, in the late 1880s these women took to the "underground" with little hope that they might soon emerge to lead more normal lives.[4]

Thus, to conceal the birth of her first child, Emily had sought refuge in Liverpool, England, at 42 Islington, the Church's dilapidated and supposedly ghost-ridden mission headquarters. As United States authorities continued to eye her husband's activities, she had stayed in England an additional sixteen months. Her circumstances had not improved upon her return to America. Heber briefly sequestered her in a specially constructed apartment hidden in her mother's home, and for a long period she was on the "open"

Courtesy Church Archives, The Church of Jesus Christ of Latter-day Saints

Illus. 9-2. Because the Edmunds Act prohibited plural marriage, Emily—like many other plural wives—went into hiding in the 1880s to escape prosecution. Heber and Emily's family: *(seated)* Heber J. Grant, Emily Grant Mansen, Frances Grant Bennett; *(standing)* Grace Grant Evans, Emily Wells Grant, Dessie Grant Boyle.

underground, shifting residences throughout northern Utah and southern Idaho. During that time, her interludes with Heber were never as frequent or as extended as she wished.[5]

Emily's destination in November 1889 was Manassa, a little town in the San Luis Valley in south-central Colorado, over five hundred miles from Salt Lake City. She did not have to travel there alone. As Heber could not be seen with her publicly, he had taken an earlier train, leaving friends to navigate Emily through the D & R G depot without being arrested. John Henry Smith, a fellow member of the Twelve with Heber, escorted Emily and her two children, Deseret and Grace, who were three years and eleven months respectively. At Pueblo, Colorado, the two Grant parties met and traveled to Manassa together.[6]

Mormons had settled in the San Luis Valley only a few years earlier. While Spaniards and their Mexican descendants had lived there as early as the seventeenth century, it was not until the late 1870s that a railroad spur opened the valley to Anglo development. The Mormons responded by founding Manassa and several satellite communities. Considered solely by latitude, the Mormon settlements seemed ideally located to receive a regular flow of converts from the Southern states, and each March and November new companies of emigrants arrived. To aid them, Church leaders sent seasoned Utah pioneers, particularly Scandinavians from the Sanpete country in Utah, to the San Luis Valley.[7]

When Emily arrived in Manassa, most of the houses were small frame dwellings, only a minor improvement over the log construction of the local church. There were two schools. The village had an assortment of stores that included the Mormon co-operative and furniture, hardware, and four general merchandise establishments, most of which would vanish during the next several years. Manassa claimed four hundred inhabitants, with another two thousand scattered nearby in the valley.[8]

Emily could see little evidence of the fertility and promise the Salt Lake City *Deseret Evening News* reported in its periodic descriptions of Manassa. While its soil and 7,500-foot altitude were ideal for irrigated potatoes, legumes, and short-season grains, the town sat on a windswept and treeless flatland. The San Luis Valley was huge, almost fifty miles wide and 175 miles long, its mountain rim barely visible in the distance. The valley's magnitude dwarfed Manassa's few buildings and gave the community the aspect of a bleak Western prairie town. To someone like Emily, who delighted in the sociability and excitement of city life, it looked painfully forlorn.[9]

She hoped her stay would be for only a year or two, but Heber, who remained for two weeks setting up house, seemed intent on a longer timetable. He clearly spent on a scale that suggested permanence. He purchased a sturdy two-room house that would provide protection from the San Luis winds, had the spaces between the wall studs filled with sawdust for insulation, ordered cloth, and had new wallpaper applied to the interior. A kitchen was later built on. With new carpets, furniture, stove, and other accessories, Emily's home was one of the most comfortable in the settlement. And to further accommodate her, Heber hired a chore boy and left his mother for companionship.[10]

Emily also had the society of other Utahns. With federal pressure mounting, Manassa had become a haven for polygamist families. Mormons reasoned that territorial marshals were not apt to travel that far for their prey, and if the marshals did, advance word could be sent to the settlement. Several Mormon patriarchs accordingly settled with their extended families in the San Luis Valley, often on land remote from the larger Latter-day Saint settlements. Manassa became a popular refuge for "widows." Among Emily's neighbors were the wives of General Authorities Francis M. Lyman, John Morgan, B. H. Roberts, John Henry Smith, and Moses Thatcher. Another dozen were plurally married to prominent Utah businessmen and bishops. However, the exiles with their children constituted less than 10 percent of Manassa proper.[11]

Emily's initial feelings about her surroundings were pleasant. She admitted to being "better contented & happier than I thought I would be." Manassa's air was bracing. She enjoyed "lovely cream[,] fresh eggs[,] and chicken" on demand. With a horse and buggy, she could visit and sight-see. And her home was satisfactory, save for one unredeemable flaw. "I have got every thing in it now that I want," Emily reported to Heber upon his return to Salt Lake City, "except you." She developed leisurely routines, rising for a late breakfast, retiring early, and doing "just as we please about everything." She especially relished her liberty: "Too be able to go out in the <u>day time</u> without a thick veil and to ask at the general post office for my own mail is indeed a treat."[12]

Still, there was no denying the hard reality of Manassa. Its wind, isolation, and rustic life (not to mention its bed bugs) were formidable challenges for citified Emily. When a stranger advised that it was the proper season for one of her cows "to go South," she reportedly entrusted the animal to him—and both he and the cow "went south," never to be seen again. Clearly, she was neither prepared for nor attracted to her new life. "I realize that I am buried alive and don't know <u>nothing no how</u>," she complained with more edge than humor.[13]

When Heber gave her two expensive paintings for Christmas, she responded: "<u>Thank you sweetheart</u> but what did you send a pair of costly pictures down here for. To please me?" The pictures added greatly to the room's appearance, but they were too nice for Manassa. "I don't want anything down here that I can ever become attached to and will hate to part with," Emily wrote. "Your Christmas present, of course, I shall <u>always</u> want to keep so [I] have carefully put the box, the pictures were in, away so I can pack them up and take them <u>home</u> with me."[14]

Emily was hardly alone in her feelings. The Manassa "widows" disliked their Colorado exile, and their distaste increased with time. There was a variety of complaints. Rose Williams found only patent medicine on the store shelves. Josephine Smith complained that the local settlers had "no desire to be or do anything in the way of improvement," and during one winter wrote: "There isn't a green thing to be seen in this valley, only the house plants, and a good many of them are dead." While more stoical than most, Rhoda Lyman longed to see her handicapped son living in Utah.[15]

Local bickering also made the environment less pleasant. "I never in all my life heard of so much contending among 'Mormon' people as there is here," one wife reported. "I hardly ever hear one person speak well of another. Snubs and criticism is the order of the day." The problem lay at the roots of the settlement. The colonists arriving from the Southern states were unprepared for Manassa's chilly climate and for the earthy speech and plain habits of the Utah pioneers sent to assist them. Conflict was always present. Several times Church meetings were disrupted by near fights. In the mid-1880s

Bishop W. L. Ball left the settlement amid charges of fraud and embezzlement. Disgruntled Saints repeatedly charged Stake President Silas S. Smith with misconduct and on one occasion threatened to lynch him.[16]

Manassa's conditions were irritating, but the main source of the widows' discontent was their having to go underground. Above Josephine Smith's mantelpiece hung an old-fashioned sampler with the inscription: "What Is Home Without a Father?" Its irony may have been lost upon Josephine, but not others. Many women longed for something more than occasional marital companionship. They saw themselves as second-class wives, living outside the law and subject to arrest. "It is such a different life, than the married one that we always picture," one underground wife wrote. It was "so hard to always be alone, no one to look to but the Father of all, and sometimes He, even, seems so far away."[17]

Because of their common plight, the "widows" turned to each other for companionship. "We do a good deal of visiting," Emily wrote. "There is quite a colony of us now and we have pleasant times together." She developed a special bond with Celia Roberts and especially with Georgie Thatcher, a cousin of Lucy Grant, Heber's first wife. When the women met as a group, it usually was for an afternoon dinner party. Emily's report of one of Josephine Smith's fêtes was probably descriptive of most: "a perfect success, lovely dinner, plenty of gossip & a house running over with babies."[18]

Church activity provided another release from the local monotony. Emily's Sunday attendance was fitful, restrained by the uncertain spirit at the meetings and by the logistics of tending two babies. Special needs and recreation, however, provided more compelling reasons to leave the house. When a mother died leaving nine children, the Mormon exiles and local Relief Society sisters made clothes for them. Emily also assisted at the church fair. Dancing at the regular church socials brought back memories of her youth. The log meetinghouse could accommodate eighteen couples when the benches were removed. Three of the "widows" regaled the Thanksgiving costume ball by dressing respectively as a "Gypsy, Hun, and Indian." Emily usually attended these events for social contact or to hear "organ and fiddle," but on some occasions she became a part of the ball. "Sister [Clara] Lyman, the bride [apparently recently married], and myself were the belles," she wrote Heber. "I danced until I was positively too dizzy to know where I was and so tired for the two day's following I could hardly drag around."[19]

Other celebrations brought a more restrained response. The Fourth of July seemed small stuff to Emily, and she had only disdain for "Sister" McKay, then living with her, who thought otherwise. From ten in the morning until one, they listened to songs and speeches at the stake church house. After lunch, they "went up on the square stood around for two or three hours watching a few cranks foot race in their stocking feet, bare heads and shirt sleeves." Then in the evening, Emily took the children back to the stake house, where she paid her "two bits" and "joined in the gay festivity of the dance" until ten o'clock. Back home, Emily put the children to bed and "read until after one o'clock when the giddy sister McKay came home," saying that she had "'had such a lovely time.'" Emily was glad that her companion had "remained until the end of the programme for I think if any body can enjoy that kind of a shindig or get the least amusement out of dancing by the music of a fiddle there ought not to be a straw thrown in her way."[20]

Nor did Emily's distemper improve three weeks later when the Pioneer Day celebration was held in Manassa. "You would have died, had you seen the procession here yesterday morning," she reported to Heber. "I hurried to get the children & myself ready to go up on Main Street to get a good view of the procession and we had it too. I shall not attempt a description for I can't without laughing and am in too much of hurry this morning to spare the time."[21]

Christmastime went better. Since the stores at La Jara, Colorado, a railroad terminus a few miles from Manassa, stocked a wide variety of supplies, Emily's first Christmas lacked nothing except Heber and the traditional turkey. There were gifts, a trimmed tree, and a dinner that included such frontier delicacies as celery, cranberries, grapes, oranges, oysters, and sweet potatoes. The following year she did better. For Emily's daughter Dessie, then in her fourth year, the event was one of her earliest and most indelible memories. On the day before Christmas, a wagon stopped in front of their house, and a man "began unloading boxes, sacks, barrels, and packages." Dessie recalled that there were "oranges and bananas—great delicacies for that day—there were apples and candy, nuts and raisins. There were lovely dolls and toys and new dresses and a seal skin coat for mother." These unexpected gifts from Heber completely changed not only the family's Christmas but also that of many townspeople who were invited to share. The "widows" capped the occasion by a dance, which Emily described as "the best party I have ever attended down here."[22]

Manassa's tempo always quickened when a General Authority spouse arrived in town. "When one of the husbands is in town we don't do a thing but visit," Emily admitted. "We have a round of sociables, dinner parties and good meeting and there are so many of us here now that there is generally one or two good fellows with us." While in the valley, the General Authorities often tried to visit each plural wife in the colony, a courtesy that the First Presidency continued during their August 1890 tour. Sometimes the men did more. They invited groups of "widows" to accompany their families on outings. Camping on the upper Conejos River was a favorite. There, Emily caught six trout during one excursion.[23]

Emily lionized the male visitors. Had he not discounted her penchant for wit and sentimentality, Heber might have become concerned by her reactions. During the First Presidency's visit, she reported that Joseph F. Smith had grown "handsomer than ever I think, and is so very pleasant. We are all dead in love with him and one of the widows remarked that she wished she was not married. Brother [George Q.] Cannon was perfectly irresistible, too." Emily's attraction, however, did not center on these two. At other times she found Moses Thatcher "perfectly divine" and relished the company of B. H. Roberts, whom she had known since her Liverpool days. Francis M. Lyman, in turn, constituted a "full team in himself at any [Church] conference." After a dinner party, she was even more effusive about Lyman: "I am quite in love with him tonight—he was so interesting and looked perfectly stunning."[24]

A psychologist might find Emily's idolizing as evidence of compensation and transfer. To be sure, behind the outward whirl of the General Authority visits there existed within most of the "widows" an inner loneliness for their own husbands. Upon the departure of a distinguished visitor, their feelings deepened into despair. "It is always such a comfort to have them here," Emily remarked, "and so lonely after they have gone."[25]

Emily released her frustrations by letter writing, a task made dangerous by the "Raid" by federal prosecutors. Fearing that her correspondence, if it were intercepted, might incriminate Heber, she concealed identities with aliases (Emily was "Mary Harris" and Heber "Eli") and employed for the sake of prying marshals veiled language and out-and-out obfuscation. "Who do they accuse H[.] J[.] Grant being married to[?]" read one letter to Heber. "I heard it was rumored after my departure from home that I was his second wife. . . . I am sorry if they arrest him on my account." Emily, of course, preserved verity by being Heber's *third* wife.[26]

Emily and Heber often exchanged weekly letters, and commemorated their wedding with a "must" letter on the twenty-seventh of each month. They also agreed to avoid tainting their correspondence with arguments and faultfinding. And both insisted on promptness. She was "in a fever" when the "gawk" of the Manassa postman mislaid several of Heber's letters. Upon their receipt she "<u>devoured</u>" them. Heber's letters, she claimed, were "all that keep me up." She called them "love letters" and requested that they always be handwritten.[27]

Because Emily and Heber were separated for months, their letters during the Manassa period became the binding tie and most tangible expression of their marriage. With so much time on her hands and so much to tell, Emily wrote long, warmly anecdotal letters. She paused in the middle of one to warn: "I am not half through yet so brace up old boy." She often felt that her letters bore the aspect of a "ten cent novel" and were too frank for her Victorian time. "I . . . remember the first letters I wrote to you after our marriage," Emily recalled. "How <u>awfully bad</u> I had it then & have not entirely recovered yet." At times she wished she could "indulge in a <u>few kisses</u>" and confessed "<u>getting mighty hungry</u>" for his company. She justified their painful separation by rationalizing that it was better that love's "fire burned even if it hurts occasionally." And on occasion Emily was even more direct. "I <u>can not</u> satisfy myself telling you how I feel & <u>just wish</u> I had an opportunity to express my true sentiments in a more substantial manner than having to resort to an old stiff pen and some horrid ink to tell you that you are the <u>best</u> and <u>kindest</u> old <u>darling</u> the sun ever shone on."[28]

Heber visited Emily five times during her year-and-a-half sojourn at Manassa and met her briefly on another occasion in Denver.

The mathematics of these visits became a serious matter. However sisterly the "widows" were in most matters, they carefully compared their husbands' attentions and, at times, noted any personal advantage. For example, one wife reported her child's apparently innocent prattle that "none of the husbands came to see their families as often as papa, neither do they stay as long." Emily noted that the woman worked this thought into her conversation in as many ways and as often as possible.[29]

True, Heber did not visit as often as men with older and larger families. He was at the acme of his early business career, juggling a half-dozen Church-business enterprises. Moreover, his husbandly duties also required times with wives Lucy in Salt Lake City and Augusta in distant New York City. Emily was satisfied that he came when he could. Six weeks after her arrival in Manassa, he astonished her by unexpectedly appearing at the front door. His visits carried her emotions on a roller coaster. "I am so grateful and so happy to have you come, so homesick and forlorn when you go," she wrote. She wondered if he might best not come at all. And then she would return to reality. His visits were "all I have to look forward to or to live for, except of course my precious babies."[30]

When Heber visited Manassa, he usually was on the wing. His restlessness signaled to Emily that he was no fonder of Manassa than she. In private moments, he admitted his frustration in "running all over the country" to see his plural wives, instead of locating them openly at home. At times he sensed the futility of his best intentions. "It is almost impossible for a person," he concluded, "to make his plural wives think that he cares as much for them as he should." But he persistently tried. Blaming the federal government and not plural marriage itself for his and his wives' frustrations, he undertook his marital responsibilities with religious seriousness: "I would sooner die a hundred times than have my wives and children turn against me and depart from God's work because of my unkindness to them or [due] to my failure to be just."[31]

Heber's concern strengthened Emily, but as time passed she grew increasingly out of sorts. When in June 1890 Mother Grant, her amiable live-in companion for the past half year, left Manassa, Emily faced a crisis. She felt more alone than she had ever felt since coming to Manassa. At first she turned inward for strength. A voracious reader of novels and popular literature, she vowed to give herself a diet of "good books" and prayer. She acknowledged to Heber that her Manassa experience had been beneficial after all and resolved to be more contented and accepting of her condition. "The wind may blow and the chickens fail to hatch—Let the frost come who cares," she wrote. Emily even planted some fruit trees, which symbolized her long-term plans to stay. "I thought as long as I am doomed to live here," she explained, "the sooner some trees & fruit were put in the sooner we would have something green on the place."[32]

Yet her resolve exceeded her strength. Without her mother-in-law, Emily's nerves flared. She jumped at the slightest noise and felt unsafe in her home, especially when an adjoining house was burglarized. As time passed, her cries became plaintive. "Don't forget [to] pray for me dear one," she asked Heber, "for without the aid of my father in heaven I can not stand this much longer & be sane." Two days later, she struggled to regain her equilibrium: "I am doing the best I can to make myself contented & happy. . . . I generally succeed pretty well and with the help of the Lord I[']ll succeed entirely."[33]

Manassa gradually became more than a way station on the underground for Emily. It became a spiritual passage. "It is my desire to do right," she resolved to Heber, "and I pray to be able to meet the trials of this life in a noble manner and in a way worthy of your wife." She related a dream that conveyed the larger message of her soul-searching. She dreamed that Heber had telegraphed from Denver asking her to come at once, for he was very sick. She rushed about and reached the railway station "just in time to see the train pass me by without even stopping." At that point she awoke. "I trust the dream is not typical of how I'll get left." She continued: "I have made all sorts of new resolutions again and feel more determined than ever to accomplish something and make myself more worthy of your confidence and love and live in a manner to always to retain it."[34]

Heber sensed Emily's growing desperation and dispatched Katherine and Heber Wells, Emily's sister and brother, to Manassa. Thereafter, during most of her stay in Colorado, Emily had Katherine or her mother as company. Her relatives helped check her despondency and disorientation, but they could do little to ease the harshness of Manassa. In summer 1890, when Emily was sorely depressed, measles broke out among the children. Then came the news that diphtheria had appeared in nearby Antonito. "If it breaks out here," Emily warned, "don't blame me if I pack up and emigrate for I can never stand the stress." Six months later, smallpox closed Manassa's schools and church and claimed several lives. Fears of an epidemic became rampant when a quarantined man walked into the Manassa post office, declaring that he did not "give a damn" if he spread the pestilence.[35]

Added to these fears was the specter of the federal marshals. Despite Manassa's isolation and relative security, there was always the threat that "smarties," as adventurous lawmen were labeled, would cross the territorial line to seek evidence. Emily was prone to attract their attention because Heber had been repeatedly investigated but never charged nor convicted. He was a prime target, unlike many of her friends' husbands who had been arrested and imprisoned. In July 1890 word was telegraphed that marshals were on their way to Manassa. Two of the "widows" were the reported objects of investigation, but Emily and the others were told to "keep a little quiet." Later, a similar unconfirmed rumor sent one heavily pregnant woman scurrying. In another instance, General Authority John Morgan, visiting his plural wife at Manassa, was captured and convicted.[36]

Pressures on polygamists and the Church itself became unbearable. Like other "widows," Emily was dismayed when the Mormons lost political control of Salt Lake City to their arch-opponents, the Liberal Party. More threatening was the Supreme Court's decision to uphold the Idaho Test Oath. The ruling not only denied the vote to Idahoans who believed in polygamy but also threatened disfranchisement of the entire Latter-day Saint community. "The clouds seem to be growing blacker and thicker," Emily wrote, "but there . . . [must be] a silver lining . . . if we only have patience long enough."[37]

When Emily read in the newspapers that President Woodruff's 1890 Manifesto banned plural marriages in the future among the Latter-day Saints, she at first was quite optimistic. "I felt almost like rejoicing and I seemed to see the first ray of light I have ever seen for us through our difficulties," she wrote Heber. "You know I believe so devoutly in you sweetheart that things, done by the authorities, which I do not perhaps understand, do not try me as they might were I married to a <u>mortal</u>."[38]

Emily's second thoughts, however, were reflective and dispirited. Why had plural marriage, the ideal for which she had become a six-year fugitive, been suspended? Heber assured her that no plural marriages would be repudiated. But this provided little solace. Groping to understand the surrendering of a basic tenet of faith, she found no fault with "the principle" but with its practitioners. "I agree with you," she wrote Heber. "Very few men have made a success of plural marriage: and after the experience of our fathers and mothers before us, it seems like we ought to improve and do nearer right: though I fail to see much more justice in families now day's than existed years ago and in some respects I think they did nearer right."

When Emily realized the Manifesto promised no redemption from underground life, her rawest feelings came to the surface. It seemed like five years since she had left home, almost that long since she had come to "this detestable place." She wrote Heber: "I hope it wont be long before I have some kind of a change or I am afraid I'll do something desperate. . . . I am so tired and disgusted with the sight of cows I feel like cussing at the very thought of one. . . . I love you devotedly but my heart is nearly breaking."[39]

In response, Heber began to consider alternatives to Manassa. Unlike many San Luis polygamists, Emily had ruled out Mexico. Elder Moses Thatcher, who believed "the least said about the Manifesto the better," hoped to continue polygamy by persuading a number of Church members in the valley to join his Mexican land schemes. Emily found more attractive the proposal that she join Augusta, Heber's second wife, in New York City. Because of underground conditions, Heber's three wives previously had had little contact. Emily had exchanged letters with Lucy in Salt Lake City, but by going East she could establish a relationship with Augusta and escape Manassa.[40]

But the New York proposal quickly faded. Emily's first intimation of difficulty was "Mother" Rachel Grant's letter disapproving the move. Next, several "widows" who were discomfited by Emily's good fortune asked their husbands to intervene and change Heber's mind. When he announced his reversal, Emily was stunned by the decision. For the first time, anger and bitterness filled her heart.[41]

Emily appreciated Heber's willingness to "satisfy" her, despite the financial hardship involved and his belief that she would not like

New York any better than Manassa. She had not expected "perfect bliss in New York but only believed I would like it better and could see something occasionally [and] have a little amusement." She knew that the present circumstances had to be endured, and she was doing her "share of making the best of them," whether Heber thought so or not. She had always known him to "have made big allowance" for her, by understanding her life and the way she was brought up. But, she wrote, "I will admit your letters not only hurt my feelings but make me wish I could pay you back with interest every dollar you ever spent for me and I wish I never had to accept another cent of your money." She added, "I just adore you and hope this letter will not wound your feelings as yours did mine but sweetheart you might just as well stick a knife into my side and ask me not to notice it as to write what you did." Emily's vial of wrath was still not emptied. She composed another letter sixteen pages long, but upon reflection she burned it.[42]

Heber, who regarded "the love of wives as one of the greatest blessings," unconditionally surrendered. After several sleepless nights, he offered Emily New York City, Salt Lake City, or Manassa as options. "It will be either home, or New York," Emily dryly commented, having made up her mind "to leave this 'land of Exiles, Greasers & smallpox.'" Nor was there a contest between New York and Salt Lake City. In March 1891, sixteen months after her arrival at Manassa, Emily began to sell her furniture, pack, and prepare to return to Salt Lake City. She was scheduled to leave in April, but her father's death in late March hastened her departure.[43]

Emily Grant was neither the first nor last of the "widows" to leave Manassa. In June 1892, Elders Francis Lyman and John Henry Smith met with some of the remaining families, and "all agreed to get over the [territorial] line." But Celia Roberts and Georgie Thatcher remained two years more; and Josephine Smith, apparently the last of the "widows," did not return to Utah until 1896. The wives' frustration with Manassa depended on their backgrounds, personalities, and length of exile. None looked back.[44]

Emily learned that her Salt Lake City friends planned an "ovation" upon her return. She wanted none of it. "I only want a visit with my folks & friends without making myself conspicuous anywhere," she said. "Not to have to jump and run from every body will be too lovely for any thing if I don't go out at all." Originally, she and Heber planned that her Salt Lake stay might extend to a year, or until the possible arrival of another baby. Then, as Utah territorial law still forbade cohabitation, she would again go underground. As she traveled the D & R G tracks westward toward Salt Lake, neither Heber nor she realized that she was pregnant and within months would need another retreat.[45]

Emily's future underground adventure would not be as trying as Manassa. In that little isolated Colorado community, she and the other "widows" had experienced the worst of the "Raid." After the 1890 Manifesto, governmental pressure eased, and the plural wives gradually and cautiously emerged from the underground. When Emily died of cancer in 1908, Utah society recognized her as Heber's wife and the mother of six of his children. Heber Grant survived to become the Church's longest-tenured President in the twentieth century. At his death in 1945, after a twenty-seven year administration, the pathos and struggle of places like Manassa had long been forgotten.[46]

Notes

This article was originally published in *Arizona and the West* 25 (Spring 1983): 5–22.

1. Heber J. Grant, Diary, November 1, 1887; October 25–26, 28, and November 9, 1889, typescript, Heber J. Grant Papers, Church Archives, The Church of Jesus Christ of Latter-day Saints, Salt Lake City. Emily Grant to Heber J. Grant, November 7, 1889, Family Correspondence, Grant Papers, Church Archives. As most of the letters in the Grant Papers are listed chronologically and easily located, box and folder numbers are indicated only for those out of sequence. Strangely, the distaff side of plural marriage has received limited attention. Two pertinent articles are Lawrence Foster, "Polygamy and the Frontier: Mormon Women in Early Utah," *Utah Historical Quarterly* 50 (summer 1982): 268–89; and Kimberly Jensen James, "'Between Two Fires': Women on the 'Underground' of Mormon Polygamy," *Journal of Mormon History* 8 (1981): 49–61. Broader treatments are in Lawrence Foster, *Religion and Sexuality: Three American Communal Experiments of the Nineteenth Century* (New York: University of Illinois Press, 1981); and Kimball Young, *Isn't One Wife Enough?* (New York: Henry Holt, 1954).

2. Andrew Jenson, "Heber Jeddy Grant" and "Daniel Hamner Wells," in *Latter-day Saint Biographical Encyclopedia: A Compilation of Biographical*

Sketches of Prominent Men and Women in The Church of Jesus Christ of Latter-day Saints, 4 vols. (Salt Lake City: Andrew Jenson History, 1901–36), 1:64, 147, 149.

3. Heber J. Grant to Dessie [Deseret Grant Boyle], March 1, 1935, Heber J. Grant Letterpress Copybook, 72:280–81, Grant Papers; and Heber J. Grant to Ray O. Wyland, December 12, 1936, Grant Letterpress Copybook, 74:532–34.

4. Gustive O. Larson, *The "Americanization" of Utah for Statehood* (San Marino, Calif.: Huntington Library, 1971), esp. 207–22.

5. Emily's feelings and experiences during her early underground days are found in her letters to her husband and family, box 121, Grant Papers, Church Archives.

6. John Henry Smith, Diary, November 22, 1889, John Henry Smith Papers, Special Collections, J. Willard Marriott Library, University of Utah, Salt Lake City; Grant, Diary, November 20–21, 1889.

7. Judson Harold Flower Jr., "Mormon Colonization of the San Luis Valley, Colorado, 1878–1900" (master's thesis, Brigham Young University, 1966), esp. 172; Hanna Daphne Smith Dalton, *"Pretty Is As Pretty Does"* (South Africa: privately published, n.d.), 26; "Manassa, Conejos County, Colorado," *Deseret Evening News,* May 5, 1880, [4]; John Morgan, "Gathering Saints—Good News from Colorado," *Deseret Evening News,* November 30, 1881, [2]; Andrew Jenson, "San Luis Stake, Colorado," *Deseret Evening News,* December 21, 1893, [9]; Andrew Jenson, "The Founding of Mormon Settlements in the San Luis Valley, Colorado," *Colorado Magazine* 17 (September 1940): 174–80.

8. Jenson, "San Luis Stake, Colorado," [9]; Heber J. Grant, "Manassa Matters," *Salt Lake Herald,* December 8, 1889, 14.

9. *La Jara* (Colorado) *Tribune,* as quoted in "Manassa, Colorado," *Deseret Evening News,* September 5, 1888, [2].

10. Grant, Diary, November 22–December 4, 1889; Emily to May [Wells Whitney], January 5, 1890, Grant Papers.

11. Flower, "Mormon Colonization of the San Luis Valley," 172.

12. Emily to May [Whitney], January 5, 1890; Emily to Heber J. Grant, December 27, 1889, Grant Papers. Emily had a penchant for underlining. In this and subsequent citations, the emphasis is hers.

13. Emily to Heber J. Grant, December 20, 1889, Grant Papers; Emily to May [Whitney], May 18, 1890, Grant Papers. Her episode with the cow may be apocryphal, but it is very much a part of family tradition. Truman G. Madsen, interview by author, Provo, Utah, January 28, 1982, in author's possession.

14. Emily to Heber J. Grant, December 27, 1889.

15. Josephine to George A. Smith, March 26, November 5, 1893, George A. Smith Papers, Western Americana, Marriott Library. Emily to Heber J. Grant, October 3, 1890, and January 27, 1891, Grant Papers.

16. Joseph Smith to George and Lucy Smith, December 31, 1893, George A. Smith Papers; H. P. Dotson, "Manassa, Colorado, February 7th, 1881," *Deseret*

Evening News, February 15, 1881, [1]; "The San Luis Valley Affair," *Deseret Evening News,* February 27, 1884, [2]; "The Situation in the San Luis Valley," *Deseret Evening News,* April 2, 1884, [2]; "From Colorado," *Deseret Evening News,* October 2, 1885, [3]; B. H. Roberts, Diary, January 27, 1893, B. H. Roberts Papers, Special Collections, Marriott Library.

17. Louise [Stringham?] to Lou [Lucy Stringham Grant], March 25, 188[?], Grant Papers. Although the letter apparently was not written from Manassa, it aptly summarizes the feelings of the women there. Frances G. Bennett, interview by author, August 6, 1981, typescript, 48, James Moyle Oral History Program, Church Archives.

18. Emily to May [Whitney], March 10, 1890, Grant Papers; Emily to Heber J. Grant, November 19, 1890, Grant Papers; Emily to Heber J. Grant, March 20, 1891, Grant Papers.

19. Celia Roberts to "Dear Grandma," November 22, 1891, Roberts Papers; Emily to May [Whitney], March 10, 1890; Grant Papers; Emily to Heber J. Grant, February 2, 1890, Grant Papers; Emily to Heber J. Grant, July 11, 1890, Grant Papers; Emily to Heber J. Grant, October 3, 1890, Grant Papers; Emily to Heber J. Grant, October 27, 1890, Grant Papers; Emily to Heber J. Grant, November 9, 1890, Grant Papers; Emily to Heber J. Grant, December 27, 1890, Grant Papers; Emily to Heber J. Grant, January 6, 1891, Grant Papers.

20. Emily to Heber J. Grant, July 9, 1890, Grant Papers.

21. Emily to Heber J. Grant, July 25, 1890, Grant Papers.

22. Emily to Heber J. Grant, December 27, 1889; Emily to Heber J. Grant, December 27, 1890; Dessie Grant Boyle, "An Appreciation," draft in Grant Letterpress Copybook, 74:100.

23. Emily to May [Whitney], May 18, 1890, Grant Papers; Emily to Heber J. Grant, July 13, 1890, Grant Papers; Wilford Woodruff, Diary, August 10, 1890, Wilford Woodruff Papers, Church Archives; John Henry Smith, Diary, February 15, 1890; George Goddard, Diary, August 11–14, 1890, George Goddard Papers, Church Archives.

24. Emily to May [Whitney], March 10, 1890; Emily to Heber J. Grant, May 14, 1890, Grant Papers; Emily to Heber J. Grant, August 19, 1890, Grant Papers; Emily to Heber J. Grant, November 6, 9, 1890, Grant Papers.

24. Emily to Heber J. Grant, November 6, 1890.

26. Emily to Heber J. Grant, [July 1886?], Grant Papers. While in England, Emily started using pseudonyms in her correspondence. To provide footnoting clarity, actual names have been substituted for aliases.

27. Emily to Heber J. Grant, May 27, 1890, Grant Papers; Emily to Heber J. Grant, July 11, 1890; Emily to Heber J. Grant, October 3, 1890, Grant Papers; Emily to Heber J. Grant, December 1, 1890, Family Correspondence.

28. Emily to Heber J. Grant, August 11, 1890, Grant Papers; Emily to Heber J. Grant, November 19, 1890, Grant Papers; Emily to Heber J. Grant, November 27, 1890, Grant Papers.

29. Emily to Heber J. Grant, May 27, September 13, 1890, Grant Papers.

30. Grant, Letterbook Diary, January 30, 1890, Grant Papers; Emily to Heber J. Grant, February 2, 1890; Emily to Heber J. Grant, April 27, 1890, Grant Papers; Emily to Heber J. Grant, June 24, 1890, Grant Papers.

31. Emily to Heber J. Grant, March 18, 1891; Grant, Letterbook Diary, September 29, 1890; Grant, Diary, November 21, December 13, 1889; Grant, Diary, holograph, May 27, 1888, Grant Papers.

32. Emily to Heber J. Grant, June 24, 1890, Grant Papers.

33. Emily to Heber J. Grant, July 11, 13, 1890, Grant Papers.

34. Emily to Heber J. Grant, September 14, 1890, Grant Papers.

35. Grant, Letterbook Diary, June 20, July 22, 25, and 28, 1890; Emily to May [Whitney], January 27, 1891, Grant Papers; Emily to Heber J. Grant, July 16, [1890?], Grant Papers; Emily to Heber J. Grant, July 27, 1890, Grant Papers; Emily to Heber J. Grant, January 1, 1891, Grant Papers; Emily to Heber J. Grant, January 11, 1891, Grant Papers; Emily to Heber J. Grant, January 23, 1891, Grant Papers; Flower, "Mormon Colonization of the San Luis Valley," 126.

36. Emily to Heber J. Grant, January 27, 1890, Grant Papers; Emily to Heber J. Grant, July 16, 1890, Grant Papers; Emily to Heber J. Grant, February 11, 1891, Grant Papers; John Henry Smith, Diary, July 16, 24, and August 2, 1892. The feelings against Stake President Silas Smith were so strong that he was accused of aiding the lawmen.

37. Emily to Heber J. Grant, December 27, 1889, Grant Papers.

38. Emily to Heber J. Grant, October 13, 1890, Grant Papers.

39. Emily to Heber J. Grant, October 27, 1890, Grant Papers. Emily's statements are interspersed with long miscellaneous comments. By bringing them together the effect is more dramatic.

40. Emily to Heber J. Grant, November 9, 1890; Emily to Heber J. Grant, January 21, 1891; Grant, Letterbook Diary, November 29, 1890.

41. Emily to Heber J. Grant, December 10, 1890, Grant Papers; Emily to Heber J. Grant, December 27, 1890; Emily to Heber J. Grant, January 21, 1891.

42. Emily to Heber J. Grant, January 27, 1890, Grant Papers.

43. Heber J. Grant to Emily, January 27, 1891, Grant Papers; Emily to Heber J. Grant, February 11, 1891; Emily to Heber J. Grant, March 20, 1891, Grant Papers; Grant, Diary, March 23, 1891.

44. John Henry Smith, Diary, June 17, 1892; Josephine Smith to George and Lucy [A. Smith], December 31, 1893, George A. Smith Papers.

45. Emily to Heber J. Grant, March 20, 1891, Grant Papers.

46. "Death of Mrs. Grant," *Deseret Evening News*, May 26, 1908, 1; *Deseret Evening News*, May 29, 1908.

Grant's Watershed:
Succession in the Presidency, 1887–1889

Events during 1887–89, during Elder Wilford Woodruff's succession to the Presidency of The Church of Jesus Christ of Latter-day Saints, remains an important but largely untold story—a time when differing views divided the Church's General Authorities and when the policies and procedures for installing a new president of the Church were tested and confirmed. These years are also important for the insights they offer in understanding the life of Heber J. Grant, who himself regarded that time as a personal watershed. While it is clear that he acted with candor, energy, and idealism throughout the episode, with hindsight he believed that he had erred, especially in breaching a vital rule of the Quorum—collegiality—as he and other young members of the Twelve had tried too hard to make their views prevail. So deep his later anguish, he cut troubling passages from his diary, and on becoming a senior Church leader he either avoided speaking of the Woodruff episode or retold the incident without including much of its detail, a not altogether conscious handling of a painful memory. But clearly it was a lesson learned. For the rest of his life, unity among the "Brethren" was a cherished, if never fully realized, ideal.[1]

Elder Grant, a self-conscious and fretful Victorian, may have judged himself too harshly. The incident took place early in his career when he had been called upon to juggle personal, family, and institutional pressures, and at a time when he was still learning the ways of his Quorum. Nor had he been alone. To one degree or another, Grant's views were shared by several other members of the Quorum—second generation leaders like Francis M. Lyman, John Henry Smith, and especially the outspoken Moses Thatcher.[2] These four men, along with the more seasoned Quorum member, Erastus Snow—Grant's benefactor and mentor from youth—felt uneasy about the influence and personality of George Q. Cannon in the leading councils of the Church. They also were reacting to the last years of the administration of President John Taylor, which they saw as peremptory and imperious.

The behavior of Grant and his friends was affected by the times. During the 1880s, the U.S. government took punitive steps against the Church, including the passage of the Edmunds-Tucker Act (1887), which forced many Church leaders into the "underground" to avoid arrest for "cohabitating" with their plural wives. Never in the Church's history had it borne such a legal assault upon its men and institutions. As a result, encounters and meetings of the General Authorities were few and the chance for misunderstanding was real—this at a time when the Quorum of the Twelve was more fully sorting out its institutional duties and procedures (illus. 10-1). How should it interact with the First Presidency or even with the Salt Lake Stake, which its president for a time appeared to claim privileges beyond those normally exercised by such ecclesiastical units in the modern church? Only later would these questions be answered and the Twelve assume its modern organizational iden- tity. Only later would the Quorum hold regularly scheduled quo- rum meetings to promote harmony and decision-making. And more to the point, only later would the Twelve's role in presidential succession become routine.

President Taylor's "Sudden" Death

During the last week of June 1887, John W. Taylor informed Grant of the approaching death of Church President John Taylor. Young Taylor had been taken to the Thomas Roueche farmhome in Kaysville, where his father had taken "underground" refuge over a half year earlier. "John W." returned to Salt Lake City badly shaken. His father lay critically ill, he told Grant, who learned for the first time of Taylor's condition. The President's legs were cold and enlarged, his tongue swollen, and his abdomen extended. Each day he could

Illus. 8-1. Members of the Quorum of the Twelve Apostles, ca. 1882. Top row *(left to right):* Wilford Woodruff, Charles C. Rich, Lorenzo Snow, Erastus Snow. Middle row *(left to right):* Franklin D. Richards, Brigham Young Jr., Albert Carrington, Moses Thatcher. Bottom row *(left to right):* Francis M. Lyman, John Henry Smith, George Teasdale, Heber J. Grant.

accept only a little food, perhaps a mouthful of bread, a spoonful or two of ice cream, or a bracing glass of Dixie wine, which the prevailing interpretation of the Church's Word of Wisdom then did not proscribe. Taylor's attendants called the disease "dropsy," the nineteenth-century description for any kind of edema or bodily swelling.[3]

Unknown to his son or to most Church members, including many members of the Twelve, President Taylor had been ill for some time, especially since January. His sickness had ebbed and flowed, but when at its worst, First Counselor George Q. Cannon was forced to bear the burden of Church administration (illus. 10-2). "It has been apparent to me that if decisions were reached and action taken in certain directions, I must assume the responsibility, and have done so," Cannon wrote in his journal, "though there are many things that I have not been able to do which I would like to have done."[4] As a result, the disoriented Taylor at times feared his counselor might be making decisions without his full approval, and to protect himself from any later charge of misconduct, Cannon began to keep a day-to-day record of Taylor's illness and of the decisions he was forced to take. As Taylor grew weaker, he stubbornly spurned doctors, and for a time he also spurned Cannon's suggestions for the need to attest a will or to summon the family.[5] Nor did he want his condition to be made public.

At first, Cannon did not resist Taylor's demands for silence. After all, it was possible that the Church leader might recover. But silence also served Cannon's sense of policy. At the time, Utah was again pursuing the goal of statehood, and Cannon, prudently, wanted no distracting publicity. Besides, he felt that if the news of Taylor's death were sudden, it might be used to good advantage. During the federal government's raid against plural marriage, when public opinion both inside and outside Utah was crucial, the shock of Taylor's death—if it came to that—might cast a useful sense of persecution and martyrdom upon the Church, which in fact later took place.[6]

However, with Taylor's health rapidly declining, Cannon was forced to assume leadership. Before informing the Taylor family of the condition of their husband and father, he had written Joseph F. Smith, the other counselor in the First Presidency, who was then hiding in distant Hawaii. While Taylor had firmly instructed Smith to remain there, Cannon now hinted to his fellow counselor that he might do otherwise. Later, Cannon asked his fellow Quorum member Franklin D. Richards to make the matter clearer. Richards then sent Smith a second letter. "You are not likely to get [direct] counsel direct from the Presidency upon . . . [your return]," Richards wrote. "You may in view of this fact realize your liberty."[7] Smith understood the meaning of these semi-veiled messages and left for Utah, arriving about a week before Taylor's passing. Cannon, who felt the heavy responsibility of making decisions for the Church while trying to be loyal to President Taylor's wishes, was pleased to see his fellow counselor so that the two could "function as a team."[8] Emboldened, Cannon also began to alert the members of the Twelve of Taylor's condition by suggesting that they return from their various underground stations, "either to this city or to where you could be easily reached."[9]

Courtesy Church Archives, The Church of Jesus Christ of Latter-day Saints

Illus. 10-2. The First Presidency, ca. 1880. *Left to right:* George Q. Cannon, John Taylor, Joseph F. Smith.

On the evening of July 25, 1887, these anticipations were realized when President Taylor died at the Roueche farm. Shortly before midnight, attendants washed the body and later that morning placed it in an undertaker's refrigerator for a final journey to Salt Lake City. Much of another day was used to conceal Taylor's last residence and the identity of his caretakers. Then, on the evening of July 26, black crepe began to replace the bunting that had been hung to celebrate Pioneer Day, and Church members at last heard the stunning news of their leader's death.[10]

Taylor's death dissolved the old First Presidency, and the Quorum of the Twelve began to function as the Church's presiding authority, a role that it would exercise for the next twenty-one months. During this time, the Quorum would review and decide important Church issues, a cumbersome and inefficient process because of the size of the group and because of the need to operate in inconvenient secrecy due to the polygamy raids. At the time, there were fourteen Quorum members. These included the twelve regular members of the Quorum as well as the counselors, George Q. Cannon and Joseph F. Smith, who had resumed their positions in the Quorum of the Twelve. Also attending some discussions was Daniel H. Wells, formerly Brigham Young's counselor, who now served as a "Counselor to the Twelve." Thus, in theory, fifteen men could attend Quorum meetings, though in practice the numbers present were usually fewer as other assignments and personal circumstances took some of the men elsewhere.

The size of the group was not the only problem. Only four of the men had their "liberty"—the ability to appear in public without the fear of arrest on charges of "cohabitation" for the practice of plural marriage. These included Franklin D. Richards and Lorenzo Snow, who had already made their peace with prosecutors by paying fines and serving jail sentences; the monogamous John W. Taylor; and Grant, whose two plural wives were not yet known.[11] However, elaborate precautions were required for most of the Quorum to protect them from arrest, and to attend a public meeting was out of the question. Traveling from northern Arizona, Elders John Henry Smith and Francis M. Lyman "disguised" themselves by shaving their beards. Elder Erastus Snow journeyed from Mexico posing as an emigrant. Closer to home, former counselors Cannon and Smith slipped into the President's office on South Temple Street by hiding themselves in a covered wagon disguised by cluttered pipes, a chicken coop, and a few chickens roosting on piles of hay.[12] Painfully, most could not even attend Taylor's funeral. The best they could do was watch the cortege from a distance.

Grant preached one of the funeral sermons, presumably because of his speaking ability and because of his "availability." He praised Taylor's "faithful, honest and conscientious life" and was certain of his former leader's great service to the Kingdom.[13] However, he said little or nothing about Taylor's personal warmth. From the time he had entered the Quorum, Grant found his leader to be distant and unresponsive—to the point that Grant wondered if Taylor liked him or his work. As a result, Grant was constantly off balance around Taylor. Shortly before his last illness, Taylor had unexpectedly embraced Grant and had praised him. "I was never more surprised in my life," Grant said.[14]

Nor was Elder Grant alone. While President Taylor was a man of undoubted talent, especially with the written and spoken word, his personality and administrative style was stern. The problem involved culture and personality—and probably the older generation of which Taylor was a part. In contrast to the open and expressive behavior of the younger, frontier-born Quorum members, one biographer found Taylor to be "correct, reserved, and cultivated"—by no means inferior qualities, yet, nonetheless, lacking in charm.[15] It was said that he carried himself stiffly, which probably had less to do with his attitude toward the office he held than with his natural and native English reserve. And he could be firm to the point of stubbornness. "There was no power on earth that could bend the will of John Taylor," Joseph F. Smith, his counselor, recalled from experience.[16] Indeed, Taylor's independence and resolve were legends in their own time.

While Taylor was still alive, his First Presidency typically did not inform or consult with members of the Twelve—or invite their recommendations. That complaint probably could have been also leveled in some measure against Taylor's predecessors, but Taylor seemed unusually aloof, impatient—and at times impersonal. Why were not the Apostles more active in their ministries, he asked? From the first years of the Church, the Apostleship had not required full-time service. Unless serving on a formal proselytizing mission, a member of the Twelve was allowed latitude for personal as well as ecclesiastical activity. However, with the Church growing, the balance was tipping, and Taylor appeared to be dissatisfied with the proportion of the apostolic time given to Church work. Could not the men be more active in their preaching and visiting to outlaying congregations? The issue came to a head in the Church's important Salt Lake Stake, where Stake President Angus Cannon, George Q.'s brother, seemed to treat the Twelve as if they were unwelcome intruders.[17] Nowhere in the Church did members of the Quorum feel such slights, which perhaps reflected Angus Cannon's claim that Zion's central stake had special prerogatives.

Or was it because Angus was reflecting the First Presidency's views that the Apostles should be more active in visiting outlying congregations? By summer 1887, a majority of the Quorum, probably a consensus, felt the role of the Twelve needed redefinition. If Taylor and Cannon wanted them on Church preaching and visiting assignments, Quorum members felt that they should be formally assigned to do such work and that their standing in the Church should reflect the importance of their calling.

The Cannon-Wells Controversy

The more pressing problem of who would succeed Taylor as Church President was also complicated by issues of personality, which centered around George Q. Cannon. Sometimes what appears to some to be strengths may be perceived as weaknesses by others. "Perhaps no man among us . . . is as gifted as Cannon," thought fellow Quorum member John Henry Smith.[18] Yet Smith and others often found themselves irritated by his manner. "I do wish Pres C. would not impress me with my excessive littleness continually," confided Brigham Young Jr., another of Cannon's associates, to his diary. "While he is kind and good and his all is upon the altar, still he makes his brethren feel that he is too much their superior."[19] These comments were made a decade after the succession controversy, but they might have been expressed equally at the time. Although Cannon moved easily with the best talent in Utah and even on occasion with the best in Washington, D.C., where he had served as a territorial representative, it appeared to some Apostles that he, for all his capacity, had the need to assert continually his mastery.

Cannon's personality alone would not have made him a center of controversy. However, his colleagues were troubled also by Cannon's way of doing things. Some thought him too shrewd, weaving political webs and magnifying some issues out of natural proportion. Others complained that he tended to involve himself in large and sometimes needless, secret projects, where he could give full vent to his careful planning. The national press, not caring about his principles but judging his personality and talent, called him the Mormon Richelieu, after the powerful Cardinal who had done so much to influence the seventeenth-century French court. But a Richelieu is never so much loved by associates as admired, and then usually after the fact. In Cannon's case, a full appreciation for his remarkable service, even among his admirers, would come only after his death.

Had Cannon remained subject to the strong wills of Brigham Young and John Taylor, there probably would not have been much of a problem. But by 1887, with Taylor seriously ill, Cannon had to involve himself in several difficult issues. First, there was the case of his son John Q. Cannon. After completing a mission in Europe, young Cannon had been called as a counselor in the Presiding Bishopric, but the assignment did not seem to hold much attraction for him. Grant, watching the newcomer, saw him as careless and indifferent. The indictment involved church as well as personal activities.[20]

But neither Grant nor any other Church leader, including John Q's father, realized the depth of the problem. More and more, the younger Cannon was enjoying the cigars, strong drink, and billiards of the Walker House, where he also gambled. Apparently to cover his losses or to support his style of living, he forged one $1,000 check and was reported to have removed $11,000 from the Church's general and temple accounts.[21] And the misconduct went further. Setting aside President Taylor's refusal to allow him to enter plural marriage,[22] John Q. began a relationship with "Louie" Wells, the daughter of Daniel H. Wells and the sister of his wife "Annie." By September 1886, Louie had suffered a miscarriage, and when John Q. confessed his conduct to his father, the latter demanded that his son make a public admission. Several days later, with no forewarning at all, Stake President Angus Cannon and John Q. suddenly appeared at the Tabernacle pulpit during a regular weekly Sunday service. Interrupting the speaker, John Q. confessed his sin to the congregation, after which his uncle announced his excommunication. The two then left as quickly as they appeared.[23]

Public confession of a transgression like John Q. Cannon's was not unusual. However, because he was a General Authority and because the announcement had been so sudden and unexpected, it created "great sensation" and "profound impression."[24] Unfortunately, the incident at the Tabernacle was not the end of things. With anti-Mormon prosecutors looking into the case in the belief that John Q. must be guilty of cohabitation, George Q. Cannon advised his son to divorce Annie and marry Louie, whose role had not yet been made public. The hope apparently was to protect the family from further embarrassment when the cohabitation case went to trail. This, too, created public controversy when Louie died in childbirth in San Francisco, and during her funeral in Salt Lake City, Angus Cannon revealed more details of John Q. Cannon's affair, including perhaps more than an intimation of Louie's role. This news—so startling and so unfitting for the occasion—caused Annie, her mother Emmeline B. Wells, and several other women in the congregation to faint. During the troubled funeral, some tried to silence Angus by shouting, "Shame!" But the stake president held his ground by claiming he was revealing Annie's role in the affair at his brother's bidding.[25]

"The leading home topic is the death of Louie W. Cannon, . . . and . . . what occurred at the Funeral," wrote one of the Quorum members, who may have been minimizing things.[26] So deep was the Wellses' outrage that another member of the Quorum wondered if "mortal enmity" between the Cannon and the Wells families would result.[27] In fact, when "Millie" Wells, another of the Wells sisters, met Angus Cannon on the street, she struck him across the face. Not intimidated, he threatened to publish a "card" revealing more details of the affair.[28]

The Wells family was upset by more than Angus's open disclosures and their untimely manner. They also feared that Annie's rights might not have been protected. Moreover, the enforced divorce, they feared, might bring undeserving stigma upon her and possibly deprive her of a fair divorce settlement. Further, some worried about

Annie repeating her sister's difficulty of a nonsanctioned sexual relationship: after all, she still seemed very much drawn to her former husband. These problems were solved when Annie and John were remarried some time later.[29]

At the time of John Q.'s excommunication, Grant had approved of President Cannon's straight-forward, public policy toward his son. It seemed honest and just. But as more details of John Q.'s activity came to light, Grant began an about-face. Grant was hardly a disinterested or insulated party, since Emily, yet another of the Wells sisters, was one of his plural wives. To reinforce the Wellses' point of view, his father-in-law, Daniel Wells, allowed him to read the letters that had passed between himself and George Q. This correspondence, to Grant, suggested that Cannon had not been as open as he had at first seemed, especially about John Q.'s lack of honesty. Rather than taking the broad view that Cannon's policy had saved the Church from embarrassment, Grant chose to see the matter in family terms: Cannon had protected his son while at the same time revealing too much about Louie. "Unless I am greatly mistaken . . . [President Cannon's] action has been wrong and someday there will be a squaring of accounting that will be anything but pleasant."[30]

Cannon's Leadership Role

The emotions about the John Q. Cannon affair peaked about the same time the Quorum was learning the details of the First Counselor's leadership during the last months of President Taylor's administration.

At a meeting attended by a small group of Quorum members several weeks before Taylor's passing, Cannon revealed for the first time Taylor's long, incapacitating illness. While rumors may have already been in circulation, the official statement of Taylor's condition was stunning. Because Taylor had been seriously ill since January, the question naturally arose why they had not been informed earlier. Why the secrecy? When Cannon also spoke of exigencies requiring him to "arrange" certain matters, some of the Quorum members began to question President Cannon's handling of details. Was there a story behind the story? As usual, secrecy was the midwife to suspicion, however much the policy of confidentiality had been Taylor's, not Cannon's, at least in its initial stage.[31]

In short, there was little in Cannon's statements that could not be explained and justified, especially in light of Taylor's administrative style and declining health. However, the confusing and suspicious times made most members of the Quorum seek explanation. Had Cannon used his near-exclusive access to President Taylor to suppress news of his condition and in the process gain influence in the Church? Was Cannon behind the First Presidency's impatience about the personal and business activities of the Twelve? What about Angus Cannon's several awkward acts? Some even questioned whether George Q. Cannon had kept Joseph F. Smith in Hawaii so he, as the First Counselor, would not have to share power.

While there were several similar concerns, all of them centered on the question of the proper role of the Twelve. Were they entitled to be informed and consulted? Or did they exist only to react to the First Presidency's wishes? "Unless I am greatly in error," Grant wrote of George Q. Cannon, "no man can rule in the Church & Kingdom of God unless he is willing to fully and freely accord to . . . [the Twelve] all the rights and privileges belonging to his brethren."[32] Whether fair or not—and many accusations *were* unfair—Cannon had come to embody the discontent and anxiety felt by Grant and his young quorum associates, and this at a time when the Quorum was defining its procedures as an organized body.

The Bullion, Beck, and Champion Silver Mine

There was a third major concern about Cannon. A half dozen years earlier, President Taylor had received a formal revelation, confirmed by another, to invest in the Bullion, Beck, and Champion silver mine of John Beck near Eureka, Utah. Using a $25,000 Church loan, Taylor and Cannon joined Beck as proprietors and sole owners. The following October the transaction took an unusual turn. The three partners reserved 60 percent of the stock to Taylor for "any purpose he may deem wise." While the property should stand independent of Church control, it was understood that if the mine proved profitable, Taylor might reclaim the Kirtland Temple property, build the long-awaited Jackson County Temple, or perhaps endow Church education.[33] In short, the idea of this extraordinary project was to create a Church fund independent of regular budget procedures for extraordinary purposes.

While the Beck property seemed promising, it suffered from mismanagement and the litigation of rival claimants to the property.[34] The mine often threatened its owners with financial ruin, and Taylor and Cannon scurried to reduce their liability by seeking new investors from both inside and outside the Church. By March 1886, Beck had been replaced, and a group of recently acquired California stockholders used their government connections to bring about a settlement with rivals claiming a right to the property.

President Taylor and Elder Cannon also sought to raise money in Utah for the mine. Elder Moses Thatcher, William B. Preston, Marriner W. Merrill, and Charles O. Card—then leading Cache Valley churchmen—were asked to contribute to meet what was described as a pressing but undisclosed Church need. Thatcher gave $5,000, Preston and Merrill $1,000 each, and Card $500. With the possible exception of Thatcher, only later were the men told the underlying nature of their "investment" in the Beck property.[35] At the time, however, President Taylor clearly told them the general terms of their holdings. In each case, two-fifths of the stockholders' shares would be held by them personally; the rest would be placed in the pool of dedicated stock under the same conditions held by the first investors. Of the latter, Taylor had absolute control.[36]

While unusual, at first none of this was controversial. It was later learned, however, that three weeks before his death, Taylor had deeded the dedicated stock to Cannon, who now claimed the same independent and absolute control as his predecessor.[37] With the mine becoming profitable, several questions became important. Was Taylor competent to make the transfer? Why had the mine not gone to the Church? What right did Cannon have to the dedicated stock and its profits? Cannon's diary had explanations. According to this source, before Taylor died an attempt had been made to convey the property to the new Church President, but since no successor had yet been chosen, a name could not be inserted into the legal document and attorneys therefore feared that the transfer might be challenged. As a way out, according to Cannon, it was thought "eminently proper" to deed the property to him, with the stipulation that the Beck property would be used for Church purposes.[38] Whatever the merits of the arrangement, almost all these details were unknown to the Quorum during the first stages of the succession episode.

For whatever reason, Cannon failed later to convey the property to the Church when a new leader was selected. As a result, the disposition of the Bullion, Beck and Champion Silver Mine not only influenced the coming succession controversy, but it also loomed over several other important Church events during the coming decade.[39]

The Succession Question and Elder Grant

Before President Taylor died, the Saints speculated on whom might succeed him. In 1884, John T. Caine, Utah's knowledgeable Territorial Delegate, gave his views. "The office is elective," said Caine. If precedent is followed, the successor will be Wilford Woodruff. "He has great ability, and is possessed with the very demon of work. He would be a most able C[hurch] leader." But Caine thought there might be an alternative. George Q. Cannon, "one of our ablest men," would make an "excellent head of the church."[40]

Caine did not mean to suggest that the leader would be chosen democratically by the general Church membership. Everyone was clear on that point. The priesthood keys belonged with the Quorum members, who would choose Taylor's successor. Church members would then be called upon to sustain or ratify their choice. Before a new selection could take place, it was expected that the interim leader would be the current President of the Quorum, the senior Apostle. At the moment that man was Woodruff, an almost eighty-year-old Connecticut Yankee.

Including the death of Joseph Smith, there had been only two previous successions, and neither had gone smoothly. After Smith's death, Brigham Young had delayed reorganizing the First Presidency three and a half years due to the uncertain times of post–Joseph Smith Nauvoo, the Church's Exodus to the West, and the lack of a consensus within the Quorum. When he finally forced a decision in December 1847, it was done despite a lack of enthusiasm on the part of some Quorum members.[41] Taylor's succession had also been somewhat uncertain. "Some [of the Quorum] entertained ideas of one kind, some of another," recalled a participant in the Taylor deliberations, who did not give specific details. "It was thought that some should be brought to the Presidency who were not entitled to it, and we had to take a little time to learn and inquire into the mind of the Lord."[42] Therefore, three years passed before Taylor was formally sustained as President. With such an uncertain pattern in the past, some ambiguity about the process of succession remained. Before Taylor died, Cannon had asked for a clarification, an action that struck several of the Quorum members as possibly self-serving.[43]

Grant also had questions about succession, but for different reasons. He shared the hope of many Latter-day Saints that a member of the Smith family might once again lead the Church, and with Joseph Smith's own sons unavailable, he turned to Joseph F. Smith, the founding prophet's nephew.[44] During the post–Brigham Young interregnum, Daniel Wells had strongly spoken in Smith's behalf, citing an alleged revelation he had personally received. Also, Lorenzo Snow and Wilford Woodruff had predicted Smith's eventual rise to the office, which on their part was likely a speculation about Smith's eventual but not immediate destiny.[45]

Before learning of Taylor's late illness, Grant had asked Woodruff's opinion on the question. Was it absolutely necessary for Elder Woodruff to become Church President? Or might Woodruff help to select another? Perhaps startled by Grant's directness, Elder Woodruff declined an immediate response but promised a letter.[46]

Woodruff's reply on March 20, 1887, was self-effacing but determined. Claiming disinterest ("I do not expect to outlive the President of the Church"), he nevertheless insisted that if he became the senior Apostle he would not step aside. According to Woodruff, Church succession involved "plain truths" as "everlasting, unchangeable, and immovable as the pillars of heaven." The proper procedure would never be altered until the "coming of the Son of Man." Joseph Smith, Woodruff believed, had given the Quorum of the Twelve the keys of authority. Upon the death of President Taylor, the Quorum therefore would preside, and their presiding officer would be the President of the Twelve. It followed, then, that on the death of any Church President, the senior Apostle *was* the President of the Church, whatever his title. The President of the Twelve, then, of necessity would become the President of the Church and thereby would assume an incumbency ending only in the new leader's death.

Woodruff's words to Grant carried what may have been a criticism. "I have full confidence to believe that the Twelve Apostles have had experience and light enough to <u>shun any path pointed</u> out to <u>gratify</u> the <u>private</u> interest of any <u>man or set</u> of men against the interest of the Church." This sentence, with its underlined emphasis, may have aimed less at Grant's inquiries on behalf of Joseph F. than at the rumors circulating in the community about the availability of George Q. Cannon.[47]

That the kindly, saintly Woodruff should be looking over his shoulder was a commentary on the mood surrounding Cannon. A week later, Woodruff reported to Grant the rumor of Cannon's insistence that the deed of the Gardo House, the President's official residence, be transferred specifically to the future President of the Church, not to the President of the Twelve. Cannon allegedly had been overheard to say the two might not be the same.[48] The result again was the questioning of Cannon's motives, despite the fact that over the past decade Cannon in a series of sermons had argued that succession rightly belonged to the senior Apostle.[49] However, so uncertain and inflamed the atmosphere, it was apparently thought Cannon could not be taken at his word.

At the end of June, Grant huddled with Thatcher for a "long talk," and the two emerged believing that Cannon wanted the Presidency. They were equally sure, however, that the position would be denied him.[50] During the next ten days, the pressures and uncertainties of the situation seemed to grow. The day after meeting with Thatcher, Grant learned of Taylor's likely passing. The next day, he read letters from George Q. and Annie Wells Cannon, learning new, still more troubling details of Cannon's handling of John Cannon's affair. While he did not disclose the letter's contents, Grant's anger deepened. His dark mood also had him thinking about Joseph F. Smith's apparent exile. There was no one in the Church for whom Grant had a higher regard. Was Smith being treated fairly? At about this time, too, Grant heard Cannon's statement about his having made unilateral decisions, and the implication of these various reports and emotions now swept over him. The timing of Grant receiving this information heavily influenced his perceptions and feelings. On the evening of July 3, Grant was so overcome that he found sleep difficult.

During the night, he considered the "many changes" that would occur at Taylor's death. Grant also reflected upon his belief that Cannon wanted to become the new Church President. "Prest Cannon thinks I am the most ambitious young man in Utah," Grant reflected, "and I think there is no limit to his ambition." In contrast to his feelings about Cannon, Grant had "perfect" confidence in Joseph F. Smith. Certainly, in the post–John Taylor world, Grant hoped the latter's influence would prevail. At last, as often on occasion of stress, his mood turned inward. He rose from his bed and prayed for the strength to curb his own desires and ambition. He did not wish to be removed from "the path of duty."[51]

Four times during the month of July, Grant met with Woodruff, once with Thatcher present. While other questions were discussed, Church succession was very much a part of their conversation. "Prest Woodruff seemed to share my opinion that Prest Cannon had not treated our quorum with as much respect and consideration as he should have done, and also seemed to fully endorse my good opinion of Prest. Smith," Grant reported, seeing Woodruff's remarks through the prism of his own hope. According to Grant, Woodruff had no personal desire for the office and would be willing to sustain Joseph F. Smith if the Quorum should desire. Yet, it was also true that Woodruff gave little encouragement to such a move, having "no idea that such a thing would be done."

However, Grant's interviews with Woodruff left him impressed. If his brethren should move on Woodruff's candidacy, Grant claimed he would be "<u>perfectly satisfied</u>," though such an alternative seemed a distinct second in his mind to the highly preferred Joseph F. Smith.[52] Grant's preference in part was a matter of personality and relative youth; he felt drawn to Smith and his vigor, and he feared that Woodruff, whatever his sterling quality, might come to be unduly influenced by Cannon if Woodruff should become Church president. These fears were partly fueled by Cannon's leadership role after Taylor's death. The situation simply did not allow Cannon to step back into the Quorum as a regular member; as an experienced member of the First Presidency, he knew too much and was too indispensable. Cannon reported in his journal that Woodruff, recognizing his value, needed his help in the weeks and months after Taylor's death. "He felt quite unable to attend to the business, as it was all new to him. I was familiar with it, and he would be very much pleased to have me assist him."[53] While Cannon's willingness to help Woodruff may have been genuinely altruistic, some interpreted it as another sign of his grasp for influence.

The Apostles' Meetings to Determine Succession

On August 3, 1887, the Quorum had its first meeting since Taylor's death—and for several members it was their first meeting in several years. Inevitably, the recent issues and tensions, too long hedged and suppressed, broke into the open. Woodruff began by promising the Quorum that it would not be dispatched *en masse* from headquarters; nor would he seek an immediate reorganizing of the First Presidency. But Grant and Thatcher swept past these assurances to assail what they regarded as the recent slights experienced by the Quorum. Surprised and nettled, Cannon questioned the propriety of his being restored to the Quorum while such anger existed in the heart of some of its members.

For the moment, Cannon's demur was left unanswered. Wells had his own statement to make, which seemed to go in a different channel from the flow of the meeting and also from the general feeling of the Quorum. As a "Counselor of the Quorum"—John Taylor had never agreed to Wells's formal ordination to the body—Wells renewed his 1877 claim that the Quorum lacked any kind of presiding authority. Arguing with unusual power, Wells urged the Quorum to immediately choose Taylor's successor—he felt they had that much authority—but then urged them to retire from trying to manage affairs. That responsibility should lie with a newly created First Presidency, he believed.[54] Wells's speech flew in the face of the Quorum's growing sense of their role, as both individuals and as a presiding quorum.

However, most of the Quorum's discussion examined Cannon's past role. The assault continued into the late evening, and the former First Counselor was hard put to provide satisfying answers, particularly about John Q. Cannon's affair. But Cannon's explanations finally gained enough ground for most of the Quorum to offer Cannon their fellowship. Grant was less sure. On one hand, he wished to stand united with his colleagues and to show mercy. But he also thought collegial unity had left unsatisfied the demands of justice. "I am almost ashamed of myself that I did not stand [in opposition to Cannon] . . . until I was satisfied," he later said.[55] But in the end, he, too, extended his hand.

The proceedings of August 3 were the beginning of a pattern. The more senior Quorum members, seasoned by their Church service and more accepting of their usual and accepted roles, were unwilling to make a point about Cannon's recent acts. Woodruff, for instance, described the charges as mere "pointless things," matters of personality rather than as items of substance.[56] That position was unconvincing to some of the newer members of the Quorum, men like Thatcher and Grant. However, a clear majority of the Quorum—senior as well as junior members—wanted a change in several other areas of Church administration. Under their direction, many of Taylor's security guards were released and the vehicles used to serve President Taylor and other Church leaders hiding from federal marshals were sold. The Church's financial papers, previously scattered in private hands for the sake of security, were once more collected together. More pointedly, Cannon was asked to surrender the Church's financial books for auditing. He did so with some feeling, claiming pleasure at being rid of anything that might bring upon him a further attack from his colleagues.[57]

In spite of the handshakes of August 3, Cannon remained for Grant and others an uneasy presence. The problem lay not so much with settling past grievances as with planning for the future. With the exception of Wells, no one during the August 3 meeting had called for the reorganization of the First Presidency. Sensing the divisions among them, the Quorum for the time being was content to endorse Woodruff's letter to the Church proclaiming an apostolic rule.[58] But what was to be done about Cannon? If opposition in the Quorum made his selection as president unlikely—if the idea ever was a real possibility—he might, some feared, dominate Church affairs as First Counselor to an aging and perhaps too pliable Woodruff.

The possibility spawned at least one fanciful, anti-Cannon maneuver. According to the memory of Edwin D. Woolley Jr., later a stake president in Kanab, Utah, Thatcher wanted his father-in-law Erastus Snow, to lead the Church as chairman of an executive committee of the Quorum. Traveling across the northern Arizona plateau, Woolley heard Thatcher repeatedly ask Snow to make himself available for the position, and he claimed that if Snow did so, he would receive widespread support in the Quorum. For some time Snow refused to reply until Thatcher, growing impatient, complained that he was failing to grasp his chances. That finally brought a firm response from the usually impassive Snow. "I want you to understand that I will not fight my brethren," he said. He was apparently referring to fighting Woodruff, but quite possibly to Cannon also.[59]

When the Quorum met prior to the opening session of the October 1877 general conference, Woodruff hoped to defuse the growing tension. Convening at 10:00 A.M. at a pre-arranged underground station—some of the Quorum members arrived secretly before daylight—the meeting continued interminably through the afternoon and evening, ending only at 2:00 A.M. on October 6, six hours before the opening of the conference. "Prest. W. W. thought there were feelings in the Council unbecoming & wished the brethren to speak freely," commented Franklin D. Richards in his diary. Cannon spoke next. While acknowledging no specific wrongdoing, he asked for forgiveness. The months since Taylor's death, Cannon said, had brought him more personal suffering than any time in his life. His welling tears showed his emotion.

Despite Woodruff's good intention, the deliberations of October 5 and 6 did not have the desired effect. Once more the emotion of August 3 was present, and perhaps still more. Pausing to allow the senior members to speak first if they wished, Thatcher launched a warm attack on Cannon's leadership and way of doing business. Grant followed with a list of a dozen or more supposed Cannon infractions. For their part, John Henry Smith and Francis M. Lyman were less assertive. These men focused on what they felt was Cannon's disrespect for the Twelve. "Bro Cannon has been his ideal of a man until late years," said Lyman, "but . . . his confidence [in him] had been shaken," as any disagreement brought the lash.

When the junior members' accusations had run their course, even Grant saw how little their mills had ground. No single charge was of "very great importance," he admitted; only when all the irritations were added together did they seem to have much weight.[60] In fact, the opposite seems to have been true. From the evidence presented, it appeared that the controversy was mainly about apostolic perceptions, not Cannon's transgressions, and the former had their origin in Cannon's personality and administrative style.

"It was painful," Woodruff said in understatement. Still pursuing reconciliation, Woodruff reminded Cannon's critics of the human qualities of all the Church's past great leaders—yet in spite of this they had been called by God. He himself had often differed with President Taylor, he said. But Taylor was "responsible to God and not to me, and this is the key upon which I wish to treat all these matters." Likewise, Cannon of course had failings—"if he did not he would not be with us." Woodruff concluded by warning "if we did not feel to forgive and become united, the spirit of the Lord would not be with us."[61]

Clearly, nothing had been resolved. The next night, after a full schedule of general conference meetings, the Quorum again met until the early morning. It was more of the same: accusations, a Cannon defense, and senior members praying for the elusive balm of Gilead. Woodruff's secretary, L. John Nuttall, who had not attended the preceding day's meeting, was stunned by what he heard. "I <u>never</u> attended such a meeting," he said.[62] At one point, Thatcher and Cannon engaged in an exchange that Grant described as "not calcu-lated to bring them any nearer together."[63] Yet, when it was all done, some progress had been made. "Differences [were] healed and we were one again," said Brigham Young Jr. optimistically. "Thank God now we may unite the people[,] for oh they need a solid head."[64]

Grant's description of the October meetings was more per-sonal. He also had found them to be unpleasant, but seemed uncer-tain what to make of them—or of his own role in them. He sensed that he had vacillated. On one hand, he had not wished to seek "occasion against my brethren." He knew the need for mercy. How-ever, he wanted the "moral courage to say I am not satisfied [with Cannon's explanations] unless I am." When it was all over, despite his swings in emotion, he wrote a passage in his diary that bore the closest examination. "All I want is to have what I think is wrong made right," he wrote, "and if I am wrong I hope for wisdom to make amends. I desire to have the Kingdom of God first in my desires and affections and ask God's help to do this."[65]

To this point, Elder Woodruff had made no attempt to reorga-nize the First Presidency. Such a move might have increased tension. Yet as he tried to lead the Church as President of the Twelve, he found himself drawn to Cannon and not simply because no one else knew the business detail from the past administration. As Woodruff later remarked, Cannon had "the biggest and best mind in the Kingdom," which in Woodruff's new, growing estimate of the man was joined by a sense of Cannon's humility.[66] When nearly a year later Cannon accepted a plea bargain with government attorneys to serve a term in the territorial penitentiary for plural marriage, Woodruff felt his loss. "This leaves me in a Measure alone for 5 Months [Cannon's projected jail sentence]," he wrote in his diary, "but I will do the best I Can."[67]

Cannon's talents were best seen as a public speaker, a writer or, when working in a small circle, a peer or an adviser; it was within this last area—working with Woodruff—that Cannon was regaining his footing. The growing Woodruff-Cannon relationship was one reason why in mid-March 1888, before Cannon accepted his prison term, Woodruff announced his desire to reorganize the Church Presidency.[68] In a series of four business meetings of the Quorum, starting on March 20, Woodruff tried to get his brethren to approve the plan. Lorenzo Snow, Franklin D. Richards, Brigham Young Jr., John W. Taylor, and Counselor Daniel H. Wells voted to sustain the measure. In opposition were Erastus Snow, Moses Thatcher, Francis M. Lyman, John Henry Smith, and Heber J. Grant. The Quorum was badly split. As usual Cannon lay at the center of things. Everyone understood that Cannon would probably be selected as Elder Woodruff's First Counselor, and this hard fact prevented resolution.[69]

During these meetings, Cannon's record was reviewed again and again—and then again and again. The first day alone left Brigham Young Jr. wringing his hands. "Much valuable time is wasted in these comparatively groundless charges and their generally successful refutation. I tremble for the future if we continue these unrighteous proceedings."[70] The second day went no better. Woodruff recalled:

> I Called upon the Quorum to bring to light all the Accusations they had against Brother Cannon As the younger Brethren including Erastus Snow was filled with Jealousey against him And he proved ev[e]ry accusation against him to be fals[e]. He was Accused to using church Money to [pay] for his Son John Q for Embezeling Church Money. He proved them to be fals[e]. Th[en] of paying large sums of Church Money in the Iron Mine that He proved to be fals[e]. Also in dealing with the Beck Mine. That was proved fals[e] and Ev[e]ry other Accusation was proved fals[e]. It was another painful day.[71]

By the fourth day, it was clear that matters were worse, not better. "The more we tryed to get to gether the wider apart we were," wrote the despairing Woodruff. "I never saw as much bitterness manifest against one good man by 5 Apostles since the days of the Apostate Twelve against the Prophet Joseph in Kirtland."[72] In the heat of emotion, Woodruff was satisfied that those opposing Cannon were dictated by simple jealousy. "Any acts of President Taylor that five of the Twelve did not think was right was laid to George Q. Cannon," he complained.[73] In reply, Erastus Snow, the nominal leader of the anti-Cannon group, also used strong language. Apparently still upset with Cannon's attempt to minimize rumors of the financial misdeeds of John Q.—and perhaps the misdeeds of another son, the rising politician Frank J. Cannon—Snow leveled the charge of "toadyism" and "man worship" against him. These words brought a sharp rebuke from Woodruff. When it was all over, Woodruff was full of remorse. "I think I done wrong & went to far in the matter," he said of his encounter with Snow.[74] With such disunity present and with no solution in sight, on the evening of March 23, Woodruff withdrew his proposal.[75]

"Never in my life have I suffered such an ordeal," said the bruised Cannon. For months he had avoided arrest for cohabitation and the thought of serving in the penitentiary had often been on his mind. But these meetings of accusation made the fear of prison recede. "Nothing" could be compared to facing the examination of his five brethren in the Quorum, he said.[76] Yet, while wounded, Cannon acknowledged no self-doubt, steeled by a confidence in his motives and by the self-inoculation that great men often feel toward stricture. "There are none of father's actions but what he can defend, and show that his intentions were good in doing them," said Abraham Cannon, another of Elder Cannon's sons, who no doubt reflected his father's views.[77]

Grant's emotions are more difficult to gauge. While he was present and active during the March meetings, surviving diaries tell little of his role. Nevertheless, quite likely Brigham Young Jr. had Grant and Thatcher in mind when complaining of the "useless talk" engaged in by some of the younger members. "It does seem the less we know the more we have to say."[78] Young's comment may have had something to do with the new administrative policies being urged by the five dissenting Quorum members. More than raising questions about succession, these men wanted reform. During the March meetings, they worked to decentralize First Presidency authority by moving some financial functions to the Presiding Bishopric and still other activities to committees within the Twelve.[79] Woodruff's consent to these suggestions brought the first measure of truce since before Taylor's death.

By October 1888, Grant, Thatcher, and several others were appointed to raise cash for the hard-strapped Church by selling the organization's excess property. Once again their acts were annoying to the older brethren. In February 1889, Nuttall, Woodruff's secretary, recorded his displeasure at such attention to temporal things. "I went to bed," said Nuttall, "having fears in my own mind as to Moses Thatcher's integrity for the welfare of the church and Kingdom—In that financial matters have more weight with him & Bro. H. J. Grant than the things of the Kingdom."[80] However, had Nuttall and others been watching more carefully, they might have sensed a change. Erastus Snow, upset by his exchange with Woodruff, had written both Grant and Thatcher to express his personal sorrow and concern. Snow had come to the conclusion that Grant and Thatcher were on the spiritual precipice, and he wanted them to know it. They had pressed their views too strongly, and Snow believed that if they continued to do so, the two would lose their places in the Quorum.[81] Snow's letters were kind but filled with portent.

In the following months, Snow's warning slowly took hold of Grant, and he later described it as a turning point in his life. Then, too, Grant must have reacted to the contrary example of Thatcher, whose opposition did not cease. In late 1888, Thatcher surprised his colleagues by threatening to sue Cannon over the Beck property stock and profit distributions. This extraordinary act—which introduced the possibility of two General Authorities engaged in legal action—cost Thatcher much of the influence he then retained with his colleagues. When Thatcher continued to agitate the Beck issue, Grant privately warned him, much like Erastus Snow's early caution, of the possible result of his behavior. In fact, Grant did more. He went to Cannon and spoke of Thatcher's continuing hostility—news that Cannon could hardly have found too surprising.[82] But more astonishing was Grant's change. Within the year, he turned from being Cannon's opponent to being his defender.

Final Steps to Reorganize the First Presidency

By January 1889, President Woodruff made another attempt to reorganize the Presidency.[83] At the time, Quorum meetings could still be tension-filled, noisy affairs, with Thatcher and Grant insisting upon more businesslike financial procedures for the Church. Woodruff left one such meeting complaining he would rather attend a funeral.[84] But on the issue of succession, the Quorum seemed to be coming together. In February, Woodruff wrote Francis M. Lyman, then serving a cohabitation prison term, asking for his position on the question and received Lyman's approval to go forward.[85] Presumably other soundings went as well.

The growing consensus was a tribute to Woodruff's leadership. A less patient man might have forced a greater confrontation and brought open rupture. Yet, President Woodruff's quiet way had controlled events. And whatever his words about denying personal ambition, he had never yielded from his view that he, as senior Apostle, must lead the Church, temporarily and in the long-term. Faced by his resolution, the dissenting members never felt freedom to bring any of their succession alternatives to the Quorum. As a result, by 1889, only two leadership possibilities existed: (1) President Woodruff might continue to preside over the Church as President of the Twelve with Cannon at his side, or (2) he might become President of the Church with Cannon as his First Counselor. The Quorum was left with Cannon de facto or Cannon de jure. The latter had the advantage of ending the unwieldy and fractious business meetings.

One issue still had to be settled before there could be a new First Presidency. Woodruff asked Thatcher and Cannon to resolve their Bullion-Beck dispute, and, consequently, Cannon at last agreed to distribute Thatcher's portion of dedicated stock. While Thatcher remained "very persistent" on the other Bullion-Beck matters, he granted that his differences with Cannon had been resolved enough to permit the Quorum to continue with its business.[86]

Two days later, on April 5, 1889, the Quorum met and the motion to organize the First Presidency carried unanimously and with little discussion. However, when the issue of Woodruff's counselors arose, the troubled past could not be entirely forgotten. Nominated as First Counselor, Cannon rhetorically asked if he should be excused from the office. He could only accept President Woodruff's invitation, he said, with the knowledge that it was God's will and that he had the "hearty and full approval of my brethren." He assumed that his colleagues would "all understand my feelings in this matter."[87]

Woodruff provided certainty on the first question. He had prayed about counselors, he told the Quorum, and announced the Lord's "mind and will" that George Q. Cannon and Joseph F. Smith should be selected (illus. 10-3). The second question—whether Quorum members would support the nomination—ended almost as well. The men responded with expressions of good will, although if the surviving diaries give full accounts, Grant said very little. Thatcher, however, was unbowed. Because of President Woodruff's assurance of divine approval, Thatcher told his colleagues that he would vote for Cannon, although, he said, he wished he had put himself in a position to receive the "same manifestation." Nor was that the only suggestion of bygones. "There has been some matters of . . . [Cannon's] former administration which have not been approved by the Saints but I will let that pass," said Thatcher. But "when I vote for him I shall do so freely and will try and sustain him with all my might."[88] These careful words were apparently the best Thatcher could do.

Prior to being sustained by the Quorum, Cannon spoke to each of the Brethren, calling them by name, one by one, to ask their forgiveness. "I do this," he said, "as a duty, privilege and a pleasure."[89] Cannon's ascension was best served by generosity. Woodruff also had words of healing. He assured the Twelve that there was never a time when the Church needed them as much. A few days later, he also told them that they were welcome to work with the Salt Lake Stake, Angus Cannon's acts notwithstanding.[90]

The names of Presidents Woodruff, Cannon, and Smith were unanimously accepted at the Church's April general conference in 1889. One conference speech after another pled for harmony. Thus, only a hint of the rift was exposed, and that only by giving emphasis to its nonexistence. The Woodruff succession had in fact preserved unity—at least outward unity and consensus. Taking his office, President Woodruff was modest and well-meaning. "This office is placed upon me in my 83 year of my life," he said. "I pray God to Protect me during my remaining Days and give me power to Magnify my Calling to the End of my days."[91]

Conclusion and Aftermath

Although more than a century has passed since the Woodruff succession, it is still difficult to make judgments about it. Why had emotions been so strong and words so angry? On one level, some answers may be found in the issues of honor and propriety, to which

Courtesy Church Archives, The Church of Jesus Christ of Latter-day Saints

Illus. 10-3. The First Presidency, 1894. *Left to right:* George Q. Cannon, Wilford Woodruff, Joseph F. Smith. The statement at the bottom of the pictures reads: "First Presidency of the Mormon Church taken on the 87th birthday of President Wilford Woodruff, 1894."

the late nineteenth century gave such importance. While many details of the Annie and Louie Wells relationship with John Q. Cannon remain screened from view—those elusive details that Grant found so damning in the Wells family's correspondence—enough of a public record exists to suggest there were grounds for complaint, both in the commission of acts and later in the management of the affair. Further, John Q. Cannon's financial misconduct made these sensitivities irretrievably worse, involving as it did Church as well as family reputation.

The personalities of John Taylor and George Q. Cannon created their own social discord. Cannon, who bore the brunt of the succession controversy, had great intellectual and administrative gifts, as well as Christian virtue. Nevertheless, he lacked the politician's easy, personal touch that might have allowed many of his associates to like him as much as they admired him. Yet, as Woodruff observed, the charges brought against Cannon mainly concerned "personality" and not "substance."[92] The most potentially serious accusation was his gaining control of the Bullion-Beck consecrated property during Taylor's decline, the full details of which still wait extended historical analysis. However, in Cannon's defense, the matter was investigated during the Woodruff succession, and no charge of wrongdoing was leveled against him, then or later.

It is likely that each one of these factors—the John Q. Cannon affair, the personalities of John Taylor and George Q. Cannon, and Cannon's administration of Church programs—might have been managed without incident had historical circumstance not been so contrary. On one hand, the U.S. government's crusade against plural marriage left the Church's efficient governing structure in ruin, with a lack of communication that gave life to rumor and misunderstanding. Also true, the difficulty of the Woodruff succession coincided with the historic rise of the Quorum of the Twelve. Previously, except in the two eras of apostolic interregnum, its members had served the Church as individuals acting on assignment from the First Presidency. However, by Taylor's last years, it was clear that the Quorum had a budding institutional role of its own. Taylor's insistence that the Twelve be more active in their ministries was one sign of the change. Another was the Quorum's complaint that its members had not been consulted during the last months of the crippled Taylor administration and the insistence of some of the Apostles that their voices be heard during the Woodruff succession. In short, this was a time when the Quorum was gradually assuming its modern role of a regularly constituted, fully engaged organization, second only in influence to the First Presidency.

The remaining threads of the succession story wove themselves in fairly predictable patterns. During the 1890s, George Q. Cannon served as much as he had in the past, providing strong and able, and at times controversial, leadership. In 1898, when Woodruff died, Lorenzo Snow assumed the office of Church President, and Cannon's heavy influence over policy diminished within hours, although Cannon was retained as First Counselor; he died three years later.

As part of President Lorenzo Snow's administrative transition, Cannon was asked to give an accounting of the Beck property stock, which had proven enormously profitable in the 1890s. Since the Woodruff succession, the Beck, Taylor, and Thatcher interests had each forced the dispersal of their portions of the "dedicated stock" and then used the proceeds for their own purposes. Cannon's share of the pool had earned an impressive $160,000, which he had used for a variety of Church and personal projects, including the quiet repayment of John Q. Cannon's speculations. Snow and Cannon, not wishing any impropriety, agreed that Cannon should surrender assets to the trustee-in-trust to cover all Cannon's private expenditures, plus interest—despite the fact that others involved in the mine had used its dividends for their personal gain. The amount of Cannon's repayment was never announced, nor for that matter was the transfer itself. As enigmatic was the value of the dedicated stock, which by the time of the Snow-Cannon settlement may have become worthless. Thus closed the chapter that Joseph F. Smith called "one of those things that perhaps had never been heard of before, and whose parallel would never be heard of again."[93] Whatever its virtues, the Bullion and Beck endeavor had generated more than its share of ill will.

Others involved in the Woodruff succession had their own stories to tell. Moses Thatcher's alienation deepened in the 1890s. During these years, he suffered from a severe illness and a resulting drug dependency, which may have increased his instability. Increasingly unwilling to accept the Quorum's consensus, particularly in political matters, he was at last removed from the Twelve in 1896.

Grant, ironically, played a role in preferring charges and acting as a prosecuting witness against him.[94]

The voluble Grant continued to play an active role in the Twelve's discussions, just as he had done during the years 1887 to 1889. Yet, much of his persistence and assurance was gone. He also continued to make peace with Cannon, making confession both to him and to members of the Quorum, believing that "God had forgiven him" for his accusations and wishing that his brethren would do so, too.[95] To help finance the new Utah sugar industry, Grant joined Cannon as a partner in Cannon, Grant & Company. In this and other enterprises, the two maintained respectful relations, although the differences in personality that had done so much to confound them in the late 1880s were never far from the surface. If Grant worried about some of Cannon's initiatives in the 1890s, he was now willing, as a rule, to let those questions be settled by time and by senior colleagues.

Finally, Lorenzo Snow's smooth succession to the presidency in 1898 owed a great deal to the events of 1887–89. They had been decisive in strengthening the precedent of Church succession by apostolic seniority, although Snow himself, who had sustained Woodruff's succession, mused in one passing conversation in 1890 that in matters of succession the Quorum still might choose whomever it wished, even a non-Apostle.[96] In the discussion preceding Snow's selection, it was Grant who maintained the traditional view, citing Woodruff's earlier letter to him.[97] As one who had questioned the idea of succession by apostolic seniority ten years earlier, Grant's statement suggested how deeply the idea had taken root in him and in the Church itself. His words also reflected how much the episode had molded and seasoned him.

Notes

1. Grant's papers remain one of the best sources for reconstructing the succession difficulty. During the late 1880s, he maintained an extensive correspondence as well as writing two parallel copies of his diary. While destroying parts of one copy of his diary, he retained the second in full, perhaps inadvertently. For profiles of two other leading figures in the succession episode—and details about the event itself—see Thomas G. Alexander, *Things in Heaven and Earth: The Life and Times of Wilford Woodruff, a Mormon Prophet* (Salt Lake City: Signature Books, 1991), 235–45; and Davis Bitton, *George Q. Cannon: A Biography* (Salt Lake City: Deseret

Book, 1999), 286–98. For a previously published detail about the succession, see D. Michael Quinn, *The Mormon Hierarchy: Extensions of Power* (Salt Lake City: Signature Books, 1997), 45–50. Also see Reed C. Durham Jr. and Steven H. Heath *Succession in the Church* (Salt Lake City: Bookcraft, 1970), 78–102; and Todd M. Compton, "John Willard Young, Brigham Young, and the Development of Presidential Succession in the LDS Church," *Dialogue: A Journal of Mormon Thought* 35 (Winter 2002), 111–34. This last article treats the development of apostolic seniority within the Mormon tradition and assumes its general acceptance in the nineteenth-century selection of Church Presidents—an argument that this chapter underplays.

2. Heber J. Grant to Georgia Thatcher, April 18, 1896, Grant General Correspondence, Grant Papers, Church Archives, The Church of Jesus Christ of Latter-day Saints, Salt Lake City.

3. Heber J. Grant, Letterpress Diary, June 25 and 29, 1887, Grant Papers; Franklin D. Richards, Diary, June 27, 1887, Church Archives; Samuel Bateman, Diary, June and July 1887, L. Tom Perry Special Collections, Harold B. Lee Library, Brigham Young University, Provo, Utah; Abraham H. Cannon, Diary, June 25, 1887, Perry Special Collections.

4. George Q. Cannon, Journal, July 18, 1887, as cited in Bitton, *George Q. Cannon,* 287–88.

5. Grant, Letterpress Diary, July 7, 1887; Franklin D. Richards to Joseph F. Smith, June 28, 1887, Joseph F. Smith Correspondence, Church Archives.

6. George Q. Cannon to John W. Young, July 11, 1887, First Presidency Letterbooks, Church Archives.

7. George Q. Cannon to Joseph F. Smith, March 21, 1887, First Presidency Letterbooks; Franklin D. Richards to Joseph F. Smith, June 28, 1887, Joseph F. Smith Correspondence.

8. Bitton, *George Q. Cannon,* 287–88.

9. George Q. Cannon to Brigham Young, Francis M. Lyman, and John Henry Smith, July 1, 1887, First Presidency Letterbooks; George Q. Cannon to Erastus Snow, July 1 and 11, 1887, First Presidency Letterbooks; George Q. Cannon to Wilford Woodruff, July 1, 1887, First Presidency Letterbooks; John Henry Smith, Diary, July 21, 1887, J. Willard Marriott Library, University of Utah, Salt Lake City.

10. Bateman, Diary, July 25, 1887; Richards, Diary, July 25–26, 1887.

11. Franklin D. Richards to Joseph F. Smith, June 28, 1887, Joseph F. Smith Correspondence.

12. John Henry Smith, Diary, July 30, 1887; Andrew Karl Larson, *Erastus Snow: The Life of a Missionary and Pioneer for the Early Mormon Church* (Salt Lake City: University of Utah Press, 1952), 702; Bateman, Diary, August 2, 1887.

13. "Laid to Rest: The Remains of President John Taylor Consigned to the Grave," *Millennial Star* 49 (September 5, 1887): 561.

14. Heber J. Grant to J. Golden Kimball, April 23, 1903, Grant Letterpress Copybook, 36:81–83, Grant Papers.

15. Paul Thomas Smith, "John Taylor," in *The Presidents of the Church,* ed. Leonard J. Arrington (Salt Lake City: Deseret Book, 1987), 113.

16. Grant, Letterpress Diary, August 3, 1887, Grant Papers.

17. Grant, Letterpress Diary, August 3, 1887. See also John Henry Smith, Diary, August 3, 1887. The brethren charged Angus with being "tyrannical and insubmissive to apostles."

18. Grant, Typed Diary, January 4, 1898, Grant Papers.

19. Brigham Young Jr., Diary, March 2, 1897, Church Archives.

20. Grant, Letterpress Diary, June 26–27 and September 4–5, 1886.

21. Francis M. Lyman to Joseph F. Smith, May 25 and 27, 1887, Joseph F. Smith Correspondence.

22. Richards, Diary, January 30, 1888.

23. Abraham H. Cannon, Diary, September 5, 1886. To make this announcement about John Q. Cannon, Angus Cannon came out of underground hiding, which necessitated his hurried departure after the transaction of business.

24. Abraham H. Cannon, Diary, September 5, 1886.

25. Francis M. Lyman to Joseph F. Smith, May 25, 1887, Joseph F. Smith Correspondence.

26. Richards, Diary, May 22, 1887.

27. Francis H. Lyman to Joseph F. Smith, May 27, 1887, Joseph F. Smith Correspondence.

28. Abraham H. Cannon, Diary, September 14, 1887.

29. Abraham H. Cannon, Diary, May 13, 1888.

30. Grant, Letterpress Diary, June 26–27, 1887; Heber J. Grant to Daniel H. Wells, November 21, 1886, Grant Letterpress Copybook, 6:510–11.

31. Grant, Letterpress Diary, July 7, 1887.

32. Grant, Letterpress Diary, June 24, 1887.

33. Papers and Agreements, esp. those of June 11 and October 3, 1883, Papers on Bullion, Beck and Champion Manufacturing Company, 1882–84, Financial Department Papers, Church Archives; Francis M. Lyman, Diary, October 4, 1883, First Presidency's Office, Salt Lake City; Journal History of the Church of Jesus Christ of Latter-day Saints, April 27, 1899, Church Archives, microfilm copy in L. Tom Perry Special Collections, Harold B. Lee Library, Brigham Young University, Provo, Utah. See also Edward Leo Lyman, "The Alienation of an Apostle from His Quorum: The Moses Thatcher Case," *Dialogue* 18 (Summer 1985): 67–91, which treats the Bullion, Beck, and Champion Mine within its larger context.

34. Lyman, "Alienation of an Apostle," 68.

35. Statement of William B. Preston, Journal History, April 27, 1899. Thatcher may have had previous knowledge inasmuch as President Taylor

had earlier requested members of the Twelve to invest in the property. Thatcher's investment is detailed in "Statement Regarding Elder Moses Thatcher's Stock in the Bullion Beck and Champion Mining Company," Financial Department Papers, Box 23, Fd. 3.

36. John Taylor to William B. Preston, December 17, 1886; John Taylor to Moses Thatcher, April 20, 1887, First Presidency Letterbooks.

37. "Agreement of 2 July 1887," Papers on Bullion, Beck and Champion Manufacturing Company, 1882–84.

38. Diary of George Q. Cannon, July 1, 1887, as cited in Bitton, *George Q. Cannon*, 286–87.

39. This is the persuasive argument of Lyman, "Alienation of an Apostle from His Quorum," 68–72.

40. Journal History, January 9, 1884, quoting from the *Leader*, January 13, 1884.

41. Meeting of the Twelve, December 5, 1847, Minutes of Meetings, Brigham Young Papers, Church Archives.

42. Franklin D. Richards, in *69th Semi-Annual Conference of The Church of Jesus Christ of Latter-day Saints* (Salt Lake City: The Church of Jesus Christ of Latter-day Saints, 1898), 31. The Taylor succession, which requires further scholarly attention, was probably complicated by some Quorum members urging the candidacy of Joseph F. Smith. Other observers have argued, then and more recently, that Young wished his son John W. Young to succeed him, although no direct evidence suggests that Young or other Church leaders favored such a course. This argument receives some sympathy in Todd M. Compton, "John Willard Young," 111–34.

43. Wilford Woodruff to Heber J. Grant, March 28, 1887, Wilford Woodruff Papers, Church Archives. Cannon had defended the principle of apostolic seniority in the succession of John Taylor and may have continued to support the idea, although perhaps with less fervency than on the previous occasion. For an example of Cannon's earlier views, see George Q. Cannon, Remarks, October 8, 1877, George Q. Cannon, in *Journal of Discourses* 26 vols. (Liverpool: F. D. Richards, 1855–86), 19:230–7.

44. Meeting of the Twelve, October 1, 1890, Grant Letterpress Diary.

45. Woodruff to Grant, March 28, 1887.

46. Wilford Woodruff, Diary, March 20, 1887, Church Archives; Woodruff to Grant, March 28, 1887.

47. Wilford Woodruff to Grant, March 20, 1887. His passion not fully spent by his letter, Woodruff wrote a lengthy and equally firm entry in his diary on the topic, March 28, 1887.

48. Woodruff to Grant, March 28, 1887. George Q. Cannon's diary, long unavailable to researchers, might clarify his motivation, though it is also possible that he carried his penchant for confidentiality even to his private papers.

49. George Q. Cannon, Remarks, October 8, 1877, in *Journal of*

Discourses 19:230–37; October 19, 1882, 23:357–67; and August 17, 1883, 24:274–76.

50. Grant, Letterpress Diary, June 24, 1887.

51. Grant, Letterpress Diary, June 25–27, and July 3, 1887.

52. Woodruff, Diary, July 14–15, and 31, 1887. See Grant, Letterpress Diary, July 25, 1887.

53. George Q. Cannon, Diary, August 5, 1889, as cited in Bitton, *George Q. Cannon*, 289.

54. While Grant's Letterpress Diary, August 3, 1887, provides the fullest account of the meeting, the journals of L. John Nuttall, Franklin D. Richards, John Henry Smith, and Wilford Woodruff each contain additional details.

55. Grant, Letterpress Diary, August 3, 1887.

56. Woodruff, Diary, August 3, 1887.

57. Abraham H. Cannon, Diary, September 8, 1887; Grant, Letterpress Diary, September 21, 1887.

58. "A Communication from President Woodruff to the Saints of God throughout the World," *Millennial Star* 49 (August 29, 1887): 545–46. The letter is reprinted in James R. Clark, comp., *Messages of the First Presidency*, 6 vols. (Salt Lake City: Bookcraft, 1966), 3:130–32.

59. Journal History, March 8, 1897.

60. Grant, Letterpress Diary, October 5, 1887. The diaries of John Henry Smith, Franklin D. Richards, Brigham Young Jr., and Wilford Woodruff provide additional documentation of the proceedings.

61. Grant, Letterpress Diary, October 5, 1887.

62. L. John Nuttall, Diary, October 6, 1887, Nuttall Papers.

63. Grant, Letterpress Diary, October 10, 1887, detailing events of October 6, 1887.

64. Young, Diary, October 6, 1887.

65. Grant, Letterpress Diary, October 10, 1887, detailing events of October 6, 1887.

66. Abraham H. Cannon, Diary, February 22, 1889.

67. Woodruff, Diary, September 17, 1888.

68. Richards, Diary, March 14, 1888.

69. Woodruff, Diary, March 20, 1888.

70. Young, Diary, March 20, 1888.

71. Woodruff, Diary, March 21, 1888.

72. Woodruff, Diary, March 23, 1888.

73. Woodruff, Diary, March 23, 1888.

74. Woodruff, Diary, March 23, 1888.

75. Woodruff, Diary, March 23, 1888; Richards, Diary, March 23, 1888.

76. George Q. Cannon to Joseph F. Smith, April 18, 1888, Joseph F. Smith Correspondence; Richards, Diary, March 23, 1888.

77. Abraham H. Cannon, Diary, March 23, 1888.

78. Young, Diary, March 28, 1888.

79. Kenneth W. Godfrey, "Was There More to the Moses Thatcher Case Than Politics?" unpublished paper in author's possession, makes the argument that Thatcher held a long-time commitment to personal freedom and a fear of authoritarian control.

80. Nuttall, Diary, February 27, 1889, see also December 3 and 17, 1888; Woodruff, Diary, October 10, 1888. Nuttall's comment suggests a clue that helps unravel the larger controversy. Since the founding of Utah, the Church had been heavily involved in economics, largely for the sake of promoting the social and economic well-being of the Saints, which contemporaries generically called "the Kingdom." In this regime, early Church leaders like Brigham Young and George Q. Cannon were less concerned about business efficiency for the sake of maximizing profits than in establishing programs of social and economic benefit to Church members. The newer and younger Apostles seemed less driven by this vision. The standard work for the early nineteenth-century Mormon social and economic vision remains Leonard J. Arrington, *Great Basin Kingdom: An Economic History of the Latter-day Saints, 1830–1900* (Cambridge, Mass.: Harvard University Press, 1958), see esp. p. 292.

81. Grant to Thatcher, April 18, 1896; Journal History, November 26, 1896.

82. Grant, "Saving the Ogden Bank," undated memorandum, Box 145, Folder 4, Grant Collection. Lyman, "Alienation of an Apostle," 71–72.

83. Nuttall, Diary, January 23, 1889.

84. Nuttall, Diary, February 27, 1889.

85. Nuttall, Diary, February 18 and 20, 1889.

86. Richards, Diary, March 14 and April 3, 1889; Nuttall, Diary, April 3, 1889.

87. Nuttall, Diary, April 5, 1889.

88. Nuttall, Diary, April 5, 1889.

89. Nuttall, Diary, April 5, 1889.

90. Nuttall, Diary, April 5 and 10, 1889.

91. Woodruff, Diary, April 7, 1889.

92. Woodruff, Diary, August 3, 1887.

93. Journal History, April 14, 24, and 27, 1899.

94. Lyman, "Alienation of an Apostle," 73–88; Journal History, May 7 and August 7, 1897.

95. Grant, Typed Diary, April 20, 1893, see also January 29, 1891.

96. Grant, Letterpress Diary, October 1, 1890. Also in 1890, Thatcher, still in the Quorum, thought that some future difficult time might require a younger man without seniority.

97. Grant, Letterpress Diary, October 1, 1890.

Strangers in a Strange Land:
Heber J. Grant and
the Opening of the Japan Mission

When Heber J. Grant returned from a two-week vacation in Pacific Grove, California, in February 1901, the news he heard at first seemed favorable. One of his associates in the Quorum of the Twelve, Francis M. Lyman, had been asked to preside over the Church's European Mission. Elder Grant congratulated himself that "missionary lightning had once more escaped me," "heaved a sigh of relief," and embraced Lyman in mock celebration.[1]

Since Grant's appointment as a General Authority, rumors had often circulated about a forthcoming proselytizing mission. Each time, however, the reports died stillborn. During the 1880s, the Church and its opponents warred relentlessly on theological, political, and even commercial terrain, and Elder Grant's business acumen was repeatedly deemed too important to the Utah scene to allow a foreign assignment.

The repose given to Elder Grant by Lyman's assignment to the Liverpool office was short-lived. Two days after his return from California, during the General Authorities' regular temple meeting, he heard George Q. Cannon, First Counselor in the First Presidency, announce the decision to open a new mission in Japan. "The moment he made this remark," Grant later recalled, "I felt impressed that I would be called to open up this mission." This prescience, however, brought a flood of reasons why he should reject the call. The Panic of 1893 and its subsequent depression had crippled his finances. He calculated his net worth to be a negative $30,000. Moreover, he had co-signed financial notes making him responsible for another $100,000 in nonpersonal debt. Because of his strained circumstance, neither of his wives had a home of her own, while his mother's house was mortgaged to assist with his obligations.[2]

As President Cannon continued for twenty-five minutes, Grant quietly weighed financial and religious commitments. Then came the call he expected from Cannon: "We hear that Brother Grant has overcome all his great financial difficulties and has announced that he is going to take a trip around the world to celebrate his financial freedom, and we have decided to stop him half way around at Japan, to preside."[3]

Having extended a call to Grant, President Cannon yielded to President Lorenzo Snow, who, since becoming the Church's prophet, seer, and revelator in 1898, had slashed at every unnecessary expenditure to save money. Fearing that Elder Grant's precarious finances might somehow encumber the Church, President Snow had some specific questions in mind.[4] First he wanted to know whether President Cannon had accurately quoted the Apostle about touring the world.

"Heber, did you make that statement?"

"Yes, I did, but there was an extra word in it, and the word was 'if.'" Grant had no plans to leave if he was unable to retire the rest of his debt.

"Well, then, you are not free?"

"No, I am not free, I owe a few dollars."

President Snow wanted specifics. "Well, what are you making?"

"A little better than $5,000 a year."

"Can you afford to lose that $5,000 for three years while you are in Japan?"

"Yes, I can."

In later years, Grant's memory of this incident remained very much alive. "[President Snow] tried for ten minutes to get something out of me [about my debts] and could not do it," Grant remembered.

Finally I said, "President Snow, with the blessing of the Lord I think I can arrange all my affairs to go on this mission, . . . and it will be time enough for me to come and tell you I cannot when I feel in my heart I can't."

"The Lord bless you, my boy," said President Snow, obviously pleased. "We will give you a whole year. You go right to work and fix up your affairs to go on this mission."[5]

As the meeting concluded, President Snow assured Grant that if he worked diligently, he "would accomplish a greater labor than any I had ever accomplished before in my life" and hinted that China might soon be opened for proselytizing as well as Japan.[6]

The decision to launch a Far East mission had not come precipitously. As early as 1851, when Salt Lake City was not much more than a pioneer outpost, the First Presidency had written that "the way is fast preparing for the introduction of the Gospel into China, Japan, and other nations."[7] Nine years later Brigham Young dispatched Walter Murray Gibson to Japan, but the missionary stopped en route in Hawaii, where his religious impulses receded and he carved for himself a political career.[8]

Curiously, there had also been contacts between Church leaders and high-level Japanese leaders. In spring 1871, Salt Lake Stake President Angus Cannon met Prince Itō Hirobumi as they traveled together on the Union Pacific. Already a major actor in Meiji politics, Itō would later serve as a special envoy, as a proconsul, and several times as prime minister.[9] During their several-day journey across the Great Plains, the Japanese minister repeatedly inquired after Mormonism. "He listened most attentively . . . and expressed a desire to learn more," Cannon reported.[10]

Even more auspicious, Church leaders in 1872 had cordial discussions with members of the high-ranking Iwakura mission. Headed by Prince Iwakura Tomomi and composed of over one hundred Japanese government leaders and functionaries making a reconnaissance of the United States and Europe, the traveling embassy became snowbound in Utah for two weeks. With nothing else to do, they visited Utah points of interest, attended Latter-day Saint religious services, and called on several prominent Church leaders, including Brigham Young, Speaker of the House John Taylor, and Lorenzo Snow, then president of the Legislative Council. Snow recalled that their visit was "very pleasant," and the officials "expressed considerable wonderment as to why we had not sent missionaries to Japan." The diaries of several of the visitors as well as the embassy's official five-volume report contained little of the prejudice normally accorded Mormons of the period.[11]

Subsequent contacts ensued. In 1888 the Japanese Consul at San Francisco, Koya Saburō, visited the territory, followed the next year by another party of dignitaries.[12] Seven years later, when Elder Abraham H. Cannon, Grant's associate in the Quorum of the Twelve, called on Koya, he was urged to open a Latter-day Saint mission in Japan. Considering the favorable opinion of Utah held by Prime Minister Itō, Cannon said, Koya "thought it very probable that we might secure permission to preach the Gospel in Japan without any government interference; in fact his people are anxious to hear the Christian religion proclaimed, as they have an idea that the success of the English-speaking people is due to their language and their religion."[13]

All this was prologue to Elder Grant's call. At the time of his selection, he was forty-four years old, the husband of two plural wives (a third had died seven years earlier), and a leading business-man. He was president of the State Bank of Utah, the Salt Lake Theatre Company, three insurance companies, and the Cooperative Wagon and Machine Company, one of the largest retail outlets in the territory. In addition, Grant served as chairman of the Utah Sugar Company and Zion's Cooperative Mercantile Institution, which were two leading Utah businesses, and was a board or com-mittee member of a half dozen other organizations.

Grant had left school while a teenager, and the hectic pace of his business life had subsequently given him little opportunity for read-ing and reflection. At the time of his call, he was the only Apostle who had not served a regular proselytizing mission.[14] Most had served several. All these circumstances left Grant feeling unprepared and inadequate. "I do not know when anything has struck me much harder than being called to Japan," he confided. "I really dreaded being called to the British mission . . . , but I look upon the European mis-sion in comparison to opening up the work in Japan, as a picnic on the one hand and a great labor on the other. However, I shall go and do the best I possibly can."[15]

Part of Elder Grant's hesitancy, of course, could be explained by his finances, which he set about to improve within an hour or two after the meeting of the Twelve. Locking his bedroom door, he prayed for relief. "I told the Lord I did not want to wait until tomorrow morning to make some money, but I wanted to put in that afternoon making a little." An impression came. "Get the Sugar Company to pay a stock dividend, that they can pay the same [money] dividend on the watered stock as they were doing on the original."

The Utah Sugar Company, founded only a decade earlier to provide Utah's farmers with a much needed cash crop, was at last reaping large profits, which in turn fueled ever increasing stock splits, higher dividends, and feverish speculation. Although the company's reserves hardly warranted the action, Grant hoped for another round of share splitting and dividend boosting. With the board scheduled to meet the following day, the timing was exquisite. After concluding his meditation, he hired a buggy and went to entreat the Salt Lake City–based directors, informing them of his mission call to Japan and pointedly reminding them how in the early 1890s he had gone into debt to support the company, only to face the onslaught of the great panic. The next day the board unanimously approved Grant's proposals and his securities jumped $16,000, an increase that temporarily left him incredulous. Catching his breath, during the next several weeks he further speculated in the stock and reaped enough profit to pay all his debts, including a $13,000 note that he had owed for over twenty years.[16]

With his finances under control, Grant turned to organizing his mission. He hand-picked three men to go with him. First, he requested the twenty-nine-year-old Horace S. Ensign, who had earlier served as his private secretary and most recently had returned from a three-year mission in Colorado. In addition to his business and church experience, Ensign possessed a magnificent baritone voice that Grant hoped would attract Japanese attention.[17] Second, he selected the mustachioed, bespectacled Louis A. Kelsch, who after his conversion to the Church had filled missions to the Southern States, the Pacific Northwest, England, and Germany. Since 1896 he had presided over the Northern States Mission, whose headquarters were in Chicago. Elder Kelsch accepted Grant's invitation with alacrity.[18] Finally, Grant asked Alma O. Taylor, an eighteen-year-old living in his own Salt Lake City congregation, to join the mission. Taylor, who was cherubic-faced but serious-minded, had studied at Chicago Harvey Medical College and worked in his family's undertaking business. Upon receipt of his call, Taylor sought Japanese-language textbooks and began studying Buddhist philosophy.[19]

These four men constituted what became known as the "Japanese Quartet," the first wave of the intended Latter-day Saint missionary force to Japan (illus. 11-1). It was hoped that they would "go on ahead," Grant noted, "look over the country, see what we can do, and if everything is all right and conditions are propitious we will then send for our wives and will probably need more Elders."[20] During this first stage, the missionaries planned to spend a year learning the language and then begin proselytizing.[21]

Grant approached his mission in his usual ambitious style. He first planned to ask his business and banking friends in New York to prevail on United States President William McKinley to speak to the Japanese ambassador on his behalf. Perhaps the ambassador would in turn write favorable letters of recommendation. In another idea variation still more bold, Grant considered the possibility of getting himself appointed to head the American legation in Tokyo. But his fellow General Authorities vetoed these and other

Courtesy Church Archives, The Church of Jesus Christ of Latter-day Saints

Illus. 11-1. The first Latter-day Saint missionaries called to Japan posed for this picture in summer 1901 in Salt Lake City. Standing (*left to right*): Horace S. Ensign, Alma O. Taylor. Seated (*left to right*): Heber J. Grant, Louis A. Kelsch.

ideas as too extravagant, advising that the mission start out in a "humble way."[22]

Shortly after 11:00 P.M. on July 24, 1901, Grant and his companions boarded the train for Portland, en route to Japan. The date had not come by chance. Suggestive of the weight that the Mormon community placed upon the mission, Grant had chosen to start on Pioneer Day, the anniversary of Brigham Young's 1847 entrance into the Salt Lake Valley. Because of the possibility of cohabitation prosecution, neither of Grant's wives was there to see him off. There was, however, a partially compensating crowd of one hundred and fifty friends and relatives, including Grant's mother, Rachel; eight of his ten children; and six of the General Authorities, all of whom partially compensated for his wives' absence. As the train pulled away from the station, Grant claimed he had never been happier in his life. He was now, with the support and love of hundreds of friends and relatives, off to introduce the gospel of Jesus Christ to Japan.[23]

Months before Elder Grant's arrival in Japan, the mainline Protestant clergy had planned a major campaign to mark the turn of the new century in Japan. In early 1901 they began with a series of neighborhood prayer meetings in the nation's largest cities. These failed to stir enthusiasm. But when the Whitsunday festivals began in early summer, their program gained momentum. To advertise their planned revivals, the staid ministers adopted the flamboyant methods of the Salvation Army, which had entered Japan only recently. The Protestants placed notices of their meetings in newspapers and posted eye-catching placards. They canvassed house-to-house, extending special invitations to those who were thought to be open to Christian influence. Capping their preparations, an hour or two before their scheduled meeting they hoisted banners and lanterns along the street, loudly chanted Christian hymns, and distributed broadsides.

Although the Protestants' "Forward Evangelistic Campaign" earned a relatively small harvest for a nation of forty million, most clergymen were buoyed. They had been about their task since at least the mid-1870s, when the government had granted the Christians religious tolerance, but gains were always hard won. During the last decade, progress had become still more difficult. Part of the problem lay with Meiji policy. When the nation ended its self-imposed isolation and embraced Western culture, some government leaders had

equated Christianity with material progress and had looked upon
the ministers with favor. But by the 1890s Japan again turned
inward. The popular watchwords of the time became: "Down with
frivolous Europeanization!" "Keep to our national heritage!" "Japan
for the Japanese!"[24]

These were not the only conditions working against the missionaries. The setting of rural Japan was especially restrictive. There,
tenant farmers who comprised half of the nation's population until
the middle of the twentieth century were fettered by feudal social
structures and the historic family system, both of which were refor-
mulated and given new life during the period of anti-Christian reaction. Religious and social change became increasingly difficult, with
many Christian congregations, which had begun optimistically only
a few years earlier, waning and eventually closing. Even in the more
fluid urban society, there were challenges. By the beginning of the
twentieth century, the nation's military expenditures exacted heavy
and impoverishing levies. Under this burden, some former Christian
converts, who had hoped that their new faith would assist them in
getting ahead, recanted. Thus, at the very time that the Latter-day
Saints launched their mission, despite the Protestants' public clamor
and mass rallies, the Christian churches were afflicted by decreased
attendance at their mission schools, slower conversion rates, and
widespread apostasy.[25]

Part of the problem lay with the Christian missionaries themselves, who too often failed to separate their own Western and
national ways from their Christian message. Many Japanese bridled
under such ethnocentrism, complaining that the Christian
churches were "mere importations," with titles, organizations,
methods, and teachings that had "nothing to do with the interests
or needs of the Japanese."[26] All this created stony soil. When Grant
and his companions approached Japan, Christianity had at best a
toehold. The Greek Orthodox denomination may have had thirty
thousand Japanese members; the Roman Catholics, fifty-five thousand (many of these descended from families who had practiced
Christianity underground for three hundred years); and the
Protestants, who had been most active since the Meiji Restoration,
seventy thousand. Taken together, the Christian population constituted a little more than one-third of 1 percent, and, given the

ephemeral discipleship of many Japanese, even these figures were probably inflated.[27]

* * *

Yet this did not stop Grant and his fellow laborers (illus. 11-2). Early in the morning of August 12, land was sighted, and at 10:00 A.M. the *Empress of India* dropped anchor at Yokohama on the western coast of Tokyo Bay's expansive waters. Quarantine checks required about an hour, following which the "Japanese Quartet" took a steam launch for shore. For Grant, their arrival came none too soon. "I said good bye to the <u>Empress of India</u> without any regrets," he said.[28] He had been seasick much of the way.

Several days after landing, the missionaries found themselves in the center of a growing controversy. Learning that a local boarding-house had turned them away because they were Mormons, a Yokohama newspaper charged the innkeeper with religious "fanaticism." Another journal quickly defended the act, with charges and countercharges soon filling the press.[29] "A heavy war is raging," wrote Alma Taylor only eight days after the missionaries' arrival. While many of the newspaper features were "severe" or "slanderous" against the missionaries, the dispute in Taylor's mind, nevertheless brought invaluable publicity.[30]

Courtesy Church Archives, The Church of Jesus Christ of Latter-day Saints

Illus. 11-2. The missionaries at the Yokohama, Japan, dedication site. Left to right: Louis A. Kelsch, Heber J. Grant, Alma O. Taylor, and Horace S. Ensign.

During the following weeks, Grant worked long hours defending the Church in the press. Not understanding the toil involved in composition, he grew frustrated that his writing required time-consuming draft after time-consuming draft. "I have never felt my own lack of literary knowledge so keenly as since I came here," he confided to his Utah friends.[31] And as he had so often expressed since the beginning of his mission, he also lamented his unfamiliarity with the finer points of Latter-day Saint theology. He found topics such as original sin and the Church's view of premortal life "difficult to fully explain."[32]

With newspaper publicity came letters and visitors, the receipt of which soon began to be a part of the missionaries' daily routine. While claiming a lively interest in the missionaries' religious message, many of their visitors, once their motives were searched more deeply, seemed merely curious about the Americans. Others revealed what appeared to be a crass self-interest, seeking position, salary, or the opportunity to sharpen their English language skills.[33]

This experience was certainly a factor in Grant's decision to vacate Yokohama for Tokyo, which, it was reported, had "fewer foreigners, a higher class of natives, a more religious sentiment, and by far better instructors in the language and much cheaper living."[34] Thus, two months after the missionaries had debarked, they secured accommodations in Tokyo's leading hotel, the eleven-year-old Metropole, and settled into an established routine.[35]

During his mission, Grant studied as he had never before. He read and reread the standard scriptural works, Church history and apologetics, Christian homilies, and several books dealing with Japanese history and culture. In candid moments he admitted that such a steady diet of studying was "just about the hardest thing on earth for me to do," though on other occasions he put forward the best possible face.[36]

But no amount of good cheer could camouflage the distress he felt over the Japanese language; its unusual syntax and thousands of Chinese ideographs posed a massive challenge for the tone-deaf Grant.[37] Though he toiled hundreds of hours studying the language and eventually compiled a detailed, one-hundred-page notebook filled with Japanese vocabulary, his progress was virtually nil.[38] "I do not seem to be able to remember anything that I learn and even the words that I have learned when I hear someone else use them I do not recognize," he complained. For such an achievement-oriented man, who preached the universal virtue of pluck and application, the unyielding, flint-hard language exacted a heavy emotional toil. With considerable pain, he finally reconciled himself to his language failure and devoted himself to what seemed more profitable pursuits.[39]

Yet the language study of his colleagues continued, and on the missionaries' move to Tokyo, Grant hired their prime Japanese investigator, Hiroi T., whom they had met in Yokohama, to serve as tutor. But the man's talents failed to speed the younger men's progress, and Taylor and Ensign argued for living among the Japanese in order to learn the language. Grant was reluctant. From the beginning, he had hoped that the mission could "start at the top" with the country's more influential citizenry. That would require learning "standard" or literary Japanese and not the dialects of the people.[40]

The tension between the missionaries and their leader unsettled Grant. He slept fitfully four nights in the middle of November, and he admitted to friends back in Utah that, while he seldom was attacked with "the blues," he could "almost get up an attack this morning and not half try."[41] With Ensign and Taylor increasingly restive and even demanding, Grant finally yielded to having the missionaries learn the language among the people, though the decision went against his better judgment.

Grant's decision was confirmed the next day by what seemed a cold and distant letter from the First Presidency that appeared to contradict everything he had done since arriving in Japan. The missionaries were told to avoid newspaper controversy and to mingle among the people, and, in Elder Grant's case, they were pointedly instructed to resume language study.[42] "I would have appreciate[d] ONE word of approval," he lamented, "but as it was not written I had to accept it as an evidence that there was none to give."[43] His reaction probably owed as much to his own emotional state as to the letter's actual contents. Obviously written in haste and without full attention to Grant's various reports, it gave offense where none was intended. Nevertheless, he hastened to implement its directions. "I know that to obey is the only way for an apostle," he told a friend.[44] He and Kelsch secured accommodations at a nearby boardinghouse, while Ensign and Taylor moved to a hotel catering to the Japanese trade.

Before their separation, the missionaries had entertained at Hiroi's request two men of unusual demeanor, Miyazaki Toranosuke and Takahashi Gorō. Miyazaki, the scion of a prominent family, who would later distinguish himself as the self-proclaimed "Messiah-Buddhist," a spiritual leader who mixed Christian primitivism with the native culture.[45] But it was Takahashi who clearly attracted Grant's eye. He had already gained the Saints' confidence by publishing on his own initiative a defense of their mission in the *Sun,* a leading Japanese periodical.[46] Takahashi spoke English well, read Hebrew and French, and even understood some Egyptian. He had distinguished himself as an educator, a lexicographer, a translator of the Protestant New Testament edition, and a prominent Christian polemicist.[47] While resisting Grant's pleas to convert, Takahashi volunteered to write a book introducing the Latter-day Saint missionaries and their message to the Japanese public.[48]

There were other impressive investigators, too. In mid-February 1902, Grant and the other missionaries dined at the home of Ichiki S., who, according to Taylor, had "figured prominently in many of the wars in Japan especially during the troubles of the Meiji restoration." Also present were Miyasaki and a Mr. Suyenaga, a newspaper editor. The Japanese appeared drawn to Latter-day Saint teachings, especially to the missionaries' description of Mormon economics and group life in the many villages established in the Intermountain West. Ichiki and his friends promised to arrange a hearing for the Utahns before a group of literati drawn from the national press and members of the lower house of the national Diet.[49]

Ichiki's presence was obviously formidable. Hiroi, who claimed to know him well, noted that in his circle Ichiki "speaks and the rest obey" and reported that the man "executes whatever he decides to do no matter how hard or what the odds." Takahashi, obviously overwhelmed, found Ichiki to be "a man such as is rarely found in Japan."[50]

Suddenly, almost in spite of themselves and certainly contrary to the low-profile language-training mission they had at first conceived, the missionaries seemed on the verge of considerable success. The momentum continued when Nakazawa Hajime, who described himself as a Shintō priest with influence over fifteen hundred followers, appeared at Grant's rooms. In previous visits Nakazawa had expressed dissatisfaction with his religion and voiced a desire to investigate the Church. When his superiors learned of his conduct, they severely rebuked him and eventually expelled him from his order.[51] This hastened his search for the truth. On March 8, 1902, Nakazawa became the missionaries' first formal convert, baptized along the shoreline of Tokyo Bay.

Other candidates were also petitioning for baptism. Attracted by the newspaper publicity, men who knew little of the missionaries' beliefs sought baptism, and Grant found that the chance for adding names to the Church's rolls was ample if he merely accepted every request made of him. But in each case he put them off, demanding they receive formal instruction.[52] Some candidates had impressive credentials. Mr. Koshiishi, editor of the newly established *Tokyo Shimbun* and apparently a compeer of Ichiki, petitioned Grant several days after Nakazawa's conversion, but a catechizing of the applicant found that he knew "practically nothing of the gospel" and that he would be "stepping blindly into the church." Like others before him, Koshiishi was refused.[53]

More persistent in the quest for baptism was Kikuchi Saburō, a Christian preacher who, the missionaries were informed, held open-air meetings in Ueno Park attended by five hundred to fifteen hundred people. Unlike others before him, Kikuchi would not be dissuaded, declaring his determination by vaingloriously offering himself to be crucified, if necessary, for the faith. Grant yielded before such ardor. Two days after Nakazawa's rite, the missionaries rowed into the nearby bay, and baptized Kikuchi. In keeping with the Latter-day Saint practice of conferring priesthood authority on its male laity, both converts were ordained to the office of elder.[54]

Kelsch, Ensign, and Taylor must have observed these events with troubled feelings because of a major change that was in the offing. The day before Nakazawa's baptism, just as the mission appeared to be gaining success, they learned that Grant would be returning to Salt Lake City for a visit. When Ensign woke Taylor with the news, the zealous Taylor could hardly believe it. "The idea, I thought to myself, of Bro. Grant thinking of returning home. Why he has only been here it seems for a week or two."[55] However, the time had not passed so quickly for Grant. Imprisoned by his inability to learn the language and ill-fitted by temperament to the slow, almost monastic life of his mission, he greeted the opportunity to return home as a welcome relief. Moreover, with his eldest daughter Rachel announcing her engagement and a new Church president about to be sustained, the Apostle also had personal and official reasons for leaving. He sailed for America in March 1902.

Nearly a half-year later, Grant was back in Japan, accompanied by several new missionaries: Frederick A. Caine, Erastus L. Jarvis, John W. Stoker, Sandford Wells Hedges, and Joseph Featherstone. In addition, some of these missionaries brought family members with them, an acceptable practice for foreign missionaries serving long missions in the nineteenth century. Grant's wife Augusta and his daughter Mary came, as did Ensign's wife, Mary, and Featherstone's wife, Marie. Marie and Joseph Featherstone had just been sealed. Mary Ensign was called to join her husband. The presence of the women, Grant thought, would add a sense of permanence to the mission (illus. 11-3).[56]

Grant and Augusta, along with the other married missionaries, secured a "semi-Japanese" house, only a block or two from the residence of the crown prince, that had five Westernized rooms and six Japanese ones.[57] While the Japanese section was clean and pleasant, its sliding doors and shutters seemed too confining to the Americans. When walking through this part of the house, they felt as though they were "in a box" and consequently used it only for storage.[58] The unmarried elders joined Alma Taylor at a Japanese hotel that provided room accommodations and one Western and two Japanese meals a day for fifteen dollars a month.

The mission headquarters at Grant's house was surrounded by a high board fence and sat on a small hill. Immediately outside the front gate was a rickshaw stall, which was normally occupied by half a dozen cabmen waiting for fares. Still further beyond, situated immediately in front of the house, lay a four-hundred-acre Japanese army parade ground, with barracks in the far-off distance.[59] From their vantage on the hill, the missionaries could observe the soldiers, who sometimes drilled from dawn to dusk. During the summer season, the troops wore white duck suits with contrasting navy blue caps trimmed in red. Augusta thought the young recruits picturesque, sitting as they often did "on the green grass, their guns

Courtesy Church Archives, The Church of Jesus Christ of Latter-day Saints

Illus. 11-3. Heber J. Grant with several missionaries and their wives, including Grant's wife Augusta *(seated, second from left)* and their daughter Mary *(seated, far left)*, in Japan.

stacked and [their] bugles hanging on them."[60] The troops were preparing for the nation's impending conflict with Russia.

Elder Grant used a highly personal reason to secure permission for Augusta to travel with him to Japan. Though his three wives had borne him an even dozen children, Grant's only two sons had died in childhood. In the Church's turn-of-the-century patriarchal society, the prospect of having his name "blotted out when I die" was deeply distressing.[61] Accordingly, he had appealed to his superiors that Augusta "will soon be past all hope [of bearing a son] . . . , unless in the near future we can be together."[62] But even this chance was slim. Their only child, Mary, had been born thirteen years earlier.

Perhaps for the first time since their marriage eighteen years earlier, Augusta and Heber now experienced what could be described as a normal and unhurried relationship. Each evening, they strolled through the neighborhood, walking across the parade ground or maybe down close to an adjoining railroad track.[63] The couple noticed new things about each other. For one thing, Augusta sensed that Heber's patience did not run as deep as she supposed. Heber readily conceded the point. "When a man is at his office and away from the little annoying things that come in a home almost every hour, he may be very patient," he reflected. "But the change comes when he has his office [in his home] and these things [are] with him all the time."[64] Augusta found it strange to see her husband study, take so much rest, and, for that matter, be so closely tied to the mission home and its domestic concerns. Once she discovered him scrubbing the kitchen floor, an act that an offended domestic servant immediately halted.[65]

Elder Grant had hoped that the literary-inclined Augusta could assist with his official mission correspondence, but the newspaper controversy had lapsed in his absence in Salt Lake City. Augusta's writing ability, however, did fill an important function. Her many letters to friends and relatives in Utah chronicled their everyday life. After one rain shower, she found their shoes "moss grown," while their clothing had "patches of mould . . . that looked like small vegetable gardens." The offending articles of clothing had to be brushed, shaken, and sunned. "The houses smell mouldy," she complained; "every one that I have been in has the same smell and the ground is never dry around the yard. When we get into bed the sheets and clothing feel perfectly wet, as all our clothing does when we put it on in the morning."[66]

The carnivorous mosquitoes were especially troublesome. On Augusta's first night in Japan, she set aside her protective netting. As a result, the insects kept her awake most of the night, and upon arising she was a "perfect sight." There were numerous other pests, "strange and marvelous." Augusta wrote:

> When we keep the mosquitoes out the fleas have their turn, and we saw outside our windows three immense spiders. . . . One night a rat ran across the net over the bed, and then there was a great scrimmage to catch it, and the bravest man who was 'not afraid of a rat,' skipped up on the bed in a hurry when the pest ran over his bare foot.

There seemed to be no end to such afflictions. Once, she insisted, the men in the mission home caught in the dead of night "two of the strangest looking great big things" imaginable, which they took outside and tied to a tree. According to Augusta's excited and perhaps imaginative report, some of the irritating creatures had forked tails, while others had long horns or hoods over their heads. Still others had a "thousand legs."[67]

As the months progressed, the missionaries developed an established Sunday regimen. They reserved mornings for themselves, when the entire contingent gathered at the Grant home for Sunday School. These services were conducted in English, with a choir, consisting of everyone present, lending musical counterpoint (Grant joined Caine, Ensign, and the women in establishing the melody).[68] At 2:00 P.M., the Saints invited the Japanese to worship with them, and six to a dozen usually did so. The visitors, who were often different young male students every week, closely observed the missionaries' mannerisms, inquired about Western music and culture, and asked occasional questions about religion. To place them at ease, the Americans eventually held this meeting in the Japanese part of their home, trading chairs for native floor cushions and forgoing the use of the Western piano.[69]

Such low-key and low-profile dealings with the Japanese were a major change from the excited and publicized moments that had followed the missionaries' first arrival. Not only had the newspaper controversy passed, but so also had the opportunity to teach Ichiki and his supposedly influential friends. During Grant's absence in the United States, Japanese authorities had placed Ichiki's friends under arrest, possibly as a result of their political beliefs or activity. Chagrined by having had contact with men who had become felons and apparently fearing adverse publicity, Elder Grant accepted their imprisonment as *prima facie* evidence of insincerity. "I have to smile when I think of the important men we thought we had made friends with, now being under arrest," he wrote. He made no further effort to contact or teach them.[70]

Efforts to introduce the gospel in Japan were beginning to unravel. The leading Japanese who had befriended the missionaries were now in prison. Despite his initial expressions of interest and sympathy, Hiroi, the missionaries' salaried translator, had grown increasingly aloof and uncooperative. He was eventually dismissed with two months' notice and what was hoped to be an assuaging dinner at the Metropole Hotel.[71] The missionaries' converts were even less satisfying. Shortly after his baptism, Kikuchi proposed that the Americans underwrite his venture to sell patent medicine. When they declined, the Japanese proselyte announced the need to "set aside religious duties for a time." He was seen rarely again by the missionaries.[72] Nakazawa Hajime seemed similarly motivated. Following his conversion, he requested fifteen hundred dollars to start a job-printing office. When his proposition was rejected, Nakazawa threatened to revert to his Shintō vocation unless the missionaries employed him. Begrudgingly, Elder Grant extended to him a loan, but when Nakazawa's wife sought further monetary support, the missionary declined. "My impression is that the only interest either one of . . . [the Nakazawas] have in the Church or us is to try and get some money," he confided to his diary.[73] Months later events appeared to confirm Grant's judgment; Nakazawa was captured while attempting to burglarize the mission home.

With several converts being similarly unproductive, Grant's overall assessment was dour. "I think we have had some fearfully poor material join the Church," he concluded.[74] "The way some Japanese jump at the gospel and then drop it as soon as they learn there is no pay in it or no employment is really amusing."[75] Undoubtedly, the Japanese view of the matter was different. Accustomed to the Protestant practice of allowing some of their converts active and often paid leadership roles, they saw no inconsistency between religious quest and personal advancement. Indeed, many Japanese Christians expected it.

This certainly was the case of Takahashi Gorō, the scholarly polemicist and self-styled Church advisor and critic. He hotly criticized Grant for not supporting Nakazawa's printing venture, and following the burglary of the mission headquarters he compared Nakazawa with Victor Hugo's tragically impoverished Jean Valjean. "Of course, speaking intellectually, you have no responsibility for . . . [Nakazawa's] doing, but intellect is not all and all. Everybody knows that Nakazawa lost his lucrative profession for sympathizing with 'Mormonism.' . . . But Mr. Grant quite cold bloodily, has left him destitute of help."[76]

The missionaries were not swayed by Takahashi's argument, preferring to believe that the scholar's scorn reflected his own failed ambition. Elder Taylor had a plausible explanation: because President Grant had first entertained the Japanese scholar at the prestigious Metropole Hotel and talked expansively about the Church's past achievements, Takahashi had assumed that they intended to spend millions of dollars funding Japanese charitable projects, which might in turn provide him a sinecure. According to Taylor, Takahashi "dreamed himself into the position of [the Church's] chief Japanese advisor, director, or something else with a mint and a name."[77]

In the missionaries' eyes, Takahashi had been treated fairly. Shortly after their initial meeting, Elder Grant had advanced Takahashi about four hundred yen (two hundred dollars) for his proposed book, after which Takahashi had further exposed himself by borrowing against his royalties. When the book failed to sell, he sought another loan from Grant. Rather than advance more money, Grant at length decided to relieve the man's financial embarrassment by buying most of the 700-volume run. Eventually the missionaries placed 362 books with members of the National Diet's House of Peers and another 8 to high-level functionaries. The rest were apparently used in their proselytizing.[78]

Takahashi's *Morumon Kyō to Morumon Kyōto (Mormons and Mormonism)* was, in fact, an able, several-hundred-page work that introduced the basic story and history of the Church to the Japanese audience, but it was also filled with archaeological and philological excursions, a philosophical defense of polygamy, and an extended discussion of the Church's ability to meet modern social ills. These topics gave the volume a heavy quality that no doubt dampened sales in a market that already found Mormon topics passé.[79]

The failure of *Morumon Kyō to Morumon Kyōto* and the younger missionaries' growing estrangement from their former contacts failed to dampen their enthusiasm. During a conference in early 1903, they politely challenged Grant's cautious policy that more time and preparation were required before active proselytizing could begin. Describing himself as "surprised and pleased" by their attitude, Grant immediately rescinded his request to tour Latter-day Saint churches in Samoa, New Zealand, and Australia—a long-standing personal goal—and began preparation for the start of formal preaching of the gospel.[80]

After producing a tract that introduced the Church to the Japanese public in broad terms, Grant hired the Kinki Kan Hall for the formal inauguration of Latter-day Saint preaching in Japan. The history-conscious missionaries carefully recorded their proceedings.

Two of them tried to deliver their message in Japanese. Caine's effort drew muffled titters, but Taylor flawlessly recited the content of the Mormons' new tract. Then Grant followed with a sixty-five-minute sermon. Setting aside his carefully selected Bible references, the mission leader spoke with "very good liberty" on such basic gospel themes as the mission of Joseph Smith and the Articles of Faith.[81] Hearty applause followed each song and talk, despite the missionaries' initial protests; and when the crowd learned that an English text of Taylor's remarks was available, the response was immediate. According to Grant, "there was a rush like those trying to get to a bargain counter at a Z. C. M. I. special sale."[82]

Several weeks later, the elders were dispatched to their fields of labor. Two went to Naoetsu on the Japan Sea coast, two were assigned to Nagano, where Grant had toured during his first months in Japan, and four, including Grant himself, remained in or near Tokyo.[83] The day after he and his companion began distributing tracts, Ensign reported himself "happy and contented."[84] But such enthusiasm was hard to sustain. At one location, the missionaries learned that impostors calling themselves Mormons had already preceded them, leaving behind "a bad record" and a ruined image. Elsewhere rumors circulated that the Mormons were Russian spies, which may have partially accounted for the people's sometimes hostile behavior.[85] After distributing tracts in a small village, Elder Hedges reported that initial receptivity had quickly turned negative. At one house, "the door was slammed so quickly in my face that I did not know what struck me."[86]

The missionaries' lack of success deeply troubled Grant and brought on one of his periodic dark moods. He wondered if the lack of discernible progress could be traced to a possible failure in his leadership, and though the First Presidency had long released him from the mandate of learning Japanese, he still brooded over his inability to grasp the language. "To the end of my life I may feel that I have not done what He expected of me, and what I was sent here to do," he complained.[87]

His increasing isolation may have contributed to his negative feelings. With his elders now in the field and his own movement restricted by the barriers of language and culture, Grant, in the words of Taylor, "irked at the leash, as any man of energy and action would do."[88] During late spring and early summer 1903, Grant's emotions oscillated widely, sometimes within the narrow range of a single letter. He might first petition the First Presidency for eight or ten more missionaries, for he clearly hoped for concrete results before leaving his mission.[89] Then, a paragraph or two later, as the reality of the Japanese mission once again imposed itself, his steadfastness wavered. Wasn't his time "being thrown away"? Couldn't he be more productive elsewhere? Such ruminations about leaving were probably encouraged by Brigham F., his half-brother, and by others who repeatedly assured him of his imminent release.[90]

Grant himself may have precipitated this prospect, but in a way consistent with his sense of duty. In early May 1903 he had written to Anthon H. Lund, President Joseph F. Smith's newly called counselor in the First Presidency, hinting of his availability to succeed Francis M. Lyman as head of the European Mission. Grant did not wish the Presidency to think that he was calling himself on a mission or releasing himself from another. "I am well and happy and as contented as I ever was in my life, and feel that I can live here for years with pleasure," he wrote. Still, and here he made his point explicit: "I would love to be where I could have something to do."[91]

Nor was he prepared to leave the question entirely in the hands of the First Presidency. Frustrated and anguished, he retired to some woods for prayer. "I told the Lord that whenever He was through with me . . . [in Japan], where I was accomplishing nothing, I would be very glad and thankful if He would call me home and send me to Europe to preside over the European mission." By his own account, it was only the second time during his life that he had sought a Church position (the other was an earlier plea to serve on the board of the Young Men's Mutual Improvement Association to serve the youth).[92]

Presumably Grant's personal struggle was kept from most of his missionary associates, who, in contrast to his own self-doubts, seemed to have a high estimate of his labor. Certainly his leadership often left them moved.[93] Once, after Elder Stoker had turned his ankle and the sprain discolored with infection, Grant suggested that the missionaries fast and pray in Stoker's behalf. He called them into a meeting, where he began with singing and more prayer. Then he and others spoke of the spiritual healing that they had witnessed. "The feeling that characterized the meeting grew stronger & stronger,"

Stoker reported. "I was almost overcome." Elder Ensign then took some consecrated oil and rubbed it on the afflicted limb and asked for an immediate healing as a "testimony" for all present. As the final act, Grant laid his hands on Stoker's head and promised the "free & perfect usage" of the foot. As he spoke, Stoker sensed a movement within the limb and heard a snapping sound. The conclusion was as spectacular: the missionary "involuntarily" stood on his feet and walked for the first time in ten days.[94]

Despite his accomplishments, Grant was ready to move on. Yet by the third week of August, Grant had surrendered any hope that he might soon leave the country. A recent letter from Abraham O. Woodruff, his associate in the Quorum of the Twelve, carried no intimation of a release, despite an earlier request for discreet information. News from Grant's family was more to the point. These sources suggested that while President Smith had not yet decided the timing of his return, the most likely possibility was not until early 1904—the next year. Grant claimed himself "not in the least disappointed" with this information. With his sense of duty again paramount, he expressed the hope for six more months of service in order to get things "moving."[95]

To avoid the extremes of the Tokyo summer and to position himself in what appeared the mission's most promising area, Grant took his family to Hojo, a seaside resort in Chiba Ken. There, on August 23, he received a registered letter informing him that a cable was being held in Yokohama. Its contents could only be relayed to him in Tokyo. He left for Tokyo at once, arriving at the Metropole sometime after midnight. The decoded message left him stunned. "You are now released," it cryptically read. "Leave the business in the hands of Ensign," wrote the First Presidency.[96] Rather than the emotional relief that Grant had long assumed his release would bring, he now felt deep and painful regret. His tearful prayers that evening contrasted the seeming "failure" of his mission with the larger-than-life successes of his apostolic predecessors. It was 5:00 A.M. before he was able to set aside his thoughts and fall asleep.[97]

Two hours later he was somewhat refreshed and had a more objective view. Writing several letters, he acknowledged the success of his earlier ministry and was also confident about upcoming events. "I have a willing heart," he reflected, and "know that I will do more [good work]." But his mind clearly remained troubled. "I am in hopes that I am not released, . . . that it is only a call to come home," he wrote the First Presidency. But his resolve vanished before he ended his sentence. "I have done so little here," he concluded, "it may be felt that it is better to use me in some other field where I can do more good."[98]

Grant already knew that there was only one available steamer that could get him to America in time for the October 1903 general conference, and he quickly booked passage. He also requested that other missionaries return to mission headquarters for a two-week farewell conference, the highlight of which took place in the wooded terrain above Yokohama harbor. Commemorating the dedication of the mission exactly two years earlier, the missionaries rehearsed their original program, repeating the same hymns and reading an outline of Elder Grant's dedicatory prayer. There was, however, a significance to the site that was probably unknown to any of the group besides Grant himself. At the beginning of the mission, he now explained, he had often come to the place to dissipate his melancholy in prayer.[99]

The three-hour meeting, in Grant's words, was "the one meeting of all meetings ever held in this land." While all twelve missionaries were "blessed with remarkable demonstrations of the Spirit," he seemed specially endowed. Invoking his apostolic authority, he blessed his missionaries and reminded them of their duty. "I never saw a man that was as full of the Spirit of God as he was then," recounted one of the young men.[100]

Eight days later, Augusta, Mary, and Grant embarked on the S.S. *Aki Maru*. He left with a surprisingly high view of the Japanese. From his many contacts and experiences, he sensed the nation's great military potential. Moreover, he saw the Japanese as "patriotic beyond any people" he had ever known, and described them as "workers." Their ambition and curiosity seemed limitless except, lamentably, on the paramount matter of religion.[101] Yet, there was something within Grant that suggested that he himself had not experienced the last chapter. To the end of his career, he would remember the emotion he had felt during the pronouncement of his dedicatory prayer. "I feel impressed that there is yet a great work to be accomplished there. How soon this may come I do not know."[102] He also felt that "there will yet be a great and important work accomplished in the land. . . . there is to be a wonderful work accomplished in Japan; that there will be many, yea, even thousands of that people that will receive the gospel of Jesus Christ."[103]

He departed with the hope of returning someday. His experience, he realized, had not been entirely negative. He had placed on his frame a precious fifteen pounds, and his quieted nerves once again permitted Spenserian writing. Moreover, he had outfitted himself with a pair of spectacles that corrected an astigmatism that for many years had hindered reading and studying.[104] Nevertheless, despite listing all the positive things he could muster, he knew that Japan had aged him "at least ten years" although he had spent only two in the land of the Mikado.[105]

As the ship departed, his missionary friends walked to the edge of the bund to see him off. At first they shouted pleasantries across the mooring. Then, as the *Aki Maru* gradually steamed from port, they waved handkerchiefs until the passengers could no longer be seen.[106]

Notes

This article was originally published in *Journal of Mormon History* 13 (1986–87): 20–43.

1. Heber J. Grant to Louis A. Kelsch, March 2, 1901, Heber J. Grant Letterpress Copybook, 31:373, Grant Papers, Church Archives, The Church of Jesus Christ of Latter-day Saints, Salt Lake City. Also see Grant to Rachel Ivins Grant, February 16, 1901, Grant Letterpress Copybook, 31:321.

2. Undated and untitled memorandum, box 144, fd. 4, Grant Papers. See also Heber J. Grant, Typed Diary, February 14 and 16, 1901, Grant Papers; Heber J. Grant to Rachel Ivins Grant, February 16, 1901, Grant Letterpress Copybook, 31:321; Heber J. Grant, "Ram in the Thicket," *Improvement Era* 44 (December 1941): 713.

3. Grant, "Ram in the Thicket," 713. Nearly identical wording is found in Undated and untitled memorandum, 1. Also see Grant, Typed Diary, February 14, 1901.

4. Précis of First Presidency proceedings, Journal History of the Church, February 12, 1901, Church Archives, microfilm copy in L. Tom Perry Special Collections, Harold B. Lee Library, Brigham Young University, Provo, Utah.

5. Undated and untitled memorandum, 3. Grant provided several variations of this dialogue in several published reminiscences. See Heber J. Grant, "Response," *Improvement Era* 44 (October 1941): 585; Grant, "Ram in the Thicket," 713.

6. Grant, Typed Diary, February 14, 1901. The Mormon press subsequently confirmed the possibility of a Chinese mission. "Missions to the Orient," *Deseret Evening News,* February 16, 1901, 4; "Opening of a Mission in Japan," *Deseret Evening News,* April 6, 1901, 9.

7. Alma O. Taylor, "Memories of Far-Off Japan: President Grant's First Foreign Mission, 1901 to 1903," *Improvement Era* 39 (November 1936): 690.

8. Heber J. Grant to Anthony W. Ivins, February 15, 1901, Grant Letterpress Copybook, 31:315.

9. James A. B. Scherer, *Three Meiji Leaders: Ito, Togo, Nogi* (Tokyo: Hokuseido Press, 1936), 1–2, claims that "next to the great Emperor Meijo, Hirobumi Ito had the lion's share in shaping modern Japan." Kengi Hamada, *Prince Ito* (Tokyo: Sanseido Co., 1936).

10. Angus Cannon, quoted in "Opening of a Mission in Japan," *Deseret Evening News,* April 6, 1901, 9. Also Angus M. Cannon to Marquis Ito, July 23, 1901, Grant Papers.

11. John Updike, "The Iwakura Mission" (graduate paper, Department of History, Brigham Young University, 1968), provides a preliminary treatment of the Iwakura Embassy in Utah. For a contemporary Utah discussion, see Junius Wells to Heber J. Grant, April 21, 1901, General Correspondence, Grant Papers; "Missions to the Orient," *Deseret Evening News,* February 16, 1901, 4; and "Opening of a Mission in Japan," 9. A wider context of the mission is found in Richard Henry Drummond, *A History of Christianity in Japan* (Grand Rapids, Mich.: William B. Eerdmans Publishing, 1971), 162–63.

12. "A Party from Japan," *Salt Lake Herald,* March 17, 1889, 7.

13. Abraham H. Cannon, Diary, April 19, 1895, Abraham H. Cannon Papers, L. Tom Perry Special Collections, Harold B. Lee Library, Brigham Young University, Provo, Utah. It is uncertain if Koya was serving as consul at the time of his 1888 visit.

14. Alma O. Taylor, "Memories of Far-off Japan: President Grant's First Foreign Mission, 1901 to 1903," *Improvement Era* 39 (November 1936): 690.

15. Heber J. Grant to Anthony W. Ivins, February 15, 1901, Grant Letterpress Copybook, 31:315.

16. Heber J. Grant, Remarks at New York Chapel, May 22, 1938, Grant Papers; Undated and untitled memorandum, 7; Grant, Typed Diary, February 23, 1901.

17. Ensign had been before the Salt Lake City public as a singer since the age of ten. "Opening of a Mission in Japan," 9, provides a biographical sketch. Also see Heber J. Grant to Joseph A. McRae, n.d. but about March 18, 1904, Grant Letterpress Copybook, 38:468; and Biographical Sketch contained in Grant Letterpress Copybook, 33.

18. "Opening of a Mission in Japan," 9; Biographical Sketch. A copy of Kelsch's *A Practical Reference Arranged Especially for Missionaries of The Church of Jesus Christ of Latter-day Saints* can be found in Grant Papers. For his reaction to the call, Louis A. Kelsch to Heber J. Grant, March 11, 1901, Grant Letterpress Copybook, 31:419.

19. Grant, Typed Diary, May 10, 1901; Biographical Sketch; Heber J. Grant, in *74th Semi-Annual Conference of The Church of Jesus Christ of Latter-day Saints* (Salt Lake City: The Church of Jesus Christ of Latter-day Saints, 1903), 12; Heber J. Grant to Joseph E. Taylor, June 2, 1912, Grant Letterpress Copybook, 45:463; Heber J. Grant to Francis Grant, February 13, 1934, Family Correspondence, Grant Papers.

20. "Opening of a Mission in Japan," 9; Heber J. Grant to Anthony W. Ivins, September 15, 1901, Grant Letterpress Copybook, 33:233; Heber J. Grant to Frederick Beesley, March 29, 1901, Grant Letterpress Copybook, 33:423.

21. Alma O. Taylor to his mother, contained in the Alma O. Taylor, Diary, October 3, 1901, Alma O. Taylor Papers, Church Archives.

22. Heber J. Grant to Louis A. Kelsch, March 18, 1901, Grant Letterpress Copybook, 31:421; Heber J. Grant to Junius F. Wells, September 30, 1901, Grant Letterpress Copybook, 33:267.

23. Grant diary entries inserted in Grant Letterpress Copybook, 34:1, July 25, 1901.

24. Masaharu Anesaki, *History of Japanese Religion* (Rutland, Vt.: Charles E. Tuttle, 1971), 360; Ohata Kiyoshi and Kdado Fujio, "Christianity," in *Japanese Religion in the Meiji Era*, trans. and adapted John F. Howes, Centenary Culture Council Series (Tokyo: Obunsha, 1956), 251–52, 255–57.

25. Drummond, *History of Christianity in Japan*, 220–21; Kiyoshi and Fujio, "Christianity," 259.

26. Anesaki, *History of Japanese Religion*, 405. See also Kiyoshi and Fujio, "Christianity," 296–97; and Joseph M. Kitagawa, *Religion in Japanese History* (New York: Columbia University Press, 1966), 241.

27. Otis Cary, *History of Christianity in Japan*, 2 vols. (New York: Fleming H. Revell, 1909), 1:359; Kiyoshi and Fujio, "Christianity," 308. These estimates are extrapolated from 1907 and 1909 estimates.

28. Grant, Diary, August 12, 1901, Grant Letterpress Copybook, 34:8.

29. Cary, *History of Christianity in Japan*, 1:309–10.

30. Taylor, Diary, August 20, 1901; Taylor, "Memories of Far-Off Japan," 690–91. The controversy is best chronicled in Frederick R. Brady, "The Japanese Reaction to Mormonism and the Translation of Mormon Scripture into Japanese" (master's thesis, Sophia University, 1979).

31. Heber J. Grant to Joseph F. Smith, October 14, 1901, Grant Letterpress Copybook, 33:287–89.

32. Heber J. Grant to B. F. Grant, August 24, 1901, Grant Letterpress Copybook, 33:149.

33. Taylor, Diary, August 19, 1901; see also Heber J. Grant to Lorenzo Snow and Joseph F. Smith, August 26, 1901, Grant Letterpress Copybook, 33:141. Their experiences were by no means unlike those of their earlier Protestant counterparts.

34. Taylor, Diary, August 28, 1901.

35. Edward Seidensticker, *Low City, High City: Tokyo from Edo to the Earthquake* (New York: Alfred A. Knopf, 1983), 42; Heber J. Grant to Brother Hull, October 18, 1901, Grant Letterpress Copybook, 33:292.

36. Heber J. Grant to Francis M. Lyman, March 6, 1903, General Correspondence.

37. Protestant missionaries also found the Japanese language to be formidable. "Sherwood Eddy concluded, on the basis of his long experience with missionaries in every part of the world, that if one were to include reading and writing as well as speaking, Japanese is probably the most difficult language in the world for a foreigner to learn." Drummond, *History of Christianity in Japan*, 148, footnote. The language-gifted Alma Taylor described the task of learning Japanese akin to "striking a pick against flint rock." Alma O. Taylor to Heber J. Grant, May 2, 1902, General Correspondence.

38. Richard L. Evans, "Strange Language," *Improvement Era* 45 (November 1942): 709.

39. Grant, Diary, September 18–20, 1901 [single entry], Grant Letterpress Copybook, 34:36.

40. Heber J. Grant to Junius F. Wells, September 30, 1901, Grant Letterpress Copybook, 33:268.

41. Grant, Diary, November 5–17, 1901 [single entry], Grant Letterpress Copybook, 34:76; Heber J. Grant to Francis M. Lyman, November 15, 1901, Grant Letterpress Copybook, 34:427–30.

42. General Authorities to Heber J. Grant, November 8, 1901, Grant Letterpress Copybook, 34:108.

43. When Anthon H. Lund, a newly called counselor in the First Presidency, wrote a softer letter to Grant several weeks later, Grant's anger was still not spent. He told Lund that he took the Presidency's letter as "a polite way of telling me I had been wasting my time in the past" and then complained, "When a man is thousands of miles away from home and done his best and all that he has done has been done with the full approval of his associates a letter like the one I got from you is appreciated more than words can tell, especially when it came in connection with the official letter of the Presidency which gently but kindly 'sat on me.'" Had parts of the original letter been written by George Gibbs, the Presidency's sharp-tongued secretary, Heber claimed that he would have merely dismissed its contents with the ejaculation, "Confound Gibbs' sarcasm." Heber J. Grant to Anthon H. Lund, December 22, 1901, Grant Letterpress Copybook, 34:149–50.

44. Heber J. Grant to Francis M. Lyman, February 21, 1902, Grant Letterpress Copybook, 35:3.

45. Anesaki, *History of Japanese Religion*, 385–86.

46. Heber J. Grant, in *72nd Annual Conference of The Church of Jesus Christ of Latter-day Saints* (Salt Lake City: The Church of Jesus Christ of Latter-day Saints, 1902), 47–48.

47. Senichi Hisametsu, "Kambara Ariake," *Biographical Dictionary of Japanese Literature* (Tokyo: Kodansha International Ltd., 1976), 276; Cary, *History of Christianity in Japan,* 1:148–49; G. B. Sansom, *The Western World and Japan: A Study in the Interaction of European and Asiatic Cultures* (New York: Alfred A. Knopf, 1951), 480. In the several years prior to the coming of the Mormons, Takahashi had published the *Japanese Alphabetical Dictionary with Chinese & English Equivalents* and a second volume, *A New Pocket Dictionary of the Japanese and English Languages.* In 1869 he may also have been the first Christian converted in Tokyo if Drummond, *History of Christianity in Japan,* 165, typographically errs in giving "Toru Takahashi" the honor.

48. Grant, in *72nd Annual Conference,* 47–48; Heber J. Grant to Gorō Takahashi, December 13, 1901, Grant Letterpress Copybook, 34:140; Grant, Diary, December 7–19, 1901 [single entry], Grant Letterpress Copybook, 34:145.

49. Taylor, Diary, February 13 and 16, 1902.

50. Taylor, Diary, February 16, 1902.

51. Taylor, Diary, February 23, 1902.

52. Occasionally Grant recorded such incidents; see Grant, Diary, December 7–19, 1901, Grant Letterpress Copybook, 34:147.

53. Taylor, Diary, March 10, 1902. After Grant's refusal to approve the request, several of Koshiishi's associates described Koshiishi as insincere and self-seeking.

54. S. C. Richardson notebooks, Church Archives; Heber J. Grant to Kelsch, Ensign, and Taylor, April 4, 1902, Grant Letterpress Copybook, 32:192; Grant, in *72nd Annual Conference,* 45–46.

55. Taylor, Diary, March 7, 1902[?].

56. Heber J. Grant to Nakazawa Hajime, May 2, 1902, Grant Letterpress Copybook, 35:204.

57. Heber J. Grant to Smith, Winder, and Lund, n.d., excerpts in Grant, Diary, July 23, 1902; Heber J. Grant to "All the Loved Ones at Home," July 20, 1902, Grant Letterpress Copybook, 35:362; Augusta Grant to "My Dear People," September 17, 1902, Grant Letterpress Copybook, 35:478; Heber J. Grant to B. F. Grant, July 24, 1902, Grant Letterpress Copybook, 35:365.

58. Augusta Grant to "All the Dear Folks at Home," July 29, 1902, Grant Letterpress Copybook, 35:427–29.

59. Augusta Grant to "All the Dear Folks at Home," July 29, 1902; Augusta Grant to "All the Dear Folks at Home," August 8, 1902, Grant Letterpress Copybook, 35:442–43.

60. Augusta Grant to "Family at Home[?]," May 11, 1903, General Correspondence.

61. Heber J. Grant to Charles W. Nibley, March 4, 1905, Grant Letterpress Copybook, 39:418; Heber J. Grant to Ellen Stoddard Eccles, December 17, 1912, Grant Letterpress Copybook, 48:43; Heber J. Grant to B. H. Roberts, December 16, 1922, Grant Letterpress Copybook, 60:57.

62. Heber J. Grant to Joseph F. Smith, October 14, 1901, Grant Letterpress Copybook, 33:287–89.

63. Augusta Grant to "All the Dear Folks at Home," July 29, 1902.

64. Heber J. Grant to Lucy Grant Cannon, December 1, 1905, Grant Letterpress Copybook, 40:592.

65. Augusta Grant to "My Dear People," September 17, 1902.

66. Augusta Grant to "Folks at Home," August 8, 1902, Grant Letterpress Copybook, 35:442–43.

67. Augusta Grant to "Folks at Home," August 8, 1902. Reading Augusta's description before it was posted, Heber and Mary complained that the account suggested the Japanese pests were as "big as cows." Augusta refused to budge. "I tell them to write their [own] version."

68. "The Work in Japan," *Deseret Evening News,* June 5, 1903, 4; Grant, Typed Diary, March 1–10, 1903; Mary Grant to Fannie Gardiner, August 10, 1902, Grant Letterpress Copybook, 35:446.

69. Heber J. Grant to Sandford W. Hedges, May 19, 1903, Japanese Mission Letterpress Copybook, 1:39, Church Archives; letter of Augusta Grant, May 11, 1903, Family Correspondence; Grant, Diary, May 24, 1903, Grant Letterpress Copybook, 36:321.

70. Heber J. Grant to Kelsch, Ensign, and Taylor, June 18, 1902, Grant Letterpress Copybook, 35:260; see also Heber J. Grant to Joseph F. Smith, John R. Winder, and Anthon H. Lund, October 1, 1902, General Correspondence.

71. Taylor, Diary, May 17–19 [single entry], 1902; Heber J. Grant to Kelsch, Ensign, and Taylor, April 16 and June 18, 1902, Grant Letterpress Copybook, 35:146, 260. Grant responded to Hiroi's demands with an even hand. "We did all we could to make things pleasant for you while you were in our employ," he wrote.

> Surely you must not blame us that you could not get the empl[o]yment that you wished at the time you stopped teaching us, neither must you blame us for what people say. We never gave any one to understand that you had joined our Church. We would have been proud to have had you do so, had you been converted to the truths which we have to offer, but as you know we have no desire to have any one join with us unless they have become convinced that we have in very deed the plan of life and salvation as again restored to earth direct from heaven. (Heber J. Grant to T. Hiroi, July 28, 1902, Grant Letterpress Copybook, 35:441)

Almost two decades later, Hiroi, who at the time was studying in New York, sought a $1,000 loan from Grant, claiming a monied and influential group now supported him. T. Hiroi to Heber J. Grant, June 23, 1920, General Correspondence.

72. Taylor, Diary, October 20, 1903; February 28, 1904; Grant, in *74th Semi-Annual Conference,* 13.

73. Grant, in *74th Semi-Annual Conference,* 13; Grant, Typed Diary, March 11–20 [single entry], 1903; Grant, Diary, July 2, 1903, Grant Letterpress Copybook, 36:490.

74. Heber J. Grant to Horace S. Ensign, January 20, 1905, Grant Letterpress Copybook, 39:269–70.

75. Heber J. Grant, Manuscript Diary, June 22, 1903, Grant Papers.

76. Gorō Takahashi to Horace Ensign, December 20, 1903, in Taylor, Diary, December 20, 1903.

77. Taylor, Diary, December 20, 1903.

78. Heber J. Grant to Joseph F. Smith, John R. Winder, and Anthon H. Lund, January 20, 1903, General Correspondence; Taylor, Diary, March 22, 1906; Brady, "Japanese Reaction to Mormonism," 165. The distribution of *Morumon Kyō to Morumon Kyōto* to Diet members was not consummated until 1906, three years after Grant's departure from Japan.

79. Brady, "The Japanese Reaction to Mormonism," translates large portions of *Morumon Kyō to Morumon Kyōto.* Brady also discusses the first Japanese book about Mormonism, *Morumon Shu,* a ninety-four-page, pocket-sized volume written by Uchida Akira under the pen name Uchida Yu. Rough translations of several chapters of Takahashi's work are found in box 148, folder 2, Grant Papers. For Takahashi's proposed ten-chapter table of contents, see Grant, in *72nd Annual Conference,* 48.

80. Grant, Typed Diary, February 1–28, 1903 [single entry]; Heber J. Grant to Joseph F. Smith, John R. Winder, and Anthon H. Lund, February 19, 1903, General Correspondence.

81. Grant, Diary, April 18, 1903, Grant Letterpress Copybook, 36:149; Heber J. Grant to Joseph F. Smith, John R. Winder, and Anthon H. Lund, April 20, 1903, Grant Letterpress Copybook, 36:61–62; Heber J. Grant to J. Golden Kimball, April 23, 1903, Grant Letterpress Copybook, 36:81–83. Grant variously estimated the size of the crowd to be as high as 650.

82. Heber J. Grant to Joseph J. Cannon, April 25, 1903, Grant Letterpress Copybook, 36:102.

83. Heber J. Grant to Joseph F. Smith, John R. Winder, and Anthon H. Lund, and Heber J. Grant to J. Golden Kimball, April 20 and 23, Grant Letterpress Copybook, 36:61–62, 81–83; Taylor, Diary, April 9–22 [single entry], 1903.

84. Grant, Diary, April 30, 1903, Grant Letterpress Copybook, 36:155; Grant, Manuscript Diary, May 9, 1903.

85. Heber J. Grant to Horace Ensign and Frederick Caine, May 22, 1903, Grant Letterpress Copybook, 36:300; Grant, Manuscript Diary, May 9, 1903.

86. Sandford Wells Hedges, "Scenery and Customs of Japan," *Improvement Era* 6 (September 1903): 818–19.

87. Heber J. Grant to Francis M. Lyman, November 15, 1901, Grant Letterpress Copybook, 34:430; Heber J. Grant to Matthias F. Cowley, May 12, 1903, Grant Letterpress Copybook, 36:239–41.

88. Taylor, "Memories of Far-Off Japan," 691.

89. Heber J. Grant to Francis M. Lyman, June 10, 1903, Grant Letterpress Copybook, 36:385–86; Heber J. Grant to Joseph F. Smith, John R. Winder, and Anthon H. Lund, June 10, 1903, Grant Letterpress Copybook, 36:394–95.

90. Grant to Cowley, May 12, 1903, Grant Letterpress Copybook, 36:240; Heber J. Grant to "Brother" Tanner, July 15, 1903, General Correspondence; Heber J. Grant to Frederick Caine and Sandford Hedges, July 17, 1903, General Correspondence; Heber J. Grant to Rachel Grant, July 28, 1903, Family Correspondence.

91. Heber J. Grant to Anthon H. Lund, May 8, 1903, Grant Letterpress Copybook, 36:205.

92. Heber J. Grant, "Greetings across the Sea," *Improvement Era* 40 (July 1937): 405.

93. John W. Stoker, Diary, July 20, 1902, Church Archives.

94. Stoker, Diary, March 11, 1903; Horace S. Ensign, "Incidents Connected with the Japan Mission," April 12, 1904, Grant Papers; Mary Grant to "My Dear Sisters," March 14, 1903, Grant Papers; Grant, Typed Diary, March 11–20, 1903; Heber J. Grant to Joseph F. Smith, John R. Winder, and Anthon H. Lund, March 19, 1903, General Correspondence.

95. Heber J. Grant to Anthony W. Ivins, April 24, 1903, Grant Letterpress Copybook, 36:84; Heber J. Grant to Abraham O. Woodruff, August 17, 1903, General Correspondence; Grant, Manuscript Diary, August 20, 1903; Heber J. Grant to Rachel Grant, September 2, 1903, Family Correspondence.

96. Heber J. Grant to Horace S. Ensign, August 24, 1903, General Correspondence; Grant, Manuscript Diary, August 23, 1903; Taylor, Diary, July 11–August 31, 1903 [single entry].

97. Grant, Manuscript Diary, August 23 and 24, 1903; Heber J. Grant to Joseph F. Smith, John R. Winder, and Anthon H. Lund, August 24, 1903, General Correspondence; Heber J. Grant to Rachel Grant, August 24, 1903, Family Correspondence.

98. Grant to Joseph F. Smith, John R. Winder, and Anthon H. Lund, August 24, 1903, General Correspondence; Grant to Rachel Grant, August 24, 1903.

99. Horace Ensign to Joseph H. Felt, September 12, 1903, General Correspondence; Taylor, Diary, September 1, 1903.

100. Stoker, Diary, September 1, 1903; Horace Ensign to Joseph H. Felt, September 12, 1903; Ensign, "Incidents Connected with the Japan Mission."

101. Heber J. Grant to Anthony W. Ivins, June 20, 1904, Grant Letterpress Copybook, 38:635.

102. For early expressions of this sentiment, Heber J. Grant to Joseph E. Taylor, January 25, 1904, Grant Letterpress Copybook, 38:217; Heber J. Grant to Alma O. Taylor, September 28, 1905, Grant Letterpress Copybook, 40:312.

103. Heber J. Grant, in *72nd Annual Conference of The Church of Jesus*

Christ of Latter-day Saints (Salt Lake City: Deseret News, 1902), 46.

104. Remarks of Rachel Grant, February 13, 1902, Relief Society Minute Book B, 1898–1902, Thirteenth Ward Papers, Church Archives; Heber J. Grant to Junius F. Wells, September 30, 1901, Grant Letterpress Copybook, 33:267–68; Heber J. Grant to Eva[?] Grant Moss, January 10, 1915, Grant Letterpress Copybook, 50:478.

105. Heber J. Grant to J. Wilford Booth, March 1, 1906, Grant Letterpress Copybook, 40:912.

106. Stoker, Diary, September 8, 1903.

Heber J. Grant's European Mission, 1903–1906

Elder Heber J. Grant landed in Liverpool, England, in November 1903, and by the first of the year he officially assumed his new position as president of the European Mission. The mission began at Tromso, Norway; and ran to Cape Town, South Africa; with Iceland and India serving as distant east-west meridians.[1] While the church had branches in each of these extremities, Grant's field of labor was more compact. Most of the mission's effort was reserved to the Netherlands, Germany, Scandinavia, and Switzerland, where he had a general superintendency, and especially in the British Isles, where he had duties that were immediate and day-to-day.

Upon his arrival, he immediately had a sense of déjà vu. Waiting for him at the foot of the pier was Elder Francis M. Lyman, his brusque, good-natured, 250-pound friend, now retiring from the European Mission to assume the presidency of the Quorum of the Twelve Apostles. As in Tooele two and a half decades earlier, when Grant had succeeded Elder Lyman as stake president, Grant now found his predecessor had "filled up the mud-holes, removed the rocks, and left a good road for us to travel on."[2] There was another familiar aspect: time had not altered Lyman's capacity for firm opinion, which, during the next six weeks before he finally sailed for America, flowed readily and at times disconcertingly. Grant wondered if Lyman still regarded him as the Tooele novice, despite Grant's two decades of service in the Quorum of the Twelve.

There was an immediate issue. "What in the world are you doing, bringing six girls over here?" Elder Lyman asked when he saw Grant, Grant's wife Emily, and a half-dozen of the Grant children disembark from the ship. Lyman's opposition continued as the family drove to the mission home. Wouldn't the blossoming Dessie and Grace distract the young elders? How in the world did Grant expect to get any work done? Lyman was defending established procedure. At the turn of the twentieth century, many Church authorities saw leading a mission as an ascetic obligation, and most mission presidents served without the companionship of a wife, much less children. Grant, unimpressed with the precedent, had previously secured the approval of President Joseph F. Smith for his family's presence. Nevertheless, to the moment of Lyman's departure, the presence of the Grant family was a continuing irritant between the two men.[3]

There was yet another problem: Grant badly wanted to be rid of the old mission home at 42 Islington. For half a century, the building had served as the European headquarters of the Church, while both it and its neighborhood had deteriorated. Universal consensus labeled it a byword, if not a hiss. "At first the din from the street kept me awake," one missionary wrote ironically about his stay at "Old '42," "but ere long it acted as a soporific, lulling me to rest, my slumber being broken only when the noise ceased, as it did for a short while between midnight and daybreak."[4] The three-story structure sat on a stone-paved intersection through which a heavy traffic of trams, buses, cabs, and trucks rumbled. Discolored by Liverpool's sodden atmosphere, 42 Islington also had a reputation for lingering derelicts and even an occasional haunting ghost.

The Grant family had long entertained colorful and disapproving stories about the old mission home, ever since Emily had fled there during the Raid of the 1880s to give birth to Dessie, the couple's firstborn. Years had not softened her feelings. Learning of Grant's call and her expected role as "mission mother," Emily firmly announced that neither she nor her children would live in the building.[5]

Before he left Salt Lake City, Heber had tried to persuade his fellow General Authorities to approve a $25,000 public subscription to fund a new headquarters.[6] Apparently dismissing the plan as too public and grandiose, they at length quietly instructed Lyman to buy a new building from Church funds.[7] Lyman accordingly located a property, but after he learned that its deed covenants were restrictive, he lost interest. Grant, however, was not to be denied. He hurried through the city looking for another house, and on finding one that was "very comfortable indeed," he succeeded in getting Lyman's approval the day before Lyman left for America.[8] Grant believed his predecessor's approbation was important, the senior Apostle's judgment faring better at home than his own.[9]

As the new home was made over for the Church's use, the Grants, despite Emily's earlier protest, briefly endured the perils of 42 Islington. The interval prompted some doggerel: "The horrors of that place you no doubt have heard," one of the Grant daughters penned, "Of the drunkards, the noise and the grime. / The three months we spent there just served to make us / Feel that 10 Holly Road was sublime."[10] Grant claimed the old place failed to yield him a single "good night's sleep."[11]

On the other hand, Grant thought the new residence as quiet as "any of the farm houses in Waterloo." "I sleep fine and enjoy hearing the birds sing in the morning," he noted. He chose an upstairs bedroom for his sleeping quarters and office redoubt. When working in the city, he often stationed himself there from early morning to past ten in the evening, his index fingers pounding correspondence on his diminutive "Blick" typewriter. Not counting an attic and basement, there were nine other rooms. The greeting room, or parlor, served as the meeting hall for the Saints in Liverpool, with religious services scheduled several times on Sunday and a service on Wednesday evening. The basement housed the clamorous presses of the mission periodical, the *Millennial Star*. Outside the house, the Grant girls planted flowers and a vegetable garden of lettuce and radishes. "No. 10, Holly Road" would be the Grants' home for the rest of their Liverpool stay.[12]

Grant approached his official duties soberly. "I am in England in answer to my prayers to the Lord and I hope to do all the good that it is possible for me to do."[13] Such avowals, coupled with his gaunt and hurried exterior, might have seemed forbidding to his youthful missionaries. As it was, his outward austerity vanished on acquaintance. A day or two after Lyman's departure, a member of the Liverpool staff inquired about the possibility of shaving his beard.

Elder Lyman, thinking facial hair added dignity, had made beards a matter of mission discipline.[14] Grant, in contrast, immediately awarded the elder's request, feigning fear that the young man's crimson whiskers might occasion a fire.[15] Such bonhomie became the rule. The mission president and his staff (most of whom soon appeared close-shaven) good-naturedly teased the elders in the mission, pointing out an elder's heavy Scottish diction or deflating another's prolonged and pompous phrases.[16] Nor did Grant object to occasional diversion. First the elders tried cricket in the mission headquarters' high-walled, spacious backyard.[17] But cricket was soon forgotten with the installation of a tennis court. "'Member how you used to whack 'em over the netting with the speed of a Colt .45? Wham!" recalled one of the missionaries years later.[18]

Despite Liverpool's "rich brown November mists," tennis became an office passion. Grant found it to be his best sport since baseball. For one thing it was efficient. "With tennis one can step out and play for a short time and then drop it," he analyzed.[19] But if his enthusiastic letters to friends in Salt Lake City were an accurate index, his playing was not so discreetly programmed into his schedule. One of his daughters agreed, writing, "Our father just loved . . . [the game] and played all he could, between conferences, meetings, and trips."[20] Always conscious of his fragile nerves, Grant had no difficulty justifying the activity. "I eat and sleep better by taking this pleasure. Physical exercise by using dumb bells may be equally as beneficial but it certainly is very annoying to me," he wrote to his mother at home.[21]

The new mission president refused to stand on ceremony or allow his age or high office to distance him from his subordinates. Perhaps as a result, a bond quickly grew between the impressionable missionaries and their leader. New elders usually first met him at the Holly Road meeting room, where one recalled that his instructions were "brief, inspiring, lovable, and full of the spirit of the Lord."[22] Rather than exhortation or pulpit pounding, Grant's style was democratic. He typically would ask each novice to join in a covenant with him to do their best and serve their mutual God.[23] During the missionaries' later experience, he was equally open, sharing both the problems of the mission and details of his own personal or business life. Unfortunately, talk soon begat talk, and echoes of his conversation were heard in distant Salt Lake City, where some Church officials murmured disapprovingly of his undignified talkativeness.[24]

Much of his talk to missionaries was fatherly counsel, with two themes dominating. First, he repeatedly urged his young charges to observe standards and keep commandments. And there was a frequent corollary: "We were . . . [told] to avoid wine and women like we would the gates of hell," recalled future General Authority LeGrand Richards.[25] Among Grant's most distressing tasks was excommunicating a handful of elders who strayed sexually. "I would a hundred times rather send the body of an Elder home in a coffin than to have to notify his family that he had transgressed the laws of chastity and been cut off from the Church," he wrote in his diary.[26] Of course, Church law on the matter was inexorable.

A second theme was as much to the point. Grant counseled the missionaries to work hard. "It did not take long to find out [what kind of leadership you would provide]," mused one of Elder Lyman's holdovers. "For with characteristic frankness you struck straight out from the shoulder and showed by your leadership that the way to go ahead was to push and keep on pushing."[27] Everywhere the trump sounded. "Work, work, work," proclaimed the *Millennial Star.* Grant's private correspondence was as firm. "You both have my love and respect," he wrote to two wayward missionaries, "but I have felt for many months that you were taking things altogether too easy."[28] Grant himself set the example. In happy contrast to languid Japan, where he had previously served as mission president, he now discovered himself outpacing even his old entrepreneurial pace. "I can truthfully say that I have never worked more hours in my life per day than I have since I arrived in Liverpool," he wrote to a colleague in Salt Lake City.[29]

Grant's openness, friendship, advice, and example were powerful tonics to his youthful cohorts. "Nothing unusual happened," wrote a member of the office staff one day. "We observed Pres. Grant's golden rule today—'Work. Work. Work.'" Throughout the mission, productivity soared. Each year of his presidency, despite a slight decline in his missionary force, the British Mission increased its street meetings, private gospel conversions, baptisms, and especially distribution of literature, which by 1906, the last year of his presidency, assumed avalanche proportions. That year four million tracts were distributed, or about eighteen thousand for each elder.[30]

To Elder Lyman, who from Salt Lake City was monitoring his successor's work in Liverpool, the tempo appeared "super human," perhaps immoderate. Grant, however, was confident he had not lost perspective. Most elders, he said, were not overworked one bit. They might put in at most six hours of "real work" daily, hardly sufficient to maintain a business position back home at ZCMI. Assuring President Lyman, Grant stated his only wish: that each elder sense the holy spirit in his life and "satisfy his own conscience that he was a diligent worker for the spread of truth."[31]

None of the activity of Grant and his missionaries, however, produced the conversions Church leaders desired. "It is the gleaning after the vintage is over," one leader despaired. A young elder put the matter more quaintly, commenting that the Mormon missionary effort was "gleaning the wheat field after the chickens have been turned in."[32] President Lyman's last year netted 472 baptisms, down from 581 the year before. Grant's first year saw convert baptisms rise to 602, and from there the total grew with annual 10 percent increases.[33] These numbers, while significant to the struggling missionaries, were dwarfed by Great Britain's 37 million turn-of-the-century population.

The main reason for the Church's poor showing lay with their image. The British public saw the Saints as strange, if not licentious, an image stemming largely from the practice of plural marriage, which the Fleet Street tabloids played on with merciless delight. Grant had been in England only a few months when one of the press's periodic outbursts began. Riding a train from London's St. Pancreas station to the mission headquarters in Liverpool, he noticed a disturbing advertisement on newspaper placards at each succeeding railroad station, "London *Sun:* A Protest against Mormonism." The editorial was in response to the possible seating of Elder Reed Smoot to the United States Senate.[34]

At length Grant himself also became a target. He had hastily left Salt Lake City for Europe to avoid cohabitation charges that had been drawn to embarrass the Church and Smoot just prior to the Senate hearings. Now the press used the matter for lurid suggestion. And with newspapers selling, still more imaginative stories were published. One supposedly told of an English girl's conversion to Mormonism and her subsequent life in Utah. According to the narrative, when she arrived in Utah she had been shackled, stripped, and displayed before the wife-hunting Church authorities, who "treated [her] worse than the coes on the farm." Forced to work the fields under the flogging watch of the first wife, the woman toiled "harder than the brutes which drew the plow." Then there was a fortunate turn of events. The "monster to whom she was married" died, a victim of appetite and overindulgence. Back in England where her tale could be told, the heroine later learned of the fate of her sister, who had also joined the Church. This woman had been found dead, broken by similar brutalities, with a lifeless babe pressed to her breast.[35]

In other times the fanciful melodrama might have been allowed to die of its own weight. But with emotions running high, Grant determined that the story and others like it had to be checked. Counseling with his youthful staff, he decided to visit the London editors immediately and engaged a railroad berth for that evening. At the editorial office of one of the most active anti-Mormon newspapers, he asked for a single column to rebut the ten or twelve stories already published. To buttress his position, Grant laid before the editor several letters of recommendation and asked the newspaper to get similar certificates from those attacking the Church.

"It does not make any difference what you have," was the response. "We will not publish anything that you have to say."

Grant started for the door, then paused. "The young man who ushered me upstairs told me your name was Robinson. Is that correct?" he said.

"It is."

"Do you know Phil Robinson?"

"Everybody knows Phil Robinson."

"Did he represent the London *Telegraph,* one of the *two* greatest . . . London newspapers during the Boer War?"

Grant's questions had less to do with establishing Robinson's credentials than drawing a distinction between the *Telegraph* and the editor's own newspaper. He then produced a copy of Robinson's kindly treatment of the Church, *Sinners and Saints,* and challenged the editor to buy the book and to read it, commenting, "You will find everything in your paper is a lie pure and simple. It will only cost you two shillings, and if that is too expensive I will be very glad to purchase it and present it to you with my compliments." Grant's efforts, however, brought no results. Though Robinson promised Church leaders a half column, the editor returned the proposed article two or three months later, claiming that he had been unable to find space.[36]

British fair play was not always so muted, and Grant, with several of his talented elders providing copy, managed to place several items with the press. But the tide flowed strongly against them. During the height of the anti-Mormon crusade, a "howling" and rock-throwing mob gathered outside the London headquarters. At a Church meeting in Finsbury, an agitator grabbed the podium, harangued for two hours, and then concluded by putting on a large belt and slouch hat (he apologized for not carrying a revolver) and proclaimed himself a Mormon "Danite." Outside the hall, two thoroughly incensed ladies, each representing the Mormon and anti-Mormon view, had to be pulled apart by their husbands.[37] Following the incident, the Church was refused further use of the building, despite their record of almost ten years of responsible use.[38]

Tensions were almost as high in other parts of Europe. "The papers are full of the Mormon question," Grant's subordinate, President Hugh J. Cannon of the German Mission, reported, "and almost without exception the reports are unfavorable." Four elders were banished from Saxony, and Prussian officials made ominous inquiries about the missionaries' day-to-day activities. The city of Dresden forbade any Church meetings and threatened the Saints with a fine of three hundred marks and six months' imprisonment if they ignored the ordinance. Scurrying to maintain their presence in Germany, the missionaries quietly changed their passport registration from clerical to student status, a maneuver that Grant's conscience admitted was "somewhat underhanded," though seemingly necessary.[39]

In Britain the tumult was over within three weeks, but for the rest of Grant's presidency, harassment and difficulty continued as a matter of course.[40] During one two-week period, police at both Swindon and Sunderland advised the elders that they would be unable to protect their proselyting, citing overwhelmingly adverse public opinion.⁴¹ At Bristol, Watford, and Southampton, Church services were broken up by sectarian opponents. In Southampton, small boys were given candy to encourage rowdyism.⁴² Opponents at Bedford used a similar scheme. Conditions were peaceful until the elders mentioned the name of Joseph Smith. Then Protestant Sunday School children, well coached and imported for the occasion, interrupted the service with songs and shouting. Eventually the adult leaders of the disturbance were marched off by the town's constabulary.⁴³

The Church often won support by its good behavior. The *Daily Mail* noted members' "quiet conviction" and "apparent absence of enthusiasm," even as the cries of protesters disrupted their meeting. When agitators seized control of a meeting at Bradford, the elders quietly passed out tracts and then left the scene, thereby earning police praise for "the proper Christian spirit" and the promise of future protection. In Liverpool, Detective Inspector Yates, first dispatched to investigate the Mormons, later became a friend. The gap between the Mormons' actual behavior and their public caricature was so wide as to be disarming.⁴⁴

Grant's presidency reflected the prevailing persecution. Though he had little hope of securing popular acceptance for his people, his sermons repeatedly spoke of Christian burden. "His faith will not be shaken by the wave of persecution that is spreading over the country," he declared. "Persecution is the heritage of every faithful follower of Christ." Opposition carried virtue. It strengthened and refined, making the Latter-day Saints, whatever their public image, a growing "factor for good in the earth."⁴⁵

His sermons also emphasized the Church's uniqueness, speaking less of the Bible than of the Book of Mormon, and often less of Jesus Christ than of Joseph Smith, for the Church's founding prophet conveyed for Grant the whole gospel. Outward observance, such as the payment of tithing or compliance with the Word of Wisdom, also drew his attention. In a time of siege, external manifestations of discipleship were important. His most frequent speaking device was to comment item by item on Joseph Smith's thirteen Articles of Faith, sprinkled with illustrative stories and personal anecdotes. Invariably, the allotted time proved insufficient for his rapid-fire delivery.

It was while he was behind the pulpit that some thought him at his best.[46] Here he could give range to his conviction and personality—testifying, admonishing, rebuking, persuading, assuring, sometimes all in a single torrent. He was not given to precision or forethought, for like his father, Jedediah M. Grant, he was not an intellectual. He was an exhorter. Words were meant to motivate, not just to inform. The result was often successful. "I have never [since] doubted that you are a servant of the Lord," wrote one missionary after hearing one of Grant's impassioned sermons. "You spoke . . . as one having authority, and you spoke with power."[47]

Behind his forceful public words, a softer view often prevailed. When he was questioned about his Word of Wisdom proscriptions, his response was pliant: preferably, the Saints should drink cocoa or a beverage such as "hot water milk and sugar." But for the life long English tea drinker, he counseled patience. "I have not felt to keep after them to that extent that they would feel that they were not worthy of being counted as good saints," he said. On another occasion he acknowledged the superior virtue of many who had been unable to keep the health code. Indeed, he thought the struggling nonobserver might be considered for Church office as the "Spirit of the Lord should direct" when more worthy candidates could not be found.[48]

Grant was seldom content with the status quo. To the First Presidency, he dispatched unwelcome suggestions aimed at improving Salt Lake City office procedures.[49] He was convinced that Great Britain should have a small Latter-day Saint temple to administer the higher ordinances. "This may be a day dream," he conceded, "but I can't quite get it out of my head."[50] To burnish the Church's public image, he asked young Church members studying music in Europe to perform at missionary conferences and even staged a favorably reviewed but scantly attended concert at Hull. The program featured three Utah artists: Arvilla Clark, Willard Andelin, and Martha Read.[51]

He was constantly on the move, traveling third-class on British rail. He once joked, "People ask why 'Mormons' always travel third class, and the answer is, 'Because there is no fourth class.'"[52] During one eight-month period, he was in Liverpool only one Sunday. He hoped to go to South Africa, Turkey, and India, and perhaps to revisit Japan, but for the time being he was preoccupied with western Europe. Not quite halfway through his mission, he had toured each of the British conferences three times. By 1905 he had visited Holland five times, Scandinavia and Germany three times, Switzerland twice, and France at least once. "I have been kept very busy," he said. Far from a lament, especially after his ordeal in Japan, his words carried satisfaction.[53]

There was a private life to these years, centering on Emily. When Grant was called to Japan in 1901, the seniority of his wife Augusta gave her claim to that exotic and exciting experience. But his typical fair dealing with his wives reasserted itself when, after returning from Japan, he received the European Mission assignment. Augusta had accompanied him to Japan, now it was Emily's turn to be with him.[54]

Had the choice of the two tours been hers, Emily certainly would have selected Europe. European tradition and culture had fascinated her from childhood, and now she was eager to experience Europe's sites and sounds. She traveled often with her husband on his preaching assignments, leaving the younger children with Fia Wahlgren, the family's nanny. This gave her the opportunity to sightsee while her husband conducted meetings and interviews. At first, when time and business permitted, he joined her, but as his mission progressed he was content to attend to duty and grant Emily her leave. Her pace was indefatigable, testing the limits of even the older Grant children, who sometimes accompanied her.[55]

Although graying with middle age, Emily remained very much alive. Her energy stemmed not only from the legendary curiosity she had inherited from her Wells ancestors but also from a sense of liberation. The days of clandestine living on the underground were behind her. For half a dozen years she had lived openly in Salt Lake City society; yet, whatever her improving station, England offered emotional release. For the first time, polygamy was not an overriding concern. She and Heber had each other to themselves, and they both felt a new intimacy. "I am getting better acquainted with Emily," he confided in a letter home.[56] It was as if the couple were honeymooning instead of beginning the nineteenth year of their marriage. They both later remembered their English experience as idyllic, a time of "perfect home life."[57] For Emily, these were certainly her

Courtesy Church Archives, The Church of Jesus Christ of Latter-day Saints

Illus. 12-1. Group of missionaries in England in 1906 with Joseph F. Smith (*center, with beard*) and members of Heber J. Grant's family, including (*back row, third from left*) Deseret (Dessie) Grant; (*back row, sixth from left*) Emily Grant; (*middle row, third from left*) Charles W. Nibley (*middle row, far right*) Heber J. Grant; (*front row, third from left*) Grace Grant.

happiest years. "Mamma did so thoroughly enjoy every minute of the time there," Dessie wrote to her father many years later. "She said she had enjoyed being with you more than anyone on earth could possibly know."[58]

It was also an exciting time for the Grant children. Without formal or higher schooling himself, their father nevertheless prized education and hoped that his family could make the best of his calling by encountering Europe firsthand. Within weeks of his arrival in England, he had sent Dessie and Grace to London for vocal training.[59] He later enrolled two of his daughters in schools in Berlin, and always, especially under Emily's enthusiastic prodding, the children were encouraged to see historic sites and attend concerts. There was, however, a limit to Grant's enthusiasm for culture. When Edith's voice teacher in Liverpool recommended that she get advanced study for a possible professional career, the churchman wanted none of it. Instead of a professional career, he hoped that his daughter might use her talent in a more conventional role, singing "lullabies to her own babies."[60] He was unmistakably relieved when Edith, who no doubt sensed her father's feelings, decided to forgo advanced training.

Not wishing to limit Europe's advantages to just Emily's children, Grant at first hoped that all ten of his daughters might join him, and he even considered having Augusta cross the Atlantic as well. But with Church officials in Salt Lake City expressing growing misgiving about his family's activities, he finally imposed a limit on the number of his children who could be in Europe at a single moment, giving each a turn by rotating them in and out of the Liverpool mission home[61] (illus. 12-1). New arrivals brought excitement. "Have been counting the hours all day," he once wrote in his diary. "Day moved like the gait of a snail. My daughters Anna and Mary will be here this evening."[62]

Grant later conceded the wisdom of the warnings he received about limiting the number of his children in the mission field, as even his diminished involvement in his family's activities brought criticism from some impoverished Saints who saw them as extravagant. Others assumed that the family's expenses were met by the Church. Grant, however, prided himself that he had paid every mite and farthing himself, including the children's boarding costs while they lived at Holly Road. These and other expenses were substantial. The final cost of the family's European experience was some ten thousand dollars.[63]

There were interludes that were biographically revealing. Emily, bright and confident in private relationships, sometimes faltered in her new setting. While visiting London with some of the girls, she was approached by a young man selling strawberries. At two shillings a box, the berries were expensive but attractive. The elders would certainly enjoy them. Surrendering a ten-shilling gold piece, she waited while the vendor went to a nearby store to make change. Minutes passed. Finally Grace went to learn the reason for the delay. "Yes, I saw the boy come in," the man behind the counter said, "but he didn't buy anything. He just walked through the store and out the back door." To make matters worse, Emily learned that the box of berries had a single layer of fruit. The boy had propped up a few strawberries on several layers of leaves.[64]

Grant had his own embarrassment. Shortly after the family arrived in Liverpool, six-year-old Frances proved herself an able mimic of Liverpool's accents and street talk. "My dear," her father corrected, "those are not nice words and I don't want you to use them. I'll have to wash out your mouth."

At breakfast several days later, Grant, always a spirited raconteur, told a story containing a few words of colorful dialogue. Little Frances overheard and commented, "Papa, you washed my mouth out for saying those words, and now you're saying them."

Wondering how he might explain to the little child the distinction of using words as opposed to recounting them, her father pled guilty. "So I did, my dear," he said, "and I shouldn't say them any more than you should. Would you like to wash my mouth out?"

She would—and did. "From that moment I knew that my father would be absolutely fair in all his dealings with me," she later remembered. Heber also learned a lesson. When telling future stories, he invariably substituted the phrase "*with emphasis*" for any objectionable four-letter words.[65]

Grant often fretted about his health. Though his tensions eased while he was in England, as his mission progressed he found himself unable to sleep past three or four in the morning. He learned to live with this disability, reading and writing during the early morning hours and then taking a compensating nap after lunch.[66] This unheard-of allowance was part of a new health-care program that apparently had begun with a prescription from Francis M. Lyman. Before dressing, Grant accordingly took breathing exercises—one hundred deep breaths. Then he kneaded his stomach for five minutes, followed by fifteen minutes of "physical culture," mild calisthenics that stretched and toned his muscles.[67] He would continue these exercises the rest of his life.

Later in the afternoon, if he felt tired, he might sit at the mission home piano and pick out a few hymns with his index finger. After a refreshing thirty or forty-five minutes, he would then return to work.[68] Clearly, he wished to slow his pace. "I try to eat slow and think slow and walk deliberately," he declared. "These things are all new to my way of living."[69]

As always, Grant measured his health by the ebbs and flows of his waistline. At first he thought he might put on weight by sheer perseverance, by strictly maintaining his exercise and tension-reducing program. He was rewarded by a quick twenty-pound gain. But as his mission continued, he slimmed down to his former 137 pounds and found, to his disappointment, that he could once more wear the clothes he had brought from America.[70] There was, however, one important byproduct to his efforts. Now feeling rested and stronger, he could, for the first time since his physical breakdown in Tooele almost twenty years earlier, pass a couch or chair without wanting to rest. For years he had pushed himself onward through the force of his strong will.[71]

He had thought that his European mission might allow him to continue a long-postponed study program he had started in Japan. During the early months, he tried to navigate ten pages a day in such faith-promoting books as Heber C. Kimball's *Journal* and George Q. Cannon's *My First Mission.* He augmented these selections with five pages in the Doctrine and Covenants and by memorizing one verse daily. But like his weight-increasing program, he found that the longer he remained in Liverpool, the less successful he was. He increasingly allowed other priorities to crowd out his studies.[72]

While in England, Grant encountered another book that had great influence on him, not only because of its contents but also for the practice it began. Pausing one day in the editorial office of the

Millennial Star, he casually thumbed through a slender volume, *The Power of Truth* by William George Jordan, a former editor of the *Saturday Evening Post.* Grant found himself captured by the author's simple phrases and practical lessons. He read the volume seven times and began to liberally salt his sermons with its messages. "I know of no book of the same size, that has made a more profound impression upon my mind," he wrote enthusiastically to Jordan, "and whose teachings I consider of greater value."[73]

Grant decided the book deserved wide circulation. Inquiring of the publishers, he learned that of the original five thousand copies printed, only a few hundred had been sold. The rest of the copies were scheduled for the incinerator. Grant immediately purchased these as well as the book's copyright and began to mark and inscribe copies for friends. Before leaving Europe he ordered another one thousand copies printed.[74] Due to his constant and impassioned boosting, the book eventually gained popularity in Utah.

Thus began one of Grant's characteristic hobbies: buying hundreds and sometimes thousands of copies of books for distribution to friends (illus. 12-2). More than simple book-giving on a grand scale, the activity fit into his view of what a man of his interests and standing should do. Despite his ecclesiastical calling, he continued to dress, act, and conform to the best standards of the Gilded Age's entrepreneurs, standards which meant, at least in his eyes, employing personal means for social and cultural betterment. He had long shown an interest in the paintings of Utah naturalist John Hafen, and while in Europe Grant's patronage continued with the promising mezzo-soprano Arvilla Clark and with two Utah artists studying in Paris, Mahonri Young and Leo Fairbanks.[75]

Grant's dealings with Fairbanks showed how strong his sense of social obligation was. The Apostle did not enjoy Fairbanks's technique and chided him for his frequent violation of Victorian mood and sensibility. "The height of art in the estimation of most men is to me the height of that which all modest people should resent," Grant said.[76] Yet he was repeatedly supportive, attempting to find Salt Lake City buyers for Fairbanks's work and personally subsidizing it. "You do not need to worry about not having enough money to take you home [from France]," he assured the artist. "You can spend all of your money [for study], and I promise to let you have money to take you home."[77]

Grant's sightseeing activities bore little of the small-town cant and forced obligation that characterized some *nouveau riche* of the period. He clearly took pleasure in cultural affairs, though his descriptive comments sometimes betrayed the eye of a beginner.[78] He noted that he "enjoyed . . . very much" *Much Ado about Nothing* at His

Courtesy Church Archives, The Church of Jesus Christ of Latter-day Saints

Illus. 12-2. Heber J. Grant signing books to give away as gifts.

Majesty's Theatre and used the same phrase a week later to describe *The Scarlet Pimpernel.* He found an unnamed opera at Covent Gardens to be "too classical" and to lack "sweet music," but he had a decidedly warmer reaction to his introduction to Wagner's *Lohengrin.* He labeled the singing of world-renowned contralto Clara Butt "splendid entertainment"; and after hearing Handel's oratorio *Elijah,* he enthusiastically resolved to "get something of this kind" performed by the Mormon Tabernacle Choir.[79]

He explored the wonders of the continent with equal gusto (illus. 12-3). Seeing Rembrandt's *Night Drill* in Rotterdam so impressed Grant that he wanted a copy.[80] In Paris he thought the Sacré Coeur "the most magnificent architectural structure I have ever seen," and the Louvre left him literally speechless. "The painting and sculpture must be seen to be appreciated—I shall attempt no description of what I saw," he wrote. In France he also visited the Cluny Museum, Sainte Chapelle, the Palace of Justice, Les Invalides, Versailles, the Eiffel Tower (going to the top), and the Tuilleries.[81] In Dresden, Germany, he attended the Royal Opera House, the circus, and the beer gardens. The latter afforded "some beautiful music by one of the finest bands in Germany," but of course no transgressing alcohol. He did, however, ruefully concede that the spectacle of "apostle Grant" spending a Sunday evening at a German beer garden would be enough, if the news leaked to Salt Lake City, to make some Saints faint.[82]

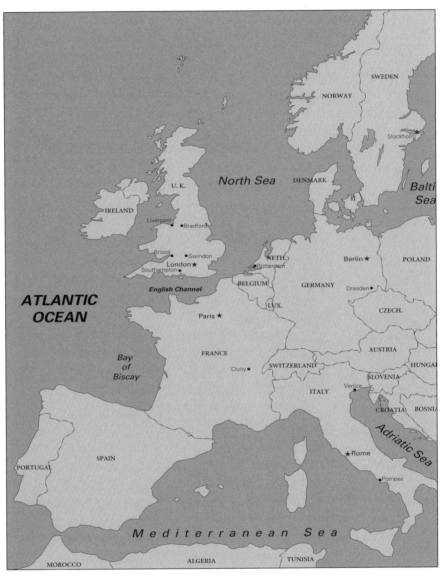

Illus. 12-3. Cities that Heber J. Grant visited while on his European mission, November 1903 to August 1906.

With Emily at his side, he noted that at times "sight seeing is about the hardest work I have ever done."[83] But there were other moments of almost boyish romp. On his fourth tour of the Scandinavian branches, he asked his companions how they wished to celebrate the Fourth of July. He answered his own question by announcing an intention to call on King Oscar of Sweden. When they arrived at Rosendal Palace, the king's summer residence, Grant and his group noted how scanty security seemed. Grant waited until the guard in front of the palace reached the edge of his prescribed back-and-forth march and pivoted to return. Taking a single Swedish-speaking elder with him, he fell quickly behind the guard for a few steps and then hastily made for the door.

"I wish to see the king," Grant told the startled chamberlain. To buttress his case, Grant quickly penciled a note: "To His Majesty King Oscar. I am here with a party from Utah, U.S.A.—fifteen in number. If you will allow us the pleasure of shaking hands with you on this day we Americans celebrate we shall feel highly honored and duly grateful." He enclosed a letter of introduction from Heber Wells, Governor of Utah, and mentioned additional letters from both Utah senators, if needed.

Grant's daring paid off. To the surprise of everyone in the party, with the possible exception of their leader, the king soon appeared— "a magnificent specimen of humanity," Grant thought. He first spoke in Swedish, but graciously switched to English on learning that the majority of the Americans could not understand him.

The interview consisted largely of pleasantries, but there was one subject that the Americans found reassuring. Thanking His Majesty for the religious liberty they enjoyed in his Norwegian and Swedish realms, the party received a forceful reply. "Liberty! yes, that is best," Oscar responded. "I do not desire in any way to hinder any from worshiping God as their conscience leads them." He then added a statement that perhaps explained his willingness to meet with them. "I have representatives traveling in various sections of the United States," the party in later years remembered him saying, "and the reports I receive indicate that my former subjects in Utah are happier and more prosperous, and getting along better [there] than in any other part of the United States." With this, he broke off the ten-minute exchange with a "God be with you all" and an "adieu," then stepped back into his residence.[84]

Illus. 12-4. Heber and Emily in front of St. Mark's Cathedral in Venice, Italy, in 1906.

Near the end of his mission, Grant received permission from President Joseph F. Smith for a final sightseeing foray into Italy. Surviving photographs show Emily and Heber exploring the wonders of Venice's St. Mark's and the ruins of Pompeii. "The day has been one of the most intensely interesting of my life," he noted (illus. 12-4). They also explored the catacombs and toured St. Peter's Cathedral in the Vatican. Heber declared St. Peter's Cathedral to be "more wonderful than any building I have ever seen." Even the weather smiled benediction, with the sky bright and crystal blue. If the European Mission years were the *crème* of their marriage, their twenty-three-day trip to Italy was the *crème de la crème*.

Grant returned from his Italian travels sobered by news of his deteriorating finances. With Philippine sugar steadily dominating American markets, his portfolio of intermountain sugar stocks had badly slumped. He attempted to be philosophical. "I am now worse off than when I came on this mission. . . . Such is life."[85]

For a moment he wondered if his Italian trip had been wise. But the costs of his touring, whether in Italy or elsewhere, were easily justified. He had traveled widely in America as a businessman and

churchman, but his European experience was an important supplement to his education. It introduced him to European grandeur,
history, and achievement. His travels also provided cultural balance
and perspective. Perhaps as important, his travels also gave him a
renewed appreciation for his own heritage. As he watched people in
Italy genuflect before icons, he expressed quiet appreciation for the
simple worship of his own faith.[86] The socially conscious entrepreneur within him sensed something terribly disproportionate about
Europe's bejeweled shrines. Couldn't the precious gems and obvious
wealth of the cathedrals finance manufacturing institution after manufacturing institution to "furnish the poor people employment"?[87]

With the exception of his Italian tour, most of Grant's sightseeing and concert-going was at an end after his first three or four
months in Europe. Following his initial excitement, he was surprised by how little the theater billboards interested him as he bore
in on the demands of his mission.[88] As his mission drew to a close,
there was no looking back. "I shall be able to go home feeling that I
have done about as well as I could have," he wrote a friend. "I did
not go home from Japan with this feeling."[89]

The mission ended with a spiritual crescendo. During his presidency, he found his meetings with mission leaders to be especially
helpful. By summer 1906 he resolved to hold at Bradford the first
modern assembly of all elders stationed in Britain. To supplement
costs, he requested money from Utah donors; and when accommodations proved inadequate, the elders volunteered to sleep three in a
bed if necessary. The results were Pentecostal. The conference was
"the best and most spirited . . . I have ever attended," remembered
young Hugh B. Brown. "President Grant spoke with great power. . . .
Most every elder wept with joy." Others confirmed the extraordinary spirit. "Some [missionaries] whose testimonies were weak said,
'Now I know.' Many even of the most energetic Elders were heard to
say that they had received a great awakening touch."[90]

One elder thought Grant's face glowed with special luminescence
when he addressed the conference. Grant could never recall laboring
under such a spiritual endowment. He struggled repeatedly to retain
emotional control. "I do not know that I have ever felt my own
insignificance and the magnitude of the work in which I am engaged,"
he reported to his mother. The experience seemed to validate his

entire mission experience. "I can now realize more fully than I have ever done before that it is impossible to have greater joy than one experiences in the missionary field."[91]

Late in the evening one elder wondered if another spiritual event might be taking place. He awakened to hear what seemed like distant singing. Rising up on an elbow, he felt the reassuring hand of Grant, his bed companion, who confessed he had been trying to sing himself to sleep after the heavily charged conference.[92] Indeed, for several days the excited leader found it hard to return to a normal routine. Instead, he walked through the mission home and repeatedly rejoiced with his office staff over their experience.[93] The conference also stirred the missionaries. The total of distributed tracts jumped each month to an unprecedented 450,000, or more than five hundred for each missionary.[94]

By the end of 1905, Grant was ready to return home to Utah. Except for two short intervals, and counting his service in Japan, he had been away from headquarters for four years. He had already served in England twice as long as the one-year mission that President Smith had first promised at the time of Grant's call. "I have had about as much of . . . [missionary service] as I care for in one dose," he admitted, "but I feel that I can and will be happy just as long as the Lord wants me here."[95] First he thought his release might come in the spring; then he hoped for the summer. But with the Smoot controversy continuing in America, Church authorities were in no hurry to disturb already troubled waters by releasing Grant with cohabitation charges against him still pending.[96]

Finally, in October 1906, Grant learned that he would be permitted to return to Salt Lake City in time for Christmas. There were the usual farewell fêtes. The British missionaries presented him with a Rembrandt print and an engraved gold watch. There was also a party at the Holly Road meeting room with recitations, vocal and piano solos, speeches, and refreshments. As the Grant family drove to the Liverpool docks, rain and wind pushed against their omnibus.[97] The seas would be heavy for their trip home.

In later years, there was an afterglow to Grant's three years in Europe, in part, no doubt, because of the approaching death of Emily, who even as they sailed from Liverpool was ill with undiagnosed stomach cancer. England, finally, had been her time, a time when she and her husband culminated their relationship. Grant also sensed a spiritual bequest. Over succeeding years, until his death almost forty years later, his judgment of his years in Europe never wavered. "I got nearer to the Lord, and accomplished more, and had more joy while in the mission field than ever before or since," he said.[98]

Notes

This article was originally published in *Journal of Mormon History* 14 (1988): 16–33.

1. "President Grant's Arrival," *Millennial Star* 65 (December 3, 1903): 778–79. Because current Church Archive policy limits the access and use of materials, many footnote citations have not been verified. When citing material from the Heber J. Grant Papers, which are lodged at the Church Archives, The Church of Jesus Christ of Latter-day Saints, Salt Lake City, I have supplied box and folder information only in those cases where access cannot be established by using the Grant register.

2. "Conference of British Elders: An Account of the Proceedings at Bradford, July 22nd and 23rd, 1906," *Millennial Star* 68 (August 2, 1906): 492; Heber J. Grant to Joseph E. Taylor, January 25, 1904, Grant Letterpress Copybook, 38:217, Grant Papers.

3. Frances Grant Bennett, *Glimpses of a Mormon Family* (Salt Lake City: Deseret Book, 1968), 7–8.

4. Orson F. Whitney, *Through Memory's Halls: The Life Story of Orson F. Whitney as Told By Himself* (Independence, Missouri: Zion's Printing and Publishing Company, 1930), 141–42.

5. Heber J. Grant to Joseph Hyrum Grant, March 4, 1904, Grant Letterpress Copybook, 38:408.

6. Anthon H. Lund, Diary, October 8, 1903, Church Archives; Journal History of The Church of Jesus Christ of Latter-day Saints, October 9, 1903, Church Archives, microfilm copy in Harold B. Lee Library, Brigham Young University, Provo, Utah.

7. First Presidency to Francis M. Lyman, November 12, 1903, First Presidency Letterbooks, Church Archives.

8. Heber J. Grant Remarks at the funeral of Henry M. O'Gorman, August 21, 1930, Grant Papers; Heber J. Grant, Typed Diary, January 17, 1904, Grant Papers.

9. Heber J. Grant to Anthon H. Lund, September 30, 1904, General Correspondence, Grant Papers; Heber J. Grant to Jesse N. Smith, December 8, 1904, Grant Letterpress Copybook, 39:177–78.

10. Emily Grant Madsen, "The European Mission," written in commemoration of Grant's seventy-first birthday, November 22, 1927, in Grant Letterpress Copybook, 66:2.

11. Heber J. Grant to Jesse N. Smith, December 8, 1904; Heber J. Grant to Alma O. Taylor, May 5, 1904, Grant Letterpress Copybook, 38:614.

12. Heber J. Grant to Jesse N. Smith, December 8, 1904; Heber J. Grant to Hamilton G. Park, June 16, 1905, Grant Letterpress Copybook, 39:867; Heber J. Grant to John T. Caine, November 28, 1905, Grant Letterpress Copybook, 40:574–75.

13. Grant, Typed Diary, January 1, 1904.

14. Bennett, *Glimpses of a Mormon Family*, 16.

15. Heber J. Grant to Rufus D. Johnson, January 30, 1935, Grant Letterpress Copybook, 72:146.

16. Rufus D. Johnson to Heber J. Grant, November 21, 1940, General Correspondence, Grant Papers.

17. Madsen, "European Mission."

18. Rufus Johnson to Heber J. Grant, November 22, 1937, incoming correspondence, Grant Papers; Heber J. Grant to Rufus Johnson, December 3, 1937, Grant Papers.

19. Rufus Johnson to Heber J. Grant, November 22, 1937; Heber J. Grant to Rachel Ivins Grant, October 11, 1905, Grant Letterpress Copybook, 40:365.

20. Madsen, "European Mission."

21. Heber J. Grant to Rachel Ivins Grant, October 17, 1905, Grant Letterpress Copybook, 40:400.

22. R. Eugene Allen, "The Mission President in Europe," *Improvement Era* 39 (November 1936): 694.

23. Grant, Typed Diary, May 6, 1905.

24. B. F. Grant to Heber J. Grant, August 5, 1905, General Correspondence.

25. LeGrand Richards to Gordon Irving, February 2, 1982, letter intended as a postscript to an oral interview by Ronald W. Walker, in author's possession.

26. Grant, Typed Diary, August 19, 1904.

27. Nicholas G. Smith to Heber J. Grant, February 19, 1917, General Correspondence.

28. Heber J. Grant, "Work and Keep Your Promises," *Millennial Star* 66 (May 5, 1904): 274; Heber J. Grant to D. W. J. and S. G. S., February 3, 1906, Grant Letterpress Copybook, 40:864.

29. Heber J. Grant to George Teasdale, January 18, 1906, Grant Letterpress Copybook, 40:818.

30. Heber J. Grant, in *78th Annual Conference of The Church of Jesus Christ of Latter-day Saints* (Salt Lake City: The Church of Jesus Christ of Latter-day Saints, 1907), 36; Heber J. Grant to Hyrum S. Woolley, May 19, 1905, Grant Letterpress Copybook, 39:746; Heber J. Grant to Matthias F. Cowley, June 10, 1905, Grant Letterpress Copybook, 39:848.

31. Francis M. Lyman to Heber J. Grant, October 19, 1906, General Correspondence; for Grant's reply, see October 31, 1906, Grant Letterpress

Copybook, 42:926–27. Grant had often made the same point to his missionaries. Without "the fire of the Spirit of the Lord," their labor, he assured them, was nothing. "Report of Priesthood Meeting in Netherlands and Belgium," in Grant, Typed Diary, February 10, 1906.

32. Orson F. Whitney, letter printed in *Deseret Evening News,* November 10, 1882, 2.

33. "Editorial: The Annual Statistical Report," *Millennial Star* 66 (March 24, 1904): 183–84; "Statistical Report of the British Mission," *Millennial Star* 67 (March 30, 1905): 202–3, 205; "Statistical Report of the British Mission for the Year Ending December 31st, 1906," *Millennial Star* 69 (February 28, 1907): 135; Richard L. Evans, *A Century of Mormonism in Great Britain* (Salt Lake City: Deseret Book, 1937), 244.

34. Grant, Typed Diary, April 3 and 11, 1904; Heber J. Grant to the First Presidency, April 19, 1904, Grant Letterpress Copybook, 38:556–57.

35. Copied in Grant, Typed Diary, April 11, 1904.

36. Grant recounted his experience several times: Salt Lake Tabernacle Address, April 13, 1930, in Grant Letterpress Copybook, 67:766–68; and "Elder Heber J. Grant," in *79th Annual Conference of The Church of Jesus Christ of Latter-day Saints* (Salt Lake City: The Church of Jesus Christ of Latter-day Saints, 1909), 115. See also Grant, Typed Diary, April 14, 1904; and Heber J. Grant to E. C. Branson, March 2, 1926, Grant Letterpress Copybook, 64:136–37.

37. London *Daily Mail,* April 11, 1904, 3.

38. Heber J. Grant to First Presidency, April 19, 1904, Joseph F. Smith Correspondence, Smith Papers, Church Archives; "Notes from the Mission Field," *Millennial Star* 66 (June 2, 1904): 348.

39. Heber J. Grant to First Presidency, June 21, 1904, Joseph F. Smith Correspondence; "Notes from the Mission Field," *Millennial Star* 66 (May 19, 1904): 315; "Notes From the Mission Field," *Millennial Star* 66 (September 1, 1904): 555; "The Sheffield Conference," *Millennial Star* 66 (October 6, 1904): 619.

40. Heber J. Grant to First Presidency, May 4, 1904, Joseph F. Smith Correspondence.

41. Vincent F. Wooton, "Success Amid Opposition in Sunderland," *Millennial Star* 67 (November 16, 1905): 733; "Notes from the Mission Field," *Millennial Star* 68 (January 4, 1906): 11.

42. "Notes from the Mission Field," *Millennial Star* 66 (June 2 1904): 348; "Notes from the Mission Field," *Millennial Star* 66 (July 21, 1904): 459; "From the Mission Field: District Meeting at Watford," *Millennial Star* 68 (January 18, 1906): 42; London *Daily Mail,* April 11, 1904, 3.

43. Jesse W. Hoopes, "From the Mission Field: A Big Meeting at Bedford," *Millennial Star* 67 (August 24, 1905): 539–40.

44. London *Daily Mail,* April 11, 1904, 3; "Jesse W. Hoopes, "From the Mission Field: A Big Meeting at Bedford," *Millennial Star* 67 (August 24, 1905): 539–40; Rufus D. Johnson to Heber J. Grant, November 20, 1943,

General Correspondence.

45. "The Liverpool Conference," *Millennial Star* 66 (April 14, 1904): 237; "The Nottingham Conference," *Millennial Star* 66 (April 21, 1904): 252; "The Leeds Conference," *Millennial Star* 66 (April 28, 1904): 268; "The Scottish Conference," *Millennial Star* 66 (May 12, 1904): 300; "The Manchester Conference," *Millennial Star* 67 (March 16, 1905): 175; "The Nottingham Conference," *Millennial Star* 68 (May 17, 1906): 315.

46. Allen, "Mission President in Europe," 695.

47. Ed. M. Rowe to Heber J. Grant, January 25, 1932, General Correspondence.

48. Heber J. Grant to H. J. Lilley, November 22, 1904, Grant Letterpress Copybook, 39:120; Heber J. Grant to Wilford Booth, February 10, 1904, Grant Letterpress Copybook, 38:279.

49. Heber J. Grant to the First Presidency, January 30 1904, Joseph F. Smith Correspondence; Heber J. Grant to the First Presidency, September 28, 1904, Joseph F. Smith Correspondence.

50. Heber J. Grant to R. W. Bryce Thomas, August 28 and October 4, 1906, Grant Letterpress Copybook, 42:759, 903.

51. Hull *Daily Mail,* quoted in "The Singers of Utah," *Millennial Star* 67 (March 9, 1905): 156–57.

52. "Elder Heber J. Grant," in *82nd Semi-Annual Conference of The Church of Jesus Christ of Latter-day Saints* (Salt Lake City: The Church of Jesus Christ of Latter-day Saints, 1911), 24.

53. Grant, Typed Diary, December 31, 1904; Heber J. Grant to Hyrum S. Woolley, May 19, 1905, Grant Letterpress Copybook, 39:746; Heber J. Grant to Marriner W. Merrill, November 3, 1905, Grant Letterpress Copybook, 40:467; Heber J. Grant to Anthony W. Ivins, August 2, 1906, Grant Letterpress Copybook, 42:484.

54. Bennett, *Glimpses of a Mormon Family,* 1–2.

55. Heber J. Grant to Susan Noble, November 18, 1904, Grant Letterpress Copybook, 39:110; Heber J. Grant to Grace Grant Evans, April 24, 1910, Famliy Correspondence.

56. Grant to Noble, November 18, 1894.

57. Grant to Evans, April 24, 1910, Family Correspondence.

58. Dessie Grant Boyle to Heber J. Grant, January 1, 1911, Family Correspondence; see also Lyde Wells to Heber J. Grant, September 7, 1938, General Correspondence.

59. Francis M. Lyman to Joseph F. Smith, January 2, 1904, Joseph F. Smith Correspondence.

60. Grant, Typed Diary, June 2, 1932.

61. Francis M. Lyman to Heber J. Grant, June 29, 1905, First Presidency Letterbooks.

62. Grant, Typed Diary, May, 5, 1905.

63. Heber J. Grant to Samuel B. Spry, March 22, 1937, First Presidency Letterbooks.

64. Bennett, *Glimpses of a Mormon Family,* 17–18.

65. Frances Grant Bennett, "Interview by the Author," Salt Lake City, August 6, 1981, typescript, Church Archives; Bennett, *Glimpses of a Mormon Family*, 15–16.

66. Heber J. Grant to Joseph M. Tanner, September 22, 1906, Grant Letterpress Copybook, 42:665–75; Heber J. Grant to John A. and Leah D. Widtsoe, November 26, 1935, General Correspondence.

67. Heber J. Grant to Rachel Ivins Grant, January 8, 1904, Grant Letterpress Copybook, 38:10; Heber J. Grant to Joseph E. Taylor, January 25, 1904, Grant Letterpress Copybook, 38:218.

68. Heber J. Grant to Van Grant, December 30, 1919, Grant Letterpress Copybook, 55:320.

69. Heber J. Grant to Anthony W. Ivins, January 21, 1904, Grant Letterpress Copybook, 38:151–52.

70. Heber J. Grant to Joseph E. Taylor, January 25, 1904, Grant Letterpress Copybook, 38:218; Heber J. Grant to John B. Maiben, April 22, 1905, Grant Letterpress Copybook, 39:597; Heber J. Grant to George Albert Smith, September 16, 1905, Grant Letterpress Copybook, 40:190.

71. Heber J. Grant to Grace Grant Evans, April 12, 1925, Grant Letterpress Copybook, 63:146.

72. Grant, Typed Diary, March 9 and 11 and April 1, 1904; Heber J. Grant to Edward H. Anderson, October 20, 1906, Grant Letterpress Copybook, 42:865.

73. Heber J. Grant to William George Jordan, October 5, 1907, General Correspondence.

74. Grant, Typed Diary, January 1, 1906; Heber J. Grant to Rudger Clawson, August 14, 1911, General Correspondence; Heber J. Grant to Holman, March 25, 1939, Grant Letterpress Copybook, 77:568; Heber J. Grant to J. William Knight, December 19, 1940, Grant Letterpress Copybook, 79:502.

75. Grant, Typed Diary, May 29, 1905.

76. Heber J. Grant to J. Leo Fairbanks, September 27, 1904, Grant Letterpress Copybook, 38:754.

77. Heber J. Grant to J. Leo Fairbanks, January 24, 1905, Grant Letterpress Copybook, 39:282; Heber J. Grant to J. Leo Fairbanks, July 6, 1904, Grant Letterpress Copybook, 38:663.

78. Heber J. Grant to B. F. Grant, June 28, 1904, Grant Letterpress Copybook, 38:672.

79. Grant, Typed Diary, March 30, 1904; February 21 and 27 and March 7, 1905; Grant, Manuscript Diary, June 10 and May 13, 1905.

80. Grant, Typed Diary, February 12, 1904.

81. Grant, Typed Diary, May 13, 1904.

82. Grant, Typed Diary, June 5 and 11, 1904.

83. Grant, Typed Diary, May 13, 1904.

84. Neither Grant's contemporary diary nor the *Millennial Star* report the conversation with Oscar's statement about Scandinavian immigrants. It is preserved in reminiscent accounts by Grant and another Mormon

who was present, Alex Nibley. For various accounts of the episode, see Grant, Typed Diary, July 4, 1906; "An Audience with King Oscar II: President Grant and Party Visit the Sweedish Monarch at Stockholm," *Millennial Star* 68 (July 19, 1906): 460–61; Heber J. Grant, Memorandum, n.d., box 145, fd. 4; Memorandum, n.d., in Grant Letterpress Copybook, 73:806–8; Alex Nibley to Heber J. Grant, July 22, 1926, General Correspondence; Heber J. Grant, "Remarks to a Boy Scout Convention, 1924," in Grant Letterpress Copybook, 61:807–8; Lucy Grant Cannon, "The Log of a European Tour," *Improvement Era* 40 (November 1937): 688.

85. Heber J. Grant to Matthias F. Cowley, December 22, 1905, Grant Letterpress Copybook, 40:702.

86. Heber J. Grant to James Dwyer, April 18, 1906, Grant Letterpress Copybook, 41:2.

87. Grant, Typed Diary, March 1906.

88. Heber J. Grant to Mary Grant, December 28, 1904, Grant Letterpress Copybook, 39:216.

89. Heber J. Grant to John H. Taylor, October 5, 1906, Grant Letterpress Copybook, 42:783.

90. Grant, Typed Diary, July 7 and 21, 1906; Heber J. Grant to Alpha J. Higgs, July 16, 1906, Grant Letterpress Copybook, 42:429; Heber J. Grant to Benjamin Goddard, n.d. [about July 26, 1906]; Grant Letterpress Copybook, 42:443 "The General Conference at Bradford," *Millennial Star* 68 (August 2, 1906): 488–89; Eugene E. Campell and Richard D. Poll, *Hugh B. Brown: His Life and Thought* (Salt Late City: Bookcraft, 1975), 37.

91. Heber J. Grant to Rachel Grant, July 25, 1906, Grant Letterpress Copybook, 42:469–70.

92. James R. Glenn to Heber J. Grant, December 16, 1944, General Correspondence.

93. Heber J. Grant to Ray Grant Taylor, July 28, 1906, Grant Letterpress Copybook, 42:450.

94. Heber J. Grant to Francis M. Lyman, September 27, 1906, Grant Letterpress Copybook, 42:752.

95. Heber J. Grant to Rachel Grant, October 4, 1905, Grant Letterpress Copybook, 40:324.

96. Heber J. Grant to Emily Grant, June 27, 1906, General Correspondence; Heber J. Grant to John Henry Smith, August 1, 1906, Grant Letterpress Copybook, 42:465.

97. Heber J. Grant to First Presidency, November 30, 1906, Grant Letterpress Copybook, 43:43; Grant, Typed Diary, November 22, 1906; Charles W. Penrose, Diary, November 1906, Penrose Papers, Utah State Historical Society, Salt Lake City.

98. Quoted in Allen, "Mission President in Europe," 694–95.

Index

This book has been produced and edited by the Joseph Fielding Smith Institute for Latter-day Saint History and BYU Studies at Brigham Young University.

The Smith Institute is a faculty research department at BYU that writes, promotes, and publishes Latter-day Saint history from the perspective of faith and according to the highest scholarly standards. Visit smithinstitute.byu.edu for more information about the organization and its endeavors.

BYU Studies publishes a quarterly journal, *BYU Studies,* as well as books and monographs that openly reflect a Latter-day Saint point of view while conforming to rigorous academic guidelines. For further information or to subscribe to the journal, visit byustudies.byu.edu.

Selected works published or produced by BYU Studies and the Joseph Fielding Smith Institute for Latter-day Saint History

Allen, James B. *No Toil nor Labor Fear: The Story of William Clayton.*

Allen, James B., Ronald K. Esplin, and David J. Whittaker. *Men with a Mission: The Quorum of the Twelve Apostles in the British Isles, 1837–1841.*

Derr, Jill Mulvay, Janath Russell Cannon, and Maureen Ursenbach Beecher. *Women of Convenant: The Story of Relief Society.*

Hartley, William G. *"Stand by My Servant Joseph": The Story of the Joseph Knight Family and The Restoration.*

Jessee, Dean C., ed. *Personal Writings of Joseph Smith, 1805–1844.*

Leonard, Glen M. *Nauvoo: A Place of Peace, A People of Promise.*

Lyon, T. Edgar, Jr. *T. Edgar Lyon: A Teacher in Zion.*

Madsen, Carol Cornwall. *In Their Own Words: Women and the Story of Nauvoo.*

Madsen, Carol Cornwall. *Journey to Zion: Voices from the Mormon Trail.*

Mehr, Kahlile B. *Mormon Missionaries Enter Eastern Europe.*

Mulder, William. *Homeward to Zion: The Mormon Migration from Scandinavia.*

Roberts, B. H. *The Truth, The Way, The Life.* John W. Welch, ed.

Robison, Elwin C. *First Mormon Temple: Design, Construction, and Historic Context of the Kirtland Temple.*

Shipps, Jan, and John W. Welch, eds. *The Journals of William E. McLellin, 1831–1836.*

Shirts, Morris A. and Kathryn H. Shirts. *A Trial Furnace: Southern Utah's Iron Mission.*

Smart, Donna Toland, ed. *Exemplary Elder: The Life and Missionary Diaries of Perrigrine Sessions, 1814-1893.*

Underwood, Grant, ed. *Voyages of Faith: Explorations in Mormon Pacific History.*

Walker, Ronald W., and Doris R. Dant, eds. *Nearly Everything Imaginable: The Everyday Life of Utah's Mormon Pioneers.*

Walker, Ronald W., James B. Allen, and David J. Whittaker. *Studies in Mormon History, 1830–1997.*

Walker, Ronald W., David J. Whittaker, and James B. Allen. *Mormon History.*

Whittaker, David J., ed. *Mormon Americana: A Guide to Sources and Collections in the United States.*

About the Author

RONALD W. WALKER is a professor of history at Brigham Young University, where he also serves as a senior research associate in the Joseph Fielding Smith Institute for Latter-day Saint History. He earned a Ph.D. in American history from the University of Utah.

Professor Walker has published more than six dozen historical articles. He has also authored or co-authored four books, including the prize-winning *Wayward Saints: The Godbeites and Brigham Young* (Urbana: University of Illinois Press, 1998). With Doris R. Dant, he co-edited *Nearly Everything Imaginable: The Everyday Life of Utah's Mormon Pioneers* (Provo, Utah: Brigham Young University Press, 1999). His other two books, written with James B. Allen and David J. Whittaker, have dealt with Mormon bibliography and historiography: *Studies in Mormon History, 1830–1997*, received a special award for distinction from the Mormon History Assocation, and *Mormon History*, which surveyed the writing of Mormon history and biography.

Professor Walker has been active in the Mormon History Association and has served as the organization's president.

He and his wife, Nelani Midgley Walker, live in Salt Lake City and are the parents of seven children.